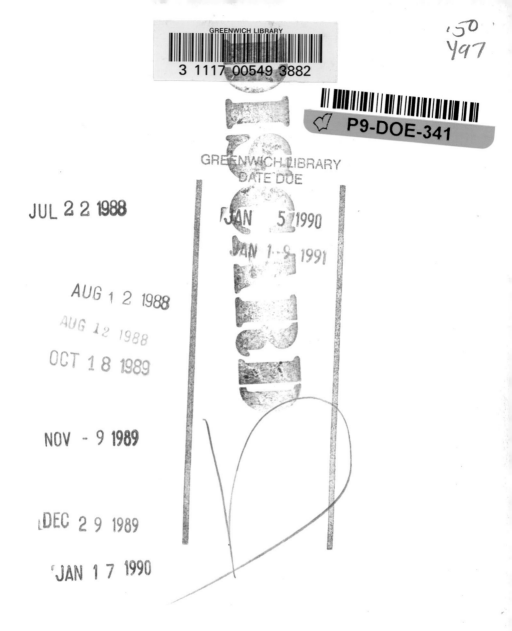

THE
MAKING
OF
McPAPER

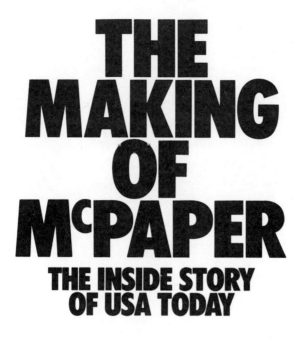

THE MAKING OF McPAPER

THE INSIDE STORY OF USA TODAY

by Peter Prichard

Foreword by Charles Kuralt

Andrews, McMeel & Parker
A Universal Press Syndicate Affiliate
Kansas City • New York

The Making of McPaper: The Inside Story of USA TODAY copyright © 1987 by Gannett New Media Services. All rights reserved. Printed in the United States of America. No part of this book may be used or reproduced in any manner whatsoever except in the case of reprints in the context of reviews. For information write Andrews, McMeel & Parker, a Universal Press Syndicate Affiliate, 4900 Main Street, Kansas City, Missouri 64112.

Library of Congress Cataloging-in-Publication Data

Prichard, Peter.
    The making of McPaper.

    Includes index.
    1. USA today (Arlington, Va.)   I. Title.
PN4899.A635U837   1987   071'.3   87-17537
ISBN 0-8362-7939-5

"It's a hard-driving company, isn't it?"

—Thomas Winship, editor,
The Boston Globe, in a 1980 conversation

Contents

Acknowledgments

When I joined USA TODAY in 1982, becoming its Boswell was the furthest thing from my mind. My daily challenge as columns editor for the editorial page was to convince four people from four different states to write short but persuasive opinion pieces. It was not easy to find writers; back then, most people had never heard of USA TODAY. Some days it was a struggle to avoid blank space.

Four years later, Al Neuharth asked me if I wanted to write the "history" of USA TODAY. He said he wanted "an honest book, a candid book." He added, with his usual modesty, that he thought the tale would make "a damn good entrepreneurial story and a pretty good journalism story."

And that was all he said. That was the end of his charge. He wrote a memo to some of the people I would later interview, asking them to cooperate. His last words in that memo were: "If you have any doubts about how to handle Peter's snooping, just tell the truth."

After he had seen the first draft of two early chapters, Neuharth told me: "I'm not sure I'm the best person to judge this." He said his role would be limited to correction of factual errors, and it was. Other than giving me his interpretation of events, as everyone else did, he made no attempt to control the manuscript. He threw open his files, which helped tell the story. The book is also based on more than one hundred in-depth interviews, and more than fifty shorter interviews. The resulting oral history was an invaluable source, as were people's private files, diaries, and notebooks.

The Making of McPaper was written by an insider, but I had complete editorial freedom. It is my view of USA TODAY's birth and its struggle to succeed—not Neuharth's view or corporate Gannett's view, but mine alone. I take responsibility for any errors, mistakes, or omissions.

I must add that I have worked for Gannett, except for one year in television, since 1972. To paraphrase a comment by Arthur Schlesinger in his foreword to *Robert Kennedy and His Times,* if it is necessary to believe that the Gannett Company is evil to write its history, then I am not qualified to be its historian. And I agree with Schlesinger that sympathy for a subject may illumine as well as distort. In this book, I hope that is the case, for I have tried hard to distort nothing. My first loyalty in writing it has been to what must be a journalist's first commitment—to the truth.

Because I am sensitive to my position as an insider, I have taken pains to make the book an honest, unflinching portrait of an enterprise; it is as straightforward and candid as I could make it.

This book could not have been written without help. First, I must express my deep gratitude to Phil Pruitt, the able journalist who did dozens of interviews, tracked down thousands of facts, and helped draft portions of chapters dealing with the News department. Pruitt is a tireless reporter and a fine critic, and his help was invaluable.

Ashley Barnes had the patience and skill to transcribe more than one hundred interviews; the transcripts filled five massive volumes. She also double-checked thousands of facts and spent days in the Library of Congress doing important research, organized our extensive files, and kept our computers humming. Without the hard work and dedication of Pruitt and Barnes, there would be no inside story of USA TODAY.

I am deeply grateful, too, to my wife Ann, a literate and loving woman who read the manuscript closely and offered valuable suggestions throughout. And I thank the many others who read the manuscript and added insights, corrections, and improvements, especially John Seigenthaler, John Quinn, John Curley, and Taylor Buckley.

My thanks, too, to the Gannett and USA TODAY photographers, artists, and librarians who helped with research, photos, and graphics, including Richard Curtis, Barbara Feininger, Phyllis Harris, Bob Laird, Dave Leonard, Karren Loeb, Lynne Perri, Bob Roller, Rick Sass, Maggie Somerville, Susan Watson, and many others. And thanks to executives at the Audit Bureau of Circulations, the Goss Company, and the American Newspaper Publishers Association who answered our questions.

I am also grateful to the people at Andrews, McMeel & Parker for their help and encouragement, especially to Donna Martin for her editorial leadership, and to George Parker, Jean Lowe, Patty Dingus, and to Barrie Maguire, the book's designer.

And finally, thanks to all of the people at USA TODAY and around Gannett who took the time and trouble to talk to us, and told the truth. It seems to me that it is unusual for a company to hold up a mirror and take a look at itself. If some people saw things differently and take offense at this portrait, I apologize. But I know that for many, looking back was therapeutic.

—PETER PRICHARD

Foreword
by Charles Kuralt

I suppose I have plunked more quarters into USA TODAY vending machines than most people—the one outside the Holiday Inn in Klamath Falls; the one at the 7-11 store in Great Bridge, Virginia; the one at the last bus stop before the road runs out at Homestead Valley, California; the one that is chained to the light pole at Eighth Avenue and Fourteenth Street in the city of New York; the one that stands as the only paper box in Lincoln, Missouri, right under the only stoplight. I am a steady and grateful customer.

I know that a lot of heavy hitters of big-time journalism sneer at USA TODAY for its breeziness and that it is lamented by certain professors and critics. Their problem is that they have only a few minutes to spend with the paper each weekday morning, busy as they are with important enterprises of their own, fraught with significance for the nation. I, on the other hand, meandering across the land seeking out rural "On The Road" stories for CBS News, have time to linger over breakfast with the four familiar sections of USA TODAY, check the weather in North Dakota, marvel over the census statistics, absorb the baseball scores, maybe even work the crossword puzzle. I can make USA TODAY last till lunchtime, easy.

Maybe I should add—and this is the rather important fact that most of the stuffy criticism overlooks—that in the small towns where I usually wake up in the morning, I can't learn about the weather, the sports, the stock market, or even the important news of the day anywhere else. I have reason to think Al Neuharth has made a bright and inventive addition to the newsstands and light poles of America. If his critics were on the road with me, they'd think so too.

What's more, I occasionally steal ideas from USA TODAY. On a shelf of the "On The Road" bus, I have a tall free-standing stack of yellowing back copies held for the purpose of stealing further ideas. (Actually, alone among American newspapers, USA TODAY doesn't yellow as it ages; it fades in more attractive hues of blue and pink and green.)

I remember sitting on Alf Landon's porch in Topeka talking about the people and the press. The wise old former governor and presidential candidate said he could remember the changes that had the most effect on life for the farmers. The first, he said, was Rural Free Delivery. It meant that the farmer no longer had to wait for Saturday to go into town and hear all the news. The news came to him every day, in the form of the big city newspaper, no more than a day late.

Then radio came along, a wonderful addition to rural life. "Think of it," Alf Landon said, "the news of the world delivered right at noontime, along with the farm prices, only a few minutes old!"

Television, in its best moments, did even more to bring people together. No longer was there any reason for the farm family not to be as well informed as the steel worker in Pittsburgh or the broker in Wall Street or the longshoreman in San Francisco.

And now there has come, as a kind of apotheosis, available to nearly everybody, all splashy and bold in the wrapping, but serious and responsible in its content, this four-section, four-color gift from Al Neuharth. It's like the gifts we used to give one another in grammar school at Christmas: You couldn't pay more than fifty cents for it, so you had to use your imagination and give something nobody else ever thought of giving.

I think of the Kansas farmer who had to wait until Saturday to learn the news. And had to guess from the shape of the clouds whether it would rain. And had to wait until he took his wheat to market to know the price they were paying for wheat. Now USA TODAY gives him— and millions of other readers, from the small towns to the biggest cities—a pretty good summary of the news every morning for half a dollar, and a weather map that tells him better than he can discover anywhere else just what the weather will be where he lives, and in several pages, the price of wheat and anything else he might wish to buy or sell, gives him a decent editorial every day, and a whole page of debate about the editorial, gives him the good news that the Royals beat the Yankees, and tells him what's going to be on television tonight, if he happens to care.

This is not just good for journalism; it's good for the country. This kind of country can't work unless people have a reliable way of finding out what's going on. Television, especially at the local level, isn't doing a good enough job of it; there's many a sorry local newspaper; and not everybody can tune in to the useful programs that do exist, or lay hold of the good newspapers that people in New York or Washington or Los Angeles are used to. USA TODAY tells us things about ourselves and about the great, wide world, that we would never learn if Al Neuharth a man I don't know—hadn't taken the big gamble of chaining all those white newspaper boxes to all those out-of-the-way lampposts.

I have always wondered why he did it. And now—thanks to Peter Prichard's candid account—I understand much more about the conflicts that were overcome, the sacrifices that were made, and how thousands of people struggled to create a new newspaper. Now you can turn the pages and find out, too.

Launch

Allen H. Neuharth sat alone in the back seat of a limousine as it slipped across a bridge into Washington, moving against the sluggish flow of commuters heading home at the end of another muggy, late summer day in the nation's capital.

For Neuharth, that Wednesday—September 15, 1982—was a momentous day. He was chairman and president of the Gannett Company, which already published eighty-eight daily newspapers. That morning, his company had launched USA TODAY, the country's first national, general-interest daily newspaper. Its first edition had sold out. Readers in the Washington-Baltimore area, its initial market, had snapped up all 155,000 copies.

The night before, Neuharth had been up until 4 A.M. He rewrote headlines in the newsroom until midnight, checked the first copies that came off the press at 1:30 A.M., did some television interviews, ate linguine with clams at 3 A.M., and went to bed in his suite at the Capital Hilton Hotel. At 6 A.M. he was up, jogging in Lafayette Park and checking the USA TODAY newsracks around the White House.

Now, at dusk, he was on the way to the Washington Mall to promote the birth of what was, in many ways, his newspaper. The launch gala was an extraordinary event: Neuharth, the head of the nation's largest newspaper chain, a man who was the closest thing the country had to a press lord, had managed to persuade the president of the United States, the Speaker of the House of Representatives, and the Senate majority leader to stand together on the same dais in a tent at the foot of Capitol Hill to celebrate the arrival of Vol. 1, No. 1, of USA TODAY.

Speaker of the House Thomas P. "Tip" O'Neill, Senate Majority Leader Howard H. Baker, Jr., and President Ronald Reagan joined Allen H. Neuharth, at the microphone, at the launch bash by the Capitol reflecting pool.

Neuharth later told his son Dan—then a USA TODAY reporter—that this day seemed too good to be true. Here he was, "a little guy from South Dakota," and the three most important leaders of the most powerful nation on earth were standing under his tent, promoting the birth of his newspaper. In his speech, the Speaker of the House, Thomas P. "Tip" O'Neill, remarked that these three leaders were not together often. That was true, and they certainly had never gathered before to promote the introduction of a commercial product.

Although Ronald Reagan, Howard Baker, and O'Neill had come to praise USA TODAY, plenty of others wanted to bury it. In the American newspaper establishment, Neuharth had more than his share of critics. They sneered at this new newspaper, his pet project. They were also put off by his vaulting ambition, his drive to acquire so many newspapers, his desire to leave his mark on journalism. Many of them distrusted Gannett, disliked Neuharth, and despised USA TODAY.

Neuharth's flair for showmanship was well known in the newspaper business, and that, too, offended his critics. The launch of this newspaper was his ultimate promotion. The centerpiece was a huge tent, 140 feet long and 60 feet wide, with "USA TODAY" banners draped all over it.

The tent's flaps had been left up, despite early objections from the Secret Service. They had to be up; Neuharth wanted to make sure everyone could see the Capitol and the Washington Monument. This christening had to come off just as he had choreographed it, with liberal doses of drama and patriotism. "The Nation's Newspaper" would debut in the nation's capital, flanked by the nation's two greatest monuments, surrounded by the nation's highest leaders, all of it wrapped up in red, white, and blue.

The eight hundred guests invited to USA TODAY's "Salute to Congress" included senators and representatives, cabinet members, and the board of directors of the American Newspaper Publishers Association. That board included some of the most powerful publishers in the country, and many of them thought the new newspaper would surely fail. After the reception, the publishers and their spouses were coming to dinner at USA TODAY's new headquarters in a thirty-story silver skyscraper in Rosslyn, a section of Arlington, Virginia, across the Potomac River from the Mall. Construction crews had been working day and night to finish the seventeenth floor executive dining room, catching naps when they could in sleeping bags on the floor. The work had been completed that very day, and the view of the Mall and the monuments from its windows was gorgeous. "From here we can look down on Washington," Neuharth liked to joke.

But on the afternoon of USA TODAY's first day, much of official Washington was busy checking out this lavish bash on the Mall. No expense had been spared; the food alone cost $45,000. Like the newspaper, the buffet had an "Across the USA" theme. Just as there was news from every state, there was food from every state. The guests ate king crab from Alaska, walleyed pike from Minnesota, crab cakes from Maryland, oysters from New York and barbecued beef from Texas—washed down with wine from California. Then President Reagan stepped to the microphone, and for a moment the crowd was still.

The president's toast was short and simple. USA TODAY, he said, is "a testimony to the kind of dreams free men and women can dream and turn into reality here in America."

Neuharth thought the president had struck just the right note. For him, this new newspaper's first day was the beginning of a dream come true, a fairy tale he hoped would have a happy ending.

■

That same week in 1982, thousands of miles across the Atlantic, another modern fairy tale was ending in tragedy. Shortly before noon on Monday, September 13, movie star Grace Kelly—Her Serene Highness, Princess Grace of Monaco—and her daughter Stephanie, seventeen, got into a car for a short trip down a steep, twisting mountain road. The route was familiar; the princess often drove the half mile between the family's summer home on a cliff and their two-hundred-room pink palace below in Monte Carlo.

While negotiating her 1972 Rover 3500 around a hairpin curve, Princess Grace suffered a hemorrhage in a blood vessel in her brain; that probably caused a brief dizzy spell or a blackout. Her car missed the curve and crashed down a ravine, bursting into flames in a farmer's garden. Doctors said if she had been anywhere else but driving a car down a dangerous road, she probably would have survived.

The first reports from Monaco that Monday were optimistic: Her condition was listed as "stationary." In fact, Princess Grace had suffered additional brain damage from the crash, and she never recovered consciousness. At 10 P.M. Tuesday in Monaco—late afternoon in the United States—her family decided to disconnect her life-support system.

Grace Kelly had not made a movie in twenty-six years, but her fans remembered her cool, elegant glamour. In moviegoers' memories, she was still that daring, romantic young woman who charmed Cary Grant in the roadside picnic in *To Catch a Thief.* Then she had done the most romantic thing of all—she had married a Prince. The Philadelphia girl with the regal looks and the Main Line manners was dead, at fifty-two.

That Monday, about the same time that Princess Grace was taking her fateful drive, Chip Peterson of St. Paul, Minnesota—an avid amateur photographer—was aboard a chartered DC-10 in Malaga, Spain, that was taking off for the States. The big jet lost power just after liftoff, crashed in a field, and burned. Fifty-five of the 382 people aboard were killed.

Peterson was sitting near an emergency door; he stepped quickly through it onto the wing and jumped to safety. He was a compulsive picture-taker, so he started shooting. Before he left Spain, an ABC radio reporter offered him $10 a shot. Peterson held out for a better offer. When he arrived in New York later that night, he got it; the freelance photo agency Sygma eventually paid him $32,000 for his film.

On Tuesday, hopes for peace in Lebanon were dashed. Bashir Gemayel, the handsome president-elect from the Christian Phalange Party, was killed, along with a number of his supporters, when a half-ton of TNT placed beneath the third floor of his party headquarters in Beirut was detonated by remote control. The top two floors crashed down on the first floor, where Gemayel was holding a party meeting; his body was dug out of the rubble. A president was dead, one more casualty in the never-ending tragedy that is Lebanon.

■

Back on the fourteenth floor of the USA TODAY building, at 5 P.M. on Tuesday, September 14, the daily news meeting—the first one held with live news and a real newspaper to put out, after months of practice sessions—was under way. Neuharth and his three top editors—the editor, John J. Curley, the executive editor, Ron Martin, and Gannett's chief news executive, John C. Quinn—were in the conference room. Sitting and standing around the room were several managing editors and their deputies. This meeting would become a daily ritual to decide which stories and photos would go where in USA TODAY. The editors had expected that a piece written by pollster Lou Harris, pegged to that Tuesday's primary elections, would work for the lead story of the first edition Wednesday.

Editors learned at the first 5 P.M. news meeting that every detail counted. Clockwise from left, Nancy Woodhull, Anne Saul, John Quinn, Al Neuharth, Don Brandt, Taylor Buckley, and Ron Martin. Henry Freeman and Sheryl Bills have their backs to the camera.

Weighed against the news of the day—the deaths of Princess Grace and Bashir Gemayel—the Harris piece did not stand up. It had to be shortened and moved to the bottom of the front page. The struggle to end Lebanon's bloody civil war had been front-page news for weeks. USA TODAY's editors could expect almost every major metropolitan newspaper—including The New York Times, The Washington Post, and the Los Angeles Times—to lead with Gemayel. "We weren't too sure what to lead with," recalls Neuharth.

For Nancy Woodhull, who was managing editor for news, the lead was never in doubt: "More readers will want to know about Princess Grace than Gemayel," she said. She was adamant, and she was the only editor who argued strongly that Princess Grace was a page one story for USA TODAY—the story most people wanted to know about. At about 6 P.M., with the lead story issue still unresolved, Neuharth went downstairs to be driven in his limo for a brief break at a Capital Hilton Hotel suite, one of his homes away from home. He stopped at the bar for a martini and to chat with his favorite bartender and the patrons. "They were all talking about Princess Grace," he recalls. He told the people around the bar that Lebanon's new president, Bashir Gemayel, had been assassinated. The news evoked only shrugs.

Then he went upstairs to the ballroom, where supporters of the mayor of Washington, D.C., Marion Barry, were holding a rally to celebrate his victory in that day's primary election. Neuharth talked to several people about the two top news stories; they were shocked by Princess Grace's death. He had always thought of himself as a good reporter, someone who could get the facts and read the mood of a room or a town. "The Lebanon thing didn't get a spark out of anyone," he recalls. "So I went back to the newsroom and told everyone, 'No question, the lead story has to be Princess Grace.'"

USA TODAY editors had already agreed to pay Sygma $5,000 for two of Chip Peterson's color photos of the plane crash in Spain. These were dummied into the center of the front page, with the story on Princess Grace in the upper right, the traditional position for the lead story. Now the editors were struggling to write a headline for the photos. The first try was "55 die in fiery crash"—old news that had been in newspapers and on radio and television all day. Executive Editor Ron Martin saw that and said, "That's not the story; it's how many lived." And so the final headline, which Neuharth wrote on his old manual typewriter, read: "Miracle: 327 survive, 55 die." Gemayel's assassination became a brief, the second item in the Newsline column on page one, with readers referred to the details inside on the World news page.

Thus in its first edition, USA TODAY had unmistakably announced it was going to be different. And a "different" newspaper was what Neuharth had always intended. Its front page would boldly pick homegrown princesses over foreign presidents, its headlines could single out survivors as well as victims. USA TODAY would be edited, its creators maintained, not for the nation's editors, but for the nation's readers.

Its aim, Neuharth wrote in his page one letter in the first edition, using the frequent alliteration that was his trademark, was to be "enlightening and enjoyable to the nation's readers; informative and impelling to the nation's leaders; challenging and competitive to the nation's journalists; refreshing and rewarding to the nation's advertisers." And then he added, in a new twist on what was an old theme for him: "USA TODAY hopes to serve as a forum for better understanding and unity to make the USA truly one nation."

From left, Mitch Koppelman, photo editor; Richard Curtis; John Quinn; and Jackie Greene, assistant photo editor, review color for the first Page 1A. The strongest color art had to be on the top half of the page so that it would show up in the newsrack window and attract readers.

The new newspaper used color extensively, and most of its news stories were short. The only stories that were continued on other pages—or "jumped," in newspaper lingo—were the cover stories on the four section fronts: the News or "A" section, Money, Sports, and Life. It devoted a whole page on the back of the A section to weather news, dominated by a color weather map of the United States. It de-emphasized foreign news in favor of domestic news culled from every corner of the country, which was reported in state-by-state round-ups on its "Across the USA" pages. And it had a large, thorough Sports section, with every result and every detail on "how they scored."

USA TODAY was so different from what some journalists were used to and were comfortable with that within months, they would derisively dub it "McPaper"—"the fast food of the newspaper business." They denounced it as junk-food journalism, tasty but without substance.

■

Neuharth had staked his reputation and many millions of Gannett's dollars on making USA TODAY a success, but he also was having fun. Instead of spending all of his time on a chief executive's traditional duties, he had an opportunity to work nights in a role that he loved— that of city editor. He was doing what he liked to do best, going to news meetings, second-guessing editors, shaping a newspaper.

The chairman, president and chief executive of a media company with more than $1.5 billion in revenues had taken the unusual step of moving his own typewriter—a 1926 black Royal—into the fourteenth-floor newsroom. The clunky machine looked ancient in a room filled with computerized, state-of-the-art editing equipment, but Neuharth did not like the light touch of electric typewriters or computer key-boards. He was launching a high-tech, satellite-delivered newspaper, yet he had never learned to use a modern word processor.

Every night for several weeks he was in the newsroom until 11 P.M. or midnight, rewriting leads, polishing headlines, reading proofs. He edited hard copies of stories—printouts—with a black felt-tip pen, ignoring the winking, green video display terminals around him. Neu-harth clearly intended to stay for a while, a prospect that made many young editors and reporters uncomfortable.

Those early days were tense, heavy with the pressure to succeed. About 65 percent of the 218 reporters and editors were "loan-

"Mix," typically a broadcast word, quickly became a key term, especially when it came to page one. The page had to have the right mix of hard news, features of wide interest, and promotional items. It had to say, "Read me."

Ron Martin and Sheryl Bills at one of many meetings. Bills wrote in her diary of working at USA TODAY: "I'll do it until Oct. 1, and then I'm going to have some of my own life and sometime later, next year probably, I'm going to leave altogether."

ers" from other Gannett newspapers, and uncertainty filled their lives. They didn't know if they would win lasting jobs, or even if USA TODAY would last. They didn't know what they would end up doing if it failed and they had to go home—but at least they had jobs to go back to.

Those who were "permanent" hires had been told Gannett would try to place them at its other newspapers if USA TODAY failed, and it was unsettling to think about that. To add to the general feeling of impermanence, workmen hammered away at the unfinished newsroom. Stepladders stood everywhere, packing boxes littered the floor, wires hung from ceilings. Most of the loaners—many of them separated from their families—were living rent-free in River Place, a drab, high-rise apartment building right next to the USA TODAY building. Gannett had rented scores of apartments there, and the loaners had vulgarly dubbed these rooms "stay-free mini-pads." In the newsroom, hardly anyone knew each other, so everyone wore name tags, even Neuharth.

The pervasive uncertainty and relentless intensity of the launch added up to a pressure-cooker atmosphere, and that took its toll. Just after midnight on September 14, Sheryl Bills, the managing editor of USA TODAY's Life section, sat on her bed in a rare quiet moment and wrote in her journal:

"This is one night before the launch of USA TODAY, The Nation's Newspaper. It is also the night of my pledge that this is the last newspaper job I want to have."

A few days earlier, Bills had written in her journal: "I've lost all concept of what a day is. I continue to work 8:30 A.M. to midnight daily, pushing constantly. I can't get enough done. Can't even make phone calls. It's hard to believe what we're really doing, how much we can endure mentally, physically. All else has stopped. It's difficult to talk on the phone. I have no contact with friends."

A month later, things were no better. Bills wrote: "I'm convinced that because of our tiredness and exhaustion, and in some cases blind ambition, we are all brainwashed and intimidated. I've never been one to believe that management does things cruelly by design, but I do wonder here about the psychological impact of what's happening. They make us feel guilty about leaving, about taking more than one day a weekend off, about working less than twelve-to-fifteen hours a day regularly, about asking for time off, about everything that's human. [John] Curley gives looks that could pierce, and says things to questions with a flash of the eyes and irritation in his voice. We all respond to that with fear and trembling and sometimes tears. Actually, all of that should stop. We should stop being so bowled over by any of them and stand on our own two feet. [Ron] Martin intimidates by suggesting that nothing is good enough, always beating us down. Nothing is up to standard."

J. Taylor Buckley, the Money section managing editor who had come from Gannett's Wilmington, Delaware, newspapers, was banished from the news meeting one day because he had not brought a budget with him—a list of the Money section stories. This requirement had never been mentioned. Neuharth just told Buckley: "A budget is the ticket for admission to this meeting, Taylor." Other editors had brought budgets that day; Buckley figured they must have held some secret meeting.

"I was terrified," Buckley says. "We feared the feedback from the chiefs. Always negative. They had these cattle prods out, zapping us every minute. One day John Curley almost took my head off for making some undetectable change in the typeface of the stock tables."

On weekends, Buckley thought he was on "work release." He would stop on the way to his home on Maryland's Eastern Shore, buy a six-pack of Genesee Cream Ale, and drink it while he drove. "About

*Members of the Money
staff had no idea that
Taylor Buckley was
feeling the pressure,
but he was. "I felt
terrorized," he says.*

*Nancy Woodhull was
determined to succeed as
A-section managing
editor, even though she
felt some people did not
trust her in that position.*

*Nancy Monaghan was
described by one
colleague as a person
who would "never say
die."*

halfway through the second one it would all hit me at once and I would
cry for fifteen or twenty minutes. I could hardly drive. Then I'd pop
another one and drink a silent toast to all those people back in Rosslyn
hammering away on Al's Spruce Goose."

Nancy Woodhull, the managing editor of the A section, had an eigh-
teen-month-old daughter, but she wasn't seeing her much. Woodhull
would leave her home early in the morning and not get back until 11
P.M. or later. Finally she arranged to have her daughter Tennie brought
each evening to the USA TODAY building about 6 P.M. She would spend
forty-five minutes with her baby in the Great Eatery, the restaurant on
the mall-level of the building. Woodhull was afraid to tell Ron Martin
what she was doing, so she always left an assistant on standby who was
supposed to run down and fetch Woodhull if Martin wanted anything.

During those early days, Nancy Monaghan, the day-side national
editor, was struggling to cope with what had become a daily ritual that
would last for weeks. Every morning before coming to work, she
threw up. "Nerves," she explained. Monaghan, who had been an outstanding reporter and editor at Gannett's Democrat & Chronicle in
Rochester, New York, was discovering that at USA TODAY, confidence
was hard to hang on to. The constant second-guessing, the feeling that

nothing midlevel editors and reporters could do was good enough, wore people down. Maybe it was wise, as some of the aspiring writers hoping to write long pieces had been told, to "check your ego at the door."

The pounding some editors took affected their news judgment. "We developed a real strange sense of what was good," recalls Monte Trammer, an editor in Money who came from the Detroit Free Press. "We were so used to being beaten up that we were scared to say anything was good. Your first line of defense was to criticize everything."

Gene Policinski, who had worked for Gannett News Service in Indiana and was now USA TODAY's Washington editor, had been working with a cold for weeks. He ignored it. Then late one night he was driving home and he felt so awful he decided to pull into a clinic for a checkup. The doctor X-rayed his lungs, which were full of pneumonia, and said: "You're thirty-two years old but you're going to die if you don't take care of this." During his illness, Policinski lost thirty-five pounds. He recovered, but within a month he asked to be moved to another position.

Midlevel editors weren't the only ones who felt the intense pressure. A colleague once asked John Curley, the newspaper's first editor, who loved to jog, why he didn't take forty-five minutes in the middle of the day to go for a relaxing run. "I can't leave," he explained. "Quinn

In September 1982, Gene Policinski was thirty-two. "I thought I was immortal," he says. But in a few weeks, the pressure and tension changed his mind.

Before Monte Trammer left the Detroit Free Press for USA TODAY, a friend said to him, "I don't blame you. If I wanted a job for six months, I'd go there, too."

Having Neuharth, John Curley, and John Quinn in the newsroom let the staff know that everybody—no matter what the title—was pitching in. But it also made some reporters and editors feel they were being second-guessed—and they were.

has to be updated constantly." And Quinn would say the same thing about Neuharth: He had to be updated constantly. If USA TODAY failed, it was not going to be because of lack of effort or hands-off management.

In August 1982, Curley worked a non-stop stretch of eighteen-hour days. Tall and athletic, his goal was to run at least thirty miles a week, but he was having trouble getting his miles in. He spent so much time in the office he treated it like his living room. He stopped wearing a tie, came to work in his New Balance running shoes, and walked around in his stocking feet a lot. Above his typewriter in his fifteenth floor office he kept an array of vitamins and natural foods.

One day, during another marathon meeting about what to put in a prototype edition, Curley got up from the meeting table. This was not unusual. Neuharth, Quinn, and Curley often paced the conference room during meetings. But that day Curley did something new: He lay down on the floor and passed out.

Someone looked over and said: "He's not breathing!" Donna Rome, the newsroom administrator, left the room and told others in the newsroom: "John Curley may have died." The fire department was called, and someone remembered that a news assistant, Jack Kelley, had taken CPR training. Kelley ripped Curley's shirt off, tearing off several buttons. He was beginning resuscitation when Curley came to and looked down at his torn shirt. "I'm terribly sorry, Mr. Curley," Kelley said. "Here are your buttons." Then the firemen arrived with their yellow coats and oxygen masks.

It turned out Curley had been out late the night before wining and dining new USA TODAY news staffers, had gone running in the morning, and had not eaten anything. Taylor Buckley brought Curley a vanilla pudding and a banana from the restaurant downstairs. Curley took a couple of bites and tried to go on with the meeting but kept nodding off. Finally he went home, took a nap, and came back to work that night.

A memo that Neuharth wrote in November to Curley and Martin, with a copy to Quinn, reflects some of the heat that USA TODAY's founder put on his top editors. It was marked "private and confidential," and it said:

> As we agreed, I am to have the following in my in-basket on the Front Page Desk every night when I am in town:
>
> 1. The *very latest* Page 1 dummy, starting at the end of the 4:30 news conference and updated as the night wears on.
>
> 2. The *very latest* printouts on every Page 1:
>
> Story
> Headline
> Overline
> Cutline
> Newsline
> Promo Ear
>
> Page 1 still works for us too irregularly or infrequently, in terms of the total look and content. There are two ways to improve on this:
>
> 1. The Page 1 news conference should not adjourn until there is a clear understanding on all color cropping, sizing, positioning—with due consideration to overline space, headline space and cutline space. A full-page-size dummy should be used. Graphics sizing and cropping must be very precise. (Editors, not artists, must decide this!)
>
> 2. We absolutely must not allow ourselves to be satisfied with any Page 1 headlines (including ears, overlines, etc.) until they have been rewritten and massaged to perfection.

Too often we accept something that is far less than the best.
We must view every word in every headline from the point of
view of the potential reader, totally unfamiliar with the content of that day's newspaper, walking up to the vending
machine and wanting to be grabbed by what is seen in the top
half of Page 1.

If we can do the above act together—regularly and consistently—with the present setup and present actors, great. If
we cannot, we must change or add to the setup or some
actors or both. . . . Thanks.

Then he had scribbled, in heavy black marker, at the bottom of the
memo: "Last night was the most *disorganized* front page desk operation I have seen. We *will not* tolerate such in the future."

Neuharth read and critiqued every edition of USA TODAY in those
early days and sent dozens of notes to Curley, Martin, and Quinn. The
founder's memos were always typed or scrawled on peach-colored
paper, which stood out in the sea of white paper. People always knew
to open the peach envelopes first; Quinn called them "orange meanies." Others called Neuharth's notes "zap mail" or "Pumpkingrams."

*Before she joined USA TODAY, Donna
Rome worked in the music industry,
including a stint with the Beatles Music
Publishing Company. She was instru-
mental in organizing the loaner
program so that it ran smoothly.*

*Jack Kelley's duties as a news assistant
didn't include writing stories, but he
was determined to succeed. He often
stayed late to help out or write his own
stories. He was promoted to reporter
after he helped cover the Challenger
disaster in January 1986.*

Bob Barbrow, an editor who was the statistics expert in the Sports department, summed up all of those demanding days in one neat sentence: "When Al wants to water ski, we all row a little harder."

■

Launch day was crazy for Carolyn Vesper, but no crazier than any other day leading up to it. Vesper, twenty-nine, had left a good job in computer sales with Xerox, even taken a pay cut to sell this snazzy new newspaper. She had been selling million-dollar computer systems; she figured selling a 25-cent newspaper would be a breeze. Her job was to convince hotel chains and airlines to buy USA TODAY at a wholesale price—12.5 cents a copy instead of 25 cents—and give it to their customers as a courtesy.

For the last few weeks, however, Vesper had spent more time loading newspaper racks into vans than she had selling. Loading vans was certainly not part of her job description, but after all, she had gone to work for Gannett on April Fool's Day, 1982.

In what had become typical for many USA TODAY employees, Vesper had left her office in the silver tower at 2 A.M. on Wednesday, September 15, just as the first edition was rolling off the presses eight miles away in Springfield, Virginia. After a couple of hours of sleep, she was back at work at 5:30 A.M. Finally, she thought, she could start selling full-time, so she had put on her best summer outfit—a white linen suit. The sun wasn't up yet, but Vesper looked like the prototypical executive in Savvy magazine.

On the way in, she heard a disc jockey for WMAL radio say: "There's a beautiful new newspaper that's hitting the stands—USA TODAY." Her day had started on a nice note—until she got to the office and saw the first edition. The front page color photos showed an airliner that had crashed in flames, with people injured or killed—the last thing Vesper wanted to see on the front page.

For weeks, she had worked to convince Eastern and Delta airlines to give copies of the first edition of USA TODAY to their customers leaving from Washington. She knew many airlines had an unwritten rule that they wouldn't distribute a newspaper that prominently featured an airplane crash—even if it said, "Miracle, 327 survive . . ."

She went straight to National Airport, where she discovered there had been a delivery foul-up. The newsstands had newspapers, but the

Carolyn Vesper says, "The last week before we started publishing got totally frenzied. The nights blended in with the days."

airlines didn't. Vesper knew she had to tell the airline managers something, so she did the most expedient thing. She lied.

Vesper told the Delta and Eastern managers the newspapers had not been delivered because of the crash photos. "We knew about your rule. We thought you should decide. Do you still want to put the papers on the flights?"

They did. "I'll be right back with them," Vesper said. She walked back to the stacks of newspapers that were outside the newsstands—it was 6:15 A.M. and they weren't open yet—and began unbundling newspapers. Clutching the papers against her white linen suit, she made several trips and carried hundreds of copies to the airline counters.

By 7:30 she was back in Rosslyn and the circulation office on the sixth floor began to get calls saying that newsracks around Washington and Baltimore were selling out. There were thousands of extra papers on the loading dock downstairs, but there was no truck to carry them. Vesper and Tom Crowley, another circulation sales executive, got Crowley's station wagon, backed it up to the dock, and began loading papers. They drove all over Washington, refilling racks, and when they ran out of papers, they went back to get more. They did that all day until after dark, when Vesper finally went home, exhausted.

She looked at herself in the mirror and discovered that her white linen suit was no longer white—it was covered with newspaper ink. She threw it in the garbage.

■

John Garvey, USA TODAY's production director, couldn't believe it. One of the new composing room cameras, which was used to shoot everything that went into the newspaper, had slipped off its mounts during one night in August. The camera weighed nearly three thousand pounds, so it had crashed right through the wall and it was leaning out into a hallway. The launch was imminent, so it was imperative to get it up and operating.

Garvey was in a hurry, so he grabbed a long crowbar and joined two helpers trying to jack the camera up. They did it, but Garvey threw out his back. In the frenzy of work to get ready to print the first edition, he ignored the injury for weeks, until his leg went numb and he began dragging his foot when he walked. Finally he saw a doctor, and a year later he had surgery to fuse the two broken discs in his back.

■

Joe Welty, USA TODAY's vice president/advertising, had been up and down Madison Avenue a hundred times, knocked on a thousand doors, and he still couldn't sell any ads.

"What niche does USA TODAY have?" asked Phil Guarascio, then senior vice president of Benton & Bowles, an advertising agency. "Where is the hook?"

John Garvey was an executive, but he did what had to be done to get USA TODAY to press on time—even if it meant picking up a pica pole and pasting up type himself.

Joe Welty was trying to sell advertising space that nobody wanted to buy.

Welty had heard that over and over from advertising executives. Pushing discounts and special deals, he had been trying for more than four months to sell them on USA TODAY—with little success.

Neuharth had told him not to worry about getting much advertising revenue the first year. They would get the readers first, he said, and the advertising would follow. Welty was grateful for Neuharth's patience, but he had his pride—he wanted to see ads in this new national newspaper. A few advertisers wanted to be in the first edition, but after that the interest died. The people who made advertising decisions for a living were very skeptical.

"Why do we need to be in this newspaper?" the Madison Avenue types asked. "Who's going to read it? I've got The New York Times, The Wall Street Journal—why do I need USA TODAY?

"Is this thing a newspaper or a magazine? What budget do I take the money out of? What's the circulation? What do you mean, it's not audited circulation yet? So who needs it?"

Welty had left a secure job at McCall's, where he had worked for eleven years, rising to advertising director. He had wanted a new challenge, and he got one. Actually, it was more like "Mission Impossible" than a challenge. And in the fall of 1982, there were some bleak days when he wondered why he ever accepted it.

■

Leading the first edition with the death of Princess Grace proved to be a controversial choice. The critics just couldn't understand how editors could see that as the most important story of the day. Their com ments reflected an attitude many journalists took toward the new newspaper—they didn't like it.

As soon as Neuharth stepped out of the limousine onto the Mall on September 15, reporters gathered around him and demanded: "Why did you lead with Princess Grace?"

Why, indeed, asked the reporter for The Washington Post in her story the next day—"when virtually every other newspaper gave greater prominence to the killing of Lebanese President-elect Bashir Gemayel?"

And then the reporter wrote: "Answer. Because Al Neuharth wanted to. 'Al did his own survey,' explained Executive Vice President Vincent Spezzano. 'He asked around town, different people. He asked me. He said that he thought Princess Grace was the most important story in the minds of the people.'"

It certainly wasn't the most important story in the minds of other journalists. Within a week, in the September 20 edition of Adweek magazine, Ray White, a former editor of Washington Journalism Review, would write: "It is difficult to define news in such a way that Princess Grace's death is more important than Gemayel's."

Neuharth often explained the choice this way: "Gemayel was Lebanon's president, but Princess Grace was our princess; she belonged to the people of the USA."

From the first edition on, Neuharth set an example with his eighteen-hour days, and nearly everyone else, from top editors and executives down to district managers and news assistants, followed it. They worked ten, twelve, fourteen hours a day—whatever it took to get the job done.

They worked hard because they had to. Starting a new newspaper was a Herculean task. They had designed it from scratch, assembled a staff, transformed a skyscraper, installed computers, set up satellite links, modified presses, designed newsracks and put them on thousands of street corners. They had produced, printed, and sold a brand-new newspaper, and they were proud of their work.

So naturally everyone at USA TODAY was interested in what the critics and their peers in the media business thought. As the months passed, the reactions poured in, and much of what was said and written stung them.

Ben Bradlee, the executive editor of The Washington Post, was asked if USA TODAY could qualify as one of the top newspapers in the country. "If it can," Bradlee said, "then I'm in the wrong business."

In The New Republic, Jason DeParle offered this observation: "Gannett is known for expert marketing and mediocre journalism, and its latest endeavor is the product of both. . . . USA TODAY is Gannett's version of 'Good Morning, America'—easily digestible, visually captivating, and broadcast via satellite five days a week in living color. Television fans can now have their tube and read it too."

A.M. Rosenthal, then the executive editor of The New York Times, said several months after the launch, "I really do not want to evaluate USA TODAY. I almost never see it, and I really am not in a position to judge."

David Hall, executive editor of the St. Paul Pioneer Press, concluded that reading USA TODAY was like "reading the radio."

Edward Sears, a managing editor at the Atlanta Journal and Constitution newspapers, went even further. He said reading USA TODAY was "like reading the phone book."

Ben Bagdikian, a journalism professor and longtime critic of newspaper chains and Gannett, made the pages of the Columbia Journalism Review sizzle with his indignation.

"Unfortunately, the country's first truly national daily newspaper of general circulation is a mediocre piece of journalism," Bagdikian wrote. "It has no serious sense of priorities: stories are played up or down not because of their inherent importance but on the basis of their potential for jazzy graphics or offbeat features.

"If USA TODAY accomplishes only partly what its promotion predicts, which is to make a major impact on newspaper reading, it will be no gain for the reading public, which gets a flawed picture of the world each day from the new paper, and a serious blow to American journalism, since the paper represents the primacy of packagers and market analysts in a realm where the news judgment of reporters and editors has traditionally prevailed."

Some of the sharpest criticism focused on Al Neuharth. His critics knew that this newspaper was Neuharth's baby, and many of them were cheering for it to fail—for personal reasons, if not for competitive ones. They thought he was too pushy, too full of himself. They saw his aggressive, hard-driving style as ruthlessness; they said Neuharth would climb over his own mother to get to the top.

In 1978, in one of the first long profiles of Neuharth, the Los

Angeles Times media critic David Shaw wrote: "Critics see Neuharth as a bit of a hustler, a huckster. Even a good friend says, 'When Al wears a sharkskin suit, it's hard to tell where the shark stops and where he begins.'"

Otis Chandler, the scion of the family that owned the Los Angeles Times, told reporters he thought Neuharth started USA TODAY because "Al always wanted to be the publisher of a newspaper of importance, and he doesn't have any."

And at the cocktail parties at the newspaper conventions, the publishers joked about USA TODAY and wrote it off. It's Neuharth's ego trip, they said. He'll be lucky if it lasts a year. They'll have to repaint all those boxes and use them at their newspapers in places like Chillicothe, Ohio, and Coffeyville, Kansas, they said.

Even The Associated Press story on the first edition exuded uncertainty:

> SPRINGFIELD, Va. Sept. 15 (AP)—USA TODAY, Gannett's
> multimillion-dollar attempt to create a national daily news-
> paper for a general audience, rolled off rented presses today.

No one was more aware of the risks than Neuharth, for it was a disastrous early failure that had helped shape his life and work. He read the criticism more closely than anyone, and some of it hurt. The doubters seemed to have the field to themselves. As John Morton, the respected analyst of newspaper companies and their stocks, noted in April 1982: "The list of large-circulation daily newspapers successfully established since World War II is not just short—it is nonexistent."

No matter what the critics called the new newspaper—Neuharth's folly, Neuharth's nonsense, Neuharth's ego trip—it was clear that many of them were cheering for USA TODAY to fail. They thought McPaper would never make it.

CHAPTER TWO

Rich and famous

Although few people outside Gannett realized it, launching a newspaper was not a new experience for Al Neuharth. On his first "launch night" thirty years earlier, a little sports weekly printed on peach-colored paper hit a few hundred newsstands in sparsely populated South Dakota.

It was the fall of 1952. Despite the war in Korea, the nation was optimistic. World War II had transformed the economy, companies were learning to think on a national scale, and business was good. Dwight D. Eisenhower had just won the presidency in a landslide. Norman Vincent Peale's *The Power of Positive Thinking* topped the nonfiction bestseller lists. The Dow Jones Industrial Average had reached a twenty-two-year high—at 281. Headlines reported the fantastic wealth of the newspaper baron William Randolph Hearst, dead at eighty-eight. He left an estate of $40 million.

Al Neuharth, who was destined to build a modern media empire himself, had just quit a steady seventy-five-dollar-a-week job with The Associated Press. Too impatient to spend years banging out wire stories, at twenty-eight Neuharth had decided to embark on a risky venture. He was going to start his own newspaper, and he was worlds away from corporate jets and limousines.

The son of a farmer who worked eighty acres near Eureka, South Dakota, two hundred miles northwest of Sioux Falls, Neuharth had a hard childhood. When he was two, his father died. Daniel J. Neuharth had been hurt when his leg got tangled in some farm machinery; then he developed tuberculosis. Daniel Neuharth had to travel to and from

Neuharth learned on the plains of South Dakota that he was a reporter who didn't know how to pay the rent.

the Mayo Clinic in Rochester, Minnesota, for treatment, so the family moved off of the farm and into the tiny town of Eureka, population twelve hundred, where Al Neuharth was born in 1924.

A few years after his father died, the family moved to Alpena, an even smaller town in Eastern South Dakota. To support her two children, Christina Neuharth took in sewing and laundry and waited on tables at Alpena's only restaurant. Al and his brother Walter, seven years older, taught their mother, the daughter of German immigrants, how to speak English. As soon as the boys were old enough, they went to work—it was the middle of the Great Depression.

"We didn't have any money," Neuharth recalls. "I guess we were poor. I learned that things are not given to you—that you've got to go after them and you've got to make your way and be prepared to scratch or scream or do whatever's necessary to survive."

That drive to survive came from his mother, who died in 1981, at the age of eighty-six. "She was a very tough woman," he says. "She decided that survival was the name of the game, and she survived. Her philosophy was that you ought to do a little bit more tomorrow than you did today, a little better next year than you did this year. Not a bad philosophy."

In 1935, when he was eleven, Neuharth delivered the Minneapolis Tribune, increasing the number of customers on his route from two to eleven. At thirteen, he began working after school in the composing room of the Alpena Journal, a weekly. Then he got a better-paying job for one dollar a week as a butcher's helper, and then became a soda-jerk in the drugstore that had the local off-sale liquor license. "I was the first guy in town to know who was drinking what," he recalls. He was also the editor of his high school newspaper, The Echo.

Neuharth loved sports, and wanted to play on Alpena's basketball team. His high school was so small, he says, that "every male who could walk and breathe played." But during an outdoor pick-up game he slipped on some ice and a much bigger kid fell on his leg, dislocating his knee, which healed slowly. He longed to participate, so he came up with a creative solution: He became a cheerleader—the first male cheerleader at Alpena High School.

By cheering the team on, Neuharth had found a way to attend all of the "away" games. It was at a basketball game between Alpena and Woonsocket that he met Loretta Fay Helgeland, whom he later married. They were divorced in 1972, and she lives in Rochester, New York. "He was a noisy little devil," Loretta says. "I knew right away that he was different. He was brighter than all of the other boys, advanced in his thinking."

In 1942, Neuharth graduated from high school and won a one-year scholarship to Northern State Teachers College in the South Dakota Boys' State competition. He lasted three months. Quarter-final exams were coming at Northern State, and the world was at war. Just before exams, Neuharth and ten of his friends enlisted together. They didn't want to wait for the draft.

Christina and Al Neuharth
not long after he hurt his leg.

He served more than three years as a combat infantryman, rising to sergeant. The army trained his unit for amphibious assaults in the Pacific, but his first assignment was on dry land in Germany, with a reconnaissance and intelligence platoon in the 86th Blackhawk Infantry Division. They fought the Germans in 1945, and Neuharth won a Bronze Star for carrying out "many missions throughout the combat period, under blackout conditions and often through enemy artillery and sniper fire."

He came home in February 1946. That June, he and Loretta were married. They bought a trailer house, and that summer they worked together in a traveling carnival, running a darts stand—three throws for a nickel—and a game where contestants pulled strings to win the usual worthless prizes. In the fall he enrolled at the University of South Dakota at Vermillion; the G.I. Bill paid his tuition. Loretta had finished a year of college, so she got a job teaching in a one-room schoolhouse, grades one through eight, north of Vermillion.

When he first went to college, Neuharth thought his future was in the law. "He was going to be a feisty lawyer, a Clarence Darrow type, helping the poor and downtrodden," Loretta says. But now that he was twenty-two and married, the idea of three extra years in law school after he had given three to the army did not appeal to a young man—a young man in a hurry. He decided to major in journalism. His aim was to become "rich and famous"—as quickly as possible.

Even then, Neuharth was very aggressive. At the University of South Dakota in the late 1940s, he cut a flamboyant figure. A combat veteran, he was older and brasher than many other students. He made a special effort to look distinctive, to be noticed. Although he had been a foot soldier, his trademark in college was a leather air force flight jacket, worn with an aviator's long white scarf, which he knotted and let hang down in front. Neuharth was only five feet, eight inches tall, but he was alert and assertive, with wavy black hair and rich brown eyes. "He was a striking guy, striking looking," recalls Craig Stolze, a retired sportswriter who was also at USD then.

Neuharth tried broadcasting first. It seemed natural to combine journalism and his love of sports, so he became a football announcer on KUSD, the college radio station. First he did the color, and later the play-by-play. He found out what people thought of his broadcasting talents when his older brother Walter, who ran a clothing store in Wessington Springs, brought a portable radio to a home game. Walter

Neuharth, in flight jacket and white scarf, with two Volante editors, Craig Stolze and Jim Kuehn, in 1950.

turned up the volume so he could hear Al call the plays. Nearby fans told him to turn it off. "Don't you want to hear the game while you're watching it?" Walter asked. "Not with that goddamn idiot broadcasting it," came the reply. Always sensitive to his public, Neuharth exchanged the microphone for a seat behind a black Royal typewriter in the office of the college newspaper, the Volante.

Neuharth and a friend, Bill Porter, concocted a plan to "control" the University of South Dakota. Porter was supposed to seize the student government, while Neuharth took over the media. They engineered a "draft Porter" movement that got Porter elected student body president. Neuharth became the Volante's editor; Porter was its business manager. "We were having a lot of fun controlling this and that," Porter recalls. "It was very sneaky. We manipulated the whole thing; we were power brokers."

Neuharth's official biography says he became editor of the Volante "partly because he needed the $15-a-week salary the job paid." But he liked being in charge, too. Craig Stolze was sports editor of the Volante then; he remembers Neuharth as a real mover and shaker. "He was intelligent, ultra-aggressive and had an inbred desire to succeed. When he became editor of the school paper, he immediately revamped it."

The 1949 University of South Dakota Yearbook shows Neuharth taking a Volante from the "newstyle offset press." The caption read: "The college publication gets a complete check before being distributed."

In a few months, Neuharth switched the Volante from letterpress printing to offset and changed its format from a broadsheet to a tabloid. The 1949 University of South Dakota Yearbook shows him examining a paper that has just rolled off the press, a scene that was to be repeated often in the future.

Stolze remembers Neuharth was always a prankster. In 1948, the two of them hitchhiked the 350 miles from Vermillion to Grand Forks, North Dakota. It was the University of North Dakota's homecoming game, and they were almost the only South Dakota fans there. Neuharth spotted a North Dakota pennant on a pole above the stadium and said, "Let's get that thing down." He shinnied up the pole, got it, and ran away, dodging hostile fans. "It showed the guy has got guts galore," Stolze says.

After the game, they began hitchhiking back. They spent the night in a cold train station in Wahpeton, North Dakota, and the next morning, the South Dakota team bus picked them up on the barren prairie highway. Neuharth had the pennant in his pocket. Loretta remembers that as typical. "He was very, very serious about his goals in life, but he wanted to have fun along the way."

In college, Neuharth worked to make the Volante into a lively newspaper, and Porter did a good job selling the ads and managing the finances. The two of them began to believe that they might be able to build a publishing empire. "We decided we were such hotshots that we would become rich and famous in the publishing business after we got out of school," Neuharth recalls.

They sat around and "gassed" a lot. In one bull session, Neuharth introduced his big new idea: A statewide sports weekly to be called SoDak Sports, patterned after his favorite, the national Sporting News. He thought the idea was a natural. South Dakota was wild about high school and college sports, and none of the state's daily newspapers, not even the big one—the Argus Leader in Sioux Falls—did a thorough job of covering sports throughout the state.

In 1950, Neuharth was elected to Phi Beta Kappa, graduated from USD, and joined The Associated Press as a reporter. While Neuharth established his reputation around the state as a reporter, Porter finished law school. They planned to launch SoDak Sports in 1952.

Neuharth had no doubt it would succeed. He and Porter saw SoDak Sports as just an interim step on the way to a publishing empire. Their plan was to publish and prosper in South Dakota, start a similar sports newspaper in Minnesota, and then go national and "develop an empire." Not everybody was so sure they could do it. Porter recalls that when he told his father, a successful merchant, about SoDak Sports, "he just about decked me."

During his two years as a wire service reporter, Neuharth worked hard. The Associated Press had only three people in South Dakota, so he covered everything—from car accidents to sports. His editors thought he was a sharp reporter and a clear, logical writer. They offered him promotions to Minneapolis and later to New York, but he turned them down. Neuharth was too restless, too ambitious, and too impatient to want to climb any corporate ladder rung by rung. He was determined to find fame and fortune the fast way.

With Neuharth as editor and Porter as business manager, the first issue of SoDak Sports appeared on November 21, 1952. It sold for a dime, and it was printed on peach-colored newsprint—an idea Neuharth stole from the Minneapolis Tribune and The Des Moines Register, which used peach newsprint in their Sports sections. He even stole a promotional slogan—"Reach for the peach"—from the Des Moines paper.

To raise $50,000 to start SoDak Sports, Porter and Neuharth went around South Dakota selling hundred-dollar blocks of stock to sports nuts. The most anyone invested was four hundred dollars. "Our idea was that with each one-hundred dollar shareholder you had a real prestigious shareholder, a real fan," said Porter, now a successful lawyer in Rapid City, South Dakota.

SoDak Sports was a zippy little newspaper. Its masthead featured an outline of the state, with SoDak Sports emblazoned across it, and an underline proclaimed: "The COMPLETE Weekly Sports Paper for ALL South Dakota." When it came to promotion, there was NOTHING SUBTLE about Neuharth's style.

SoDak Sports spent a lot of time and energy promoting itself. Neuharth's instinct for blowing his own horn was obvious then, and it proved to be a trait that helped shape Gannett and ignite his critics for years to come. But his promotional claim was true: SoDak Sports was a COMPLETE sports newspaper. It had every score, every result in South Dakota. To encourage readership, Neuharth and Gordon Aadland, the newspaper's humor columnist, revived an old trick from political campaigns. "We wrote complimentary and provoking letters to the editor over a pseudonym," Aadland recalls.

Sodak Sports carried in-depth stories on every sport and every important game played in South Dakota. In the fall, it reviewed football and previewed basketball. It covered the outdoors—hunting and fishing—in depth. Long before women's sports were popular, it devoted extensive space to women's basketball—which it called "the gals' game." The newspaper even took some heat from ardent male fans for taking "the gals" seriously.

It had its own all-star teams, its own coaches-of-the-year, its own team rankings, its own predictions, even its own mascot—the leggy, busty Mamie Van Doren. She was in Hollywood by then, but she hailed from Rowena, South Dakota. Neuharth knew that a little cheesecake never hurt sales, so SoDak Sports ran pictures of Mamie in short-shorts when football and basketball were over and things were slow. The jocks thought Mamie made a nice contrast when the sports news was about the pheasant population or where the walleyes were biting.

SoDak Sports had a feature, "We asked 'em," where the inquiring photographer—Neuharth with his reliable Rolleiflex—would ask fans about a sports issue. Neuharth knew how to generate extracurricular interest in his newspaper, as when he asked six female cheerleaders: "When you're at a basketball game, who do you watch the most, the

It's New! *SoDak Sports* 10¢

The COMPLETE Weekly Sports Paper for ALL South Dakota

VOLUME I   SIOUX FALLS, S. D., NOVEMBER 21, 1952   NUMBER 1

All-State Grid Teams Honored

★ 1952 ★ ALL-SO DAK FOOTBALL STARS

FIRST TEAM

Wayne Simons, Sturgis — Back
Jack Becker, Yankton — Back
Meredith Mitchell, Milbank — Captain, Back
Bob Berguin, Sioux Falls — Center

Jim Staggs, Sioux Falls — Guard
Nip Johnson, Brookings — Back
Jim Kuchmann, Lead — Guard

Deane Rykhus, Brookings — End
Ken Schulte, Mitchell — Tackle
Bill Vogt, Watertown — Tackle
Wayne Fix, Aberdeen — End

★ Second Team ★

Jerry Keffeler, End	Sturgis
Jack Neuroth, End	Sioux Falls
Merle Aamot, Tackle	Brookings
Dean Willard, Tackle	Spearfish
Leonard Spanjers, Guard	Milbank
Don Englebrecht, Guard	Tyndall
Johnny Meyers, Center	Huron
Dave Christensen, Back	Brookings
Billy Jones, Back	Deadwood
Gordon Englert, Back	Cathedral, Sioux Falls
Billy Cone, Back	Flandreau

★ Third Team ★

Roger Laubak, End	Sisseton
Billy Geis, End	Belle Fourche
John Brown, Tackle	Watertown
Ross Omen, Tackle	Chamberlain
Jim Larsen, Guard	Britton
Bill Huddleston, Guard	Sturgis
Dick Boettcher, Center	Aberdeen
Arlo Grass, Back	Rapid City
Duane Leach, Back	Sioux Falls
Jack Spargur, Back	Pierre
Don Barnhart, Back	Mitchell

On the Inside

● All the latest waterfowl and deer hunting tips plus an exclusive "inside story" on the fish poaching racket are included in the big outdoor section, pages 12, 13 and 14.

● The All-SoDak College football team is on page 4. The All-SoDak six-man stars are on page 2.

● There's a big Class "B" basketball preview and roundup on pages 8 and 9.

● You'll find more about the 11-man All-SoDak football team on page 2.

● Keglers, your bowling news is on page 11.

SoDak Sports' weekly mission was to blanket South Dakota. "All-State" teams and results from across the state, shown on next page, were two devices used to give the paper a statewide flavor.

June 5, 1953   SODAK SPORTS   Page Eleven

Two No-Hitters Highlight Heavy Amateur Action

Emery, Lily Hurlers Toss Perfect Games

By The
SODAK SPORTS STAFF

It was a fine weekend, with the first cooperation of the season from the weatherman, and SoDak's amateur baseball players got in their first good lick of the season over the Memorial Day holiday weekend.

Two no-hit games and some wild scoring splurges headlined the parade. The no-hitters were picked up by Gordon Smith of Emery and Walter Kruse of Lily.

Here's the way the action went around the state—a complete report on the playing activity of nearly 150 of SoDak's amateur teams, from every corner of the state:

LITTLE EIGHT

Wallace blasted 13 hits and runs to win a free-scoring contest from Turton, 16-12. Elmore and Brekke teamed up to hurl the seven-hit win.

Florence edged Garden City, 3-2, as Kessler allowed only three hits in getting the victory. Billy Stenwedel doubled for the winners.

Bradley topped Turton, 13-0, with Fritz and Bill Obermier both collecting home runs.

DAY REFUGE

Grenville blasted Enemy Swim, 28-3 as Henry Koslowski got two home runs and R. Henning added one.

Roslyn added two wins over the weekend, defeating Enemy Swim 6-3 and Ortley 3-1. A home run by Lyarpeya led the Roslyn win over Enemy Swim. Jerde struck out 15 Roslyn batters in losing.

HILLSIDE VALLEY

Corona crushed Big Coulee, 20-5, with a home run by Vic Settje leading the winner's 12-hit attack.

Big Stone won over Wilmot, 14-6, as Lynn Bruna and Lloyd Howell each got a single and a double to pace the hitting.

It took Marvin 11 innings to get the best of Milbank Dokeya. A punch hit single by Herman Reyelts scored the winning run for Marvin.

CORN BELT

A no-hit, no-run game by Emery's Gordon Smith highlighted loop action. Smith's no-hitter was a 15-0 win over Alexandria.

Salem came from behind to beat Humboldt, 6-4 when Fetert, Salem pitcher, homered with a man on and Byrd added another. Spencer bested visiting Freeman, 11-6. Spencer's starting hurler, Scarborough, chalked up strikeouts in the first seven frames. Freeman's Walters led hitters with a perfect four-for-four.

Canistota defeated Montrose

11-5, although the losers outhit the winners, 12 to 11. Four Montrose errors hurt.

UPPER SIOUX VALLEY

Arlington's 11 hits paid off for 11 runs and an 11-2 win over Castlewood. Ringgaard gave up just six hits to get the victory.

Toronto topped Bruce, 8-6 with Rynerson and Richie teaming up to get credit for the win.

Estelline edged Dempster, 5-4. The winners got eight hits to four for Dempster.

OAHE

Ten Onida hits gave that club 9-3 win over Ft. Pierre at Onida. Lamb started on the hill for the winners, with P. Kane going the last six innings and getting credit for the win.

Blunt bested Ft. Thompson, 6-3. Smith collected 13 strikeouts in hurling the win for Blunt. Robert Engle, Ft. Thompson manager says he's looking for weekday games and teams interested should contact him at Ft. Thompson.

SUNSHINE

Tripp scored five runs in the first inning and went on to defeat Ethan, 10-2. Ollie Isaak, starting his first loop game of the season, allowed only three scattered hits in getting the win. Willie Hoff got an inside-the-park homer for Tripp.

Parkston won over Delmont, 12-5 to give them a record of 2-2 in loop play. Louis Fergen got a third inning homer for the winners.

NORTHERN HILLS

Peterson hurled no-hit ball for seven innings as he pitched Sturgis to a 7-2 win over Spearfish Sunday. He allowed six hits and two runs in the final two frames. Moistad collected three hits for the winners, including a round-tripper.

Ft. Meade pounded out an 18-5 win over Vale, with Salzen getting four hits in six trips to lead the winners. L. Land and Wood each got 2 for 5 for Vale.

LAKE REGION

Walter Kruse hurled no-hit ball for Lily to get a 2-0 win over Bruseport. He walked two and gave up eight, with only four opponents getting on base. Holmquist split two games winning from Pierpont, 16-7. Seven Pierpont errors hurt in their loss.

Andover got two-hit pitching from Rich Marske and Morehouse for its 10-6 win over Bristol. The winners collected eight straight hits during a five-run rally in the seventh.

PONY HILLS

Woonsocket took an 8-5 Pony Hills loop win over Letcher with Gene Bentz going all the way and giving up eight hits for the win. In a memorial day non-league game, Woonsocket dumped previously unbeaten Howard, 7-5 at Woonsocket.

Dick Hackett went the route for the winners in that one.

Mitchell's Cobbs bested Mt. Vernon, 9-1. Shaw got 17 strikeouts in hurling the win.

Wessington Springs banished Plankinton its first loop loss of the season, 13-4. The winners collected 15 hits off the offerings of A. Strand, Anderson and L. Strand.

Alpena scored a 27-16 win over Forestburg in a contest marred by errors. Alpena had 14 hits and nine errors while Forestburg had 10 hits and committed 14 errors.

ROSEBUD

Bill Amacher made it two in a row for Burke as he hurled an 18-2 win over Wewela. Amacher had a no-hitter for 7 1/2 innings. He struck out 11.

JAMES VALLEY

Huron's Stahla Flyers edged Redfield, 7-6. Redfield led through most of the game but four hits and three runs in the 9th gave Huron the win. Highmore broke up a 4-4 deadlock with Faulkton in the 8th inning to take a 6-4 win. Brewer of Faulkton collected a three-bagger for the game's longest hit.

PHEASANT

Howard continued to ride high with a 4-0 record to lead the loop. The leaders rolled to a 21-4 win over Oldham in a game called at the end of six because of rain.

Madison VFW bested Ramona 5-2 to also remain undefeated in league play.

Carthage bested Winfred, 8-2. The standings:

Team	W	L
Howard	4	0
Madison	2	0
Canova	2	2
Ramona	2	2
Carthage	1	2
Winfred	1	3
Oldham	1	3

WHETSTONE VALLEY

Summit bested Strandburg, 3-1 as Zachonier struck out 10 to get the win. Webster's Rodney Soyland allowed only one hit in hurling his team to a 2-0 win over La-Bolt. He struck out 13. Milton Nelson, LaBolt pitcher, struck out 15 but allowed seven hits for two runs.

South Shore bested Milbank's Fire Chiefs 8-6 as the losers left 12 men stranded on the bases.

EASTERN DAKOTA

Gary broke up a 1-1 deadlock in the 7th inning to topple Clear Lake, 3-1. It was a well-played game with Milton getting credit for the win. Clear Lake committed two errors while Gary played flawless ball.

EDMUNDS COUNTY

Ipswich pounded out SoDak's biggest score of the weekend with a 55-2 win over Loyalton. Mel Tuscher and Beselich each

hit two home runs for the winners. LeRoy Tuscher added one homer. In a non-loop game, Ipswich bested Mound City, 17-15 in 11 innings on Memorial Day. Leola collected a 12-6 win over Hosmer, despite 11 errors. Jim Rath got his first homer of the season for the winners with two men on. Schumacher was the winning hurler with a six-hitter.

SAND LAKE

Hecla scored the winning run in the last of the 8th to down Westport, 3-2 after Ed Schaumann of Westport had homered in the top of the 8th to make it 2-all.

Pat Vickers got a homer for Claremont but it wasn't enough as his team lost to Frederick, 7-5. Britton remained undefeated in the loop with a 7-0 win over Columbia. The two-hit hurling of G. Jonsman got the shutout for Britton.

LAND O' DUCK

Browns Valley pounded two Sisseton pitchers for 17 hits and a 16-7 win. Dingman of Choklo hurled a two-hit shutout to beat Wheaton, 5-0. Wilmot defeated Dumont 4-3 and Rosholt downed New Effington 4-0 as Gabrielson hurled a three-hitter.

SOUTHERN HILLS

Igloo nipped Hot Springs, 9-8. The hits were identical to the runs, with Igloo getting nine and Hot Springs eight. Bangart got 15 strikeouts in eight innings.

HUB CITY

Aberdeen's defending State Amateur champion Preds blasted Bradburya, 18-1 in a Hub City loop game. It was their league opener.

The Harbor team pounded out 12 hits for an 11-1 win over McPearya. Gunderson got the win on a neat three-hit job.

STANDING ROCK

Bullhead blasted Little Eagle, 13-1, with 18 hits figuring in the win. Red Bear got the lone round tripper for the winners.

CENTRAL STATE

Bowdle took over a first place tie in the Central-State loop by defeating Hoven, 10-8. Hoven had been alone at the top going into the game. Bowdle got its 10 runs on seven hits and

Hoven errors.

Lowry bested Onaka, 10-4 as H. Perman famed 17 Onaka stickers. C. Perman, M. Huber and H. Perman each collected two hits for the winners.

REE VALLEY

Orient toppled Ames 14-11 as Bob Hansen pounded out four hits, including a triple, for the winners. Orient got 10 hits to eight for the losers.

YELLOWSTONE TRAIL

Mobridge and Eureka both won Sunday in the Yellowstone Trail loop to set the stage for their big clash at Eureka next Sunday.

Mobridge blasted Mound City, 31-3, with a 26-hit attack telling the story.

Eureka downed Selby, 11-3. A big 5-run fifth inning spelled the win. Stoebner threw a five-hitter for Eureka.

SOUTH MOREAU RIVER

Marcus matched its 17 hits with 17 runs for a 17-7 win over Iron Lightning. H. Klinss collected 11 strikeouts in hurling the win, while losing pitcher Co Carley fanned 10.

MEDICINE CREEK

Kennebec took over sole possession of first place in the Medicine Creek loop with a convincing 17-2 win over Vivian. The combined three-hit pitching of Hehn and Halverson gave the leaders the win. Jack Pier doubled and tripled to lead the Kennebec hitting.

Presho got its first win of the season with a 14-6 triumph over Cacoma. Lower Burle moved up to a second place tie by beating Murdo.

The Standings:

Team	W	L
Kennebec	3	0
Vivian	2	1
Lower Brule	2	1
Presho	1	2
Cacoma	1	2
Murdo	0	3

PRAIRIE

Dean Boskelheide pitched and batted Northville to a 5-3 decision over Ferney. Boskelheide hurled three-hit ball and chipped in two hits, including a home run with one man on base which provided the winning margin.

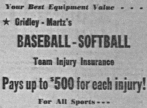

WE ASKED 'EM

Gals Agree: All Talent, No Looks, Makes Jack Dull Boy

"We Asked 'Em" got real people into the weekly talking about sports issues. It was one of many ideas in SoDak Sports that Neuharth would use later in his career.

best looking boys or the best basketball players?" The cheerleaders cared more about good looks than good set shots.

The little peach tabloid ran sports news from every little town that managed to field a team. It had news from New Effington and Wallace and Pierpont and Agar and Florence and Hayti, all neatly organized on one page. As a result, SoDak Sports gained instant loyalty from readers in the small towns not served by one of South Dakota's thirteen dailies. "People who lived in the boondocks waited with bated breath to get it," Craig Stolze says.

Bob Yackley, a rancher who lives in Onida, South Dakota, remembers waiting for SoDak Sports. "Everybody looked forward to getting that paper. I was only thirteen then, but I remember they would spread the pages across the windows of the drugstore, so we could see where they had ranked Onida and Agar." The paper was living up to its motto: "SoDak Sports Blankets the State!"

Tom Brokaw, now of NBC News, was a regular reader. Brokaw grew up in Pickstown, South Dakota, where he was a 135-pound second-string quarterback on a six-man football team. Brokaw decided to play a joke on a teammate, George Hall. After talking to Brokaw, Hall became convinced that he was going to make the SoDak Sports Class C all-star team. So when Friday came, "like a big bass rising to the bait," Hall ran down to the drugstore to get the latest copy of SoDak Sports. Brokaw and his friends stood off to one side and laughed at

SoDak Sports ran many game pictures to attract fans.

Hall's disappointment, as only teenagers can. "SoDak Sports was a real Bible," Brokaw says. "It was very important to us during its brief run."

In Vol. 1, No. 1, of SoDak Sports, Neuharth wrote that one of the goals of that newspaper was to "bridge the gap between east and west, north and south and make South Dakota one big 'sports family.'" That was a theme that he would return to, again and again.

Even with his considerable energy, Neuharth couldn't cover all of South Dakota by himself. So he organized an advisory board composed of sports editors from many South Dakota dailies. The little weekly wasn't considered competition, so the editors became SoDak Sports stringers and made sure it had all the scores. They also contributed ideas and occasional stories.

Jerry Tippens, now an editorial writer with The Oregonian in Portland, thinks the idea for a news network came from Neuharth's experiences on the Mitchell (S.D.) Daily Republic, where he worked one summer during his college vacation. That newspaper had a circulation of about twenty thousand in a town of only twelve thousand. The Daily Republic covered that lightly populated area like a blanket. It had a huge network of stringers and a company plane, which it used to fly copies of extra editions to distant towns.

In 1953, as part of a circulation drive, SoDak Sports gave away an all-expenses-paid trip to the Rose Bowl. Neuharth went along with the lucky fan, and the experience confirmed his instinct that good promotion was essential to success. When he got back to Sioux Falls he gushed in an editorial that Rose Bowl officials "are as fine a group of promoters as you'll ever find. These people don't overlook a bet in the promotion of their project. They're proud of that Rose Bowl, they tell people so constantly and they made every effort to satisfy each Rose Bowl visitor so he'll go back home and 'talk up' this event. And, those public relations efforts certainly have paid off for them. To us that's further proof that proper promotion is the key to the 'selling' of anything."

Neuharth took his own advice. A full-page promotional ad in SoDak Sports in 1953 proclaimed: "We're crowing . . . Because . . . We're growing."

It continued: "Yes, SoDak Sports has moved into a NEW and LARGER office location. And we're crowing about it because it is the first in a series of steps to be taken in an expansion program designed to bring you an even BIGGER and BETTER SoDak Sports every Friday."

we're crowing

Because . . .

We're Growing

Here's the view of the NEW SoDak Sports offices as you come down Main Avenue from the North in Sioux Falls. Located just one block South of the Coliseum, the NEW location of SoDak Sports represents a 300% increase in office facilities. The move to the NEW offices is the first in a series of steps in the SoDak Sports expansion program.

We're Crowing . . because We're Growing — Yes, SoDak Sports has moved into a NEW and LARGER office location. And we're Crowing about it because it is the first in a series of steps to be taken in an expansion program designed to bring you an even BIGGER and BETTER SoDak Sports every Friday.

★ WE STARTED FROM SCRATCH . . .

Actually, all we had to start with in Issue Number One of SoDak Sports was an idea. We had no way of knowing what your reaction would be to a COMPLETE Weekly Sports Paper for ALL South Dakota. The venture was an "experimental" one. We could only hope to be able to fulfill the need we were confident existed — the need for statewide coverage of the greatest citizen builder in our society — SPORTS. During the "Trial" period of SoDak Sports, we made our share of mistakes. You've been very patient with us about those. And you've been most kind about acknowledging our accomplishments. It is because of YOU we were able to say . . .

★ TO GIVE BETTER SERVICE . . .

SoDak Sports has moved into the NEW location you see pictured above. This is step number one in a planned series of expansion moves soon to be completed which are designed to step up our ability to give you a better product. Our NEW offices, with a capacity over three times greater than our old location, will enable us to adequately house our increased staff and the facilities necessary to complete preparations for the next move forward. In our NEW location, we are in a position to serve more actively as the clearing house for the information which goes into the complete, statewide picture of the SoDak Sports scene.

★ WE'RE HERE TO STAY . . .

SoDak Sports has been accepted as an institution by the sports loving public of our state. As we near the end of our first year of publication, we are increasingly aware of our responsibility — our debt to you. Without the support of our many thousands of loyal readers and increasing number of advertisers, it would not have been possible to attain our present position. The fact that you have continued to "Reach for the Peach" every Friday has given us the confidence and ability to actively plan and — as of this date — actually undertake an expansion program geared to give you a better SoDak Sports each week.

★ WE'RE STILL "ON TRIAL" . . .

with you readers. Even though the initial "Trial" phase of our operation has been completed for some time, you may rest assured that we won't lose sight of the fact that we are constantly "on trial" with you readers. Throughout our whole operation, we will always be striving to give you a product which will enable you to give us a favorable verdict week after week. That's why when "We're Crowing" we will be doing a lot of "Crowing" about it. We want you to know that we are placing ourselves in the position of being able to offer greater and more complete services to our readers and advertisers. We want to do more FOR you and WITH you, for therein lies our responsibility to YOU.

When You Are In Sioux Falls . . STOP IN AND VISIT WITH US . . At The NEW SoDak Sports Office — Just a Block South of The Coliseum.

SoDak Sports' founder was never shy about promoting his newspaper.

SoDak Sports was a typical weekly newspaper operation: Porter handled the business side, Neuharth handled the news side, and they did everything themselves. "We put in a lot of thirty-six- and forty-eight-hour days," Porter recalls.

On a winter weekend, Neuharth would climb into one of their two light-green Plymouth station wagons, which had a map of South Dakota and the SoDak Sports logo emblazoned in peach paint across the side. On a single Friday night, he sometimes covered four high school basketball games. Starting in eastern South Dakota, he photographed the pregame in one town. Then he drove twenty miles and did the second half of another preliminary game, then drove another fifteen miles and hit the second game of a doubleheader in another town, and then headed west. South Dakota is divided by a time zone; you gain an hour west of the Missouri River, and sometimes Neuharth could use that to catch the end of a fourth game.

"In the beginning, I did all the reporting, writing, picture-taking, and editing alone," he says. "Then on Tuesday we'd go to the composing room and help them make up the pages, help them run the press, and bring the papers down to the post office and mail them."

Neuharth and Porter were truly underpaid and overworked—they paid themselves one hundred dollars a month. "We took virtually nothing out of the paper, only what it cost to live," Porter says. By then, Loretta Neuharth was the assistant to the credit manager at a Sioux Falls clothing store, so they had enough to live on. Instead of money, Porter and Neuharth took their salaries in stock. They rapidly became the largest shareholders in SoDak Sports: Al and Loretta had more than ten thousand shares, and Porter had just under ten thousand.

Neuharth developed his management style at SoDak Sports, too. Don Lindner, who worked for the weekly in 1953 and later became sports editor of The Rapid City Journal, says they all worked long hours, "but Al was probably working harder than anyone else. Things were to be done his way. He was demanding about that. He wanted perfection. He can be charming, but he also can be very firm."

Bill Porter says of Neuharth's style: "Al was very methodical, very objective, and ruthless as can be. He had an ability to see circumstances clearly and turn them to his advantage."

SoDak Sports' circulation grew fast, from a few hundred a week to eighteen thousand after about a year. Things were going so well that Neuharth decided to celebrate in an editorial marking SoDak Sports' first anniversary: "A year ago SoDak Sports was a brand new experiment. The odds were heavy against a new publication such as this 'living' beyond a trial period of two or three months. The only reason we're still here, and here to stay, is because you fans and readers have demonstrated, overwhelmingly, that SoDak Sports fills a want and need in the South Dakota publication field."

In that same issue—November 20, 1953—he announced the birth of his son, Daniel J. Neuharth, II. "He 'reached for the peach' on his very first day in camp and used enough diapers the first two days to 'Blanket the State'!" Neuharth wrote in his regular column, "SoDak Sports Slants."

In his annual report to readers, Neuharth didn't mention advertisers. That's because there weren't many. But if times were tough, the reader didn't notice it in the newspaper's tone. The young entrepreneurs got a bit cocky; they started talking about bigger things. They told people that they were thinking about launching a daily, general-interest newspaper, a tabloid to compete with South Dakota's biggest daily, the Argus Leader, which had a circulation of about thirty-five thousand.

Neuharth wasn't shy about attacking his opposition. When the Argus Leader mistakenly awarded the "fisherman of the year" title to a man who had caught a fifteen-pound Northern Pike, Neuharth wrote that three newspapers, including SoDak Sports, had reported that an Aberdeen man had caught a twenty-four-pounder. He couldn't resist adding a jab: "It's embarrassments like that which we expect will cause the Argus to return to its former and rightful role as a South Dakota regional newspaper and leave the business of statewide reporting and statewide awards to a statewide publication like SoDak Sports."

For the 1953 World Series, Neuharth went to New York with a Buick dealer who had won a SoDak Sports promotion. Neuharth didn't even have tickets. He expected to buy them from scalpers, and then the Buick dealer managed to get better seats for everybody from General Motors. After Neuharth watched his beloved Yankees win their fifth straight World Series title, he unloaded again on the Argus Leader. Its editor, Fred C. Christopherson, had written a column saying it was a "myth" that a left-handed pitcher enjoyed an advantage over a left-handed batter.

Neuharth answered that in an editorial with the headline, "Another

Strikeout for the Argus Leader." Neuharth wrote: "For your information, Mr. Editor, here is the No. 1 fundamental of baseball strategy, as recognized by any six-year-old boy on the sandlot baseball diamonds." He explained a "cardinal principle of baseball science." Left-handed pitchers enjoy an advantage because their curve ball breaks away from left-handed hitters. Neuharth closed by writing: "If you still insist on trying to enter this field of sports which is so completely foreign to you, may we make one suggestion? Before you put yourself back in the lineup next time, call SoDak Sports, telephone 2-8012.

"A friendly group of good sports stands ready there to answer any questions you might have. We don't like to see those big goose eggs after anyone's name in the lineup. In the interests of a better batting average for you, Mr. Editor, SoDak Sports will be happy to give you any information you might want concerning any sports subject before you take another wild swing at the plate."

Christopherson was furious. He ordered his staff not to mention SoDak Sports in the Argus Leader's news columns. Neuharth had learned how to needle critics or competitors.

Months passed, and circulation remained steady. On the news side everything was fine, but the business side was in sad shape. SoDak Sports wasn't making any money. Their problem was simple: They weren't getting enough advertising. The longer Neuharth and Porter studied the situation, the clearer it became that they could not get enough ad revenue to support SoDak Sports.

They had no consistent, regular advertising contracts. They had a few cigarette ads, and they tried a lot of promotions. If a team won the state basketball championship, they sold merchants one-shot ads congratulating the team. But almost all the ads were small and time-consuming and expensive to sell.

"Advertising was catch as catch can," says Porter, who handled it. "We would sign up advertisers for fourteen-dollar contributions: 'Casey's Drug Store salutes the Clark Comets.'"

The young entrepreneurs got one bad break, too. By 1953, television had come to Sioux Falls. The few auto dealers who had sales in more than one part of the state liked seeing themselves on the small screen, so they canceled the tiny schedules they had been running with SoDak Sports.

Circulation revenue was no answer. Since many newspapers still sold for a nickel then, it was unrealistic to try to raise the price of

SoDak Sports, which already sold for a dime, to a level that would bring in a lot more revenue, like twenty-five cents. "We were losing and losing and losing and we didn't have a hell of a lot to lose because we never had more than fifty thousand dollars in capital," Neuharth says.

In the spring of 1954, Jerry Tippens returned from Korea and stopped in Sioux Falls to see Neuharth, his old friend from the Mitchell Daily Republic. Tippens could tell from Neuharth's comments that SoDak Sports was in tough shape financially, but as the drinks flowed they began to dream a little. "We talked about how you would go about putting out a national newspaper, in a country that was so large and so diverse," Tippens recalls. They talked about the transportation problems, the time zones, the great challenge it would be.

But Neuharth's Dakota dreams were a long way from coming true. In the summer of 1954, he and Porter realized they didn't have enough money to keep going. They had to sell a lot more stock, or raise a lot more money some other way, or fold. They announced that SoDak Sports was going to take a "time out" for six weeks. It would come back stronger than ever, Neuharth pledged. They tried to find more investors. They found a few and took pledges, but never collected the money.

Their failure was a bitter disappointment, but especially to Neuharth. SoDak Sports was his dream. "So we sat down and said, 'It hurts like hell, but we better admit it ain't gonna work,'" he recalls.

They got a lawyer who outlined their options. They could just quit and seek protection under the bankruptcy laws. Or they could try to sell SoDak Sports and see if they could recover the investment.

They tried to sell it—to Fred Christopherson, the editor and part-owner of the Argus Leader, the same newspaper Neuharth had been picking on so persistently in the news columns. Christopherson was not interested in buying SoDak Sports. Instead of seeing it as a business opportunity, he seemed to take some pleasure in the failure of these cocky young kids. "He just laughed at us," Neuharth says. "He wanted to see us go belly-up."

So they did. They held a bankruptcy sale. They didn't have much: a few desks, some typewriters. They couldn't raise enough money to pay all of their bills, so the creditors got less than thirty-five cents on the dollar. The shareholders' stock was worthless.

Neuharth remembers it this way: "It was pretty sad. The thing that surprised us both was that a lot of our stockholders were in Sioux Falls, and a lot of them came by when we were selling off equipment, not to buy, but to thank us for all the fun. Hell of a surprise, because we thought we'd be run out of town on a rail."

In the winter of 1954 on the treeless, windswept South Dakota plains, Porter and Neuharth, the would-be media moguls, had to figure out what to do next. Porter had a law degree, so he decided to stay in South Dakota and join a law firm. Neuharth decided to seek his fortune elsewhere—as far from South Dakota as he could get.

SODAK SPORTS CALLS. . .

Time Out!

. . .FOR A MONTH

Take a break, catch your breath, then come back and give 'em all you've got.

That's the standard procedure for a "time out" situation in sports events. And that's what SoDak Sports will be doing, starting next week.

With this issue, SoDak Sport begins a one-month period during which publication will be suspended. We'll be back in your mailboxes and on your favorite newsstand starting Friday, Nov. 5.

We have decided, reluctantly, that the "time out" period is necessary to allow us to reorganize and put into reality a number of topnotch ideas we have to bring you a bigger and better sports paper every Friday.

During our initial two years of publication which we are now completing, the constant routine requirements in producing a weekly statewide paper on the scope of SoDak Sports have added up to a tremendous task. They have kept us from devoting as much time as we would like to the development of new ideas, new experiments in this brand new field of a weekly statewide sports paper.

Those are the things we'll catch up on during the month of October.

Among the contemplated changes before November 5 are a re-location of our center of operation, developments of new editorial contacts and features, and other reorganizational steps designed to move us full speed ahead on the road toward a better organized, bigger, more interesting weekly sports paper.

We had hoped we could make the operational changes while continuing regular publication. But we've found that would be impossible, without the quality of the paper suffering. So we've decided it's better to call "time out," quickly take care of the necessary reorganization and changes, then come back in full force.

Naturally, all SoDak Sports subscribers will be compensated for the loss of a month's issues. Five weeks will be added to the subscription period of all subscribers.

Our staffers will continue in the field during this "time out" period, keeping their fingers on the sports pulse of the entire state, preparing themselves for the newer, bigger sports paper coming up.

We'll see you November 5. We hope you'll agree THE NEW SODAK SPORTS we bring you then was worth the "time out" period.

. . . the Publishers

From the last issue of SoDak sports.

Before he left, the two of them tried to figure out what went wrong. "We mismanaged it," Neuharth says. "We misjudged what kind of revenue we could get. We had an idea for a sports newspaper that was popular, but we had no business plan. We had no idea what percentage of our revenues would have to come from advertising or from circulation, in which year or in which month. We just had an idea without a plan."

The young editor landed on his feet. He had a cousin who lived in Fort Lauderdale who knew someone to write to at The Miami Herald. Neuharth put together a resume, dug out his back copies of SoDak Sports, and solicited a letter of recommendation from South Dakota's governor, Sigurd Anderson, who was a loyal reader. "Everyone needs some diversion from his work," the governor had explained, and Neuharth had run a picture of Anderson reading SoDak Sports under the headline, "Our No. 1 Reader."

With those credentials, Neuharth got a reporting job on The Miami Herald. The Herald offered him ninety-five dollars a week, pretty good for 1954. He was happy to be getting out. "After the thing went belly-up, I left. I didn't want that shame hanging over my head."

Broke and in debt, but wiser about the way a business works, Neuharth left South Dakota for Florida. And buried in the ashes of his failure were the seeds of a much bigger idea.

CHAPTER THREE

Space-age
newspaper

George Beebe, managing editor of The Miami Herald, was opening his mail one day in the fall of 1954 when he came across a letter from Al Neuharth, asking for a job. Beebe had read thousands of resumes from young journalists who wanted to work in sunny Miami, and the volume from "snowbirds" always increased when it got cold up North. This application was a little different: It included a recommendation from South Dakota's governor. And when Beebe looked at SoDak Sports, he was impressed; it was a good newspaper, and it wasn't all sports news.

For example, when President Eisenhower vacationed in South Dakota in June 1953, Neuharth appointed himself White House correspondent for SoDak Sports. On the trip out to the Black Hills, he economized by sleeping in the car. He covered Eisenhower's fishing trip in detail, including the political aspects, and made sure Ike had copies of SoDak Sports to read when he wasn't fly casting.

The news side of SoDak Sports was virtually a one-man show, and Neuharth's high energy level impressed Beebe. But The Herald didn't have an opening for a reporter just then, so Beebe stuffed Neuharth's resume in a drawer and forgot about it.

While out of work, Neuharth began to worry. He had one offer, for ninety dollars a week, to go back to The Rapid City Journal, where he had worked one summer. The money was fine, but he really wanted to leave South Dakota. His other possibility was to edit a trade magazine for a steel company in Duluth, Minnesota, but he saw that as a last resort.

Then Beebe had an opening. He placed a call to Alpena, South Dakota, looking for Neuharth. Christina Neuharth told Beebe her son had gone to Minneapolis; he was staying at the Nicollet Hotel. The trip was for an interview with the steel company. When Neuharth walked into his Minneapolis hotel room, the phone rang. It was Beebe: "Would you be interested in this reporting job?"

You would have expected Neuharth to leap at it. He had just seen his dream of a statewide paper die; he desperately wanted a win to counterbalance that loss. Instead, he was cool and careful. He told Beebe he had been planning to visit his cousin in Fort Lauderdale: "Let me come down to Miami, take a look around, get a feel for the place," Neuharth said. "I'll pay my own way."

Neuharth bought a train ticket in Sioux Falls and rode the two thousand miles to Miami, sitting up for two nights. He couldn't afford a sleeper. When he walked through The Herald's newsroom, he was impressed and a little scared. It was bigger than anything he had ever seen, but it was a big opportunity, too. He told Beebe he'd take the job; he just wanted a few days to look around town, to talk to a few people before he went to work.

This was Neuharth, checking out the local scene. It became a lifelong habit. "He used to tell us that he could go into any town in this country and in a day or less find out what the passions of the town were, the mood, what they liked and didn't like," says Jim Head, who had joined The Miami Herald in 1954, two months before Neuharth. "He would spend time in diners talking to waitresses and countermen. He would talk to cab drivers, bus drivers, people on the street. And then he'd go to the Chamber of Commerce and talk to them. But most of the people he talked to were working-class. He knew what they were thinking."

His mind made up, Neuharth went back to Sioux Falls and borrowed two hundred dollars from Loretta's brother, Les Helgeland, who was sports editor of the Mitchell Daily Republic. He and Loretta, who was then pregnant with their second child, loaded their belongings into a U-Haul trailer and put little Danny in the car. Off they drove to Miami, to a new state and a new life.

In The Herald newsroom, Neuharth made an immediate impression. His first big scoop was a story about two brothers, the Kramms, who were running a mail-order scam. They had rented a small office in a seedy area and put in a few phones. They hired women to go through phone books from major cities and pick out people with Italian or Irish last names. The women called and tried to sell their marks plastic crucifixes: "Just send five dollars, in cash, in the mail. It's a benefit to help veterans."

Neuharth's exposé ran on The Herald's front page, and the postal authorities shut the Kramms down. The Herald followed up with editorials condemning this outrageous fraud and congratulating itself and its reporter. A few months later, Neuharth discovered that the Kramms were back in business at a new location. He wrote the story again, and this time the Kramms went to jail. Neuharth won several awards, and a citation from the postmaster. "It was a real coup," says Jim Head, who later became executive editor at King Features. "Everybody took notice of the kid reporter."

Head was from Kansas. He had graduated from the University of Kansas Journalism School, and stayed in Lawrence to work at the Journal-World. He had mailed resumes all over the country, and George Beebe hired him over the phone, without ever meeting him. Head was on The Herald's copy desk one night when a man walked in off the street, distraught. In those days, newspapers had no security guards. The man said, "I just shot my girlfriend."

Art Himbert, an assistant city editor, saw Neuharth sitting in the back of the city room, finishing up a story. Himbert brought the man back to the kid reporter and said: "Talk to him. See what he's got." Then Himbert went back to his desk and told the copy editors on the rim that the walk-in was probably just another nut.

Five minutes later, Neuharth reported back: "You better call the police. This guy shot his girl. He's got a gun. It's back there at my desk." Then he walked back to his typewriter and kept the guy talking until the police came.

The cops found the girlfriend, shot several times and barely alive, in the man's apartment. Neuharth pounded out the story, right on deadline. It went take-by-take to the desk and on out to the composing room. "It was a great story," Head remembers. "He was star-kissed on some of those things. A lot of guys can be in the right place for the lightning to strike, but no one knows any better than Neuharth what to do with it when it does hit. That's his great magic. He can exploit a situation as well as anyone I ever saw."

Neuharth's career took off. After two years as a general assignment reporter, several months in The Herald's Washington bureau, and some time as an assistant city editor, Beebe told his young star he wanted to make him executive city editor. Neuharth sized up the situation and calculated how he could get the most out of it. Instead of taking the job immediately and basking in the glow of a quick promotion, he asked that the news be kept secret for a couple of months, while he worked at the side of the acting city editor he was slated to replace. The day before Neuharth's promotion was announced, the acting city editor—who was popular in the newsroom—was deposed. The editor was upset; he turned to his friend Neuharth for solace. Neuharth listened and sympathized, but didn't let on that he was taking the man's job. When it became clear what had happened, some reporters were angry. "It was the mark of a sharpster," Head says. "That's what he was and is today. He makes no apologies for that."

A few reporters thought Neuharth was too ambitious to be trusted. His detractors gave him a nickname, the Black Knight. Later, they began calling him the Black Prince. It seemed likely he would inherit the throne some day, and they didn't like that. "One of the reporters who didn't like him said it was because wherever he goes he leaves a field littered with dead," Head recalls. "He was ruthless and unscrupulous and a hell of a good operator on top of everything else. There was a lot of bitterness in the city room because of the way he had vaulted over everyone."

Then in 1957, thousands of miles from Miami, a rocket was launched that would help change Neuharth's career.

The Russians surprised the world by placing in orbit the first artificial satellite, *Sputnik*. Their success came on October 5, just four months before the United States was supposed to launch its satellite, which everyone had expected would be the world's first. The nation was in shock: Sen. Henry Jackson, a Democrat from Washington, called it "a devastating blow to the prestige of the U.S. as the leader in the scientific and technical world." Sen. Styles Bridges, a Republican from New Hampshire, sounded even more ominous. He said it was time for Americans "to be less concerned with the depth of the pile on the new broadloom rug or the height of the tail fin on the new car and to be more prepared to shed blood, sweat and tears if this country and the free world are to survive."

The space race was on. And one place where blood, sweat and tears were being shed was at Cape Canaveral, the main U.S. launchpad midway down Florida's Atlantic coast. Before the space program, Cape

Canaveral had been a sleepy fishing village nestled among the orange groves of Brevard County. The local resort town was Cocoa Beach, just south of the Cape. Cocoa Beach was a resort all right, but it was—as Tom Wolfe described it later in *The Right Stuff*—a low-rent resort. Wolfe wrote that Cocoa Beach was so low-rent that the vacation houses there were "little boxes with front porches or 'verandas' nailed onto them and a 1952 DeSoto coupe with venetian blinds in the rear window rusting in the salt air out back by the septic tank."

Cocoa Beach was being transformed from forgotten backwater to boomtown. Engineers from Los Angeles and Seattle and Detroit were flocking to the place, to operate the huge *Jupiter* and *Atlas* rockets that roared off the launchpads at Cape Canaveral. Officers and technicians were pouring into Patrick Air Force Base, along route A1A just south of Cocoa Beach, to install the radar dishes that would track the big rockets across the heavens.

The government was throwing money at the space program, and the word was out that Cocoa Beach was the place to be. There were jobs there, guys there, girls there, and you could sleep outside under the stars and life was just one big party, one big beach. Bars and strip joints were springing up everywhere to cater to space workers who were working double and triple shifts and had money to burn, and closing time was 4 A.M. Housing was in such short supply that people camped on the beach until they could find somewhere to stay, or someone to move in with.

That was the scene Al Neuharth walked into in 1959. By then, he had been promoted to assistant managing editor of The Miami Herald and he was there to open its new Brevard County bureau. The Herald was looking for ways to increase its circulation 180 miles from home. Cocoa Beach had up-to-date entertainment, but its newspapers seemed closer to the Stone Age than the Space Age.

Along the Atlantic Coast, there was no daily newspaper between Daytona Beach on the north and West Palm Beach on the south, a distance of 180 miles. Brevard had three little weekly or biweekly newspapers—in Cocoa, Melbourne, and Titusville—but no local daily. And the county was bursting with well-traveled, well-educated, and well-paid people: By 1960, its population had more than doubled in a decade, to 111,000. It was the fastest growing county in the country.

Neuharth sensed a big opportunity. It was clear that the Space Coast was about to explode with growth. And when it came to newspapers, there was an obvious vacuum. Orlando was sixty miles to the west, and while the Sentinel Star reported on Brevard County, its coverage was sparse and spotty. The Miami Herald sold a few thousand copies of an early edition in Brevard, but it carried almost no local news, no late news, and no late sports scores. The answer, Neuharth thought, was to start a new daily newspaper.

He took his bright idea back to Miami. The Knight brothers ran The Miami Herald and Knight Newspapers then. John S. (Jack) Knight, the crusty, aggressive editor-publisher who had built the chain into a national company, was editor-in-chief of The Herald, splitting his time between newspapers in Miami and Akron. Neuharth had caught Jack Knight's attention, partly because he had been a star reporter, but also because they were both avid sports fans. They had discovered that when Neuharth ran into Jack Knight prowling around the newsroom, looking for the racing results on the wire.

As Neuharth moved up in the Knight organization, he served on newspaper-wide committees and met Jim Knight, the Herald's business manager. So it was natural for Neuharth to go to Jim Knight and say: "You ought to start a newspaper up in Brevard County because that's where people are going to come, from all over the country."

Jim Knight reacted the way many of the senior executives in Neuharth's life have when they heard one of his crazy ideas—he laughed. Then he said: "Kid, we're doing pretty well already."

Neuharth refused to quit. He pushed: "Well, if you don't want to start a new newspaper you ought to buy one of those papers up there that's a weekly, turn it into a daily, and make that part of your network." Jim Knight thought Neuharth might have something there. The Knights tried to buy the Melbourne Times, but its owner wouldn't sell. "They didn't pursue it very aggressively," Neuharth says now.

At Knight Newspapers, Neuharth kept on moving. In 1960, he was appointed assistant to Lee Hills, executive editor of the Detroit Free Press. Hills' title was deceptive: he was really the publisher of the Free Press, in charge of the business side as well as the news side. Hills was moving up fast in the Knight organization and likely to be promoted; as Hills' heir-apparent in Detroit, Neuharth split his time between the news and business operations.

Just before Neuharth left for Detroit, Jack Knight saw him off. Knight took Neuharth aside and told him: "You've done all right playing softball in Miami. Now it's time to see if you can play hard-

John S. "Jack" Knight built the newspaper chain that evolved into Knight-Ridder Newspapers, Inc., from the Akron (Ohio) Beacon Journal, which he inherited from his father in 1932.

ball in Detroit."

Knight wanted Neuharth to play hardball. "I was the corporate bad news guy from Miami," Neuharth says of his role in Detroit. "Lee Hills superimposed me on top of the managing editor, and we retired some folks who had been retired on the job for a long time. They were anything but Neuharth fans." That episode enhanced Neuharth's reputation as a ruthless corporate climber.

Detroit was a tough newspaper town. The Detroit News, owned by the Evening News Association, and the Free Press, which Knight had purchased in 1940, were fiercely competitive. The Free Press had large, strong unions which didn't make managing it any easier.

One Saturday night Neuharth was attending a formal Chamber of Commerce dinner when the pressmen called a "chapel" meeting and announced they were stopping work, on the spot. An editor called Neuharth back from the dinner, and a few minutes later he stepped off the freight elevator into the Free Press pressroom, resplendent in his black tuxedo. "You've finished your comic books," he told the disgruntled men, who liked to do a little light reading during breaks between editions, "so why don't you go back to work. We've got a newspaper to put out. We can talk about this on Monday." Maybe it was his tuxedo or his promise to talk later, but it worked, and the presses rolled.

In 1963, unbeknownst to Neuharth, Paul Miller began looking for bright young people to help him run Gannett Newspapers. The company had been started by an upstate New York entrepreneur, Frank E. Gannett, who bought a half-interest in his first daily in Elmira in 1906,

In 1931, Time magazine
speculated that Frank E.
Gannett could play a key role
in starting a national daily
newspaper.

for three thousand dollars in cash and seventeen thousand dollars in loans. He later bought several other newspapers, and by 1950 owned eighteen in New York State and others in Connecticut, Illinois, and New Jersey.

Frank Gannett was a teetotaler. He refused to let his newspapers accept liquor advertising, but he did allow them a significant degree of local autonomy. Editors and publishers of Gannett's newspapers made their own news and editorial decisions, while operating under tight, centralized financial controls. For example, in 1950, sixteen of the eighteen Gannett newspapers in New York State endorsed Thomas E. Dewey for governor, even though Frank Gannett opposed him.

Gannett died in 1957. As his successor, he had chosen Paul Miller, who had been Washington bureau chief for The Associated Press. The son of an Oklahoma minister, Miller was a charming chief executive and seemed, on the surface, to be easygoing. But he had a short fuse and, when crossed, his temper was fierce. He took a strong interest in the news and editorial policies of the newspapers, especially Gannett's Rochester newspapers, which had become the company's flagships soon after Frank Gannett moved to Rochester in 1918. Gannett kept the title of editor of one Rochester newspaper, The Times-Union, until 1948, when he retired in favor of Miller. When Miller became chief executive in 1957, the chain—it insisted on calling itself the Gannett Group then—owned twenty-three newspapers in five states.

Frank Gannett, and Paul Miller after him, were among the first executives to appreciate what a superior investment small- and medium-size newspapers could be. Most of these newspapers were very profitable, and many had no direct competition. They were usually owned by families or small companies, and as the years passed, many of them came up for sale. Sometimes family members lost interest in running the newspaper. Sometimes there was a family fight over how to run things. Or sometimes high inheritance taxes made it more attractive to sell the newspaper instead of keeping it in the family.

In addition to his Gannett role, for many years Miller was chairman of The Associated Press. He traveled widely on Gannett and AP business; he was on a first-name basis with nearly every newspaper owner of consequence in the country, and he played golf regularly with many of them. As a result, Miller was often the first to know when a newspaper was for sale. David Shaw of the Los Angeles Times wrote that when it came time for a family to sell, "Miller was often the first man many of them thought to entrust their life's work to."

By 1963, Neuharth was beginning to make a name for himself in the newspaper world. He had become a frequent lecturer at seminars run by the American Press Institute at Columbia University in New York, an independent group which sponsors seminars to improve the editing and business skills of newspaper executives, and he had made friends with API's director, J. Montgomery Curtis.

Curtis had grown up under the stern regime of A.H. Kirchhofer, who for nearly forty years was a powerful editor at the Buffalo Evening News, the newspaper of record for western New York. Beside his editor's desk in the middle of the newsroom, Kirchhofer had bolted a chair to the floor. When Kirchhofer summoned a sub-editor to sit for a chat,

Paul Miller, who traveled widely and met the leaders of many nations, started as an editor of The Okemah (Okla.) Daily Leader in 1926 for thirty dollars a week.

the wretch was forced to keep his distance. Monty Curtis had been Kirchhofer's city editor in that autocratic system, but he had one of the most creative minds in newspapers.

Casting about for help, Paul Miller asked Curtis who were the best and the brightest young people in American newspapers. Neuharth was one of the first names he mentioned, so Miller approached him. At first, Neuharth was reluctant to make a move. He told Miller he had a good job in Detroit, and Knight Newspapers was likely to promote him to run the operation there. But Miller was persistent and persuasive: He told Neuharth this was a rare opportunity, one that he ought to consider seriously. When Neuharth weighed his prospects with Knight and Gannett, he realized that the smaller New York company had one clear advantage. For a strong, ambitious executive like himself, there was a clear path to the top—there were no family members, no Gannetts, in the business. And the little company was aggressive; it seemed willing to reach a little farther and strive a little harder for success.

So in the spring of 1963, Neuharth took the job Miller offered: general manager of the Rochester newspapers. By taking over the chain's flagships—the Times-Union and the Democrat & Chronicle—Neuharth was following in the footsteps of Miller and Gannett. He was seen by outsiders as the heir apparent, but some insiders saw him as a threat to their hopes to be chief executive. His salary was $35,000 a year.

As usual, Neuharth wasn't satisfied with the status quo. He began changing the Rochester newspapers, improving their organization for the reader. He took all of the ads off the fronts of the sections, positions that advertisers had held for years and paid premiums to get. "He antagonized every one of the major advertisers," recalls Vince Spezzano, who was covering politics for the Times-Union when Neuharth was there. Spezzano was a very short, very popular political reporter who seemed to know everybody who was anybody in Rochester. Neuharth would have an occasional late dinner with Spezzano and pick his brain about the local power structure.

In changing the Rochester newspapers, Spezzano says, "Neuharth wasn't timid. He believed that any newspaper ought to be a reader's paper first, and that the advertiser ought to recognize that if people read the paper, they read the ads."

Editors in Rochester were also uncomfortable with Neuharth. John

Dougherty, the Times-Union's managing editor, called Neuharth the "space-age editor." Dougherty told his friends, "He's going up like a rocket, and he'll come down just like a rocket, too."

And, perhaps because he was caught in the gray gloom and salty slush of a Rochester winter, Neuharth thought about Cocoa Beach, too. He still dreamed of starting a newspaper there.

Neuharth needed someone else who was interested in a new venture in Florida, and in Paul Miller, he had found a natural. Miller wanted Gannett to be in Florida; he had tried to convince some Florida publishers to sell to Gannett, but it was hard for Yankees to buy newspapers there. Neuharth told Miller it wasn't necessary to buy an existing daily newspaper—you could just start one. Neuharth added with his usual modesty, "I know the state." He kept pushing and pushing, and finally Miller told him: "Okay, okay. Figure out how to do it."

Neuharth developed a plan. Gannett could buy one of the three existing small newspapers in Brevard County and either convert it to a seven-day-a-week publication or use it as a base to start a brand-new daily. Miller liked that idea, so he shared it with Gannett's two top financial executives, Lynn Bitner and Cy Williams. Bitner was the general manager of the company; Williams was its treasurer.

"They both thought it was the craziest scheme they had ever heard of in their lives," Neuharth says. The company was consistently profitable. It now owned twenty-six newspapers and had just bought the Westchester-Rockland newspapers, north of New York City. Gannett paid $15 million for those papers in 1965; by 1987 they were worth more than $200 million.

Everything's fine, the financial people said, let's not do anything dumb. Miller temporarily pacified Bitner and Williams by telling them the company would merely "explore" the idea of starting a newspaper in Florida.

By volunteering to start a new newspaper, Neuharth was going against a national trend. Daily newspapers were dying, not being born—especially in the big cities. In 1960, New York City was served by seven daily newspapers. By 1967, it had only three. One of its great newspapers, the proud Herald Tribune, published its last edition in April 1966. Labor problems, the growth of the suburbs, and competition from television were killing big-city dailies.

Back in 1959, Neuharth had met Marie Holderman, the elderly widow who owned the Cocoa Tribune, a small newspaper that was based in Cocoa, just inland from Cocoa Beach. In the spring of 1965, he went back down to talk to her again. By now, the Space Coast was really booming. Cape Canaveral had been renamed Cape Kennedy, in honor of the late president.

Mrs. Holderman was in her eighties now, and she was willing to listen to Neuharth. After a while, they began to discuss the outlines of a deal. With the reluctant cooperation of Bitner and Williams, Neuharth developed a sketchy financial plan for what it might cost to buy the Cocoa Tribune and use it as a base to start a new newspaper.

Moving carefully, Neuharth began to share his idea with others. He called in Vince Spezzano, the former Times-Union reporter whom he had promoted to head research and publicity for the Rochester newspapers, and swore him to secrecy. "He was pretty sure he could get the board to commit the money," Spezzano remembers. "They were going to buy Cocoa and start a daily. He laid out the whole scenario." Neuharth told Spezzano to go down to Cocoa and make a list of the five hundred most influential people in Brevard County—without mentioning the Cocoa Tribune or Gannett. "That's how I met and got to know every bartender and waitress in Brevard," Spezzano says.

Weeks passed, and finally Neuharth persuaded Mrs. Holderman to sell the Cocoa Tribune to Gannett for $1.9 million. By then, the Tribune was publishing five days a week, up from twice weekly. It claimed a circulation of sixteen thousand, but the real number turned out to be only nine thousand. They closed the deal one hot night in Cocoa. As they were driving off to dinner, Cy Williams looked at Neuharth and said: "Okay, we bought you the fucking thing. Now what are you going to do with it?" It was Neuharth's first glimpse of how far-sighted the financial department could be.

As Neuharth weighed the two options—converting the Tribune to seven days a week or starting an entirely new newspaper—he became convinced that a start-up was the way to go. He told Paul Miller: "We can't convert the Tribune to seven days a week and really have fun and do something exciting. We'll be taking something that's already there and changing it a little bit. I don't think that will excite the space community."

With Miller's support, and over the objections of the financial department, Neuharth persuaded Gannett's board of directors to spend between $3 million and $5 million, over five years, to start a new newspaper in Florida. It was a big bet for the little newspaper chain, but Gannett was still a private company then, and it didn't have to worry about maintaining a perfect record of quarter-to-quarter earnings gains for its shareholders. Neuharth was satisfied with the business plan. "We didn't make the mistakes we had made at SoDak Sports," he says. "This was a solid business plan. We knew how much advertising revenue, how much circulation revenue we had to get to survive."

And this time he had enough capital. He had found out at SoDak Sports why most new businesses fail—they don't have enough money at start-up. Neuharth didn't have to go to Harvard Business School to learn that lesson; he had learned it the hard way on the streets of Sioux Falls. "I was a reporter who didn't know how to pay the rent," he would say later of his SoDak Sports experience. He was determined not to let history repeat itself.

Gannett bought the Cocoa Tribune in June 1965, and Neuharth began planning to launch the new newspaper. First he invented a cover story. If anyone asked, they were to be told that Gannett was going to start a Sunday edition of the Cocoa Tribune. Neuharth hoped this deception would explain why Gannett was expanding the Tribune's little plant, installing bigger presses, and hiring a large staff. If they announced early on that they were starting a new newspaper, he reasoned, it would sap some of the drama and might provoke a bigger competitive response. The Orlando Sentinel Star was then selling twenty-nine thousand copies a day in Brevard County and had a bureau there.

Then Neuharth ordered some research. At the Detroit Free Press he had met Lou Harris, the pollster whose opinion samplings had helped convince John F. Kennedy to seek the presidency in 1960. In Detroit, Neuharth and Harris had designed the first thorough readership survey for a newspaper. It told them what the readers liked, what they didn't like, and what they expected from their newspaper.

Drawing on that experience, Neuharth asked Harris to survey Brevard County's readers. His passion for secrecy carried over to the research: Respondents were told the survey was being done for a department store. The results confirmed Neuharth's instinct that the way to go was to start a new newspaper; the readers there "weren't interested in local traditions or old stuff." Instead, many were newcomers from metropolitan areas; they were a cosmopolitan bunch, interested in change and science and space.

*Moe Hickey already had
been general manager and
publisher of a group of
weeklies in Philadelphia
and worked for Gannett as
business manager in Elmira,
New York.*

Neuharth began hiring. From Gannett's newspaper in Elmira, New York, he brought in Maurice L. "Moe" Hickey, a bright thirty-year-old, and named him business manager. Hickey was a strong number two to Neuharth, who was really the publisher. From Orlando, he stole the Sentinel Star's state editor, Bill Bunge, to be managing editor. Then Neuharth had to take care of another important detail: what to name his brainchild.

He wanted a name that would encompass more than just the little town of Cocoa or Cocoa Beach. This was to be a countywide newspaper. It was going to cover everything that happened in Brevard County, in depth and in detail. This time, Neuharth planned to blanket a county instead of a state. They kicked around different names—The Brevard World, The Brevard Sun—but nothing seemed to fit. Moe Hickey was in Orlando for a Florida Press Association meeting when he was awakened in the middle of the night by a phone call. Unable to sleep, he sat up thinking. Hickey hit on a simple name that night, but it rang right: TODAY.

Always the promoter, Neuharth added the explanatory underline: "Florida's Space Age Newspaper." To emphasize that, they put Saturn-like rings around the letter *O* in TODAY's masthead.

Hickey helped assemble the staff, doing much of the hiring in semi-secrecy. As an anniversary issue of the new newspaper noted later, with a hint of pride: "In late 1965 the new paper was such a well-guarded secret that many newsmen were hired without knowing they were going to work for TODAY." In the meantime, the staff improved the Cocoa Tribune, increased its circulation, and tried to get a feel for Florida.

Then, on January 27, 1966, at what TODAY later described as "a gigantic banquet at the Carriage House on Cocoa Beach," Neuharth and Miller told four hundred business, civic, and political leaders that TODAY would be launched in March. Spezzano's list of Brevard's top five hundred had come in handy; it formed the nucleus of heavy hitters for his first "launch party."

Neuharth knew that by starting a new newspaper, he was taking a career risk. "People in Rochester said I would come back as either the president of Gannett or as a copy boy," he says. The next two months were exceptionally hectic, even by Neuharth's hard-driving standards. An article Neuharth edited in 1967 for the first anniversary of TODAY captured some of the atmosphere of the start-up:

> This was the situation for Gannett Florida on Jan. 28,
> 1966: Brevard County knew there would be a new daily news-
> paper in less than two months, there was only part of a staff in
> Cocoa, there wasn't enough working space, construction was
> in progress, no one was quite sure how the new paper would
> look and there were as many ideas on how to get ready as
> there were people on the staff.
>
> From that unsteady beginning, the fledgling staff of your
> Space-Age newspaper geared up and in less than two months
> whipped into shape the paper you saw on March 21, 1966.
> How we did it remains a mystery even to those of us who
> were here. We lived in a nightmare of mistakes, correc-
> tions, conferences, critiques, shredded paper and sleepless
> nights.

During the start-up period, Neuharth spent most of every week in

The Saturn rings in TODAY's *nameplate gave the newspaper an instant space-age look.*

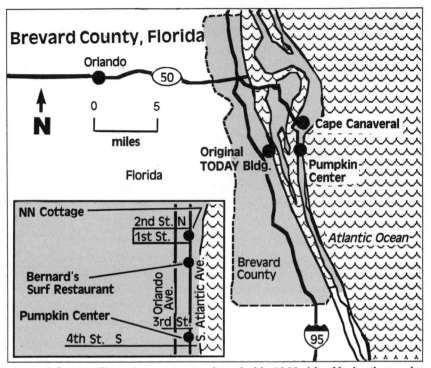

Brevard County, Fla., where TODAY was launched in 1966. After Neuharth moved to Pumpkin Center in 1973, many key corporate meetings were held at his home.

Florida. Although he was still general manager of the Rochester newspapers, he was clearly in charge in Cocoa. "We called him the Chief Architect," Moe Hickey says. "We more or less just carried out his orders."

Because he was still working part of the time in Rochester, Neuharth found it convenient to borrow people from the flagship newspapers to help on the Florida project. He borrowed editors, reporters, photographers, and artists. TODAY was the first Gannett newspaper to benefit from a "loaner" program, which later grew into a company-wide talent exchange.

As the pace of planning quickened, Neuharth decided that the original editing team wasn't strong enough. So he brought in his old friend from The Miami Herald copy desk, Jim Head, as executive editor. By then, Head was a top editor at the Detroit Free Press. To help Head, Neuharth sent in Ron Martin, a smart, ambitious young editor whom Neuharth had met in Detroit and then brought to the Rochester Demo-

Jim Head, right, first met Ron Martin, left, at the Detroit Free Press in 1959 soon after Martin graduated from the University of Missouri.

crat & Chronicle. "I may have been Gannett's first loaner," Martin says. Within a couple of months, Martin was TODAY's managing editor. Instead of dumping the people Head and Martin displaced, Neuharth made use of them elsewhere. Bill Bunge, who had been TODAY's managing editor, was shifted to editor of the Cocoa Tribune, which continued as a small local daily, Monday through Friday. Bunge remained involved in Cocoa news operations until he retired twenty years later.

Neuharth looked to outsiders for help, too. His old friend Monty Curtis, excited by the first new newspaper to attract national attention since Newsday was started on Long Island in 1940, came to Cocoa to lead two weeks of critiques of prototype editions. Edmund Arnold, a Syracuse University journalism professor who was a nationally known newspaper design expert, helped establish TODAY's 7½-column format.

As usual, Neuharth ruled on nearly every detail. He led the most intense phase of preparation, the two weeks of dry runs just before launch. The 1967 anniversary article caught this intensity: "Every other day for two weeks we put out an issue of the paper, complete with ads and run on a deadline-dictated schedule just like the real thing. Reporters covered events and wrote stories, editors edited them and wrote headlines, composing room operators set type and printers

From its first edition, the "Space Age Newspaper" gave readers in-depth coverage of the space program. The upper right corner of the first issue was used as a promotional box, giving the date of the next space shot, and a space story was stripped across the top. TODAY also had a full-time "aerospace writer."

made up pages, pressmen put on the plates and started the machinery, papers were distributed by truck to 'drop' points all over the county and the time was recorded . . . but that's where it stopped."

Neuharth was up in the early morning hours, riding in a car behind the trucks as they did their dry runs to the drop points, marking the time drivers took to execute each drop with a stopwatch. Sometimes Paul Miller rode along. The anniversary article continued:

> You never saw those dry-run papers. We printed just enough copies for our use, then destroyed the metal plates that printed them. We guarded those few copies while we studied them, then destroyed the papers themselves.
>
> We weren't entirely overjoyed with those seven dry-run issues. They weren't very pretty, and they didn't read as well as we wanted them to. More discussions, more conferences, more critique sessions with our outside experts followed. We tore each issue apart and analyzed it, vowing not to make the same mistakes in the next one.
>
> But we got better. Deadlines were moved up [to later times], type was set quicker, the holes disappeared, the paper began to take on the uniformity which now is its symbol, the product more closely resembled a professional newspaper. And then the big day came! Sunday, March 20, 1966. The day we were going to put out Monday's paper—the first issue of TODAY you would see. Everyone came to work hours earlier than necessary that Sunday. We couldn't have stayed away from the office if we'd been ordered to. We were making history.
>
> We had put together a paper in less than two months. We had done what our contemporaries in the newspaper business said was impossible—we gave you TODAY.

That launch night, Neuharth had installed his black 1926 Royal typewriter in the newsroom. By 1966, it looked strange among the new machines. He sat at a desk near Jim Head's, reading stories, rewriting headlines. "He was my chief rewrite man and critic," Head says. "If it had been anyone else but Neuharth, it would have been pretty galling. But I respected his ability, and I think he had some respect for mine."

That night, and many nights thereafter, Neuharth was in the newsroom and the composing room, reviewing stories and headlines,

*Marie Holderman, the first of
many newspaper owners Al
Neuharth would charm,
visited TODAY on launch night.*

checking things on the plates as tired compositors wiped their brows.
When the press finally rolled, he was there to get one of the first copies; he gave it the same "complete check" he had given TODAY's
ancestors, the Volante and SoDak Sports. TODAY was his baby, and this
time, he was going to make sure it grew up.

"He read every headline," Spezzano recalls. "Nothing went on the
front page without him seeing it. He approved all the radio commercials, everything."

For four weeks, they delivered the paper free to every household in
Brevard, more than fifty thousand of them. The response from the
readers was excellent: "Thank you for starting my day off a whole lot
better," wrote one reader the first week. "TODAY is as fresh and stim-
ulating as that first cup of coffee in the morning," wrote another.
Reflecting Neuharth's flair for promotion, the first issue carried letters
from Very Important Readers, including Vice President Hubert H.
Humphrey and a U.S. Senator from Florida, George Smathers.

TODAY also bought nearly every billboard in Brevard to announce its
birth. Neuharth had brought Spezzano down from Rochester to help
promote the newspaper; he hired a flatbed truck with a Dixieland band
on it to play the shopping centers, trumpeting TODAY's arrival.
Spezzano also came up with a TODAY "flying saucer"—a disc that
floated on a cushion of air. The machinery required to keep it aloft
made a terrible noise, and Spezzano and his helpers took it to school-
yards and shopping centers, where the racket drove people crazy. But
it sure got their attention.

They sponsored parties and contests and gave away Yo-Yos and bal-

loons with the TODAY logo plastered all over them. Its slogans were
everywhere:

"TODAY will be different"

"Start TODAY Right, Start TODAY Bright."

There was a lot of free promotion, too, because there were many
reporters from the cold who talked their editors into sending them on a
spring fling to Florida to write something about the new newspaper.

The initial reaction from advertisers was not nearly so encouraging.
Sears, Roebuck was the biggest newspaper advertiser in Brevard
County. A regional Sears executive told Neuharth: "We're not going to
advertise with you. We don't need another place to spend our money."

In its treatment of the news, TODAY was well organized, reflecting
Neuharth's methodical mind. The left-hand column on page one was a
summary of the news stories inside the paper. It began with headlines
"In the Area," and then moved to "In Florida," then "In the Nation"
and finally, "In the World." That left-hand column was to become a
Neuharth trademark, widely imitated by other newspapers. It was 1½
columns wide, and came out of Neuharth's desire to make TODAY's

*Putting up with Neuharth's relentless nitpicking and fine-tuning took patience, as
this tired compositor discovered. Paul Miller is in center.*

front page different. "That was a given," he says. "It had to look a hell of a lot different than Miami or Orlando or Jacksonville or Daytona."

TODAY was one of the first newspapers to be organized into three distinct, free-standing sections: News, Business, and Sports. In the beginning, when the advertising came slowly, the "local front" was included in the A section. Within weeks, local news became a separate section.

It was designed as "a reader's paper." That meant there would be no ads on the backs or fronts of sections—each section was "wrapped in news." It also had some distinctive features, like thorough weather coverage. TODAY devoted more space than most newspapers—nearly half a page—to weather news. It used photography liberally, with occasional picture pages. And it had the inquiring photographer feature that Neuharth had used at SoDak Sports.

Neuharth promoted his emphasis on organization with the slogan, "Easy to Read, Easy to Find," which he had tested when he redesigned the Rochester newspapers. A typical promotion read: "Like all your favorites in TODAY, 'Dear Abby' is always in the same place." Jim Head remembers Neuharth's flair for organization. "He regimented the hell out of the thing. Most of the concepts in TODAY were Neuharth's; what I did was implement them."

Head had some trouble hiring a staff, because there wasn't much to do in Brevard County in 1965. "There were no museums, there were no symphonies, there were no libraries to speak of," Head says. "There was nothing to do. If you didn't drink, fish, boat, surf, or screw you didn't have anything to do in that place. The wives didn't like that kind of pioneer life."

Partly because of adversity, TODAY also had a comics page that was different. When he had been in Miami, Neuharth had signed several contracts with syndicates that gave The Herald exclusive rights to the most popular comic strips for large portions of Florida. Then George Driscoll, a King Features syndicate salesman who was a friend of Neuharth's, suggested that they add color to the few daily comics they could buy—another innovation the new newspaper got credit for.

At first, people said the old press—which came from Gannett's Binghamton, New York, newspaper—was incapable of printing color. Neuharth challenged his production crew to prove that it could—and they did it.

TODAY subscribed to just about every wire service that it was possi-

TODAY was heralded by a noisy "flying saucer" that kids could ride.

ble to get, including The Associated Press, the AP Financial wire, United Press International, the New York Daily News wire, the Washington Star Service, Reuters Foreign Service, the Chicago Tribune Service, the World Book Encyclopedia Science Service, the Newspaper Enterprise Association, Copley News Service, and Gannett News Service.

That was expensive, of course. But Neuharth had decided he would spare no expense in the start-up. "It was either going to be right quick or gone quick," Spezzano says. "He had no intention of dragging the thing out for five years. He was going to spend that $3 million in a hurry because that's what you needed to make it successful, to keep that high visibility. If he had tried to spread that money out over a five-year period, TODAY probably wouldn't have succeeded."

A key pricing decision came early. After four weeks, they were going to stop giving TODAY away. The plan called for them to charge half-price for the paper, five cents a day, or twenty-five cents a week, and thousands of twenty-five-cent coupons had been printed. But Lou Harris had been polling readers, and he found they liked the new newspaper so much they were willing to pay full price, ten cents a copy or fifty cents a week for it. "You're damn fools if you discount the price," Harris said.

"So we threw away all the coupons and went for it," Neuharth recalls. That month—April 1966—Neuharth was at an American Newspaper Publishers Association dinner in New York. He drew a seat next to Jim Knight, who in 1959 had rejected his idea of starting a new newspaper in Brevard. Knight said: "Kid, you made your first and fatal mistake. You can't sell that paper for full price. You're only a month-and-a-half old. Too bad, 'cause I like you."

As it turned out, Knight was wrong. The plan called for a goal, after one year, of twenty thousand circulation. After just ten weeks, TODAY's paid circulation had passed thirty-three thousand.

They succeeded in spite of some serious problems in the circulation department. Neuharth had promised that anybody who lived in Brevard County could get "doorstep delivery." But it was hard, in a place where people were sleeping on the beach and partying all night, to find good help. In the first year, according to Head, turnover in the circulation department was running about 400 percent.

"It was amazing you could get a newspaper delivered at all under those conditions," Jim Head says. "These guys were leaving the paper in the bushes and Neuharth was peering around the potted palms to see who was screwing up and he had his stopwatch on them. Hickey was taking an incredible pounding from Neuharth for all the problems, but there was no way with that kind of monkey crew in circulation that we were ever going to have doorstep delivery. But the public was pretty understanding; they forgave a lot."

The advertisers, who had been slow to put their dollars into a new newspaper, changed their minds. The regional Sears executive who had said he would never use TODAY pulled his Brevard County advertising out of the Orlando Sentinel Star and put it all in TODAY. The new newspaper was on its way.

It soon surpassed the competition. When the new newspaper was launched, the Sentinel Star sold twenty-nine thousand papers a day in Brevard. Within a few months, that was cut to fourteen thousand. The Miami Herald's circulation was sliced, too.

TODAY succeeded, in part, because the competition didn't think it would. The Orlando newspaper was run by Martin Andersen, who had owned the Sentinel Star for years before selling it to the Chicago Tribune in 1965. Andersen expected TODAY to fail, so he didn't increase news coverage or promotion in Brevard. For six months, Orlando did nearly nothing to respond, outside of running a few in-house ads aimed at retaining advertisers. By then it was too late.

In October 1966, Andersen gave a speech at the Cocoa Rotary Club. He was a powerful man in Orlando, in Orange County, and in

Florida. In his talk, the first he had given in Brevard County in thirty-five years, Andersen emphasized the decades of cooperation Orange County had given Brevard and other smaller counties surrounding it. Andersen's theme piqued Neuharth's interest; the brash newcomer had given many speeches about how for too long in Washington and in Tallahassee, Brevard had been seen as the "stepchild" of Orlando and Orange County. It was time for Brevard to speak with "one voice" and demand its rights, Neuharth said.

In the first editorial in TODAY, Neuharth had written: "The time has come for Brevard County to speak as one voice on matters that affect the entire area. Stepchild status is no longer enough. Longtime Brevard residents are well aware of how often this stepchild status has worked against Brevard."

That message, of "one Brevard" with TODAY as its voice, was enthusiastically received by his audiences. "He could manipulate them and rabble rouse them and choreograph them," Head says. "He could have led them through the Cocoa High School fight song if he'd wanted to."

Neuharth's "one Brevard, one voice" theme was strikingly similar to the stated goal of SoDak Sports: to make South Dakota "one big sports family." Now, just as he had seen an opportunity to attack Fred Christopherson in Sioux Falls, Neuharth saw a chance to go after another competitor with a paternalistic attitude—Martin Andersen of Orlando—and blow TODAY's horn at the same time.

The Titusville Rotary Club gave Neuharth the forum he wanted. In his speech, which he described as a "grim fairy tale," Neuharth labeled Andersen "the highway man of Andersenville." He accused Andersen of diverting two key Florida highways and a university away from Brevard to Orlando and Orange County. Neuharth explained, in fairy-tale style:

> And happily for the Highway Man, there were no loud complaints from the outlanders in the provinces, for there was really no effective way to complain. Then, once upon a recent TODAY, there was. It came to pass that a young voice grew strong in the province, proclaimed its independence from the bonds of Andersenville and began to ask:
> "Why should all roads lead to Andersenville?"

Neuharth's speech got a lot of attention in Florida newspapers. For a while, he became the champion of all of the other publishers around the state who didn't like Andersen.

But there was one major problem with TODAY's rapid growth: Because its circulation was higher than expected, TODAY printed more copies and used more newsprint than it expected, and so its costs soared. In 1966, TODAY lost $2 million; Neuharth had spent 40 percent of his five-year budget in one year. Everyone wanted to know how the new baby was doing, and Neuharth would reply: "Well, we've gotten more circulation and more advertising than we'd ever dreamed of, and more red ink than we ever thought we were going to get, too."

That was the moment Neuharth's in-house critics chose to turn the screws on Paul Miller. Cy Williams and the financial people began to complain about how much Neuharth's pet project was costing the company. TODAY had doubled its planned circulation, but it had not doubled its ad rates, so its losses were mounting fast. Neuharth began to wonder if he could hold off the pressure from the corporate finance people who were saying, "cut the losses, shut it down."

Neuharth thought it was too risky to raise ad rates faster; that might have scared advertisers away. "The only question was, would Paul Miller stay the course with us or would we panic because of the pressure from the business office?" Neuharth says now. "Fortunately, he stayed the course."

In 1967, TODAY came of age journalistically. Early on, Neuharth had said to his editor, Jim Head: "Someday there's going to be a tragedy at the space center and we'd better be ready for it. We can either fall flat on our faces or do something significant about covering it."

On the night of January 26, 1967, Head was attending a meeting of the local chapter of Sigma Delta Chi, the Society of Professional Journalists. Neuharth had helped start a chapter in Brevard, and then turned around and started one in Rochester so he could explain TODAY to that audience. At the journalism meeting, Head got an emergency call from the office: "There's been a fire at the Cape. Gus Grissom, Ed White, and Roger Chaffee may have been killed." The three astronauts had died in a fire while the rocket was still on the launchpad; the accident would set the space program back for many months.

Head canceled the meeting, and the audience—almost everyone there worked for TODAY—walked out en masse and went back to the office.

TODAY
Florida's Space Age Newspaper

Three Astronauts Die In Apollo Cape Fire

Full Story Inside

White, Chaffee And Grissom Trapped in Ship

AN EYE WITNESS STORY:

'. . . Everybody Was Running'

'The Program Must Go On,' Says LBJ

After the Tragedy
AN EDITORIAL

The Apollo disaster was TODAY's first big news test, and the small newspaper won national recognition for its coverage.

TODAY pulled out all the stops. Head could not find Moe Hickey, so he made a command decision: He took all the advertising out of the main News section. TODAY's reporters and editors covered the story the way Neuharth wanted it covered—they blanketed it with seven full pages of stories and pictures. They won a National Headliners award, and the Columbia Journalism Review said that the best coverage of the tragedy was by The New York Times—and by that new little paper in Florida. In its first year, TODAY won eight first places in national and state journalism contests.

While TODAY's circulation was growing, Neuharth kept busy on other fronts. In January 1967, Neuharth was promoted to executive vice president of Gannett. He was now clearly Paul Miller's heir apparent. That April, he helped Miller acquire two newspapers in Rockford, Illinois, bringing Gannett's total to thirty. In October 1967, Gannett began selling its stock as a public company, and the two top executives began a speaking campaign to explain the newspaper business to Wall Street.

In August of 1968, twenty-eight months after it had been launched, TODAY turned the corner. The ink on its bottom line changed from red to black. Neuharth sent a telegram to Moe Hickey, who was vacationing with his family in Maine:

"TODAY MADE PROFIT FOR JULY. STOP. TWO YEARS AHEAD OF PLAN. STOP. CONGRATULATIONS. STOP. SIGNED AL NEUHARTH."

Most of the powers-that-be had thought Neuharth's new newspaper was a crazy idea, but he had gone ahead, had some fun, and done something exciting. With a mixture of guts, money, imagination, and perseverance, he had made TODAY click. The SoDak Sports monkey was off his back.

CHAPTER FOUR

Neuharth's Nonsense

On a sunny afternoon in September 1979, years after the success at Cocoa, a big black Mercedes pulled up a hill overlooking Zurich and stopped in front of the Dolder Grand, one of the world's great hotels.

The chauffeur released the locks and out of the back door stepped Neuharth, wearing a white jacket, black jeans, a white shirt, and a black ascot. He paused for a moment to stretch, flexing his legs beside the car while he gave the driver his orders. Neuharth looked like a man who was at the top of his powers, and he was. In January of that year he had added the title of chairman to his titles of president and chief executive officer of Gannett Company, Inc., the media company whose revenues were about to pass the $1 billion mark.

At the end of 1978, at the age of seventy-two, Paul Miller had retired, and the title of chairman had passed to Neuharth. He was quick to seize the reins from Miller, who was reluctant to give up an active role in Gannett. For the first time since he had become chief executive in 1973, Neuharth, at fifty-four, was alone at the top of the company. Now, unquestionably, he was Gannett's leader, and he was champing at the bit to shape its future.

Unlike many chief executives, Neuharth shunned the conservative look—the banker's gray suit or boardroom pinstripes. By this point in his life, he dressed exclusively in black and white—as did his second wife, Florida State Senator Lori Wilson, whom he married in 1973. His stark, dramatic wardrobe included jet-black jogging suits, dazzling white silk shirts, and vivid black-and-white-checked blazers. The two-tone clothes became another Neuharth trademark, and set him apart from the corporate crowd. His distinctive outfits were something of a joke among the more conventional newspaper executives, prompting the wife of one to ask: "Which family of the Mafia did you say he belongs to?"

Even though it was obvious he was trying to make a statement with his wardrobe, Neuharth's explanation was that he was just being practical. Wearing only black and white interchangeable clothes makes packing easier, he told the reporters who often traveled with him for a few hours or a few days, eager to profile the nation's most visible, most aggressive media mogul. Neuharth did do a whole lot of packing, because he traveled a quarter-of-a-million miles a year. He was on the road so much that he wore a Wittnauer wristwatch with two faces: one for the time zone he was in, and another that showed the time at corporate headquarters back in Rochester, New York.

The Dolder Grand is gracious and grand in every sense, serving tea in a great hall outside the dining room every afternoon, to the accompaniment of chamber music. It was nearly tea time when Neuharth arrived, but he had no time for cakes or classical music. He was there for a business dinner, and there were last-minute details to check.

In 1979, in addition to his array of corporate titles, Neuharth was chairman and president of the American Newspaper Publishers Association, a powerful trade group. It had become a tradition for its board, every few years, to hold a meeting outside the United States. That year the ANPA board included some of the great names in American publishing: Katharine Graham, chairman of the Washington Post Company; Warren H. Phillips, a former Wall Street Journal reporter who became president and chief executive of its parent, Dow Jones & Company; and Stanton R. Cook, president and chief executive of the Tribune Company, which published the Chicago Tribune.

In his first-class seat on the Swissair flight from New York to Zurich, Neuharth had gone over—with his characteristic intensity—every item on the meeting's agenda, weighing each issue, deciding the likely outcome of each debate. He had selected the Dolder Grand as the group's hotel, having stayed there on an earlier trip to tout Gannett's stock to European investors. Neuharth had personally planned the evening's menu—venison accompanied by North Dakota wild rice, flown five thousand miles for the occasion—and okayed the wines and champagnes that were served with each course.

Because the meeting was in Europe, Kay Graham had invited executives of the International Herald Tribune to attend. The IHT, which was jointly owned by the Washington Post Company, The New York Times Company, and Whitney Communications, had a circulation of nearly 100,000 in Europe. About 9 P.M., midway through the dinner, copies of the next day's edition were delivered to the publishers' tables.

That edition had been generated by editors working on computer terminals in the Paris headquarters of the IHT. Contact prints of each finished page were taken to the newspaper's facsimile transmission room. The pages were scanned by a laser, which converted the visual images into digital signals. This packet of electronic signals was then sent over telephone lines to a printing plant in Zurich. It took only three-and-a-half minutes to send the data for an entire newspaper page.

If that same page had been sent over land from Paris to Zurich—a distance of more than three hundred miles—it would have taken at least eight hours. In the facsimile room of the Swiss printing plant, the digital signals were decoded and converted back into a negative image of the newspaper page, which was then burned onto a plate and placed on an offset press, which printed the finished page.

The publishers, including Neuharth, were impressed by the IHT's use of this new technology. The IHT had been negotiating for several months to take the next step, and send those digital electronic signals to a satellite orbiting 22,300 miles above the equator. The satellite would bounce the signals down to a receiving dish in Hong Kong, where the IHT planned to print its Asian edition. In the United States, Time, Sports Illustrated, and The Wall Street Journal were already using this space-age technology to print magazines and newspapers.

The International Herald Tribune had always been a very readable newspaper, a good summary of U.S. and European news that was well read by Americans traveling abroad. By using electronic transmission to speed production, the IHT could now print in England and Switzerland as well as France, get later news into the paper, and sell more copies in more places.

After dinner, Neuharth stopped to have a drink at the Dolder Grand's bar with Larry Sackett, the IHT's bright young production director. Sackett had worked for Gannett at The Evening Press in Binghamton, New York. He was interested in new technology, so after some years as a reporter and copy editor, he became the newspaper's production editor—the liaison between the news and production departments—and helped install its computerized typesetting system. Then the Binghamton publisher, Robert Eckert, was named publisher of the International Herald Tribune. He tapped Sackett as his production director and brought him to Paris in 1977 to set up the Swiss printing operation. When Sackett arrived, the IHT was still trucking its papers out of Paris; the paper was usually a late arrival on Swiss and Italian newsstands, and drivers were getting killed in accidents on the treacherous mountain roads. Having solved that problem, Sackett was now setting up the new satellite link to Asia.

Always the reporter, Neuharth began asking Sackett questions: What had Larry been up to? What about the IHT's plans to use the satellite? Was it reliable? Was the printing quality consistent? How about its new marketing program to sell newspapers to the airlines in Europe?

All was going well, Sackett said, but from a personal perspective, he thought he was ready for a career change. He wanted to return to the United States. Neuharth had intended to talk longer, but by then Kay Graham had noticed that one of her employees was involved in an intense conversation with a competitor. She raised her eyebrows and strolled over to the bar to see what Neuharth was up to.

Kay Graham's instincts were correct: There was something going on. She knew Neuharth never went off duty; he didn't waste time on small talk or casual conversations. But he revealed nothing that night.

Two months later and four thousand miles away at Gannett's corporate headquarters in Rochester, Neuharth dropped a broad hint about what he had in mind. He usually spent weekends at his home in Cocoa Beach; he loved November in Florida, where it was usually warm and sunny, and hated winter in Rochester. But on this November Sunday in 1979, he had left the Florida sunshine behind to fly to Rochester for a corporate meeting, and it already looked like winter: The sky was gray, the wind off Lake Ontario had a real bite to it, and the first tiny snowflakes were beginning to swirl past.

The next morning Neuharth had a big fire going in the fireplace of the boardroom on the twenty-fifth floor of corporate headquarters, a marble-faced building that Rochester reporters called "the white tower." The mood in the room was upbeat. A few months before, Gannett had completed its biggest deal, buying the Combined Communications Corporation for $370 million. That brought in two big newspapers, The Cincinnati Enquirer and the Oakland (Calif.) Tribune, giving Gannett a total of eighty. It also made Gannett a big player in broadcasting, adding seven television stations—many in prosperous Sunbelt markets—and twelve radio stations. And it included the largest outdoor advertising company in North America.

After the merger, Karl Eller, Combined's energetic chief executive, challenged Neuharth's leadership. Eller flew around the country in his Learjet and lobbied Gannett's directors, arguing that he—not Neuharth—should be Gannett's CEO. Neuharth fought back with a vengeance and won the support of the directors. Eller quit, citing his differences with the "philosophy, policy, and style" of Gannett's management—Neuharth. For years after that, Neuharth would refer to the "philosophy, policy, and style" of the Gannett Company, much of which he set. With the addition of Combined Communications, Gannett had annual revenues of more than $1 billion, earnings of $134 million, and operations in thirty-four of the fifty states. It was truly a nationwide company.

On that cold day in Rochester, Neuharth was presiding at a regular meeting of Gannett's Office of the Chief Executive, the top management group in the company. Besides Neuharth, the OCE then was composed of three other executives: Jack Heselden, Doug McCorkindale, and John Quinn.

Heselden, then fifty-nine, was a friendly bear of a man who wore short-sleeved white shirts, even in the middle of a bitter Rochester winter. He had come up on the business side as a newspaper publisher and a corporate personnel executive, and now he headed the company's newspaper division. Each afternoon would find him curled up with his telephone, his feet on his desk, looking outwardly relaxed while he doggedly chipped away at the waste in some publisher's operation. Heselden had a sure instinct for what would help the bottom line. He would pick and prod at a publisher's budget, saving a few dollars here, a few dollars there. He hit a few newspapers every afternoon, and pretty soon it added up to millions.

McCorkindale, then forty, had left a Wall Street law firm to join Gannett in 1971, and had risen to be the company's chief financial and legal officer. In those areas, his expertise was unmatched. Neuharth liked to call McCorkindale "the best numbers man in the newspaper business," and he probably was. He had been a wrestler at Columbia University and had planned to teach history until a professor told him: "You're too combative. Better go to law school." He was a top scholar

"We're a good enough company [that] we can make bad decisions," Doug McCorkindale would later say of the decision to launch USA TODAY.

Jack Heselden remembers Neuharth asking, "Why is it we don't have the respect and the reputation some of the other major newspapers have?"

John Quinn says the reaction from the financial department to the research idea was "deadly silence."

at Columbia Law School, and his shrewd intelligence was evident in his grasp of strategy and detail during Gannett's many acquisitions. In any negotiation, McCorkindale was usually one or two steps ahead of his opponent across the table.

Quinn had spent the first twenty-three years of his career at The Providence Journal, where he had started as a copy boy, and rose through the ranks in Providence to become day managing editor. On a skiing trip in 1959, Quinn suffered a heart attack at the age of thirty-three. His wife Loie, a nurse, helped revive him. When Quinn was well enough to travel, his boss at The Journal, Mike Ogden, told him he should take some time in Florida to recuperate. Ogden called one of his editor friends—George Beebe at The Miami Herald—and asked him to take care of Quinn. Beebe told Neuharth to handle the details. Neuharth knew the p.r. man for the Deauville Hotel, and when John and Loie Quinn got to Miami Beach, they were given the hotel's presidential suite. To say thank you, the Quinns invited Al and Loretta Neuharth to dinner. Quinn and Neuharth hit it off: They both enjoyed challenging the conventional wisdom about how to edit a newspaper.

In late 1965, with plans for TODAY well along, Neuharth was looking for outside talent to strengthen his editing team at the Rochester newspapers. After looking at several candidates, he offered Quinn the job of executive editor. At first Quinn was reluctant to leave his hometown of Providence, where he had gone to college and worked for two decades. Neuharth kept after him, even sending a case of champagne at Christmas to get his attention, and in February 1966 Quinn moved to Rochester.

Thirteen years later, at the age of fifty-four, he headed the company's news division; he was a strong, detail-oriented editor, a prodigious worker, and an astute corporate politician. For defending news and editorial integrity against those with a bottom-line-only mentality, Quinn commanded great respect within the company—so much oo that in later years, Neuharth would call him "the conscience of the Gannett Company."

Pacing back and forth across the Gannett boardroom, Neuharth began to talk about Gannett's future. It had just completed its biggest merger. Eller's challenge to Neuharth was over. What next? A frequent lament among its top managers in those days was Gannett's lack of a national reputation. It was a big, profitable, well-run media company, but it was hardly a household name. Working with Paul Miller, Neuharth had helped sell Wall Street on the company's stock; the two of them had gone on a crusade to help financial analysts understand just how profitable the newspaper business was outside of New York City.

They made hundreds of speeches explaining the consistent profitability of Gannett's small- and medium-sized newspapers. That educational campaign, combined with Gannett's unbroken string of quarterly earnings gains, had made the company's stock a Wall Street favorite. When Gannett went public on October 24, 1967, its stock sold for $29. Since then, the stock had split twice. After adjusting the 1967 price for the splits, Gannett had soared from $7 to $46 by November 1979. Its shares were selling for thirteen times earnings, nearly double the average price-earnings multiple for the Standard & Poor's 500, which was then seven.

Despite Gannett's financial success, it still lacked a national reputation for journalistic excellence. In the 1970s, Jack Germond, the respected political writer who was Gannett News Service's Washington bureau chief for many years, once described the company as "a bunch of shitkicker papers."

Most of Gannett's newspapers weren't big in 1979, but that year they won more than seven hundred journalism awards. And a Gannett

News Service investigation in 1979 of the misdeeds of the Pauline
fathers, a Pennsylvania-based religious order, would win the Pulitzer-
Prize Gold Medal for public service in 1980. But Germond's perjorative
epithet had stuck.

Neuharth knew how hard it was to get a big-time reputation when all
of your newspapers were published in smaller cities and towns and
concentrated on local news. He told a reporter: "No matter how hard
you try or how well you produce in El Paso or Bridgewater, your
efforts are not as noticed as they would be in New York, Washington,
Los Angeles, Philadelphia, or Chicago." Neuharth was not about to be
satisfied with second-best in anything, and that was especially true
when it came to his company's reputation. The word was out, inside
and outside the company, that Gannett was looking to do something—
maybe anything—on a national scale.

But what? A national magazine? Gannett had looked into magazine
acquisitions. There was a possibility that U.S. News and World
Report, employee-owned and number three in the newsweekly competition, could come up for sale. Neuharth had been courting one of its
principals, Marvin Stone. The addition of Combined Communications
had given the company new reach, and Neuharth envisioned a Gannett
national advertising network that would sell packages combining newspapers, radio and television, and billboards.

But in front of a roaring fire on that cold November Monday in 1979,
Neuharth was not talking about buying magazines or selling ads.
Instead, he surprised the group with an inquiry about the budget. Gannett's budget for 1980 was already done; McCorkindale was confident
that in the coming year, Gannett would churn out another excellent
earnings gain—probably somewhere around 15 percent.

Still pacing, Neuharth asked the three executives a question. "How
would it affect the company," he asked, "if we were to set aside a
special kitty next year for research and development?" "How much?"
someone asked. "One million dollars," Neuharth said. "That's
enough to find out if this company has what it takes to publish a national
newspaper."

McCorkindale's mouth dropped. Spending an unscheduled million
was not something he relished; it would mean he would have to dig a
little deeper and press a little harder to make the profit plan in 1980. He
and the others began asking the pertinent questions: How would the
money be spent? Who would be hired? What would be explored? "I

didn't ask you how we would spend it," Neuharth replied. "I asked you how we would raise it."

That meeting persuaded Quinn that Neuharth was ready to explore launching a national newspaper. "I came out of it with a feeling that the business side was going to be expected to produce the resources for a major research project, and they were not going to like it, they were not going to understand it."

Besides the Combined Communications acquisition, there were other trends that convinced Neuharth Gannett could do much more with its own resources. TODAY in Florida was the company's most prominent example of internal growth, but it was hardly the only example. In the past decade or so, Gannett had successfully started thirteen Sunday newspapers, in Burlington, Vermont; Lafayette, Indiana; Westchester County, New York; Camden, New Jersey; and other cities. Only one, a Sunday edition of the Hartford Times, had failed. In launching that, the company killed a popular Saturday edition of the Times. The readers were furious, and they kept reading the competition, The Hartford Courant, on Sundays. The Times never recovered from that mistake. Gannett soon sold the newspaper and it later closed.

In addition to its new Sunday newspapers, Gannett had started Westchester TODAY, a morning edition of the Westchester Rockland Newspapers north of New York City. It hit the streets and the train stations on August 21, 1978, the first day of a New York City newspaper strike. Westchester TODAY was basically produced by only six editors; it relied heavily on wire-service reports and stories reported by the staff of the nine afternoon dailies. But it was a typical Gannett start-up: It was well organized, it had all of the late news and all of the late sports scores, and the commuters liked it. In the first week of November 1978, just before the New York City strike was settled, Westchester TODAY's sales hit a high of fifty-eight thousand copies a day. Then the pressmen and the mailers settled their dispute and the three New York City dailies resumed publishing. In November 1979, Westchester TODAY's circulation was holding at about thirty-five thousand.

On the West Coast that same month, Gannett was gearing up to launch a new morning edition of the Oakland Tribune, to be called Eastbay TODAY. This was a more elaborate effort. A task force of editors from other Gannett newspapers had been brought to Oakland to plan the new edition, which was going to go after single-copy sales in the Bay Area by relying on a large, thorough sports section, late news, and a low cover price—ten cents. Eastbay TODAY also revived an old gimmick from Neuharth's past—its business and sports sections were printed on peach newsprint. And its slogan was "Reach for the Peach."

In the fall of 1979, Neuharth and Quinn went to Oakland several times to help plan the launch of Eastbay TODAY. Gannett had named Bob Maynard, an outstanding journalist who had been a reporter and editorial writer at The Washington Post, as the Tribune's editor. That made Maynard the only black to hold the top editing job at a large general circulation daily in the whole country; his appointment was evidence of Gannett's oft-stated commitment, under Neuharth, to get more blacks and women into top jobs. "Gannett's leadership must reflect its readership," Neuharth said again and again. He had appointed several women as publishers of Gannett newspapers and added women and minorities to the board of directors.

On one of their frequent trips to Oakland, Neuharth and Quinn had a late-night dinner with Maynard and the Tribune's publisher, a former labor relations lawyer named Al Dolata, and a few other executives. The conversation got around to what the front page of Eastbay TODAY ought to look like. Quinn whipped out a felt-tipped pen and began drawing a layout on the tablecloth. No, no, not that way, Neuharth said. Pulling the tablecloth around to his place, Neuharth began editing Quinn's mock-up, sketching the way Eastbay TODAY should look. For the Tribune executives, this was equivalent to Moses receiving the stone tablets on Mount Sinai. At a meeting a few days later, Dolata and Maynard were arguing over what Neuharth had said at the midnight dinner. To prove his point, Dolata reached into a desk drawer and pulled out the soiled tablecloth. He had bought the tablecloth for eight dollars that night to preserve "the word" of Neuharth.

The Tribune's circulation director was a tough, cocky, combative thirty-one-year-old named Frank Vega. He had come up through the ranks of circulation departments in Tampa and Philadelphia, and he was known as a big-city street-fighter. When it came to selling newspapers, he says, "I thought I was the greatest thing since sliced bread."

To prepare for the launch of Eastbay TODAY, Vega had put together a three-by-four-foot chart, showing every truck route, every drop point, every vending machine, and the times when all of the newspapers would be delivered. Vega was proud of his detailed scenario, and his pride showed as he briefed Neuharth and the other Gannett executives. Vega claimed, of course, that all of the newspapers would be delivered on time. Midway through the presentation, Neuharth interrupted: "That's bullshit, Vega."

"What do you mean, sir?" asked Vega, trying hard to be polite.

"I've been through launches of TODAY in Florida and Westchester TODAY," Neuharth said, "and you circulation guys never deliver what you say you will."

As respectfully as he could, Vega disagreed. He told Neuharth he had been out with the trucks and that every run had been timed twelve times. "I'll bet you five bucks we deliver what we say we can, give or take five minutes."

"You're on," said Neuharth, who loved to make small wagers with his colleagues. The night of the launch, November 5, 1979, Neuharth was out in his limo, checking the truck runs. Four were on time; one was two minutes late. Vega had won his five bucks—and a place in Neuharth's million-dollar research plan.

Neuharth's blueprint for this secret national newspaper research project was really quite simple. He would invite four experts—the "young geniuses" he called them—to figure out if Gannett could create a national newspaper. He had not been very specific with his colleagues about what shape he thought it would take, and in the months to come, the Gannett grapevine began humming. Some speculated it would be a national sports newspaper; others suggested it might be a summary of national news that could be wrapped around Gannett's own newspapers, which were heavily local. Or perhaps the company would create a new Sunday supplement, like Parade or Family Weekly. Back on that November Monday in Rochester, no one in the meeting room knew for sure what would come of this "research and development" idea. But one thing was clear: Project NN—for National Newspaper— had been born.

By mid-February 1980, Eastbay TODAY was selling well. Its circulation had passed fifty thousand, and Bay Area sportscasters were raving about its Sports section. Frank Vega was about to celebrate by taking a little time off with his family when he got a mysterious phone call from Jack Heselden, the Gannett executive in charge of newspaper operations and profits. Like Neuharth, Heselden had been impressed by Vega's well-planned charts—Heselden called them "truckie

Frank Vega felt like one of
Neuharth's "chosen" executives.

When Tom Curley learned he would
be on the research team, he said,
"God, I'm excited. I'll never sleep
again."

charts"—and by his bravado in getting Eastbay TODAY all over the streets.

"What are you doing Saturday?" Heselden asked. It was already Thursday.

"I'm going skiing," Vega said.

"Can you go some other time?" Heselden asked.

"Well, the snow will be around for a few more months."

"Good. Can you be in Cocoa Beach on Saturday?"

So on Saturday morning, Frank Vega walked into Pumpkin Center, Neuharth's oceanfront estate in Cocoa Beach. His ski trip would have to wait a few years. Neuharth often described his Florida home and office, which he had built by buying several properties in the same block, as a renovated "log cabin," but it was much more than that.

Inside Pumpkin Center there was a decorative pool where Japanese Kai swam, a big fireplace, and an upstairs conference room next to Neuharth's office where many important meetings were held. The building had eleven television sets, fifteen telephones, and AP and Gannett News Service wire-service printers. Outside there was a screened-in, heated swimming pool next to the house, a tennis court, a par cours physical fitness course, and landscaped grounds and paths down to the beach. It was protected by alarms and a television surveillance system.

Paul Kessinger felt Neuharth had dropped "this bomb, this stunning bomb."

Of his decision to work on Project NN, Larry Sackett says, "Win, lose, or draw, the experience of trying to pull together something like this happens once in a lifetime."

Upstairs in Pumpkin Center's conference room, Vega met the other three researchers who had been tapped for the project: Larry Sackett, who had left the International Herald Tribune to return to Gannett; Tom Curley, a former reporter and editor who now headed Gannett's extensive reader research project; and Paul Kessinger, a former reporter who had been Heselden's marketing assistant in the newspaper division. Vega and Curley were thirty-one; Sackett was thirty; and Kessinger was twenty-nine. As their direct supervisor, Neuharth had brought in Vince Spezzano, fifty-three, the newspaper promotion expert who had helped launch TODAY in Florida; he was now its publisher.

Everyone was dressed casually; sport shirts and jeans were the rule in Cocoa Beach, and Neuharth was wearing his tropical whites. A wireservice printer was clacking away at one end of the room—Gannett News Service spewing copy. Neuharth explained that he was tape recording their meeting, to "make sure we all understand how we got here and where we want to go."

He began talking, in a calm, measured voice, about the past. He had been thinking not just about Westchester TODAY or Eastbay TODAY or all of the reader research Gannett had done, but about "a dream some of us had down in this part of the country fifteen years ago. We had a dream that maybe our little company could start a newspaper down

*Vince Spezzano remembers
Neuharth asking whether
Gannett had been slow to take
advantage of new technology.*

here. Most of you know that we did, and it worked."

It was easy to dream in Cocoa Beach. Out the window, they could see the surf breaking, pelicans gliding by, and people strolling or jogging on the beach. For Neuharth, Pumpkin Center was a refuge. He had named it after a crossroads in South Dakota where he and his friends had stopped, years earlier, for rest and refreshments after a day of pheasant hunting. It was a place to think and dream and plan for the future.

"Some of us now, for some time, have had a somewhat bigger dream," Neuharth continued, "that maybe this somewhat bigger company might be able to start a national, a nationwide daily newspaper, and we hope maybe that will work. Whether it does or not, I think there are many, many advantages that all of us around this table and the company in general can gain from this exercise."

Before deciding whether to launch, Neuharth said, there are four questions that must be answered: Can we produce and print a national newspaper? Can we distribute and sell a national newspaper? Can we design a daily newspaper that will grab readers around the country in sufficient numbers to make the effort worthwhile? Can we get the necessary advertiser support for a national newspaper?

Sackett, the satellite expert, was supposed to answer the first question. Vega, the circulation director, had the second. Curley, the research expert, took the third, and Kessinger, the marketer, the fourth.

Secrecy was paramount. No one else had heard such a specific outline of what they were supposed to investigate. Gannett's board of directors, for example, was told only that the company was going to budget a substantial sum of money for research and development work on new newspapers. "There has not been the slightest hint of a look at a national, nationwide daily publication to the Gannett board of directors, nor will there be early on," Neuharth said. The task force members had to sign nondisclosure statements, promises that they would not reveal sensitive company information.

The official Gannett release on the project was deliberately vague, taking cover in obscurity and the passive voice. The March 5, 1980, release read: "Establishment of a research and development task force on new ventures for Gannett Company, Inc., and appointment of two new general executives were announced today by Allen H. Neuharth, chairman and president." Neuharth added that the task force "will explore any and all possibilities for new ventures in the entire communications field which might even better serve readers, advertisers, viewers, or listeners." He had thrown in the broadcasting reference, even though this task force would concentrate exclusively on print ventures.

The four "geniuses" had a budget of $1.2 million, most of it to pay for formal research on why readers bought newspapers. As a base, they would use a shabby cottage that Neuharth's second wife, Lori Wilson, owned on Route A1A in Cocoa Beach, just a few blocks from Pumpkin Center. Neuharth reminded them he would be sneaking around, taking a peek at their work. And then he added a caution, about the differences between dreams and reality. "We've got to be realists. We may conclude that this dream is silly as hell and that Project NN, which is meant to stand for new newspapers, may more appropriately stand for Neuharth's Nonsense—in which case we won't go ahead with it. But if the big venture won't fly, then I hope and expect there would be many, many byproducts from your work."

Then Neuharth gave them a few hints about his own thinking. He had spent many hours thinking, daydreaming, "blue-skying" he called it, about a national newspaper. In every one of his offices—in Pumpkin Center, in Washington, in New York, in Rochester, and in his office in the air, aboard the Gulfstream jet on which he had logged millions of miles—Neuharth kept maps of the United States that showed Gannett's far-flung operations.

"When you look at a map of the United States," he told the group, "you will find that Gannett has production and distribution facilities

within two hours of at least forty very big markets." He had already
added up the markets where he thought they could get a total circulation of one million, which he viewed as the necessary minimum. But,
"two, three, four, or five million has got to be our goal if this is worth
doing and worth doing the right way in a big way."

In his travels, it had become obvious to Neuharth that not every
newspaper was doing all it could to attract and keep readers. "You
don't have to be very damn intelligent," he said, "or any genius to
realize that there are a good number of those markets that either have
lousy morning newspapers or absolute rags."

The task force settled one important issue that first day in Cocoa
Beach. In a memo the month before, Larry Sackett had fooled around
with a name for the new national newspaper. He called it "U.S.
Today." Now, at their meeting, he said "U.S. Today" should be a
"national index on the news," a quick read for the upscale commuter,
the busy executive.

That sounds fine, Neuharth said, but then he added: "So that no one
else wastes any time trying to figure out what the name of this here
newspaper is gonna be, let's just say that's one thing that's been
decided without any research. If we publish it, the name will be USA
TODAY, unless somebody can convince me that it's the wrong name,
which is highly doubtful."

It was highly doubtful that anyone would try. Once more, as he had
done in his twenties in South Dakota, and again when he was in his
thirties in Florida, Neuharth thought he had identified a vacuum that a
new newspaper might fill, a niche where a new source of information
might thrive.

CHAPTER FIVE

Cottage industry

While jogging up the beach near Pumpkin Center early one Saturday in April 1980, Neuharth decided to check on how Project NN's whiz kids were doing. He turned away from the ocean and crossed Route A1A to take a look.

The cottage was empty and locked. A high-tech security system had been installed, and if the lock was not operated perfectly, an alarm would go off in Cocoa Beach police headquarters, bringing squad cars screaming down the coastal highway.

Since he was locked out, Neuharth slipped up beside the large picture window that faced the street and tried to see in. He couldn't see anything, because that window had been covered with a reflective plastic film. But Frank Vega had resisted this security measure. He had not covered the small window in his tiny office, because he didn't want to obstruct his view of the girls who often bicycled by in bikinis. Neuharth noticed Vega's window was clear and peered inside.

What he saw did not please him. On a large blackboard, he could read the words, "Circulation projections," and just below were several numbers—1.75 million, 2 million, 2.3 million.

When Neuharth caught up with his young circulation expert, he was angry. He chewed Vega out: "This is supposed to be a secret project, Mr. Vega. Don't you realize people can *see* through that window? Any *idiot* could walk by and figure out what you guys are doing."

Vega recognized that tone of voice: It was the Black Prince at his most threatening. Neuharth did not use that tone with everyone, but if he thought histrionics would help achieve his objective, he could deliver a performance worthy of a Marine Corps drill instructor.

By that afternoon, workmen had installed the plastic film over Vega's window. The street outside had become an orange haze; he would have to stand in the doorway to watch the girls.

The cottage was not a comfortable place to work. Originally a garage, it had been a barber shop before it became Project NN's super-secret nerve center. It was a three-room shack, with a small living room and two tiny bedrooms. The living room, which the researchers called their "war room," was only twenty-by-twenty, and it was crowded with charts, blackboards, and a desk for the project's secretary, Jean Hagen.

For the first two months—March and April, often hot and muggy in Florida—the air conditioning did not work. At times the temperature in the cottage passed one hundred degrees. Their copier was a primitive, painfully slow tabletop model; it wheezed and whined and blew heat into the room, contributing to the claustrophobic atmosphere.

Books and studies of media trends were piled everywhere, and when all five of them were packed into the war room it was hot, crowded, and uncomfortable. The researchers were young, high-energy people who were embarked on the biggest project of their lives, and all of them had strong—but very different—ideas about how things should be done. This marriage had not been made in heaven; some of the team members did not like each other much, and it was not easy for them to work together.

Larry Sackett, Project NN's high-tech expert, took a highly organized, business-school approach. He began drawing charts for the project's "feasibility phase," which he divided into steps: "Step 1a—Macro Information Gathering" and "Step 1b—Micro Information Gathering."

Vega thought Sackett's business-school approach was just bunk. He scoffed at case studies and the academic approach. He was used to fighting for circulation numbers on the streets, and to him, this project was simple: "Let's figure out how many newspaper coin racks the country can hold and how much chain we're going to need to tie them down."

Sackett, too, remembers the tension. "Frank would say something, I'd have to argue with him." With his glasses and mild-mannered look, Sackett resembled a skinny Clark Kent. If Sackett seemed intellectual, Vega was physical: a short, muscular Italian-American dynamo

The four "geniuses" had a lot of flip charts in the cottage, and every time a stranger came to the door, they scrambled to cover them up.

who could swear in three languages. They had a basic personality conflict, which the hot, crowded conditions did not help. One night, after months of feuding, Vega became so enraged he grabbed Sackett in a bar, lifted him out of his seat by his necktie, and threatened to pound him into the ground.

Tom Curley had been a reporter at the Rochester newspapers, and later went to school at night to get his MBA degree. He knew his way around flow charts, but he didn't get along with Sackett either. "It got to the point where if Sackett said 'yes,' Curley would say 'no,'" recalls Paul Kessinger, the fourth member of the team.

Kessinger was slight and scholarly and his boyish enthusiasm for the project was infectious. He had been elected to Phi Beta Kappa and graduated from Stanford, been a reporter, and then gotten master's degrees in journalism and business in two years at Columbia University. In the cottage, he spent a lot of his time playing dorm counselor to keep the researchers from killing each other. "It got hot and heavy," Kessinger recalls. "Vega and Sackett were at one another's throats all the time."

In a March 1980 memo to his boss, John Quinn, Tom Curley touched on the frustration the team felt cooped up in the cottage: "We are doing the right things, but at a painfully slow pace," Curley wrote. "The situation dynamic is frightening: Someone says let's draw [market] clusters on the map up to three hours from Gannett print sites. Suddenly we are printing three or four hours from a metro market."

Curley pointed out that printing the newspaper that far away from its markets would mean the presses would have to be started very early, before midnight Eastern time. That would be too early to get all of the late news and sports scores into the newspaper, and they knew Neuharth wanted a newspaper that had the very latest news in it. Curley's memo added:

> After two days of arguing, they agree to look at clusters an
> hour or two hours away. And the "we-are-great" syndrome
> fills the hours. I don't mean to give the wrong impression.
> The talent here is enormous. The group will succeed. It's just
> that thirty-year-olds don't have the market cornered on bril-
> liance, and they don't know it.

Overseeing the team was Vince Spezzano, the Rochester reporter whom Neuharth had helped up the corporate ladder and who was now TODAY's publisher. Spezzano was intensely loyal to Neuharth, so much so that he was seen by some as a corporate yes man—eager to tell the CEO what he wanted to hear, not what he needed to know.

Neuharth knew that all was not sweetness and light in the cottage, but that did not bother him. He enjoyed putting people with different management styles together. He had learned that out of clashes and conflicts, good ideas often evolved. Some of his colleagues saw this as a perverse form of executive abuse; Neuharth saw it as a good way to arrive at the right conclusion. He encouraged aggressive debates; he liked to challenge his colleagues' ideas and test his own convictions until he was sure he was right.

And, in spite of their personal difficulties, the crowded conditions, the isolation of Cocoa Beach, and the press of an early deadline, the Project NN team members delivered. They gave Neuharth the hard facts he needed to move his dream of a national newspaper one step closer to reality.

Gannett was clearly in the best position of any media company to attempt a project this large. In 1980, it had eighty-one daily newspapers, more than any other chain. At the end of 1979, it had passed Knight-Ridder to become the largest newspaper group in circulation too, selling 3.6 million copies per day. It had the nation's largest network of journalists: More than four thousand reporters and editors worked at its newspapers, broadcast stations, and other operations. It had printing plants and distribution systems around the country, and Gannett News Service bureaus in eleven state capitals, New York City, and Washington, D.C.

In 1980, there were signs that other media companies might experiment with a national, general-interest newspaper. That August, The New York Times began printing its new national edition in the Midwest, transmitting the pages via satellite to a Chicago printing plant. It was a two-section newspaper, a slimmed-down version of the New York edition, with national and international news, sports, and features in the first section, and business news in the second section.

The Times had tried before to expand. In 1962, it had begun selling a scaled-down edition in the Far West, but its Western edition never attracted enough readers or advertisers, and in 1964, the company shut it down. Now The Times was ready to try again; this time, it could use satellite technology to lower production costs. "Our position is one step at a time," Times spokesman Leonard Harris told Fortune magazine in 1980. "Our largest attention in the Midwest will go into building our delivery system from scratch—a long, difficult process. We don't want to excite expectations." Obviously, The New York Times wanted to keep a low profile; its corporate style was far different from Gannett's.

In June 1980, The Wall Street Journal expanded to a two-section format and increased its capacity from forty-eight to fifty-six pages. It added reporters and expanded the space it devoted to general news and features.

From sources in the industry, Neuharth had learned that The Washington Post also was exploring some kind of new national publication. But he did not think that was a serious threat: "We didn't think they would have the balls to risk weakening their Washington monopoly by trying anything major nationwide." In 1983, The Post Company began publishing its National Weekly Edition, a tabloid review of the news which has a circulation of about fifty thousand.

Neuharth was more concerned that someone who understood the success of national newspapers in Europe or Japan would enter the U.S. market, someone like Rupert Murdoch, who owned newspapers in Australia and England. In 1980, the Daily Express in England had a daily circulation of 2.4 million, and the Daily Mail's was 1.9 million. In Japan, one newspaper—Yomiuri Shimbun—sold more than 8 million copies per day.

Even so, the steps by U.S. competitors added urgency to the work of the Project NN Team. The four of them pushed hard to try to answer the questions Neuharth had posed.

They traveled a lot. Sackett figured he logged about 150,000 miles in the seven months before they reported to Gannett's top management and its board of directors in October 1980. They got into a routine where they would pick up a rental car Sunday night in Cocoa Beach, get up early on Monday and drive to the Orlando airport, fly to some distant city, and return to Florida late Friday night.

Vega traveled to the Audit Bureau of Circulations offices in Chicago, where he studied single-copy sales reports of major metropolitan newspapers. By mid-May, he had digested circulation and market penetration data for newspapers and magazines in the top one hundred markets, done an overview of newspaper distribution systems across the country, with special attention to The Wall Street Journal, and prepared a timetable that showed when USA TODAY's presses had to roll in thirty big markets.

He was also beginning to sense just how big a job distributing a national newspaper would be. Vega's early calculations showed that USA TODAY would have to be sold at more than 105,000 sales outlets, most of them newsracks. He estimated that servicing all of those outlets would require more than 1,200 truck runs each day.

There were times when Vega began to wonder whether he could do it: "I would wake up at night scared shitless. How do I do this? And then I kept telling myself, 'This is Oakland times twenty-four. You just take what you did in the Eastbay launch and multiply it twenty-four times.'"

Kessinger was looking at the market for national advertising in newspapers and magazines, poring over marketing journals in the Columbia University library in New York, analyzing how the nation's top one hundred advertisers spent their money. He read so much that spring and summer he had to have his glasses strengthened. He, too, had doubts: "I hope you and everyone else involved will realize," he wrote in a memo to Spezzano, "that we can do projections and assumptions and analyses and studies and lists until hell freezes over, but we won't be able to answer 'yes' or 'no' categorically on the advertising question until we have a *prototype* and *concept* to lay down in front of the folks who spend the money."

Tom Curley was busy working with Gannett's outside researchers,

Michael and Judee Burgoon of Michigan State University, to figure out if people wanted to buy a national newspaper. That summer, the Burgoons' firm conducted eight thousand in-depth interviews with newspaper readers. Between 1978 and 1980, the researchers had surveyed another thirty-thousand readers and nonreaders in studies for Gannett newspapers. The results showed that despite the proliferation of media, people were still hungry for information. And the Burgoons' study turned up a very encouraging statistic: 23 percent of those surveyed said they read at least two newspapers during the week. "People will subscribe to a newspaper and also will buy a second newspaper off the newsstand," the Burgoons concluded.

At one point, Tom Curley suggested that Gannett should consider starting an all-sports newspaper, because the lack of a thorough, daily, nationwide sports report was a vacuum they could fill. Neuharth rejected the idea. "I thought that was too narrow," he says. "I also thought a sports newspaper would be a hell of a lot harder to sell internally and to the board. That would really have looked like a rerun of SoDak Sports and Neuharth's ego trip."

Larry Sackett was talking to satellite companies and trying to figure out where Gannett could print a national newspaper. Sackett had lunch with Harold R. "Johnny" Johnson, a retired air force general who worked for American Satellite Company, and told him Gannett wanted to explore setting up a national network. Johnson took some notes on a cocktail napkin. Johnson met Sackett a few days later in the Admirals' Club at LaGuardia Airport and handed him a design study for a satellite communications system. Sackett read it and agreed to pay American Satellite ten thousand dollars. Gannett had taken its first small step toward satellite delivery of the news.

Sackett was beginning to think they might really be able to launch a national newspaper. He wrote in a memo: "We do have printing sites in many of the major markets. The technology is certainly there to transmit the pages via satellite at a reasonable cost. So far I am very encouraged that we have a good shot at pulling this off."

After just a few weeks, Kessinger and Sackett made a discovery that radically altered the way they thought about the project. They were talking with Young & Rubicam, then Gannett's advertising agency, using their standard cover story. "We're from Gannett's new ventures task force, and we're exploring any and all possibilities in the entire communications field."

The Madison Avenue types told them that when it came to attract-
ing national advertising, newspapers had one big disadvantage: They
couldn't take color ads. Most of the nation's big newspapers, like The
New York Times and the Los Angeles Times, were produced on
presses that had to print hundreds of thousands of copies. Those
presses had to run at high speed for several hours just to get the newspaper out, and that left little time for crews to make the many adjust-
ments that good color reproduction requires. If those newspaper
presses could print color at all, it was certainly not magazine quality—
and that was what major print advertisers were used to.

Some medium-size newspapers that ran fewer copies could print
good color, but across the country, the quality was very erratic. Most
newspapers had never tried very hard to match magazine reproduction. They had not made the investments that were needed: in quality
control, in standardized inks and newsprint, in fine-tuning presses, and
training press crews.

While investigating the national advertising universe, Kessinger
had studied The Wall Street Journal. He had discovered that if all of the
special interest financial ads were removed from The Journal—the ads
from brokerage houses, mutual funds, and the "tombstone" ads that
announced various financing deals—there was not enough general
interest advertising left to support a newspaper. That meant that if
USA TODAY was going to succeed, it would have to attract nearly all of
the other print advertisers—those who used magazines. Those ads
were all in color; most magazine advertisers didn't even bother to prepare black-and-white materials. If they did want to buy space in a black-
and-white newspaper, their advertising agencies would have to create
special materials, at extra expense.

The news magazines were moving to color, too. Time's editorial
content was already all color, and in 1980 Newsweek was making the
transition. When Sackett visited executives of the Goss Company in
Chicago, the world's largest manufacturer of newspaper presses, they
told him that by carefully following a detailed quality-control program,
it was possible to print excellent color on Goss Metro presses, which
Gannett used in some cities.

In their "undercover" roles, Kessinger and Sackett met in New
York with Jim Kobak, a leading consultant to the magazine industry.
Years earlier, when he had quit his nine-to-five job, Kobak had vowed
he would wear Bermuda shorts for the rest of his life—even to black tie

dinners. Kessinger and Sackett fed him the new ventures cover story, and Kobak, sitting on a sofa in his shorts, told them in no uncertain terms that to succeed, any national magazine had to be able to print high-quality color. The message clicked for Sackett and Kessinger, who were mentally substituting the words "national newspaper" whenever Kobak said "magazine."

"I remember the two of us walking out saying, 'This sucker has got to be in color.'" Sackett recalls. They asked for a meeting with Neuharth, and a few days later rode from Florida to New York with him on a corporate jet.

Neuharth already believed that if Gannett decided to launch USA TODAY, it ought to use full color, just as TODAY in Florida had—but he had not told the team members that. It would have to be in color if Gannett was going to make a splash and get people excited about a new national newspaper. But Neuharth had been thinking about color news photos and graphics and color's promotional value, not color advertising. He had not shared any of his thoughts about color with the researchers; he didn't want them to know his preferences and prejudices. If the team knew too many details of what he thought a national newspaper should look like, they might tell him what they thought he wanted to hear instead of what their research found.

Sackett and Kessinger told Neuharth that to attract national advertisers from magazines, USA TODAY had to be in color. Why? he asked. Because color advertising had become the common currency of magazines; there weren't enough black-and-white ads out there to support a national, daily, general-interest newspaper. Neuharth, playing the role of the skeptical reporter, kept probing, trying to poke holes in their logic.

Could they print USA TODAY in color and still have late deadlines? How would color affect the satellite transmission times? How much would the use of color add to production costs?

"He really pushed us to the wall on why we had to have color," Sackett recalls. But by the time they were on final approach to the runway at LaGuardia, Neuharth said: "Okay, let's start thinking in terms of color."

The three of them probably did not realize it then, but deciding to use color meant that the nation's newspapers would never be the same. Analysts would say later that producing USA TODAY in color revolutionized newspaper printing and contributed to a significant increase in newspaper readership. And it was an expensive decision: Going with color would cost the Gannett Company millions and millions of dollars.

Back at the cottage, the "young geniuses" were not worrying about their place in history. They were trying to teach Vince Spezzano how to open the door without setting off the security system. When Spezzano arrived before the others, he inevitably triggered the alarm, setting off sirens and dispatching police cars. The police would walk into the cottage, glance at the piles of books and papers in the war room and ask Spezzano: "What are y'all so worried about? Nuthin' worth stealin' here."

There was a certain Keystone Kops quality to the project. One day Sackett opened the door to the cottage's tiny bathroom and thick gray smoke poured into the room. He closed the door and said, as calmly as he could: "Frank, I think there's a fire in the building."

Vega put a towel over his head, expecting to protect himself from the smoke, and crawled under the cottage to check for flames. "Call the fire department!" Vega shouted to Jean Hagen, the sweet, quiet woman who was the project's secretary. Lifting his towel for a moment, Vega yelled, "But don't tell them where we are! We're working on confidential files here."

Of course Hagen had to reveal their address, and it wasn't long before the cottage was surrounded by a secret agent's nightmare: a bevy of fire trucks, police cars, and curious onlookers. Vega and Sackett tried to keep as many firemen as they could at bay, while hastily hiding flip charts and circulation projections. Eventually, two workmen from the public works department arrived and explained it was a test of Cocoa Beach's sewers. Smoke had been injected into the system to figure out which pipes lacked the proper traps; the cottage merely needed some plumbing.

The Project NN task force had a habit of uncovering problems that seemed insurmountable. By mid-summer, after surveying all of its newspapers, Sackett found Gannett did not have enough offset presses to print USA TODAY in color. To do that, massive investments in new equipment would be required. In an August 5, 1980, memo to the other team members, he wrote: "I am quite confident of our ability to get a page negative to any possible U.S. printing location [via satellite]. Unfortunately, I am far less confident of our ability to print it once we get it there."

Sackett was worried enough to ask for another urgent meeting with the chairman and president. "Tell Neuharth we've run into a brick wall," Sackett urged Spezzano. "We can't print this thing unless we fix all these presses, buy a lot of new equipment, train a whole bunch of new people."

But in the meeting with Neuharth, Spezzano didn't mention any brick walls. "I knew he would just kick them down," he explained later. Instead, Spezzano said: "Al, we've hit a speed bump. We don't have enough press capacity to print this newspaper." Neuharth didn't waste much time on speed bumps; Gannett would just have to buy some new press equipment. He turned to Jack Heselden, the head of the newspaper division, and said: "We can fix that, can't we, Jack?"

Sure, Heselden said, we can fix it. At the time, no one realized what kind of an effort it would take to fix it.

They had also discovered some arresting details about costs. Publishing a thirty-two-page national newspaper of one million circulation five days a week would require huge quantities of newsprint—about fifty thousand tons a year, enough to fill more than one thousand tractor-trailer rigs. It was going to be very expensive to print a million newspapers a day, if they could sell that many. If the newspaper were expanded only four pages, from thirty-two to thirty-six pages, that would cost the company an extra $2.2 million in newsprint each year. Vega complained that it was hard to devise budgets "because so many unexpected costs are not even evident now." He had just visited Washington, D.C., and learned that to sell newspapers in the subway system, special newsracks would be required. Each rack cost one thousand dollars, and they needed at least one hundred of them.

Vega had been meeting with newsrack manufacturers, who were working on designs for a new, unique newsrack for USA TODAY. To start, Vega figured that they would need at least forty-one thousand racks. He also suggested that they hire a data processing expert to begin planning the computer system they needed. Neuharth did not have a good understanding of computers, and he ignored Vega's request. That was one of his early mistakes.

The team had been making periodic progress reports, and it was beginning to look as if the answers to Neuharth's questions were all "yes." They had come a long way in a few months, a long way from the days when they joked that Project NN stood for "Nobody Knows." Late that summer Neuharth invited John Quinn and Jack Heselden to hear an update. He left out Doug McCorkindale, the fourth member of the Office of the Chief Executive and the chief financial officer.

"At that point, Quinn was for the project no matter what the

research showed," Neuharth says. "McCorkindale was against it no
matter what the research showed. I had already decided we were going
to do it unless the research really blew up in our face. And Heselden
was neutral. I didn't want to waste a lot of time on people who just
wanted to pee on the idea of getting involved. So Doug was excluded
from a lot of those early meetings."

Two camps were forming within the company. One, led by Neuharth
and Quinn, was composed of managers who had once been newspaper
reporters and editors. They wanted to start USA TODAY; they thought
they could create a newspaper that would interest readers and eventually attract advertisers. The other camp, led by Doug McCorkindale, was composed of people who were excellent financial managers
but had no news experience. They thought starting USA TODAY was a
profoundly crazy idea that would waste millions and seriously wound
the company.

"The Quinn crowd thought, 'Maybe he's serious and by God, that's
a great idea!'" Neuharth says. "The McCorkindale crowd started saying, 'If we don't watch this, the goddamn fool will go do it.'" The split,
which would last for years, led to shouting matches and changed
careers. It also retarded USA TODAY's progress.

In mid-September, just before the researchers were supposed to
report to Gannett's top managers and its board of directors, Neuharth
sent the researchers a memo asking three more questions:

How many air travelers are there in the United States on an average
weekday? How many people stay in hotels or motels in the United
States on an average weekday? How many people have moved in the
past ten years?

The answers were a snapshot of a mobile society. In 1980, the latest
research showed that 850,000 people a day traveled on the airlines;
1.75 million people a day stayed in motels or hotels, and 100 million
people had moved in the past ten years. Neuharth filed those numbers
away for later use. He knew those millions of travelers were a prime
audience, a logical target for a national newspaper.

In late October 1980, the Project NN researchers traveled to Reno,
Nevada, to report to separate meetings of the Gannett Operating
Committee and the board of directors. At a dress rehearsal in Reno,
Neuharth told them what to expect. He was thinking ahead again:

"The Operating Committee will be wondering about the cost," he
said. "They will be wondering about the magnitude of the cost. They

will be asking themselves if this newspaper is launched, how much will they have to subsidize it from their own operations? One or two will want to show how smart they are; they might question some of your assumptions.

"The board will be interested mainly in the concept. They'll be interested in the magnitude and the timing, and what it will mean to Gannett down the road: Will we be able to afford it? The board is unlikely to question your assumptions."

With his knack for details and his insistence on orchestrating everything, Neuharth then polished each presentation. He told Vega to mention that if USA TODAY is not a success, the newsracks could be repainted and used locally. He reminded Tom Curley to put something back in: The possibility that this new newspaper could set the national agenda. "It is impressive that USA TODAY could become the first read in the White House someday," Neuharth said.

Then, Neuharth revealed how far he had thought this project through. Next year—in 1981—they would be moving to Washington, D.C. Their budget would be bigger—$3.5 million—and they would be developing prototype editions of USA TODAY. By mid-1981, Neuharth said, he expected to make a go or no-go recommendation to the board. If the studies showed the newspaper could achieve a circulation between 1 and 2 million, take in more than $200 million in revenue, and make a profit after five years, they would go ahead with it. If it could not, they would kill the idea and see what the company could gain from the research.

Neuharth was operating on two levels. On one, he had made Project NN's members feel like geniuses—the chosen executives, the four experts Gannett had picked, among hundreds of possible candidates, to find out if this newspaper could be launched. On another, higher level, he was way out ahead of them—already rehearsing, in his mind, the proposal he would make to the board of directors more than a year later. As Vince Spezzano said, whenever the researchers uncovered a new issue, they would say: "Let's see if we can catch up with Neuharth's mind on this one."

On October 28, 1980, the Project NN team reported to the board of directors. Before the meeting began, all of the directors signed non-disclosure forms, promising not to reveal company secrets. Sackett started things off by bumping into a flip chart and knocking the whole thing into the lap of Dolores Wharton, the enthusiastic arts advocate who was one of Gannett's newest directors. Sackett survived that and went on to tell the board that the researchers had looked at producing a broadsheet newspaper, thirty-two to forty pages daily, with eight pages printed in color.

"None of the equipment or technology being discussed here is Buck Rogers fantasy," Sackett told them. "The Wall Street Journal has been using a similar system since 1974 and has never lost an edition due to a satellite or facsimile failure. The International Herald Tribune is using the same equipment to transmit its newspaper simultaneously from Paris to London, Zurich, and Hong Kong via satellite."

With its printing presses in sixty-four cities, Gannett could reach a good part of the nation. The plan then was to print in twenty market clusters. Sackett estimated that twelve Gannett plants could be used to print USA TODAY, but at eight sites, commercial printers would have to be hired. He thought that if they did decide to launch this newspaper, they would not face much of a technological problem. The technology was mostly "off-the-shelf" equipment. But they would face a huge logistical problem: Printing more than 1 million copies of a newspaper every day and getting them to more than one hundred thousand sales outlets would be no easy task.

Vega gave the board the statistics on the mobile society Neuharth had identified, noting how many people travel each day. He said USA TODAY would rely on single-copy sales, sold from a distinctive, different-looking newsrack. "A business traveler in Washington, D.C., can pick up a copy on Monday and have an identical rack smiling at him in Los Angeles on Tuesday." That single-copy strategy was in tune with Neuharth's directive to the team in March. He told them not to "waste any time, at this stage, planning for home or mail delivery." That was another mistake that would hurt later.

Then Vega gave them a glimpse of how big USA TODAY could be. The research showed, he said, a circulation of about 1 million after the first year and about 2 million by 1987. "This starts us out in the same league as the Los Angeles Times on day one, and puts us at a larger circulation base in the fifth year than The Wall Street Journal with its 1.8 million circulation."

The researchers reported that the answers to the four questions Neuharth had posed at Pumpkin Center in March were all affirmative. Larry Sackett reported that Gannett could produce and print a national newspaper. Frank Vega said they could distribute it. Tom Curley's research showed that readers would buy it. And Paul Kessinger said that with the right readers—well-educated, well-paid people—a new national newspaper could attract national advertising.

Tom Curley says that he always knew the answers would be yes. "It was the way the questions were phrased," he says. "The answers had to be yes."

Looking back, Neuharth says that the results of the research could have killed USA TODAY, but his instincts and experience told him Gannett could launch it. "There really was a chance that they or the research or other things could put a negative answer on it, but their job really was not to prove that it could be done; their job was to disprove that it could not be done, because the presumption was that it could be."

But speaking to the board of directors in October 1980, Neuharth was very careful to move gradually. He knew it would take time to sell the board on the idea. He emphasized that this was only a preliminary study, that prototype editions would have to be produced and printed, and more research was needed. "We are only looking at the future, at ways to use our existing resources. We are looking for a product which will be both profitable and successful. Whether Gannett makes a major decision of this type won't be asked of you unless management feels

Andrew Brimmer says USA TODAY required enough "imagination to look at the horizon—not the near-term, not the middle ground, but the far horizon."

Of the fight to start the national newspaper, Wes Gallagher says, "When you do anything with an organization, the natural inclination of people in the bureaucracy is to resist any change."

strongly and positively about the results of further tests."

Some board members were immediately enthusiastic. E.J. "Jack" Liechty, a personable, retired circulation executive who had been president of Speidel Newspapers, a chain of thirteen dailies that Gannett had acquired in 1977, came up to Tom Curley and said: "Only Gannett could do this."

Andrew Brimmer, an economist and former member of the Federal Reserve Board who was a director of several large companies, observed that if Gannett didn't start a national newspaper, perhaps some other company would—and an opportunity would be lost.

But some board members were skeptical. Wes Gallagher, the former president of the Associated Press who had headed the wire service's coverage of the Normandy Invasion, asked several pointed questions.

"Fascinating study," Gallagher said, "but are we putting the cart before the horse?

"Why should I want another paper? What are you going to offer me that the Los Angeles Times or The Wall Street Journal doesn't already? What is USA TODAY going to have that will be so overwhelming it will replace what people are getting now?"

In 1980, no one had a pat answer for that question.

CHAPTER SIX

Tell us
what you think

If the 1960s' movie *The Graduate* had been made in the 1980s, the businessman who gave Dustin Hoffman a career tip would not have touted "plastics." He would have whispered, "satellites."

Satellites were wiring the world, turning the planet into a global village where instant communication was no longer a dream but a reality. They made long-distance telephone calls cheaper, encouraged competing phone service and allowed TV networks to flash news anywhere in the world—live via satellite. They also made it possible for newspapers to zip pages to distant printing plants at a low cost. It was a communications revolution.

So it was fitting that the first outside source to uncover Gannett's plan to start a national newspaper was Satellite Week, a Washington trade publication covering the fast-growing satellite industry. On December 5, 1980, a few days before Gannett executives were to gather in Washington, D.C., for their annual year-end meeting, Satellite Week issued an "extra edition." Its headline declared:

GANNETT CO. PLANS NATIONAL NEWSPAPER

DISTRIBUTED BY SATELLITE

Nation's largest newspaper chain, Gannett Co., plans to start national daily newspaper. . . . Paper will be first consumer-oriented, satellite-transmitted national daily newspaper, reportedly will emphasize business and sports news.

> Cost of start-up will be "mammoth" we are told, possibly
> around $100 million. Investment reflects Gannett's desire to
> take higher profile in newspaper industry.

The Washington Post reached Neuharth for a reaction: "I don't comment on newsletter items," he said. Media industry analysts were caught by surprise, The Post said. They could not quite believe that Gannett, with its reputation for steady financial performance, would seriously consider such a high-risk proposition. "I really question whether they really have that in mind," said John Morton, a leading analyst of media company stocks.

The Satellite Week report was on the right track, but premature. Ten days later, Neuharth announced that the company was establishing the Gannett Satellite Information Network, its own nationwide communications system.

He said Gannett would explore "a variety of ways to deliver more information to more people in more places" and gave some specifics. Gannett was looking at news and advertising supplements for its eighty-one newspapers, special programming for its seven television and thirteen radio stations, and high-quality national advertising transmissions for its thirty-eight thousand billboards.

But Neuharth downplayed the idea that Gannett might launch a national newspaper, way down to the seventh paragraph of the news release, which mentioned only "the possibility of a national general-interest daily newspaper."

"Preliminary research indicates favorable response to the concept," Neuharth said. "The next step will be developing and field testing prototypes with potential readers and advertisers. For planning purposes, that projected publication has been given the title USA TODAY."

Neuharth had written the press release himself. He emphasized that "no decisions have been made on the format or content of USA TODAY. It is envisioned as a 'different' national newspaper which would neither compete with existing metropolitan newspapers nor Gannett community or regional newspapers. If the response to the prototypes tested in 1981 is favorable, a 1982 launch of the new newspaper is a possibility."

In what became a pattern, the reaction from journalists, critics, and analysts to Gannett's announcement was skeptical.

"A national daily newspaper seems like a way to lose a lot of money in a hurry," media analyst Morton said. Wall Street seemed to share Morton's doubts. The day Satellite Week reported that Gannett might launch a national daily, the price of Gannett stock dropped 1.25 points. Other media stocks were basically unchanged.

The New York Times' media writer, Jonathan Friendly, observed that if Gannett created a national newspaper, then that "could give the company a major voice in national affairs." Those suggestions fueled talk among publishers that USA TODAY was just a Neuharth ego trip. Morton told The Times that he "had not detected much desire by readers for such a publication."

Newsweek's writers turned thumbs down: "There remains a very real question whether a general-interest national daily could cut sufficiently into a market dominated by local papers." Even so, the newsweekly said, "the news from Gannett stirred special excitement, thanks to Neuharth's gift for showmanship. He made the announcement at the company's year-end executive meeting amid a swirl of rumors, leaks, and last-minute press releases."

The main release announced that the company was setting up the Gannett Satellite Information Network, a separate corporation with its own executives. It was the base Neuharth would use to further explore whether Gannett could start a national newspaper. For a few days, insiders called it G-SIN, but that acronym did not last. It was soon changed to GANSAT, but not until Neuharth had rejected some more imaginative ideas from Chief News Executive John Quinn: "Astro-News," "StratoNews" and "Infosphere, Inc." Quinn also offered one other tongue-in-cheek suggestion: "Gannettnik." "I couldn't resist," he wrote in one of his frequent notes to Neuharth.

For the top jobs at GANSAT, Neuharth tapped two people who had helped him start a daily newspaper fourteen years earlier—Moe Hickey and Ron Martin. Hickey, a veteran Gannett executive who had given TODAY in Florida its name, had gone on to be publisher of Gannett newspapers in Lansing, Michigan; Rockford, Illinois; and Rochester, New York.

Ron Martin was a creative editor with wide experience. After leaving TODAY, he had held high editing posts at the Rochester Democrat & Chronicle, The Miami Herald, The New York Post, US magazine, and the Baltimore News-American. Neuharth had asked Quinn who was the best candidate, inside or outside Gannett, to be USA TODAY's

*Ron Martin left his first
interview with Quinn and
Neuharth asking himself, "I
wonder if they could be
thinking about a national
newspaper? Nah. Well, maybe
they could be."*

planning editor. "Ron Martin," Quinn said. Neuharth agreed so
quickly that Quinn thought Neuharth must have already settled on
Martin. Three Project NN people—Paul Kessinger, Larry Sackett,
and Frank Vega—retained key positions in GANSAT. Tom Curley continued to work for Quinn as research director, but within a few weeks
was working on the USA TODAY prototypes.

Just before he announced GANSAT, Neuharth called Hickey and Martin to his Capital Hilton suite for an after-dinner meeting. In a few days,
Neuharth would say that "no decisions" had been made on the format
or content of the proposed national daily. But that night, Martin recalls,
"He had a very clear idea of what he wanted." Neuharth gave them his
charge, his vision of what this new national newspaper should be.

USA TODAY would be a broadsheet newspaper of thirty-two to forty
pages, not a tabloid, Neuharth said. It would use color on every section
front. It would emphasize extensive, results-oriented sports coverage
and a thorough weather report—as much as a page per day. A regular,
standard part of the News section would be a roundup of the top news
from every one of the fifty states, every day. This would be a unique
feature.

The fifty-state idea was nothing new for Neuharth. When he
became chairman and president of the publishers' association in 1978,
he said he would speak in all fifty states. It took him two years, but he
kept his promise. His schedule was often as hectic as a presidential
candidate's. He would speak at a breakfast meeting of editors in Tennessee, hit a publishers' luncheon in Kentucky, and fly on to Illinois for
a dinner speech. Visiting every state helped him plan for USA TODAY; it

gave him a sense of which newspapers were strong and which were weak. It was also a good way to scout possible acquisitions.

That night at the Capital Hilton, Neuharth interrupted his instructions to Hickey and Martin to emphasize their target audience: "Remember, 850,000 people travel on the airlines every day; 1.75 million stay in hotels. They will be hungry for news from home."

The three of them discussed whether one of the prototypes should include a regional news section. Neuharth said no: "If we compared our California coverage with the L.A. Times', we would be playing to their strength instead of ours." He continued his charge to them:

USA TODAY should be very newsy. It should have lots of information—summaries, results, statistics, lists. It should have an upscale look. Red, white, and blue should be used subtly, as an identifier, but not in a way that would chase off nonpatriots.

Neuharth paused again. He thought about how USA TODAY's front page would look in the vending machine; he imagined a reader studying it, deciding whether to buy. He turned to Hickey and said, "Make sure the vending machines and the mastheads work together." Neuharth the promoter had that marketing idea firmly in mind. The combination should say to the customer: Buy me. Read me. Take me home.

He wanted the newspaper to mix sections that were heavy on results—what happened last night—with material that would set the agenda—what would happen next.

All of those ideas were tested later, and the readers liked them. Much of what USA TODAY evolved into grew out of the vision Neuharth had been carrying around with him, in all those hours and days he spent thinking and dreaming about a national newspaper. He thought about the newspaper when he jogged in the morning, during lulls in corporate meetings, during all those days and nights when he was alone in the corporate jet, crisscrossing the country. He thought about this national newspaper all the time, so it wasn't surprising that a full-blown vision burst forth that night with Hickey and Martin.

Later many of USA TODAY's critics would adopt the view of Ben Bagdikian, a journalism professor at the University of California at Berkeley, who wrote in the Columbia Journalism Review that "the paper represents the primacy of packagers and market analysts in a realm where the news judgment of reporters and editors has traditionally prevailed."

But in his charge to Hickey and Martin, Neuharth said their first

priority in designing USA TODAY should be "news instincts and experience." Neuharth's news instincts had been shaped by years of experience launching new daily and Sunday newspapers. He knew a lot of
what he wanted long before the first opinion survey or focus group
began.

Research, he said, would come next. And the last priority would be
"our studies of how we can supplement what the major papers do."
After they had created the prototypes, then they would use research
to make modifications.

Martin was an intellectual, intense man who seemed to read constantly—newspapers, magazines, books, anything. When he heard
about USA TODAY, he realized that he was in for the time of his life.
When they approached Martin in the fall of 1980, Neuharth and Quinn
never mentioned a national newspaper. They said only that they
wanted his help for a project that "could be more exciting than anything
you've ever been involved in." Martin was weighing another job offer,
but dropped it when Neuharth said, "You'd be crazy not to do this."

From the beginning, there had been a strong entrepreneurial spirit
to the project. USA TODAY was born and took shape in small task forces,
not large corporate bureaucracies. The ethic was not "file a report"
but "get it done." It had more in common with the garage where two
whiz kids started Apple Computer than the corporate design center
where hundreds of engineers have invented General Motors' new
cars.

But as the project grew, it lost some of its entrepreneurial momentum. In January 1981, the GANSAT crew moved into the eleventh floor of
Gannett News Service's space in a K Street office building in downtown Washington, D.C. Moe Hickey took over the executive office at
one end of the building, more or less evicting John Quinn, Gannett's
chief news executive. Quinn was based in Rochester, but he frequently
worked out of that office when he came down to edit prototypes and
supervise the wire service. Gannett News Service had given GANSAT
some of its precious space, and Hickey seized a big chunk of it for his
executive command post. When he was in town, Quinn sat at a small
desk outside Hickey's office. Then Hickey's secretaries questioned
whether they should answer Quinn's phone. Quinn didn't say anything, but he took notice.

Ron Martin set up shop in a room the size of a closet. He recognized
right away that trying to start a national newspaper from scratch was

The prototype staff gave Ron Martin this T-shirt to remind him of what a tireless, detail-oriented editor he was. He says, "My top priority was to make this the most interesting, readable, enjoyable newspaper that it was possible to produce."

an advantage, at least as far as editorial content was concerned. The usual innovation for newspapers was to add a new section, not invent a new newspaper. Journalists produced prototypes, and if the result fit the rest of the newspaper, you printed it. The creation of USA TODAY was different. Except for Neuharth's general guidelines and the name, they had no restrictions—no old traditions, no ancient nameplate, no prejudices. It was an editorial and marketing dream, but it proved to be a logistical and operating nightmare. And that brought out the best and the worst in a lot of Gannett people.

After the arduous prototype process ended, Martin's colleagues presented him with a T-shirt emblazoned with the words: "What if we try it this way?" Martin explains that because they were working with a blank piece of paper, "we did try it just about every way."

The pace was demanding. With John Quinn's help, twenty-two loaners from Gannett newsrooms around the country were brought to Washington to work on the prototypes. One was Dick Thien of the Sioux Falls Argus Leader, South Dakota's biggest daily. Fred Christopherson, the crusty co-owner of the Argus Leader whom Neuharth had needled thirty years earlier, had sold the Argus to Speidel Newspapers, and in 1977 Gannett acquired Speidel. Neuharth had returned to his home state in triumph—Gannett now owned SoDak Sports' old nemesis.

Thien had worked with Martin at the Rochester newspapers: "God, what an intense fellow," Thien says. "I think Ron even reads the little tags on mattresses. He would go home with one briefcase and come back with three loaded with stuff for us to read."

Martin was concentrating so hard on the project he was sometimes unaware of who was around him. Some mornings he would ride up to the eleventh floor of the K Street building in the little elevator and never notice the prototype editor standing next to him, never say hello. The very next morning he would recognize the same person and say a kind word or two. "Don't try to figure Martin out," Thien told the other loaners. "You'll never be able to."

Thien, who had been Martin's sports editor in Rochester, was a gruff, cigar-chewing type who barked like an oldtime city editor. But he had mischief in his eyes and enjoyed a good joke. One day he decided to lie down on the floor outside Martin's office. "Just watch," he predicted. "Martin will come out and step right over me."

Sure enough, Martin fired out of his office, intent on his latest adjustment to the weather page, and stepped right over Thien's prostrate body without a word. Laughter erupted, and Martin looked down and discovered Thien giggling on the floor. "What are you doing down there?" he asked.

Thien was in charge of producing the sports section for the prototypes. Sheryl Bills, the cool and composed managing editor from Cincinnati, handled features. Tom Curley had business news, and Martin added the main news section to his other responsibilities.

They loved starting from square one, designing a newspaper from nothing. For years, Martin and the others had known readers did not follow all the stories that "jumped," or continued to other pages. Readers did not like the tortured writing of many newspaper stories. They wanted clear, concise writing.

"People just don't have time," Martin says. "Every bit of reader research tells you that nobody reads jumps. Yet I did what every other editor did—I jumped four or five or six stories off of every section front. That's the way it's done! Even though we knew readers didn't follow jumps, we said, 'If they're smart they'll follow these stories. It's important for them to know this information.' If we think it's important, they'll read it."

The combination of their news instincts and the research told them that one way they could make USA TODAY "different" was to put readers first, to publish news that readers cared about. Certainly they would not ignore news that editors felt was important, but they would not ignore readers' feelings, either. The prototype editors knew that if they could not create something that captured people's interest, Gannett would never launch this street-sales newspaper. Editors would have to win readers' loyalty over and over again, day after day.

In their discussions, the term "second read" emerged. The planning editors knew they would have many, many readers who also read another newspaper; USA TODAY would have to offer those people something new.

Martin and his crew of loaners worked hard, under difficult conditions. The computerized typesetting system they had been given was a reject from a small Gannett newspaper, and it often failed. Each day they would try to work on a different page. On a Monday they would try to get the weather page right, on Tuesday the Washington page, on Wednesday the state-by-state roundup. They hung the finished pages on a wall and every few days Neuharth would come by to take a look, just as he had done at TODAY and other start-ups. "Neuharth had the most open mind in terms of what we would consider and what we would try," Quinn says. "He was always open to new ideas." But to the loaners, it seemed that nothing they could do was good enough for the triumvirate of editors who conducted these frequent critiques—Neuharth, Quinn, and Martin.

"Neuharth read every word of everything that was written," Thien recalls. "I rewrote one piece for the sports cover seventeen times. I never had to rewrite anything seventeen times for anybody in my life. Finally it came back approved with his mark on it—the black *N* with the circle around it. And what finally passed was version three, damn near word-for-word."

It was the same technique Neuharth had used in Cocoa: If you do something over and over, if you debate it and discuss it, eventually the best ideas emerge. Karen Howze had joined the prototype team from Rochester, where she had been an assistant managing editor. "It was like every idea was coming back fifteen times. And it was clear that Neuharth was not willing to take 'We can't do that' for an answer."

Quinn was all over the prototypes too. He wrote Martin a staccato, eight-page memo, suggesting changes: "USA TODAY must sell news/info at a fast, hard pace. Every page one inch must be packed with news/info in easiest-to-read, most comfortable, quick-glance style. No repetition, no word waste, no nonfunctioning white space. . . . Every above-fold item must work to catch reader-on-run."

John Bodette, a loaner from St. Cloud, Minnesota, remembers that they had assembled hundreds of designs for nameplates for the new newspaper, "and Martin could find something wrong with every one of them."

Once in a while things got testy. On one of the two prototype editions, some loaners objected when a sample advertisement was put on a sports page. "I don't see where it hurt us that much," Martin said.

"I don't think you will get much agreement on that from your sports staff," said John Bannon, who had worked on the page.

"That's okay," Martin replied. "I don't require much."

They began working on the prototypes in January. At first, the loaners came to Washington for three days a week. Then the standard stay was lengthened to four days, then five, and then Martin asked them to stay "for the duration." "That scared the hell out of everybody," Thien says.

"Life was not easy in the task force world of USA TODAY," John Quinn wrote in Wire Watch, his weekly bulletin to Gannett editors, after the loaners went home in mid-June 1981. "Some news staffers came on board for the very-first-of-the-year brainstorming sessions and others joined later as the prototype editions worked their way through the development of concepts, section blueprints, typographic designs, content ideas, page layouts, and finally, first draft pages.

"Then came the corporate kibitzers," Quinn wrote, "shifting emphasis here, packing in more hard news there, wearing out the sports agate with an avalanche of makeovers, tinkering with this head and that label, adding bells, whistles, and assorted innovations."

The prototypes were scheduled to go to press May 15; they finally were finished on June 11. Jim Norman, a loaner from Pensacola, wrote a poem about the long days in the prototype office at 1627 K Street:

> I once had a real life outside of 1627,
> down in Florida which now seems like heaven,
> I had a boat and a beachhouse and friends and family,
> I want to go home some day soon,
> hug my wife while we watch the moon,
> play with the kids and know how sweet life can be.

When will we be freed to see our loved ones, our families?
My youngest was a baby when I left, now he's almost four.
Quoth Ron Martin: Never more.

Despite all the hard work, the twenty-two journalists who worked on USA TODAY's prototypes shared a feeling of excitement, of camaraderie, of mission. "It was just so damn exciting to think that this country could have a national newspaper," Thien said.

In April, before the prototypes were finished, Gannett held an editors' meeting timed to coincide with the American Society of Newspaper Editors' convention in Washington.

Neuharth kicked off the meeting by repeating the rumors that were flying around: (1) Gannett wants to start USA TODAY because that was the only way it could get into Washington after Kay Graham refused to sell it The Washington Post. (2) GANSAT was set up because Gannett decided not to buy The Washington Star. (3) Neuharth needed a Washington base because he wanted to run for the U.S. Senate.

"None of these rumors is true," Neuharth said. "Washington is the news capital of the world. There ought to be a way Gannett can bring even more news resources together in Washington and find ways to send more news to people. One of the ways is via satellite." He noted that those news resources were underutilized; Gannett was delivering only about 20 percent of the news and information it gathered.

Ron Martin talked about the prototypes. It was the first time he had described them to anyone who hadn't signed a nondisclosure form. "I feel like I'm doing something illegal," he said.

John Bannon helped develop a Sports section that he would later call his "baby."

Six of the many nameplates that were rejected.

"We won't be another National Enquirer," Martin said. "We won't be another National Observer, either," referring to the national weekly newspaper that folded in 1977, after Dow Jones had struggled for fifteen years to make it a success. "I'm amazed at how many people assume that's our model. I would bet they haven't gone back to read the last several issues. It was a pretty sleepy product and we can't afford to be sleepy."

Martin explained the newspaper sought a mobile, active, well-paid, well-educated audience, probably more male than female. Many would be occasional readers of newspapers—in some markets, 25 to 50 percent of adults were not regular readers of newspapers. "That could be good news for a national paper," Martin said. "Those people don't have a strong allegiance to any one paper."

USA TODAY would aim for broad-based national coverage, with thorough sports, weather, and television reporting, all of it done from a "vigorously national" perspective. Martin said USA TODAY could learn from the way the television networks and the news magazines approach information and entertainment—a tip-off that USA TODAY would be stealing ideas from other media.

"We ought to be able to do on a daily basis some things the national weekly magazines do," Martin said. "Nobody is doing quality sports coverage on a daily basis. We think people are hungry for more information if it is packaged and presented effectively and appealingly."

In late May 1981, Neuharth spoke to the annual shareholders' meeting in Rochester. He crowed a little: Gannett News Service had won the Pulitzer Prize Gold Medal for public service in 1980, and the independent business magazine Dun's Review had named Gannett one of the five best-managed companies in the country.

One reason was Gannett's remarkable record of profitability, unmatched in the media industry. Since the company had gone public in 1967, it had never had a down quarter. By the spring of 1981, the string had reached fifty-four consecutive quarters of comparative earnings gains. And it had just announced another increase in its common stock dividend, the thirteenth increase in thirteen years. A Fortune magazine article noted that Gannett's stock price was 500 percent above the 1967 offering price, while the New York Stock Exchange composite index had gained less than 50 percent.

Neuharth told shareholders the decision to launch USA TODAY would come only after "careful study and testing of the prototypes." In a speech to financial analysts that spring, he had said: "There are no ego trips scheduled at Gannett," rebutting criticism that USA TODAY was a product of Neuharth's unbridled ambition.

When the two sets of forty-page prototypes were finally printed, their nameplates were different, but the front pages similar. Both used color pictures of the space shuttle *Columbia* being returned to Cape Canaveral, shared a "cover story" on the "super-cities of the 1980s," and had two-and-a-half pages of state-by-state news in the A section.

Prototype I had a full page of weather, in color, on the back page. Its second section was "Agenda," a mixture of an editorial page, health and science news, and two pages of business news. A thorough sports report was the third section, and the fourth was "Life," with heavy emphasis on entertainment.

Prototype II's "D" section was "Money," a complete business report including stock prices, which Prototype I omitted. The editorial page and weather pages were facing each other near the end of the "A" section, leaving the back page for an ad. Its "B" section was "Life," and "Sports" was the "C" section. Both prototypes had complete television coverage and many graphics. Neither carried comics. A national newspaper could not carry the most popular comics, since the rights to publish them had already been sold on a territorial basis to newspapers across the country.

Each prototype had large, two-page advertising spreads in full color, and samples from automotive, travel, tobacco, and liquor advertisers. Both editions were tightly organized, reflecting Neuharth's "easy to find, easy to read" philosophy.

The prototypes were mailed to 4,500 "opinion leaders" across the country—including publishers, editors, and leaders in business, government, education, and sports. The headline on Neuharth's letter to readers on the front page asked, "An idea whose time has come?" He explained that satellite transmission made a national, general-interest daily possible, and sent along a postage-paid postcard inviting readers to "tell us what you think." The card had two boxes to check:

1. "I hope you start publishing USA TODAY regularly."

2. "I hope you forget about the idea."

The reaction from other journalists was swift and, by this time, predictable.

"Perhaps the best word to describe these prototypes is shallow," said Publishers' Auxiliary, a trade newspaper for the National News-

George Rorick, who developed the weather page, and Ron Martin review pages. Moe Hickey called Rorick in Lansing, Michigan, one Tuesday and invited him to work on the prototypes. Late that same afternoon, Rorick arrived in Washington, D.C.

paper Association, which represented weekly newspapers. "How stupid do they expect their readers to be?" Its editorial concluded that USA TODAY "poses little threat" to community newspapers.

One reporter for the Los Angeles Times advised Gannett to forget about the idea: "A sampling of business leaders, analysts, and newspaper executives who received copies of the prototype last week variously described the newspaper's appearance as 'dazzling' and 'bland,'" wrote Debra Whitefield. "And the vast majority of those polled Tuesday by the Times said they would recommend that Gannett scrub the idea."

Newsday's media writer asked: "Is the country ready for a newspaper that tries to span and swallow a continent, or is Gannett trying to cover too much ground?"

Some early returns from opinion leaders were discouraging, too. Many found the heavy diet of state-by-state news boring. "I strongly urge you to scrap that section," wrote Roy M. Fisher, then dean of the

University of Missouri Journalism School. And after USA TODAY started publishing, John Morton, the stock analyst, said, "The 'Across the USA' section is the weakest conceptually—though I did read the Kansas section because I come from there."

Advertising decision-makers had trouble seeing much potential in the prototypes. "Advertising will be very, very difficult to come by," said Sheldon Taule, a senior vice president of a Baltimore advertising agency.

"Who is this newspaper going to appeal to?" asked Thurman Pierce, then a print media manager for J. Walter Thompson. "They have put design before demographics."

Marketing & Media Decisions, a trade magazine, summed up the skepticism of the advertising community: "Consensus is that Gannett's national newspaper will be a tough advertising sell."

But the reaction from some of Neuharth's old associates was quite different. Jim Head, who had worked at TODAY and who by 1981 was the top editor at King Features, wrote: "You have a winner on your hands, though it may be like opening Pandora's Box . . . something so all-encompassing will have to expend great amounts of talent and treasure. I do think it will be a ripping success."

Dolph C. Simons, Jr., editor and publisher of the Journal World in Lawrence, Kansas, told Neuharth that sports buffs might decide to read USA TODAY every day because "it would have more sports than most any daily in the U.S."

Richard K. Wager, publisher of Gannett's daily in Poughkeepsie, New York, told Neuharth that his eleven top managers read the prototypes and decided Gannett should go with USA TODAY—but the vote was six to five.

George Beebe, The Miami Herald editor who hired Neuharth when he was down and out, wrote his old protégé: "I know you wouldn't move all the way to the prototype unless you were convinced such a newspaper had a chance for success. There is no one that would be happier to see you make a success of a proposal that has most newsmen shaking their heads in wonderment."

At that Gannett editors' meeting in April 1981, Neuharth said in closing: "So far this has been very easy. The tough thing will be to decide what GANSAT should commit itself to. The Go/No-Go decision will be the toughest decision this company has ever made, and one of the toughest decisions any media company has made."

KANSAS

Great Bend estate accused of fraud

Dentist Kenneth A. Mitchell's family has been charged with not reporting nearly $600,000 found in a suitcase after his 1976 death. U.S. Attorney James Buchele says it may be "the largest tax fraud case in Kansas history." The Great Bend dentist apparently didn't like banks, Buchele said.

Session praised, panned

Republican leaders in the Kansas Legislature held three press conferences in Topeka to spread the word that the session was a great success. But Democratic Gov. John Carlin held his own press conference to declare it "a collective disaster" and vow to veto all or parts of the Legislature's school aid package. Taxpayers face property tax increases averaging 3.5 mills.

The Kansas brief from the "News from Across the USA" section in Prototype I.

It was a tough decision because it would require a big investment, both in terms of Gannett dollars and in terms of Neuharth's career. He was not far from retirement. If USA TODAY succeeded, it would be his crowning achievement. He would leave his mark as an influential journalist and a visionary entrepreneur. But if it failed, he would not end with a bang, but a whimper.

"We will not make the decision with our glands," Neuharth said over and over in 1981. Before deciding to "Go," Gannett would carefully weigh the risk/reward ratio and the results of in-depth, scientific research done on the prototypes. The mailing to opinion leaders was an interesting promotion, but those results were unscientific. If careful questioning of prospective readers proved negative, Neuharth pledged, "We will not hesitate to say, 'Well, it seemed like a hell of a good idea, but its time has not yet come.'"

Back in the summer of 1981, there were a lot of Gannett executives who would have voted "No Go." They agreed with John Morton, the most-quoted stock analyst: Starting a national newspaper was a good way to lose a lot of money in a hurry. A political battle for the future of the company was under way.

CHAPTER SEVEN

No guts, no glory

There were times when Chuck Schmitt, the young finance director of GANSAT, felt he was in no-man's land.

Schmitt had risen fast. Before moving to Washington, he was assistant controller at corporate headquarters in Rochester, working for controller Larry Miller and chief financial officer Doug McCorkindale. His job then was to analyze budgets and manage financial reports from Gannett's many newspapers and broadcast stations. Enthusiastic and energetic, Schmitt was one of the best "numbers-crunchers" in a company known for strong financial management.

Now, at thirty-three, he had been thrown into a much broader role. GANSAT President Moe Hickey was known as a great delegator of responsibility, and he had given Schmitt a very full plate.

When he arrived in Washington in January 1981, Schmitt was GANSAT's entire financial staff. He had to organize its affairs and make sure it paid the bills. For a while, he even signed all the checks himself. Hickey also put him in charge of some of the long-range planning for the possible launch of USA TODAY. Schmitt was told to search for a big block of office space—two-hundred-thousand square feet—select a computer system, and develop a budget for the proposed national newspaper.

Schmitt's budget assignment was by far the most important. USA TODAY needed a realistic, well-thought-out business plan. Because of his SoDak Sports defeat, no one was more aware of that need than Neuharth. Without a solid plan, there was little chance the board of

Larry Miller says of the early days at USA TODAY, *"We should have recognized early on that you couldn't expect people to do fifteen jobs at the same time."*

Chuck Schmitt remembers juggling a number of duties at once: "There were never enough hours in the day. It was always very busy."

directors would buy in. The people who worked on the business plan also knew Neuharth wanted to launch USA TODAY. They knew it would take some strong negative news—overwhelming rejection of the idea by readers and advertisers, for example—to change his mind. If the probable rewards justified the risk, Gannett was going to go ahead.

In late August 1981, the momentum to "Go" got a huge boost at a meeting in California—and that increased the pressure on Schmitt. Gannett's top managers and its board of directors met in Oakland to hear what readers thought about the prototypes. The results from the scientific research were stunning: Readers loved USA TODAY.

Louis Harris and Associates, the research firm Gannett had acquired in 1975, had conducted nearly two thousand personal interviews in the nation's twenty-four largest markets. It was the same kind of work Lou Harris had done for TODAY in Florida, but on a much larger scale. The conclusion of Harris' slide show was simple: USA TODAY was an idea whose time had come.

After reading the two sets of prototypes overnight, 21 percent of the people surveyed said they were "certain to buy" USA TODAY. Harris estimated that would translate into a nationwide circulation of 5 million. To be conservative, Harris cut his estimate by more than half, to 2.2 million. That would mean the newspaper would be in about 3 percent of the households in any market. Harris also concluded readers wanted more national sports coverage; if that section was the equivalent of a national daily sports newspaper, it would be a big draw.

Simmons Market Research Bureau, an independent firm with no connection to Gannett, had done 1,150 personal interviews in the nation's eight largest markets. Simmons talked to a new newspaper's toughest audience—single-copy buyers, heavy readers of national news who lived in big cities. They liked the prototypes, too; 27 percent of the Simmons sample said they "definitely would buy" USA TODAY.

Then the managers and directors heard the final tally from the unscientific research with the 4,500 opinion leaders. Seventy-four percent of those who sent back postcards checked the box that said, "I hope you start publishing USA TODAY regularly."

Taken together, this was very heartening news. After a year and a half of careful research, here was proof Gannett could create a newspaper that would grab readers. The satellite technology was there to transmit the newspaper around the country, or even around the world. Gannett had the resources to print the paper and distribute it almost everywhere. Now well-to-do, well-educated readers were saying they would buy it. And advertisers were telling Paul Kessinger that if USA TODAY could reach well-heeled readers, they would buy ads in it.

"I had the feeling most people thought it was something we could do," recalls Julian Goodman, a Gannett director and former reporter who had been the chairman of NBC. "If somebody wanted to stop it, they would have to stop the locomotive."

Neuharth's press release from the Oakland meeting said the

Regarding the vote by the board, Julian Goodman says, "A vision has a way of becoming infectious, particularly when it is engendered by the chairman."

research added up to "encouraging public response, but now we must determine whether we can translate that response into a business plan for successful regular publication." He also noted that Eastbay TODAY, the Oakland morning newspaper Gannett had launched in 1980, was going great guns. "That street sale daily has grown from zero circulation to over eighty thousand in less than two years."

John Quinn sensed the rising enthusiasm at the Oakland meeting. "People who were not hung up on tidy corporate management were fascinated," he recalls. Listening to Lou Harris, Quinn jotted a note in the margin of Harris' report: "USA TODAY is an idea whose time has come—it will fail only if its editors fail to put out a good enough newspaper."

The positive reader reaction to the idea was a turning point, Quinn says. "The question of whether Neuharth was on solid ground was now gone. The project was off and running and the board agreed with the thesis. If you had felt that there was anything frivolous about this— that it was an old man's childhood vision—Oakland was the meeting where the statistics came in and said there's a market for it if you don't screw it up. The lingering questions had been answered. You had to say to yourself, 'Your job for the company now is to make it go.' Yet that's where the foot-dragging began."

The foot-dragging came from financial executives who did not want USA TODAY to go forward. In 1981, the battle lines had been clearly drawn. As Neuharth would put it later, one side was planning for success; the other side was planning for failure. One group was trying to successfully launch USA TODAY; the other was trying to clamp down on funds for it and figure out what could be sold when it failed.

GANSAT's young managers were certainly not planning for failure. They were caught up in the enthusiasm of launching a national newspaper; their professional futures were tied to its success. In preparing a budget, they tried to make their numbers realistic, but they wanted them to be upbeat. They knew if there was no hope in their profit and loss projections there would be no hope of launching the newspaper.

Chuck Schmitt's multiple responsibilities made things hard for him. His management style was in one sense the opposite of Moe Hickey's—Schmitt did not delegate enough. He would do most of the details himself, even if he had to work eighteen hours a day. In a project that turned out to be much bigger and far more complicated than anyone had dreamed, that proved to be a key weakness.

Steve Johnson and Jean Hagen of the Circulation department, plan sales locations for a city street-by-street, corner-by-corner. Later, colored pins were placed on the map, denoting newsracks and other sales points.

During 1981, the enterprise changed from a blue-sky dream to a real business. The team worked in offices in downtown Washington now, not a cottage. The demands on key planners—Moe Hickey, Ron Martin, Chuck Schmitt, Paul Kessinger, Larry Sackett, and Frank Vega—were more precise, more detailed, more pressure packed.

Sackett had to install a transmitting earth station at the Army Times Company's printing plant outside Washington. That privately owned company published a string of suburban dailies and worldwide publications for the U.S. military. Its plant could print high-quality color, and Sackett was trying to upgrade Gannett's presses so they could match that standard.

Vega was working on newsrack designs and planning truck runs and newsrack locations—right down to the street corner for nearly every major city in the country. Kessinger took the prototypes to major advertisers and ad agencies and asked them how many pages they might buy in USA TODAY. Martin and an expanded group of editors produced one prototype after another, and each one was critiqued as closely as the originals.

And now in late 1981, there was intense pressure to finish the business plan. The board was scheduled to make the Go/No-Go decision in December. First the key planners went over the budget with Hickey, and then the corporate financial experts came in from Rochester. They picked apart newspaper budgets for a living.

The trouble with USA TODAY's business plan was that a lot of it had to be guesswork; no company had ever launched a national newspaper in such a short span of time. The Wall Street Journal had grown very gradually, over fifty years. The New York Times was building its national edition very slowly, one market at a time. There was no model for USA TODAY to follow. No one was sure how many copies they would sell, or how much it would cost to sell them. No one knew how many ad pages they would sell, if any. To make Schmitt's job even harder, all of his old friends in the corporate financial department were against the project.

"They thought it was the craziest damn thing they had ever heard of," recalls Paul Kessinger, who left Gannett in 1985 to join Urban and Associates, a Boston newspaper consulting firm. "The financial people were just shaking their heads over these numbers."

They were shaking their heads because it was clear that even at its most optimistic, the business plan showed Gannett would lose many millions of dollars if it launched USA TODAY. The prospect of pouring $40 million or $50 million a year down the drain made the corporate financial planners apoplectic. Neuharth always changed the word "losses" to "investment" whenever he saw it, but that gave them no comfort. They knew they would be expected to find the money somewhere to cover USA TODAY's losses, and that would not be easy.

Beyond their fear of huge losses, they were convinced that these projections had simply been manufactured out of thin air. Doug McCorkindale and Larry Miller thought the GANSAT people were massaging the numbers to produce unrealistic, overly optimistic estimates. They figured Schmitt and Hickey were trying to give Neuharth the rosy numbers he dreamed about. McCorkindale and Miller thought their mission was to save Neuharth from himself.

In Kessinger's view, Neuharth wanted honest estimates. "He thought the revenue estimates were too high, that the numbers weren't real. I think he expected a greater degree of precision than these numbers could ever possibly have. The budget was assumption on top of assumption on top of assumption. He probably wanted more ammunition against the financial guys than he was getting."

Schmitt was the point person who had to explain these dicey projections to his old friends in the corporate finance department, the guys who had promoted him. He knew how good they were at poking holes in a budget's faulty assumptions, but in the past he had been a poker, not a pokee.

"Chuck was in a no-win situation," Kessinger recalls. "There was no way that he could make all the people happy that he had to make happy. People would ask him, 'Where did you get that number?' Finally, he would have to admit, 'Well, you know, it's air. It's an assumption.' That's not a great answer, but it was true."

"Everybody realized that we were making up numbers," Schmitt says. To add some depth to the projections, he set up a computer simulation for every market where USA TODAY would launch. They could key in circulation projections and newsprint costs and estimate revenues and expenses for every print site.

Schmitt sat through a lot of tough meetings, trying to hang in there. "Moe would want him to be much more forceful and dynamic about his numbers," Kessinger says, "and the corporate financial people would get this look in their eyes that said: 'C'mon Chuck, this is all bullshit. Go ahead, you can tell us. You're one of *us*, Chuck.'"

McCorkindale remembers his deep distrust of the original budget projections with understatement: "I did not have a lot of confidence in their business plan. They were doing an awful lot on a guessing basis rather than on a knowledge basis. They were trying to make the numbers work, to fit answers in where they wanted it to come out."

Larry Miller was a mild-looking accountant, but in a budget session he could be a formidable adversary. He had been crunching newspaper numbers for more than twenty years, and he knew how to probe for the soft spots. When he found a budget he didn't believe, he could rip it apart, using sarcasm, ridicule, and derision. Miller was McCorkindale's top analyst, so when Miller mocked this business plan, people naturally thought the two of them were conspiring to derail Neuharth's USA TODAY express.

Miller says he was frustrated because everyone knew the numbers weren't real. GANSAT's planners "would struggle harder to find out what Al wanted them to say rather than what the real truth was. Anything that you ever got your hands on, you could just poke holes all over. Unfortunately, that then got viewed as peeing on the project instead of trying to help with the projections. But nobody really wanted to listen because they wanted the plan to say what they wanted it to say."

Jimmy Thomas says of the business plan, "Every assumption made was as optimistic as you could possibly hope to make it."

Jimmy Thomas, Gannett's treasurer, was another McCorkindale lieutenant who questioned the business plan. Thomas' analysis pointed out that the USA TODAY business plan assumed that small increases in circulation would yield large increases in revenue from both advertising and circulation sales. "Those assumptions are almost certainly wrong," Thomas wrote McCorkindale in a 1981 memo. "I have frequently heard USA TODAY referred to as a 'big risk, big reward' venture. After going through this analysis, I'm not sure the reward is that good."

The "us and them" mentality was thriving. News and GANSAT were on one side, corporate finance on the other. Neuharth and Quinn saw USA TODAY as a great opportunity to do something exciting, to add something new to journalism, to create an innovative, profitable newspaper. The financial experts, led by McCorkindale, thought launching a national newspaper might financially cripple the company and turn out to be the worst thing Gannett could possibly do.

Fights between news and finance were nothing new. Years earlier, Quinn had successfully resisted attempts by McCorkindale's predecessor as chief financial officer, John "Jack" Purcell, to allocate news budgets according to specific formulas. Purcell thought it would be orderly if the news budget of every Gannett newspaper was limited to 10 percent of operating revenues, or if every newspaper had one news staffer per one thousand circulation. Quinn argued successfully that it would be a terrible mistake to put news in a financial straitjacket; some news staffs needed proportionately more money, others relatively less.

Later Quinn and McCorkindale clashed. Quinn liked to keep a special part of his budget reserved for news department emergencies—like adding a hot reporter the newspaper had not budgeted for. He called this his "chemicals" budget, because that was where he had hidden a lot of money when he had been editor of the Rochester newspapers, in the "chemicals" line in the photo department budget. No one was sure how much "chemicals" should cost. McCorkindale did not find any of this humorous; he called Quinn's kitty a "slush fund."

Neuharth usually encouraged news-finance competition. Good arguments produced good decisions, and these lively discussions added checks and balances to the company. "McCorkindale was always policing Quinn's budget and Quinn was always trying to put one over on McCorkindale," Neuharth says. "And I was always the referee." But this time, the news-finance split was so serious it threatened the biggest project the company had ever attempted. And when it came to USA TODAY, the chief referee was somewhat less than objective.

While the budget experts manipulated millions, Frank Vega was struggling to find the right newsrack. Neuharth wanted something different, something that would stand out among all of the mundane models other newspapers used. Vega brought several different kinds of racks to Washington so Neuharth could rattle the handles.

Moe Hickey was there too. Meetings with Neuharth made nearly everyone nervous, and Hickey was no exception. A tall Irishman with a ruddy complexion, Hickey would perspire profusely when things got tense, as things often did when Neuharth was involved—especially if he began one of his Marine Corps drill instructor acts.

That day Neuharth got up and began pacing around the room, studying the newsracks. They were the traditional kind; most of them had the coin mechanism mounted on top of the box, not far from eye level, with the newspaper displayed at belt level. To read the front page in the vending machine, a customer had to bend down. As Neuharth paced about the room, Vega got up too: "I didn't want him to get the edge on me. When he's standing behind you, you feel very uncomfortable."

After checking the boxes, Neuharth finally said, "Mr. Vega, why do you circulators insist on promoting the price of the paper?" He tapped the coin mechanism. "Why can't we promote the paper up here?"

Vega explained that then the coin mechanism would have to be under the newspaper, and you would need an electric motor to open

Prototypes of USA TODAY racks were lined up in the hallway of the GANSAT office. Some were taken out on the street late at night and photographed beside other newsracks.

the newsrack. "The problem is, Al, that there aren't electric outlets on every street corner in the country."

Vega's know-it-all tone was his first mistake. His second was when he decided to explain the laws of gravity to the chairman and president. "You see, Al, you put a coin in the slot up here, gravity pulls it down and as you pull this handle the coin falls—as you see here, Al—and that allows the latch to open. Therefore, the rack works on gravity."

The longer Professor Vega talked about gravity, the lower Moe Hickey's head got. By this time the perspiration had spread down to Moe's elbow. He was fed up with Vega's smart-aleck style. So was Neuharth, who was ready to pounce.

"Mr. Vega, I understand the fucking laws of gravity. But I want that coin mechanism *under* the rack."

Vega got Neuharth's point. "I understood that I was to move the mechanism."

He went back to the drawing board. "We must have gone through forty different designs," Vega says. "We had plastic racks, we had racks that looked like showboats, we had red-white-and-blue racks."

Neuharth wanted a unique newsrack. But when Vega surveyed the handful of companies that made them he realized that building a brand-new one could be a problem. No single company could produce the tens of thousands of racks they needed—"especially if we went with the big bang theory and launched all of the markets at once."

Within a few months, with help from Neuharth, Jack Heselden, and others, Vega managed to come up with a design that put the coin slots to the right of the window that displayed the newspaper. The window that held the top half of the front page was tilted gently back, so reflected light would not impede the view. Mounted on a pedestal, this new newsrack looked like a big TV set. In the age of television, the distinctive blue-and-white newsrack became the best advertisement USA TODAY could ever have.

Managing GANSAT's team was a difficult transition for Moe Hickey. He was used to being the chief executive of a newspaper. He was good at recognizing when something was wrong at a newspaper and getting it fixed. But his style of management was remote rather than hands-on, and as the months passed, Neuharth, Heselden, and Quinn began to sense that Hickey was not up to dealing with all of the details of this new job.

Quinn told a corporate staffer to call Hickey every few days, ask for an update on GANSAT's progress, and send a confidential memo to the members of the Office of the Chief Executive. Often Hickey didn't have much to report; his answers were short and laconic and he seemed irritated by the frequent inquiries. And there were days when Hickey would lower the blinds to his office and he and Frank Vega would play a long game of Scrabble to while away the afternoon. If someone arrived unexpectedly for a meeting, they hid the game board under the newspapers.

"I think Moe was kind of stunned by the whole thing," Paul Kessinger recalls. "Stunned by working with us, since it was not the easiest group to work with. He was a real operational, hard-nosed guy, and all of a sudden he's in a think-tank kind of environment where he doesn't have to fire anybody, doesn't have to hire anybody—just try to hold this thing together. I think he was very uncomfortable with that. But he came to believe in it. You couldn't work there for as long as he did without believing."

*Fred M. Gore of Carrollton, Texas, was the principal designer of the USA TODAY
rack. Frank Vega met with Gore in 1980 and told him that Gannett wanted a rack
with a space-age look that would appeal to a generation that grew up watching
television. He also said the rack would have to stand out when placed next to other
newsracks. These are some of the designs he developed.*

A colleague once asked McCorkindale that if Hickey had such mixed feelings about USA TODAY, why did he take the job of planning it? "He probably thought he didn't have any choice," McCorkindale said.

As the months passed, the USA TODAY locomotive gathered steam. Every time the board of directors met, Neuharth gave them an update—and the directors were asking a lot of questions.

J. Warren McClure, who had sold two dailies to Gannett and had been vice president/marketing of Gannett in the 1970s, was one of Neuharth's most insistent interrogators.

McClure hated waste. He often wrote Neuharth snotty notes about how much the fruit baskets cost on the corporate jets or how much the company had paid to mail him a news release. When he ran the Burlington Free Press, McClure was so tight he wouldn't buy paper towels for the newspaper's bathrooms; his employees used waste paper from the ends of newsprint rolls instead. Although he was a millionaire, he used a computer data base to communicate with his son who lived in France, because electronic mail was cheaper than long-distance phone calls.

"I was known as the strawberry guy," McClure says. "I figured that every strawberry on the plane cost at least $2.50. Limousines bother me. I'm just a bare-bones operator."

Whenever USA TODAY came up, McClure peppered Neuharth with questions: How much would it cost? Are you sure of your numbers? How would launching USA TODAY affect acquisitions? How come only a fraction of The Wall Street Journal's circulation comes from street sales? Have you studied national newspapers abroad? How much faith are you going to put in Lou Harris' research?

Neuharth and McClure had very different management styles. If the board of directors had traveled to Europe on the *Queen Elizabeth II*, Neuharth would have put everyone in first-class cabins; McClure would have been more comfortable in steerage.

Wes Gallagher, the former war correspondent who had headed The Associated Press, had doubts about USA TODAY too. "Why should I want another newspaper?" he kept asking. "What are you going to give me that I can't get elsewhere? If you do go ahead with this, you need a Barney Kilgore."

Barney Kilgore was the legendary editor of The Wall Street Journal who improved its writing and organization and reshaped its front page to broaden The Journal's appeal beyond business readers. Kilgore later

J. Warren McClure's granddaughter was born on the day the newspaper was launched. McClure remarked at the time that she was "in better financial condition than USA TODAY."

became chief executive of The Journal's parent, Dow Jones Co., and helped The Journal grow into a truly national newspaper. He also was the force behind one of Dow Jones' few failures, The National Observer, the national weekly. The USA TODAY project did not have one editorial genius, but in the combination of Neuharth, Martin, and Quinn, it had three creative, experienced editors.

Neuharth lobbied Gallagher frequently, hitting him at receptions and dinners at board meetings. Sometimes he planted Quinn in the seat next to Gallagher at corporate dinners. Gallagher had spent his career at the AP, a news cooperative that answers to the newspapers that are its members. Neuharth kept reminding Gallagher that Gannett was not like the AP: "Quit thinking like the head of the AP, where you're never allowed to do anything because you've got a thousand bosses. This is Gannett. It's about time we had some fun."

Gallagher recognized that the board was more receptive to USA TODAY than many Gannett executives were. "If you had taken a vote of all the executives who were involved, it probably would have gone against the project," he said. "But there was only one vote that counted, and that was Al's."

Neuharth had assured Gallagher and Julian Goodman, the retired NBC executive, that if USA TODAY flopped, he would quit. He told them, "If we lay a big egg here, Gannett can recover. I cannot. Therefore, if that happens, I'll ask you guys to turn me out to pasture sooner rather than later."

If Neuharth was pushing the throttle forward on the USA TODAY locomotive, Doug McCorkindale was trying to hold it back. Once on a plane ride from New York City to Rochester, he expressed his deep frustration with the idea to a colleague. "It's the worst thing the company could do," he said. "Give me anything you can think of that will help me stop it."

McCorkindale was trying to stop it by focusing on the financial risks involved; it was his job to identify those risks. Insiders suspected that he was feeding questions to McClure, and encouraging his lieutenants on the financial staff to rein-in GANSAT's spending.

Neuharth never tried to get McCorkindale to downplay the financial risks. McCorkindale says, "Al permitted me—probably encouraged me—to be heavy-handed about showing the downside, so there was no assumption by anybody that we were trying to gloss over the risks. I indicated it was going to be a horrendous cost to the company and the return on investment was not very good."

It was very likely, McCorkindale predicted, that if Gannett launched USA TODAY it would have its first down quarter—ending one of the most remarkable profit streaks in U.S. business history. That possibility did not seem to scare Neuharth. Although he wanted to keep Gannett's financial winning streak alive, he talked of having a "down quarter party" for Wall Street analysts if McCorkindale's dire predictions came true.

In August 1981, McCorkindale complained in a memo to Neuharth that "even with the suggested 'cuts,' the GANSAT capital needs for 1982 are over $50 million." He tried to slow down the locomotive's momentum, recommending that they delay launch until the spring of 1983 and "change the overall game plan and focus on a few test markets which would exclude the heavy expenditures for newsracks, computers, etc."

While the pushing and pulling went on, there were rounds of meetings at GANSAT's offices to try to finish the five-year business plan. Neuharth walked in unexpectedly on one; Hickey, Schmitt, and Jimmy Thomas were there. Neuharth listened for a while and said, "Well, if we do decide to go ahead I can tell you this: It will cost far, far more money than anybody thinks. And if it's successful, it will make far, far more money than anybody thinks."

The fall of 1981 was hardly a propitious time to be thinking about launching a new newspaper. The economy was sluggish, interest rates were an astronomical 20 percent, and the stock market was stagnant. Some people thought the newspaper industry was dying.

Madelyn Jennings says,
"Mostly Al bets when he
knows he's going to win."

At the 1981 American Newspaper Publishers' convention, Ted Turner—the yachtsman and entrepreneur who was known as "the mouth of the South"—made a bold prediction. The owner of the year-old twenty-four-hour-a-day Cable News Network told publishers: "Newspapers as we know them today will be gone within the next ten years or certainly [will be] serving a very reduced role. . . . Unfortunately, you're becoming very rapidly technologically obsolete."

Deaths of newspapers—especially newspapers published in the afternoon—had become common. In August 1981, after years of losses and attempts to find a buyer failed, Time, Inc., pulled the plug on The Washington Star.

In October 1981, Neuharth asked the members of the Office of the Chief Executive to give him some final thoughts on USA TODAY. The OCE included Neuharth, McCorkindale, Heselden, Quinn, and Madelyn P. Jennings, the senior vice president of personnel, who had joined Gannett in 1980. Jennings was a veteran executive who had worked for General Electric and Standard Brands, and now she was one of the highest ranking women in U.S. business.

Neuharth asked for a private memo, with copies to no one, on the Go/No-Go decision. John Quinn built his vote around Tom Curley's view that USA TODAY was an opportunity to be grasped, or to be lost. Quinn thought of a whole page of reasons to launch the newspaper, including:

A viable audience has been identified, waiting for the right new newspaper. Gannett is unique in having leadership and resources to make this succeed. Biggest info group must recognize opportunity *and* obligation to meet this need. Together, USA TODAY and Gannett's local newspapers will bring renaissance to print information services. Gannett and Neuharth owe themselves, and nation, this new opportunity for success.

Exploding media have increased hunger for news/info, but none has met market for news/info-in-a-hurry that is more portable than TV news, more consistent than dailies, more general than special publications. Despite continuing exploration-only caveats, abandonment now in face of "encouraging" research would add to Gannett's no-guts, safety-first, little-league image.

Quinn's formula to achieve all this was to "Go like hell." Part of his memo emphasized the management problems they were having at GANSAT, and the potential for divisiveness:

> USA TODAY must be not a pet, but a passion. Project NN was founded on the Gannett ability and flexibility in reaching for new horizons, coupled with its proven spirit and competitive style in achieving success.
>
> The evolution from Project NN to GANSAT has diluted the groupwide interest, has abused the groupwide resources, and has under valued the groupwide potential. Even with the most optimistic business plan, USA TODAY cannot succeed on the margins alone; it must have the enthusiastic contribution of every effort every member of the group can make, whether on the fighting front or the home front. USA TODAY leadership not only has failed to recognize and develop this; it has in one way or another discouraged it.
>
> The spark must be rekindled; the venture must be rescued from its "pet project" status and "spoiled brat" style . . . the success of USA TODAY must be emblazoned as a matter of pride, of passion, of honor for all in Gannett.

McCorkindale told Neuharth that if USA TODAY went to the board, "if you want me to vote for it, I'll vote for it. If you want me not to speak at all, I will not speak at all." Neuharth replied: "I want the board to know that we are not unanimous in this."

McCorkindale's memo on USA TODAY reflected his view that the prudent thing to do was to forget it. He began with a fat paragraph entitled "No Go—*Pro.*" He noted that the economy was weak and Gannett's operating units were 6 percent below profit plan in 1981. He predicted that starting USA TODAY would be a financial disaster.

"If we miss the 1982 plan by anything close to the same percentage, we will have a down year, even assuming perfect timing from the sale of some losing operations. Even if everything works perfectly, we will have a down fourth quarter in 1982 because of the fall start of USA TODAY."

He went on to say that launching USA TODAY could even mean two down years in a row for Gannett if the "business plan is not met on revenue side or if expenses are underestimated."

McCorkindale expected negative impact for five years on earnings, dividends, capital expenditures, acquisition opportunities, other Gannett newspapers, and a reduction in the company's high return on sales ratio. He also suggested Gannett would not meet the earnings goals that triggered its long-term incentive plans; that meant executives would not get the stock payoffs they expected.

"Overall, financial risks, commitments, and impact are significant. The business plan projects modest future financial gains." For McCorkindale, the proper risk/reward ratio just wasn't there, and his view was powerful within the company.

In her memo, Madelyn Jennings noted that "the last two years have been a time of tight budgets, freezes on hiring and travel, failure to meet budgets due to circulation and advertising losses. Asking our people to tighten their belts more may elicit ennui and turnoff." She told Neuharth that since she was new to the newspaper business, she did not feel well qualified to make the decision. If forced to decide, she would vote no.

Jack Heselden, the president of the newspaper division, had listened to both sides and came down almost in the middle. But when Neuharth asked him what he would do if he were CEO, Heselden said he would have to say "No Go."

"I really wish that I could suggest that we do it," Heselden said. "Maybe I can't because I'm conservative. But if you decide to do it, I'll support you all the way. I'm one of your biggest fans. I've seen you take a lot of things that looked chancy and make them work."

"Are the circulation projections achievable?" Heselden asked in his memo. "I realize we have had two qualified research organizations involved, but many companies have launched new products based upon extensive research which inaccurately predicted results in the marketplace."

Heselden was worried they would underestimate USA TODAY's costs and the return on investment would be far smaller than projected. "I don't envy you this weekend when you are pondering the decision," he concluded. "It's a tough call."

Neuharth knew that. "It was clear I had to say to the board that the members of the Office of the Chief Executive were not unanimous in their thinking," he says. "That's when I did a little soul-searching."

To put some of his personal doubts to rest, Neuharth convened a meeting of his two children. Dan, then twenty-seven, had been a reporter and was teaching journalism. His daughter Jan, twenty-six, was in law school.

The 1981 World Series was under way. The New York Yankees were playing the Dodgers, and Neuharth was in Los Angeles for the game. He was staying at L'Ermitage, a stylish Beverly Hills hotel, and he invited Dan and Jan to dinner. That night, as he had many times before, Neuharth talked about SoDak Sports—how that early failure had taught him a valuable lesson about profits and losses, the difference between success and failure. He often told them: "Everybody ought to have a SoDak Sports; a failure is much better early in life than late in life.."

He explained that whether to launch USA TODAY was the biggest—and toughest—decision the Gannett Company had ever faced. "I told them it was a risky thing, and there would be those who would be ready to pee on it the minute it was announced and those who would be very gleeful if it didn't work."

If the newspaper went belly-up, their old man would end his career as a failure. "That would be very embarrassing for me," he said, "but it might embarrass you, too. I don't want you to suffer for something your old man did. What do you think? What's your vote?"

Dan and Jan were unanimous. They told him to go for it. They thought it would be exciting; they thought it would be fun. They thought the country needed a national newspaper.

"Good," Neuharth said, "Because the OCE is split three-to-two against it, and I needed two more votes." That was a small joke; the votes of his children, while welcome moral support, were not the decisive factor in Neuharth's decision to move forward.

When Gannett began exploring the idea, Neuharth told Dan that the odds were against USA TODAY succeeding; he estimated them at twenty–eighty. Now, after eighteen months of study, he thought it was a fifty–fifty proposition.

Despite the risks, it was obvious to Dan and Jan that their father wanted to launch USA TODAY. He knew that if Gannett did not have the guts to do it, there would be no chance for glory. "He always talks about how Gannett doesn't make glandular decisions," Dan says, "but there was a glandular side to this."

"His gut thing was he wanted to do it," Jan says.

Even so, Neuharth thought about the downside a lot. Looking back at it, he describes the decision-making process this way: "Did I want to take the risk, stick my neck out this far one more time? I'd had the second divorce, and if this blew up in my face. . . . . Didn't have to do it. Everything was going great. I was making a lot of money; I was CEO. I was going to be CEO as long as I wanted to. Didn't have to rock the boat. But I was convinced that anyone who was CEO of Gannett, given the facts that I had, had to interpret them as saying you ought to do this."

That same weekend, John Quinn had discussed the decision with his wife Loie and their children. He asked them, "Is USA TODAY going to be fun for the old man?" They said yes. "It didn't take them long to figure that out," Quinn says.

The "family summits" became a private joke between Neuharth and Quinn. Whenever they ran into a problem, Neuharth would say, "Why don't we take it home and let the kids vote on it?"

Back in Rochester, Neuharth studied the questions that the directors had raised. Tom Reynolds, a Gannett director and a partner in the big Chicago law firm of Winston and Strawn, was asking a lot of them. "Would you provide a list of assumptions upon which the business plan is based?" Reynolds asked. "What is the best case projection? What is the worst case?"

Many of Reynolds' questions reflected Doug McCorkindale's concerns. "Certainly in those days McCorkindale was playing to Tom Reynolds and J. Warren McClure," Quinn remembers.

Just before the board voted on USA TODAY, Neuharth set up an informal meeting for four outside directors: Bill Craig, the retired Rochester bank president; Julian Goodman, the retired chairman of NBC; Dolores Wharton, the director who was on the boards of the

Of her "go" vote, Dolores Wharton says USA TODAY "was fresh. It was daring. It had a lot of zing, pizzazz, style. America needed it."

Kellogg Company and Phillips Petroleum; and Tom Reynolds. The purpose of the meeting was to discuss USA TODAY's business plan, and Neuharth and Moe Hickey would answer questions.

Reynolds had taken the business plan home and studied it. When he compared its numbers with those of other Gannett newspapers, he discovered differences he could not explain. For example, the plan showed that USA TODAY would get most of its revenue from circulation, not from advertising—the reverse of a traditional newspaper. "I said to myself, 'Okay, they've got to have an explanation for it. Maybe it's a daily magazine. Maybe different ratios are appropriate. Let's see if the numbers stand up.'"

During the meeting Reynolds, an experienced trial lawyer, began to hammer away at the assumptions in the business plan. Hickey did not have an opinion about most of them. The more questions Reynolds asked, the less Hickey said. Finally, an exasperated Reynolds asked: "Mr. Hickey, what's your confidence level in this project? How confident are you?"

Reynolds was a litigator; he had fought a lot of personal injury lawsuits and that was a standard question he asked expert witnesses. Hickey didn't have an answer. "He hedged all over the place," Neuharth recalls. "He knew he had blown it." Afterwards, Hickey was just sitting there—flushed, mute. They asked him to leave the room. "Don't be too hard on him," Neuharth told the directors. "He's young." Hickey was forty-seven, but Neuharth still thought of him as the bright young executive who helped start TODAY in Florida.

It was hardly surprising that Hickey had a hard time answering

Tom Reynolds says of the dissent within the company in late 1981, "If you don't have dissent in an organization, you don't have dialogue. You've got to have it because that's what distinguishes great companies from average companies."

Reynolds' questions. No company had ever tried anything exactly like this before, so the business plan had to be based on assumptions that no one could completely support. The numbers Hickey and Chuck Schmitt had prepared were really just educated guesses. They showed that USA TODAY would lose about $30 million in 1982, about $50 million in 1983, but only $6 million in 1984, and then turn the corner and make a healthy profit in 1985.

During 1981 and 1982, the assumptions in the business plan were constantly changing. Once USA TODAY began publishing in September 1982, Neuharth announced only "that we have a five-year business plan that projects profitability by the end of 1987." That goal was based on projected revenue of more than $250 million a year and an eventual circulation of more than 2 million.

When Hickey had left the meeting, Neuharth tried to repair the damage. Of course these numbers are just assumptions, he told the directors. The losses the business plan predicts are probably under-stated. But remember, there is a very logical rationale behind this new venture. Nearly two years of research shows that the technology is there to transmit a national newspaper. We have, or can get, the presses to print it. We can distribute it nationwide. We can create a newspaper that will grab readers—the prototypes and the research prove that. If we can get the readers, the advertising is bound to follow. The risk/reward ratio is favorable. If we choose not to go forward—knowing what we know—we will surely miss a huge opportunity. And the plan contained an "escape hatch." If USA TODAY was a dismal flop, they could pull the plug while losses were modest and salvage some parts of it.

Neuharth's honesty impressed Reynolds: "The one thing I always admire is that while he was driving this enterprise, he was also cautioning, 'Guys, you don't know if this is going to make it. We've made a lot of assumptions which may prove wrong. If they are wrong, then we've got the outs.' Very seldom do you meet a salesman who points out the downside."

Reynolds told Neuharth he had no confidence in Hickey. "I'm going to support you," Reynolds said, "but I hope to hell you don't have him running it." Over the months, Neuharth had questioned Hickey's performance; this meeting confirmed his doubts. Neuharth would have to find a new spot for Hickey. The first of many management changes at USA TODAY had occurred.

To prepare for the board's vote, Neuharth wrote the directors a long memo. "I recommend we proceed with publication of USA TODAY in the fall of 1982. Nearly every measure indicates the upside potential is considerably greater than the downside risk."

As a courtesy, Neuharth sent the memo to Gannett's retired chairman, Paul Miller. But in January 1980, Miller had suffered a stroke; he had not fully recovered his ability to speak and was not a factor in the decision.

Neuharth was up-front about the differing opinions within the company. "Since we are plowing new and uncertain ground," he wrote, "there are varying degrees of enthusiasm, or lack thereof, at various levels of management. However, I can assure you that all in management stand ready to work cooperatively and effectively once the board decision is made—to salvage all we can from USA TODAY activities and

As of December 1981, Moe Hickey says he thought USA TODAY "had a difficult, but reasonably good chance of succeeding."

Rollie Melton says he remembers Doug McCorkindale's "trepidation. A financial guy is always looking for a return, and there wasn't any return in the near term."

investment to date if we abandon the project, or to work diligently toward its success if we proceed."

He sent directors two draft press releases. One said Gannett would launch the newspaper; the other said it would forget the idea because of the poor economy and internal factors. Neuharth must have been gritting his teeth when he wrote that draft.

The morning of the vote, The Washington Post ran a story in its Business section headlined: "Gannett Board May Approve National Paper." The fourth paragraph read, "Another Wall Street analyst, who asked not to be identified, said 'Gannett would be crazy to do this . . . it's ridiculous.'" Neuharth later told reporters the story provided "a light moment for our board of directors."

It was time to vote, and Neuharth had arranged the room with his customary attention to detail. From his earlier discussions, he expected most directors would vote to launch. But there was one vote he was unsure of—J. Warren McClure's. He manipulated the seating so as they went around the room, McClure would come after several "Go" votes.

The vote began. Andy Brimmer said yes: Gannett should seize this opportunity. If it did not launch a national newspaper, someone else would. He thought the company had taken a classic Harvard Business School approach to introducing a new product, although Neuharth didn't have any Harvard MBAs working on it. Wes Gallagher went along, but commented, "I hope you go first class and do whatever it takes to do it right."

Tom Reynolds puffed on his cigar and voted yes; his doubts had been answered in the Sunday afternoon meeting. He had decided there was a rational basis for the business plan's assumptions: "They were not just numbers picked out of the air." And it was important to him that Gannett was not betting the company. "We were betting the average yearly compound growth rate."

Rollie Melton, the former president of Speidel Newspapers, knew USA TODAY would result in increased recognition for Gannett. He was an enthusiastic yes. So was Dolores Wharton. Bill Craig, the conservative Rochester banker who had been a power on the board for a long time, backed it too. He thought the project had been thoroughly researched.

Then they came to McClure. He voted yes. "Pretty damn risky and I've got a lot of money at stake in this company," he had said to Neuharth. "But I told you that when you started the Sunday paper in Burlington, and it turned out all right."

Julian Goodman, the newsman who had been NBC's chairman, could not attend the meeting but was squarely behind the project. He wrote Neuharth that "it would be wrong for a growing company to shrink from any opportunity it is so uniquely qualified to undertake." The inside directors—Neuharth, McCorkindale, Heselden, and former Speidel executive Bob Whittington—all voted yes.

The vote was unanimous, twelve to zero, to launch USA TODAY. The new venture had become an adventure.

CHAPTER EIGHT

Converts and critics

John Garvey started in newspapers when he was twenty-one, as a printer's apprentice at The Yonkers (N.Y.) Herald Statesman. One of his jobs then was to lug heavy trays of metal type around the back shop; it was a dirty place that smelled of black ink and hot lead.

Now, twenty-three years later, he was GANSAT's production director, one of three hundred Gannett executives who had come to the Capital Hilton Hotel in Washington to hear Neuharth's 1981 "State of the Company" address. Garvey was deeply involved in USA TODAY, and the back shop he was helping plan would seem light years away from the one where he started. Its facsimile room would use laser scanners and satellite technology—more like a scene from *Star Trek* than *The Front Page*.

After two decades at the Westchester newspapers, Garvey had been promoted to production director at TODAY in Florida; then Sackett hired him for GANSAT. Before leaving Cocoa for Washington, Garvey happened to mention his daughter Liz to Neuharth. She was a tournament tennis player who hoped to attend college in Florida so she could play year-round. Because her parents were moving, she would have to apply as a nonresident, and that made it harder to get into Florida universities. Neuharth volunteered to help, and wrote friends at the University of South Florida.

Now Garvey was listening intently to Neuharth's year-end speech. Many in the audience suspected that Neuharth and the board had decided to publish USA TODAY, but no one was sure. Ten minutes in, Neuharth said that in 1982, Gannett would reach for new ways to grow.

Neuharth faces reporters just after announcing that Gannett would launch a
national newspaper in the fall of 1982. Larry Sackett, who worked on Project NN,
says, "I always believed in my heart that we were going to do it, but until it got said
publicly, there was always a chance that something would happen."

"One of the new ways will be the publication of 'The Nation's Newspaper.'" The crowd leaped to its feet and applauded.

When the speech ended, the crowd of Gannett managers gave him
another standing ovation. Neuharth moved away from the podium,
toward the rear of the room, and stopped next to John Garvey. The
tension seemed to flow from his body. Then he turned to Garvey and
said: "Has Liz decided what college to go to yet?"

"I was tongue-tied," Garvey said. "It's amazing how something like
that can get the hook into you." Neuharth had won another lifelong
convert.

Neuharth knew he would need a lot of converts to pull off a project
so big. In a 1981 speech to shareholders, he had listed the ingredients
that had gone into Gannett's success. One was "the priceless labor
and loyalty of Gannett people." Neuharth did not belabor the company's strong work ethic; instead he and other top executives led by
example. Long hours were a given. When they started TODAY in Florida, Moe Hickey had been struck by Neuharth's stamina: "We left
some mornings at 2 A.M. and he would stay up and critique the paper.
I'm not even sure he went to bed at night." Once in 1966, before Gannett had its fleet of corporate jets, an airline strike made it hard to get

from Cocoa to Rochester. Neuharth rented a car and drove all night rather than miss a corporate meeting.

At that year-end meeting in 1981, Neuharth unveiled his launch strategy for USA TODAY. It would begin publishing in the Washington, D.C., area and expand over six months into fifteen of the nation's top twenty markets. Neuharth and other top planners had decided that launching everywhere at once—the big bang theory—would be too difficult and too expensive. The cost would surely break Gannett's string of record profits.

USA TODAY would be a morning newspaper, selling for twenty-five cents a copy. For the first time, Neuharth said that it would be more than a street-sales newspaper: Mail and home delivery would be offered later. He said the decision to publish had been "carefully calculated" based on two years of study and tests of prototypes. Then he added:

"When we first announced the research project, we said we would begin regular publication only if we were convinced we could achieve 1 million to 2 million daily circulation and at least $250 million in annual revenues at a profit in three to five years. We have concluded these goals are not only achievable but exceedable."

USA TODAY would be financed from the company's rich cash flow. Gannett's 1981 revenues were about $1.4 billion; its profits were $173 million, up from $28 million in 1971. Ignoring Doug McCorkindale's pessimistic forecast, Neuharth predicted that Gannett could create the newspaper and still continue its long record of quarter-to-quarter earnings gains, although those gains would be "somewhat lower."

While waiting for Neuharth to confirm that Gannett would go ahead with USA TODAY, John Garvey was thinking, "What Neuharth doesn't need is a failure. He is not going to go with this if he doesn't think it's going to work."

He repeated his long-held vision that a newspaper could be a unifier: "USA TODAY will reach out to become 'The Nation's Newspaper' . . . a cohesive daily force for the mutual interests of Americans across the country."

After the USA TODAY announcement, the pace of planning quickened. Even before the meeting in which Hickey revealed his confidence level to the directors, Neuharth and Jack Heselden had been discussing how to divide the project. They needed to put the right people in the right jobs, and launching a national newspaper was turning out to be far too big a task for one person to handle.

Just before Christmas 1981, Tom Dolan—the publisher of the Westchester Rockland Newspapers and a longtime Gannett executive—lost his wife to cancer.

Phil Gialanella, Gannett's publisher in Honolulu, called to comfort his old friend Dolan. Gialanella said he couldn't make it back for the funeral, so he invited Dolan to come out to Hawaii to rest for a couple of weeks. Then Gialanella got a call from Neuharth. He said that since Gialanella and Dolan were so close, Phil really should come East for the funeral; a Gannett plane was available. After the funeral Heselden took Gialanella aside and told him there were other reasons he was wanted on the mainland. "We're flying back to Rochester," Heselden said. "Al wants to have lunch."

They went to the Top of the Plaza, a restaurant on top of a building with a good view of the gray Rochester skyline, and Neuharth told Gialanella: "I want you to be president of USA TODAY." The president was going to be in charge of everything except advertising and news. Neuharth said he expected Moe Hickey would take the title of publisher and head advertising.

Leaving Hawaii was the last thing Gialanella wanted to do. He was a tall, slim, nervous type, with a chronic ulcer. He had a dark complexion, and living in Hawaii gave him a permanent tan. He hated ties, preferring jeans and designer pullovers, which went well with his dark glasses. Gialanella was a tough, talented manager, but in his Guccis and shades, he looked more like a nightclub operator than a newspaper publisher. Neuharth appreciated his loyalty: "If there was ever a soldier who would march, it's Phil." Neuharth remembers Phil's nervous reaction to the USA TODAY job offer:

"Oh, shit, I was just getting to like Hawaii," Gialanella said. "I don't want the damn job. But look, I'll do it—on one condition. Promise me when my tour of duty is over—one year, I'll do it for just one year—I can go back to being publisher in Hawaii."

"No problem, Phil," Neuharth said. "When it's over, you go back to Hawaii."

Then Neuharth and Heselden sat down with Moe Hickey. They told him USA TODAY was too big for any one manager. They wanted him to take the title of publisher, with responsibility for advertising. He would be based in New York, where he could drum up business on Madison Avenue. "He was almost as quick to say no as Phil was to say yes," Neuharth says. "He said, 'You're asking me to be a glorified advertising director. I spent the last year on this thing and I ought to run it. If I can't run it, I don't want to be part of it.'"

Of Neuharth's offer to be USA TODAY's publisher, Hickey says only, "I'd done that before when we started Gannett Newspaper Advertising Sales," referring to the subsidiary that sells national advertisers space in Gannett's local newspapers. The advertising challenge facing USA TODAY was much larger than anything Gannett or anyone else had done before. Neuharth thought Moe Hickey had the potential to meet it, but Hickey was unwilling to try.

Six months after becoming executive vice president, Vince Spezzano, left, told Neuharth, "This has not been easy. Too many people wanting too many things in too little time. At the same time, I have loved every minute of it." Phil Gialanella, right, says, "I think Moe Hickey probably had more confidence in the project than I did."

Neuharth told Gialanella that Hickey had turned down the publisher's job because he wanted the whole thing. "Great," Gialanella said, still looking for an out. "That's fine with me. Let Moe be president and publisher. I'll do temporary duty from Hawaii, work a year on special assignment for Moe."

Neuharth counteroffered: "How about if you do both jobs and Vince Spezzano will be your assistant?" A little reluctantly, Gialanella agreed. As USA TODAY's first president, Gialanella was responsible for advertising, circulation, and the business office. As executive vice president, Spezzano took promotion—his strength—along with production and personnel. Gialanella kept his title as president and publisher in Hawaii; that gave him confidence that he would eventually return and assured regular business travel back to the islands.

At some companies—given what had happened—Moe Hickey probably would have been looking for a new job. Instead, Neuharth made Hickey publisher in Reno and president of Gannett West, with responsibility for several newspapers. The move saved Hickey's career and helped the company, because Hickey was a capable publisher.

In news, John Curley, who had headed Gannett News Service when it won the Pulitzer Prize for public service and gone on to be publisher in Wilmington, would be USA TODAY's first editor. And Ron Martin was named the executive editor—with Neuharth and Quinn looking over their shoulders, breathing down their necks, and calling many of the shots. Martin had been the top planning editor for a year, and he had trouble accepting Curley's appointment.

"There was a hell of a lot of administering to do and we didn't think one person could do it all," John Quinn says. Quinn and Neuharth were afraid that if Martin had to do all the administrative work—budgets, housing, salaries, computer systems, wire-service contracts—he would not have time to be the creative, ideas-oriented editor they needed. "Ron's first reaction was, 'I don't want to work for a newspaper edited by John Curley.' But I think they found peace together," Quinn says.

The opinion pages were a delicate subject. Neuharth and Quinn wanted to be sure that in its editorial positions, USA TODAY was not seen as a captive of corporate Gannett, or as an extension of its chief executive. Neuharth preached editorial autonomy, but he practiced it, too. He was not in the habit of dictating editorial policy to Gannett's many newspapers, and he would not do so at USA TODAY. For a man

From left, USA TODAY's *planning editors were John Curley, Bob Casey, David Doucette, Carol Richards, Richard Curtis, John Walter, Nancy Woodhull, Henry Freeman, Sheryl Bills, and Ron Martin.*

who was driven to try to control everything around him, this was uncharacteristic restraint. Some critics had long feared that because it was the nation's largest newspaper chain, Neuharth might have Gannett corporate indulging in the kind of meddling William Randolph Hearst delighted in. The most egregious example was in 1898 just before the Spanish-American War began. Hearst cabled his correspondent in Cuba about the sinking of the *Maine*: "You furnish the pictures and I'll furnish the war."

Neuharth and Quinn wanted USA TODAY's editorial page to be different, to be vibrant, but to be independent, too—to reflect "the diverse views of a diverse nation." Quinn proposed that they turn to an award-winning editor who was a legend in his home state of Tennessee, John Seigenthaler. "But will he take the job?" Neuharth asked. Quinn replied: "He will if he gets the Gialanella deal and keeps his titles as editor and publisher of The Tennessean."

Seigenthaler began as a reporter on The Tennessean in Nashville in 1949. Many successful, respected journalists learned their craft in The Tennessean's newsroom: David Halberstam, the prize-winning author; Fred P. Graham, who later became CBS's Supreme Court correspondent; Bill Kovach, former Washington bureau chief for The New York Times and later editor of the Atlanta newspapers; and Jim

In a December 1982 article in Washington Journalism Review, John Seigenthaler said, "If there is one reason I agreed on the spot to do this, it was because there was an opportunity to create from scratch a new editorial voice, without any strings, directions, or suggestions."

Squires, editor of the Chicago Tribune.

Seigenthaler had been a tenacious reporter. He once worked on a single story for months, tracking and exposing a wealthy Nashville man who appeared to commit suicide but had run off with his lover. In the early 1960s, Seigenthaler left journalism for a year-and-a-half to serve as Robert F. Kennedy's assistant in the Justice Department. At the height of the civil rights movement, he was the Justice Department's chief negotiator with the governor of Alabama, and during the 1961 Freedom Rides, he was attacked by a mob of whites in Alabama and suffered a fractured skull.

In 1962, at thirty-four, Seigenthaler was named editor of The Tennessean. He was then the youngest editor of a major daily newspaper in the country.

Ironically, before Gannett bought The Tennessean in 1979, Seigenthaler had been an outspoken critic of newspaper chains. But Neuharth recognized that Seigenthaler was an able, respected journalist and asked him to stay as editor and publisher in Nashville. He became a strong, independent, and valuable voice within the company, although he loved to joke about the day he was "sold into chains."

When Neuharth offered Seigenthaler the job as editorial director of USA TODAY, he was quick to accept, saying: "Anyone who would turn that opportunity down would have to have a serious mental disability." He kept his job in Nashville and began commuting regularly to Washington.

The year before, responding to the invitation to comment on the first prototypes, Ralph Otwell of the Chicago Sun-Times had proposed

a single-issue opinion page. Seigenthaler had never seen that suggestion, but after months of study, he came to the same conclusion. A
daily debate on a single issue would make an interesting—and different—editorial page. Next to it, Seigenthaler decided to publish a daily,
in-depth interview with a newsmaker, called "Inquiry." He also came
up with the idea for "Voices Across the USA," a feature that ran readers' pictures above their opinions on an issue. When Seigenthaler presented the "Voices" idea to Neuharth, the chairman said: "You
wouldn't have the guts to do that." Neuharth did not mention that he
had pioneered similar inquiring photographer features at SoDak Sports
and TODAY in Florida.

Seigenthaler assembled a ten-member editorial board that reflected
the nation's diversity—young and old, men and women, black and
white, liberal and conservative. Each day, the board would discuss an
issue, reach a consensus on what was USA TODAY's opinion, and publish
an opposing point of view as well. Quinn and Neuharth left
Seigenthaler alone to design the Opinion Page. "I trust you," Neuharth said.

On the business side, Gialanella was in charge—with Neuharth
standing by with his stopwatch. Gialanella had started in the circulation
department of The Binghamton (N.Y.) Press in 1946. By 1963, he had
risen to assistant to the publisher. Then the owner of The Passaic
(N.J.) Daily News lured him away from Gannett to turn a Dover, New
Jersey, weekly into a daily. Neuharth read about Gialanella's role in that
successful conversion and tried to get him to come back to Gannett.
Gialanella agreed, and Neuharth promptly sent him to Hartford on the
team that started the ill-fated Sunday edition of the Hartford Times.

Gialanella and Spezzano began a search for USA TODAY's advertising
director. Gannett's experience was in community and regional newspapers; it did not have anyone with the right national advertising expertise for the job. Armed with a list of twenty names of Madison Avenue
types who might be candidates, Gialanella and Spezzano hit the streets
of New York. No one was lining up to take the job; the prevailing
attitude among advertising executives was that USA TODAY was a crazy
idea that would never work.

Gialanella and Spezzano used a roundabout approach. They
explained what USA TODAY was and then asked each person for suggestions, names of people who could do it. They hoped some candidates would express interest.

Neuharth had heard that Cathleen Black, the young publisher of New York magazine, was very good. Black wasn't interested in USA TODAY. "She wasn't sure the damn thing would work," Vince Spezzano says. "We weren't even going to consider anyone who didn't believe in the thing." Later, she would become a believer.

One candidate who was enthusiastic about the newspaper's chances was Joe Welty, the advertising director at McCall's magazine. At fifty-two, he felt his path to the top at McCall's was blocked and he was ready for a new challenge. "The scale of it fascinated me," Welty says. "This was truly a big idea."

Welty began as USA TODAY's vice president/advertising on March 1, 1982. His first sales meeting was scheduled for mid-May; he had less than three months to hire a staff, set ad rates, and create a sales presentation. Then they would start trying to sell advertising at the end of May, about three months before launch. They could have used at least six more months to get ready. To attract advertisers, Welty helped design a "Partnership Plan." Advertisers who agreed to run regular ads for a period of 15 months, through 1983, would get the first 6 ½ months of advertising free. After that they would pay the full price—if USA TODAY was still publishing.

Welty also was taking a crash course in the philosophy, policy, and style of the Gannett Company. The extent of Neuharth's involvement in the details amazed him. In their first meeting to discuss the makeup of the newspaper—where the ads would be placed—Welty asked who would be making those important decisions. "It's going to be your decision and whoever's working with you, helping you," Neuharth said. Welty looked over at Gialanella and Spezzano, who were cracking up. "They think this is very, very funny, and I'm not getting it at all," Welty recalls. "Then it became apparent to me that the person who would be helping me would be Neuharth." For the first year of publication, Neuharth personally laid out USA TODAY every day, deciding how many pages it would have, how much news, how much advertising, and which ads would run where.

Spezzano says that Welty was just what USA TODAY needed at the outset: "He had a reputation of being able to sell any goddamn thing to anybody. We needed somebody to come in with the amphibious landing boats and take the beachhead."

In those first few months, military metaphors were common. R. Joseph Fuchs, a financial analyst who studied media stocks for Kidder,

Top executives at Pumpkin Center in 1982. From left, Ron Martin, General Manager Jerry Bean, John Curley, Phil Gialanella, and Vince Spezzano.

Peabody, said of Gannett's efforts, "If this fails, planned as it is like a Marine invasion, then nobody can do it."

Frank Vega, now vice president/circulation, was busy hiring big-city street fighters for the circulation department. By the end of March 1982, Vega had hired four hundred circulation people and had plans to hire sixteen hundred part-timers. "They were a rough, tough bunch of people who could sell," Spezzano says. "They would kick the shit out of anyone who touched their vending machines."

In the first fifteen markets, Vega expected to have one hundred thousand sales locations. As a start, he was planning to place fifty-eight thousand newsracks on street corners across the country. He had finished detailed maps of sixteen hundred distribution routes. In each market, his people had gone over every route with tape recorders and stopwatches, recording the best locations for the racks and how long it would take to put newspapers in each one. For example, route Number One in the Washington, D.C., market took two hours and one minute to serve, and it included twenty-nine newsstands and twenty-one newsracks.

J. Warren McClure, the Gannett director who had many doubts

about USA TODAY, gave Frank Vega an address in the Los Angeles area where his son was living. "Where will he be able to buy the paper?" McClure asked. Vega walked over to his giant wall map of Los Angeles with all the color-coded pins in it and quickly found a 7-11 and several newsracks within a few blocks of where McClure's son was living. "He thought that was the neatest thing he'd ever seen," Vega says. "It showed him how detailed our planning was."

Two other "young geniuses" got key USA TODAY jobs: Larry Sackett was named vice president/telecommunications and Paul Kessinger, planning and research director on the advertising side. Tom Curley became editor of Gannett's newspaper in Norwich, Connecticut, in 1982, but he was destined to come back to USA TODAY.

The months leading up to the launch were hectic for USA TODAY's leaders. They moved into the new thin silver skyscraper in Rosslyn, Virginia, just across the Potomac from Washington. They hired staffs, installed satellite dishes, improved presses, produced more prototypes, called on advertisers, and planned promotions.

There were rounds and rounds of meetings, and Neuharth led most of them. "We were living with Neuharth morning, noon, and night," Gialanella says. On weekends Gialanella and Spezzano flew to Pumpkin Center with Neuharth for more meetings, "going over everything, hashing over everything."

While immersed in the details, Neuharth kept his vision of the newspaper, his dream. He had known all along how hard people would work for it. In mid-1981, at a brainstorming session at Pumpkin Center, he said: "Anybody who is going to do this is going to feel that they have had the chance of a lifetime. We are going to expect that people will regard it as that and bust their tails and gamble on the long-term returns to them. And if we score, it will be very big."

While the Gannett people were busting their tails, the outside critics were taking target practice. The sniping had started at the news conference on December 15, 1981, right after Neuharth announced that Gannett would start USA TODAY.

"In the editorial spectrum that ranges from the National Observer to the National Enquirer," one reporter asked, "where will USA TODAY fall?"

"Somewhere in between," Neuharth said, with a smile.

The reporters laughed, but they still thought a national newspaper was a crazy idea. Debra Whitefield reported in the Los Angeles Times the next day that Gannett was going ahead with USA TODAY "despite skepticism in the industry."

She quoted an anonymous executive of a "major newspaper": "Neuharth can pull-motor this thing along, but I just don't see the need for it." Then she speculated that Gannett must have some other agenda in mind:

"Since the paper will be sold in Washington first, there was talk Tuesday that this was merely a way for Gannett to sneak in the back door and go head-to-head with The Washington Post, the city's only daily since the Star closed earlier this year."

As the new year began, the ranks of the doubters multiplied. News of more newspapers failing seemed to confirm the judgment of the naysayers. In January 1982, The Philadelphia Bulletin folded. Later in 1982, the Cleveland Press and the Buffalo Courier-Express would publish their last editions. Newspapers in Minneapolis, Des Moines, Duluth, Tampa, and Portland, Oregon, would merge with other newspapers. In all, twenty-one daily nameplates would disappear in 1982.

"At a time when several major newspapers are in deep financial trouble," wrote Jonathan Friendly of The New York Times, "starting a new one and expecting it to sell 2.5 to 3 million copies a day seemed to some to be a foolhardy exercise in swimming against the current."

John Naisbitt, the futurist who later wrote the bestseller *Megatrends*, predicted USA TODAY would drown. "All of the major trends for the last decade and a half have been in the other direction," Naisbitt told Advertising Age. "The big successes have been occurring at the other end of the spectrum with city magazines, local business publications."

USA TODAY is "producer driven," Naisbitt said. "They have gotten so enamored with the new technology and the fact that they can put out a national newspaper, that they've said, 'My God, look what we can do. . . . Let's go out and do it.' That's very seductive, and it's going to do them in."

Heavy sports coverage would not attract readers either, one advertising executive said. "Who wants national sports coverage on a daily basis?" asked John Meskil, a top advertising executive at Warwick, Welsh & Miller in New York. "I couldn't care less what happens to the Chicago White Sox."

Wall Street took the same view. "Their early attitude was that it was an absolute disaster," recalls Doug McCorkindale, who spent a lot of time on the phone trying to convince analysts Gannett could afford to launch USA TODAY. "They totally overreacted and almost came to the conclusion that Gannett was going to go under. They thought it was the dumbest idea that had come around in a long, long time."

John Reidy, an analyst of media stocks for Drexel Burnham Lambert, told a reporter: "Neuharth has quite an ego, and some analysts think this is quite an ego trip."

Gannett's stock plummeted. It had been selling at 38½ on December 14, the day before the announcement. On March 15, it hit a low of 29½, a 23 percent drop in just three months—a $477 million loss in the market value of the stock. Vol. 1, No. 1 was months away, and already Wall Street was selling USA TODAY short.

CHAPTER NINE

Skies are basically blue

In the winter of 1982 Tom Shafer walked into the pressroom at the Gainesville Times, a small daily north of Atlanta that Gannett had bought the year before. Shafer had learned how fast things could change at Gannett. A year earlier, he had been a mid-level editor at TODAY in Florida who worked closely with the composing room. Then John Garvey left and Shafer replaced him as production director. Now he was on loan to USA TODAY, in charge of improving Gainesville's press so it could print this new national newspaper for the Atlanta market. Fletcher Carter, then Gainesville's production director, was on hand to greet Shafer:

"Tom, welcome to Gainesville, Georgia. You're going to be here for the rest of your life."

There were many days when Shafer thought that was no joke. To get acclimated, Shafer spent two days watching Gainesville's press crew. What he saw shocked him: This crew had never done quality color; they lacked the training and the skills to ever be able to do it. Beyond that, the printing press was in terrible shape. Gears were worn out, cylinders were gouged, and the rubber rollers were so hard they barely carried ink. A previous foreman had tried to improve things by customizing the press; he bored new holes in a housing and changed the relative positions of the printing cylinders. That do-it-yourself approach was a disaster. The printing plates inevitably slipped, and every time the crew tried to print color, the result was a blurry mess. "Those papers were so bad," Shafer remembers. "They were just awful."

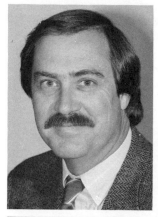

*"Now everybody in the
industry calls us and wants
our standard operating
procedures book, wants to
know how we did it,"*
Tom Shafer says.

Shafer called corporate headquarters to air his frustration. He got
Chuck Blevins, Gannett's vice president/production, on the line:
"What in the hell are you trying to do to me?" Shafer complained. "You
better go get all of the best pressmen you can find and bring them down
here, because if this thing's going to work you're going to need some
different folks with a different understanding of what we're trying to
do."

To succeed, USA TODAY had to be able to print high-quality color
consistently at every one of its print sites—nationwide. "If you bought
a paper in New York and then flew to California and bought one, the two
had to look the same," Blevins says. "If you're advertising a red Corvette, you want a red Corvette that looks the same across the country."

If Gannett could not deliver that consistency, USA TODAY was in
trouble. Readers would be turned off and advertisers would not buy
ads. National advertisers were used to the standards set by glossy
magazines, outstanding color reproduction on coated paper. Newspapers had never tried to match that high standard before.

Many advertisers did not believe newspapers could print magazine
quality color. Neither did many newspaper publishers and commercial
printers. Neither did many press crews. But Gannett said it was going
to do it.

The high-tech, space-age part of the printing process was very reliable. Western Union's *WESTAR III* satellite sat 22,300 miles out in
space above the Galápagos Islands in the South Pacific. It had been
tested repeatedly, and it worked. USA TODAY could simultaneously

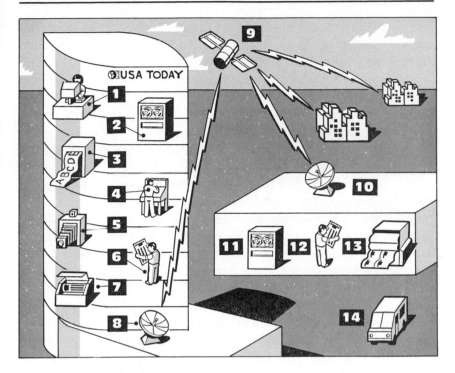

Producing a high-tech newspaper:
1) About 450 journalists write and edit copy on 325 terminals.
2) Main Atex computer processes copy and transmits it to phototypesetters.
3) One of three phototypesetters produces type.
4) Pages are pasted up.
5) Pages are photographed.
6) Photographs are full-page glossy positive prints.
7) Laser scanner converts page into electronic signal that can be transmitted to ASC-I, the satellite used for the domestic edition.
8) Rooftop satellite antenna transmits signal to satellite.
9) ASC-I, stationed 22,300 miles above the equator, then transmits signal to thirty print sites across the USA. It takes 3½ minutes to transmit a black-and-white page to the satellite and to all print sites and up to 6½ minutes for each of four separations for a full-color editorial page.
10) The earth station at each print site receives the signal.
11) Signal is sent to a computer that converts the electronic signal to a laser beam that exposes film and produces a full-page negative.
12) Film is processed and an offset printing plate is produced.
13) Presses print copies at an average rate of 18,000 an hour.
14) Some 380 trucks deliver newspapers to 120,000 newsracks, approximately 500,000 homes, and 80,000 other sales points.

beam each page at the speed of light to a multitude of print sites. But when the pages got to the plants and had to be reproduced in high-quality color, there were all kinds of obstacles.

Different print sites had different kinds of presses, yet Gannett was expecting each press to produce the same dazzling color from the same negative transmitted across the country. Shafer knew most people who worked in pressrooms had never been trained to reproduce color, and many were reluctant to learn new skills: "I've been running this press for thirty years, kid. Don't tell me what to do."

In a typical press, newsprint moves through the rollers at about forty-five miles an hour. As it does, the width of the paper stretches; it can be three-quarters of an inch wider in one press unit compared with another. And different parts of the paper may absorb water and ink at different rates, while moving at high speed. All of this makes it very difficult to get a yellow dot on one plate to line up with a magenta dot on another plate to make red; if the dots are off a fraction of an inch, the image is a muddy mess.

Newspapers had never tried to use raw materials that met the same specifications every day. The quality of newsprint, of ink, even of the water that was mixed with the ink, varied wildly from city to city and from day to day.

Even within the company, there were people who thought Gannett could never do it. Louis A. "Chip" Weil III, vice president/development for Gannett and an outspoken opponent of USA TODAY in the early days, wrote Moe Hickey in 1981 about the prototypes, which had been printed at the Army Times plant in Springfield, Virginia. "I like the liberal use of color," Weil wrote. "However, from a technical standpoint I think it will be impossible to maintain the Army Times standard nationwide. Press and camera people who do a mediocre job now aren't going to turn out first-rate work the day we throw the switch on this."

No one understood that better than Chuck Blevins. Blevins had started in the composing room of his college newspaper at Indiana University and converted the Daily Student from hot type and a flatbed press to cold type and offset printing. After college, he joined The Wall Street Journal as assistant production director in Cleveland. He came to Gannett in 1971 and worked at several newspapers before heading up the corporate production department. By mid-1981, he had taken over the job of upgrading print sites from Larry Sackett, who had his hands full setting up the satellite and facsimile network. Blevins began talking to commercial printers and press manufacturers to learn how to attack the problem.

"There was not one person we talked to who thought we could do it," Blevins says. "I guess I was lucky enough that I didn't know we couldn't do it."

In the summer of 1982, Blevins was spending more time in noisy pressrooms than in his quiet office in corporate headquarters. He was in Gainesville's plant with Shafer—and the press still didn't work. It

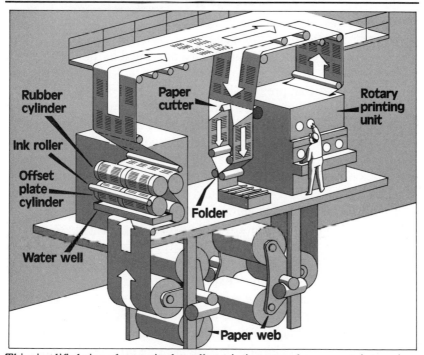

This simplified view of one unit of an offset printing press shows newsprint moving through the press to become a newspaper. The web of newsprint runs underneath the blanket cylinder, which has a rubberized blanket on it. The flexible aluminum plates which carry words and images are mounted on the offset plate cylinder. A mixture of water and ink is applied and the image of a page is transferred, or "offset," onto the blanket cylinder, which presses the image onto the newsprint. The web is sliced into pages and these are collated in the folder, and then the finished newspaper rolls off the press. USA TODAY's heavy use of color helped spur the Goss Company to develop a new press, which it calls the "Colorliner" and some USA TODAY executives call "the Gannett press," which will be able to print full color on every page.

was August and eighty-five degrees in Georgia, with just a few weeks to go before the September 20 roll-out of USA TODAY in the Atlanta area. By then Gainesville's production director and most of the press crew had either quit or been replaced. The new crew was running yet another color test, and as usual, it was not going well. Shafer stopped the press and shouted, "Hold it! Everybody come here. You can't keep running back and forth like crazy people. Let's slow down and start over."

Shafer, Blevins, and a few others had been there for days. They would arrive at the plant every day at 1 P.M., and meet until 4 P.M. to decide what had to be done that night. After a break for dinner, they would return to the pressroom and work until 5 or 6 A.M. Then they would go back to the Holiday Inn, sit at a table next to the pool, drink a few beers, and watch the sun come up. "We'd look at each other and say, 'Ain't no way that press will ever work,'" Shafer says.

The Holiday Inn had a guard with a .357 Magnum who would come by to check them out; he thought they were a little weird. Once he asked them to leave. "We will if you can carry us away," they told him. After a few nights, the guard started joining them for a beer. After dawn broke they'd get a few hours sleep and go back to the pressroom and do it again. Gannett's flying squad of production experts lived this kind of life for months and months, at print sites across the country.

One night beside the pool, after several bags of chips, several beers, and several weeks of lousy color, they finally decided the only thing to do was to junk a big part of Gainesville's press and start over. Red Henderson, Blevins' press expert, got on the phone with the people from Goss in Chicago, the world's largest manufacturer of printing presses. Ordinarily it would take a minimum of six weeks to get two new Urbanite units shipped to Gainesville, but Blevins wanted them now. The Gannett people were buying printing presses the way most people bought groceries, and they wanted them installed yesterday. A typical conversation went like this:

Goss executive: "We can get it to you in six weeks."

Henderson: "Well, we need it next week."

Goss: "Can't do it."

Henderson: "Look, are you going to work with us or not?"

Goss: "Let me go back and check."

But Goss delivered. It shipped the two units, which had been earmarked for another newspaper. Butch Tauber, the Goss Company's

*Red Henderson was in charge
of press installation and
operation. He thought from
day one that most of the press
in Gainesville, Georgia,
would have to be replaced.*

ace press erector, was there to set them up. He was a flamboyant character who wore buckskin jackets and thousand-dollar cowboy boots and traveled between the Holiday Inn and the newspaper in a white Lincoln limousine. Tauber was on top of the new units before they came off the forklift, and in two days they were installed. When a color test rolled off that press two days later, the red Corvette looked like a red Corvette.

A couple of weeks later, after 1 A.M. on Monday, September 20, 1982, Neuharth was standing next to the machinery that folded the first copies of USA TODAY as they came off Gainesville's new press. "I handed him a paper," Shafer says. "He whipped through it and then he nodded, and the papers went out the door. That press crew was so happy."

Early on, Blevins realized the only possible way to print quality color everywhere was to standardize everything. All the presses had to be set to the same specifications. The newsprint had to be the same every day, at every site. The ink had to be the same. The color had to be measured every day, at every site, so it would be the same everywhere. All of this was totally new to newspapers.

"Newspaper presses were never designed for what USA TODAY is doing," Blevins says. "They were never designed for this level of precision, for full color printed on deadline." Newspapers usually treated color as a special event. A photo for the front page—a static shot of some spring flowers was typical—would be taken far in advance. The press crew often tried to print color in advance instead of on deadline, so they could tinker and get things right. Even so, most crews didn't

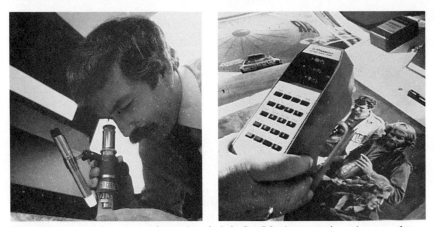

Extra steps are taken to monitor color. At left, Jon Markey examines the spread between color dots with a sixty-power microscope. The densitometer, at right, was common in commercial printing shops before USA TODAY, but its use was almost unheard of in newspaper production.

try very hard. If the color wasn't right after the first one hundred copies, they ran the press anyway and pushed the papers out the door. USA TODAY was trying to treat color just like black and white and run it routinely, on deadline, every day.

Blevins and his people set up a series of standard operating procedures. He sent many printers to school at the Rochester Institute of Technology. Instructors taught them how to use densitometers, a small hand-held device that measures the amount of ink on a page. To have something to measure, Blevins later asked that a thin blue color bar be placed at the bottom of page one every day. Neuharth soon found a use for that space and began promoting the next day's newspaper in it. As a reference, Blevins and his people wrote a six-inch-thick manual that contained the SOP for everything—from what kind of newsprint to buy to how to put the printing plates on the cylinders.

Getting consistent color required enormous effort. Blevins and his people—Jon Markey, Denny Doss, Tom Shafer, Red Henderson, and many others—traveled constantly. After Atlanta, USA TODAY launched a week later in Minneapolis-St. Paul. A week after that, they rolled the paper out in Pittsburgh. Then Neuharth decided to move up the West Coast sites by several weeks; in November, they began printing in the Seattle and San Francisco markets.

Their lives were a blur of printing plants. They installed millions of dollars' worth of printing presses and mailroom systems, remodeled buildings, and trained new people—all in record time. Gannett pumped $600,000 into press units for Gainesville; spent $200,000 to build a new mailroom in Tarentum, Pennsylvania; committed $4 million for a new press in San Bernardino, California. In 1982 alone, they expected to spend $14 million on production equipment. Many millions more would be invested in the next few years as Gannett built more offset printing plants from scratch.

There was no time to relax. Blevins was sitting in his office two weeks after the Pittsburgh launch when he got an urgent call. The Tarentum, Pennsylvania, press—the one that produced papers for Pittsburgh—could not put an image on paper. It was Friday, and the press crew was not sure it would be able to print weekend editions of the local Gannett newspaper, so USA TODAY's next pressrun on Sunday night was in doubt, too.

By 8 P.M. Friday, Blevins and Markey were in Tarentum staring at another press that wouldn't work. Friday evening was supposed to be sacred, a night off, and Markey was so dismayed at giving up yet another weekend that "he wasn't fit to live with," Blevins says. They went through dozens of hypotheses as to what could be wrong, but ended up going back to the basics. Maybe something was wrong with the water and ink mixture. Maybe it was the water.

In the middle of the night, Blevins and Markey found a supermarket that was still open. They bought every jug of distilled water on the shelf. Then they isolated one press unit and started pouring in the pure water while the press crew struggled with Sunday's local advance run. It worked.

But they still didn't know what had gone wrong with Tarentum's water; everything had gone fine during the first week USA TODAY had been printed there. By the following Sunday night, the press crew had bought all of the distilled water they could find in the Tarentum area, and they kept dumping it in while the press ran USA TODAY's Monday edition.

That week Blevins had a water conditioner installed, and he ordered conditioners for all USA TODAY presses. A few days later, Markey was talking to a former Tarentum press crew member. "Oh, yeah," the man said, "that happens every year. In the fall, when all the leaves and stuff came down the river, we always had trouble. The PH level changes in the water." Another mystery solved.

Chuck Blevins says Neuharth's charge to him was simple: "I want constant, consistent color reproduction across the country and high quality. You go do it."

Production had the resources to do the job right. Blevins remembers an early USA TODAY meeting when Neuharth asked why something had gone wrong, and an executive replied, "We were trying to save money." Neuharth started pacing, gritting his teeth, building a head of steam. "I never told you to try to save money," Neuharth said. "I've never put any restraint on your ability to do the job."

"He has never once put a limit on how we did things," Blevins says. "In production we made some mistakes when we started by trying to go too cheap, trying to conserve capital. We were penny-wise and dollar-foolish."

In USA TODAY's early issues, much of the color was dazzling. But sometimes, even when everything had been standardized, the system broke down. Neuharth traveled too, and he spent many hours personally checking racks in different cities—sometimes while jogging, sometimes riding from rack to rack in a limo with his pockets full of quarters. On October 18, he wrote Phil Gialanella:

This tearsheet of page one of the USA TODAY issue of
October 15 was picked up by me in Rochester. The purple
sky behind the autumn leaf picture is even more purple in this
one than it was in the others I saw. Skies are basically blue.
The sky I saw on the picture which the graphic arts department had processed for this picture was blue. What
happened?

More importantly, we are not getting the consistent quality control on news color pictures that we should expect and
should get. Please double the monitoring and the efforts of
our quality-control people.

On November 1, he fired off another one, advising Phil Gialanella,
Vince Spezzano, and General Manager Jerry Bean to pass around the
page one tearsheet he sent them "and then get together so that the
three of you can throw up in unison. The color is so out of register and
so bad that my very first efforts at newspapering in South Dakota
would put this to shame. Wheninhell are we going to get some quality
control on our page one editorial color reproduction? Please fix and let
me know how/when it has been fixed."

Efforts were redoubled, and consistency improved. Letters from
readers praised the newspaper's colorful look. Vivian Chung of
Hockessin, Delaware, a suburb of Wilmington, wrote Editor John
Curley in November 1982: "I would like to compliment you and your
staff for a fine job on your paper. This paper is different from any other
paper I have seen and is by far the best. For one thing, the paper is
very well organized and the layout is superior. The subdivisions under
the different sections make the paper very easy to read. The second
thing I find impressive about USA TODAY is its color. The abundance of
color in the advertisements and the pictures breaks the monotony of
reading a traditional black-and-white newspaper."

Chuck Blevins and his traveling buddies smiled when they read that
one.

CHAPTER TEN

Identity
crisis

When the first edition of USA TODAY sold out in the Washington area, its editors and reporters were jubilant: After months of trial runs, they had produced a real newspaper.

On the night Vol. 1, No. 1 was printed, many of them boarded buses for the short ride out to the Army Times printing plant in Springfield, Virginia. They sipped champagne on the way, and watched the first edition come off the press at 1:30 A.M.; John Curley was waving it over his head as he left the building. Curley went to bed at 3:30 and was up at 7 A.M. to be on "Good Morning America."

The rest of the staff got a little more rest, but woke up to realize they had to do it all over again, day after day. Those early days were difficult, because USA TODAY was a newspaper in search of an identity. "In the beginning, our toughest job was trying to convince *ourselves* that we knew what we were doing," Neuharth would say later.

USA TODAY's News department was, in Neuharth's words, "overstaffed at the top." Gannett's chief executive and its chief news executive—Neuharth and Quinn—were almost always there, working on the Page One desk with USA TODAY's top editors—John Curley and Ron Martin.

Tension was highest in the A section. In Sports, the mandate was simple: To cover every game, every score, and every statistic, and produce the most thorough sports report available. Managing Editor Henry Freeman and his staff were building a national sports daily within a newspaper. Their mission was clear; they just had to execute it.

Staffers watched the first papers come off the press shortly after 1:30 A.M. September 15, 1982.

Joe Welty, center, and Frank Vega, to the right in dark shirt, toast the new newspaper. The celebration was brief. Vega was already worried about the next launch in Atlanta.

In Money, the goal for J. Taylor Buckley's staff was to cover all the business news and add financial features that readers could use. The Life section's mission was muddled at first; Sheryl Bills and her people were struggling to strike a balance between entertainment news and more substantial issues in health, science, and medicine, but the casting about there did not compare to the agony in the A section.

In early December 1982, Nancy Woodhull, managing editor/news, went into the 5 P.M. news meeting thinking she had a 1A story. A man had driven a truck up to the Washington Monument and was threatening to blow it up. She was sure this was a national story, a 1A story.

Ron Martin said no, it was a Washington, D.C., story. It didn't belong on page one. He bumped it back to 3A. Woodhull couldn't believe it, but she didn't cut back on coverage. Then Dan Rather led with the story on the CBS Evening News, and the thinking changed. "It went back on page one as if the story had just happened," Woodhull recalls. Throughout the various newsrooms, Sony color TVs hung from the ceilings, and they were always on. Editors were very aware of what people saw and heard on the television news and shaped USA TODAY's print report to take that into account. Now that millions of viewers knew about the Washington Monument incident, it was a national story.

That was an example of a story that needed a "verification factor," or "VF," as some people called it. Throughout the newsroom, there were editors and reporters who had been stars at smaller newspapers; now they felt top editors had doubts about their news judgment. After they had been second-guessed a few times, some staffers began to feel that it didn't matter what they thought, because a story was not a story until it had been on national television or in a big newspaper.

The monument story also represented the "they" syndrome. "They" referred to the editors at the top, the "Gang of Four": Curley, Martin, Neuharth, and Quinn. That quartet spent so much time in the newsroom that a separate conference room, called the "war room," was reserved for their editing sessions, with Neuharth's black Royal prominently displayed nearby. None of the midlevel people could predict what "they" would want in those afternoon meetings. The truth was, "they" were still trying to figure out what it was "they" wanted.

Beyond USA TODAY's basic format and standing features, there was no grand blueprint, no set of rules from which the top editors worked. They were more or less making it up as they went along, following their

Quinn, Martin, Curley, and Neuharth set up the "war room" in the fourteenth-floor conference room, where they read proofs, rewrote stories, and polished headlines. Curley soon decided that they had enough people editing copy so he turned his attention to making sure the deadlines were met.

From left, John Quinn, Ron Martin, and John Curley review copy on launch night. At that point, Curley thought the odds of success were only forty-sixty, but after the enthusiastic reader reaction in the Washington–Baltimore area, he upgraded USA TODAY's chances to sixty-forty.

USA TODAY

PROTOTYPE EDITION I

'An idea whose time has come'

Welcome to a prototype edition of a new newspaper proposed to serve the nation.

FRIDAY MORNING

THE TOP STORY in this prototype edition of USA TODAY is the prototype itself, the news, information and advertising services that could be offered in a new nationwide, general interest daily newspaper.

THE CONTENT IDEAS for USA TODAY have been published in two different prototypes. These will be tested by professional research and through the invited reactions from a select group of readers.

THE RESULTS OF THESE STUDIES will help determine whether some combination of these USA TODAY ideas will be published as a daily nationwide newspaper or, beginning late in 1982. Instead of offering current news, the prototype editions demonstrate the coverage and style that might have been published on a Friday in mid-May. Many stories are more abbreviated than they would be in a normal daily edition to permit a wide variety of examples in a single prototype edition. The column below explains the kind of information USA TODAY would contain on a regular schedule.

ACROSS THE USA TODAY
NEWS OF THE NATION dominates the first two inside pages of USA TODAY, with overnight news on 2A and 3A from Boston to Miami to Houston to Riverside, Calif.
NEWS FROM EVERY STATE follows on pages 3A, 4A, 5A, a unique state-by-state report from any state the reader may have come from, may be going to or may be interested in.

WEATHER
A FULL PAGE of color-coded maps predicts the weather across the USA for today, tomorrow and the next day, plus reports for all regions and from all 50 states, up-day temperatures from the nation's travel centers, and more, every day on the back page of the first section of USA TODAY.

WHAT'S GOING ON TODAY
AGENDA IN BOTH a page and a priority in USA TODAY. The AGENDA page on 1B delivers the day's cross-country calendar — from Teamsters Union leaders meeting in Las Vegas to the Old Time Radio Reunion in Jonesboro, Tenn. THAT AGENDA TRADEMARK also is stamped on other USA TODAY pages — the agenda for the nation's capital, 8A, for foreign affairs, 10A, for business, 2B, for sports, 2C; for entertainment, 3D, for TV, 4D.

OPINIONS FROM ACROSS USA
THE EDITORIAL PAGE offers USA TODAY's views, plus opinions from 20 other newspapers across the country — north and south, east and west, large and small, group and individually owned, from liberal to conservative — on 3C.

MONEY
BUSINESS NEWS PAGES of USA TODAY offer another different approach to the news — on 6B, information on personal finances; on 7B, the morning business report.

THE NATION'S SCOREBOARD
SPORTS FANS OF ALL KINDS will find every result of every general interest sport everywhere, plus plenty of special interest detail, on the sports pages, Section C. Scores, statistics and facts that just a fan's look at upcoming action with complete 1's schedules, a page of numbers for the money player, a cross-section of columnists' viewpoints and a locker room full of sports talk.

LIFE ACROSS USA TODAY
THE HEARTBEAT of the exciting American lifestyle is recorded in LIFE, Section D, with a column of talk from across the nation and trends on 1D, with color-coded nationwide TV schedules. In between is a sampling of the good things of life in America and the people who are a part of it.

ABOUT THE PROTOTYPE
THIS EDITION of USA TODAY has been developed, edited and published by a task force of news, advertising and production talent drawn from the staffs of Gannett newspapers. This mid-May news report came from Gannett News Service, the nationwide staff of the Gannett News Service and The Associated Press and United Press International. Gannett is a nationwide information company, with 83 dailies, 22 newspaper, seven television and 13 radio stations, outdoor advertising, marketing, research operations and satellite transmission in 35 states, two US territories and in Canada.

INSIDE USA TODAY

COPYRIGHT GANNETT

Social Security plan stirs national storm

GRACEFULLY HOME AGAIN: The space shuttle Columbia arrives home at the Kennedy Space Center piggybacked on a Boeing 747, ready for its second flight on Sept. 30. The four-day, five-hour mission was made the first time a spaceship has flown more than once. Officials reported only 90 more faults during the first mission. (Soviet's latest space move, page 10A.)

White House phone calls 90% opposed

By ANN DEVROY and CHRIS COLLINS
For USA TODAY

Some older citizens are breaking down and weeping on the phone, others talk of their betrayal by a President who promised not to reduce Social Security.

The public verdict on President Reagan's proposals to save the Social Security system from probable bankruptcy by curbing benefits for future retirees poured across the country Thursday in a flood of fear, concern and confusion.

At the White House, the switchboard logged 600 calls since the plan's introduction two days ago and these were important in its running, 90 percent against the administration.

As Congressional offices around the country, telephone lines were busy.

At the Lakeland, Fla., office of Sen. Lawton Chiles, D-Fla., aide Sandra Oldham replied to queries about the number of calls: "Is the sky up? Yes, yes and yes. We've just been flooded."

In Tennessee, the four district offices of Senate Majority Leader Howard Baker received more than 150 calls, said staff assistant Carolyn Hill, the most on any one topic since the Panama Canal treaty debate.

At the Senate Committee on Aging, Minority staff director Bertita Applewhite said, "We've

Complete story on page 10A
BENEFITS continued on page 2A

The pope forgives 'poor boy'

From USA TODAY Reports
ROME — Pope John Paul II Thursday forgave the "poor man, poor boy" who shot him Wednesday as he rode through St. Peter's Square and said he would pray for the 23-year-old Turkish national who was being held in Italian authorities.

Doctors said the pope was in satisfactory condition in intensive care but there still worried about infection the bullet twisted around in the intestine.

The accused gunman, Mehmet Ali Agca, told police that he acted alone, but authorities suspect accomplices. Someone supplied the 9-mm pistol used in the shooting and financed Agca's $150-a-day travels through Europe before the shooting.

Agca has been free since his escape from a Turkish prison in 1979 following the assassination of an editor. A military tribunal sentenced him to death in absentia, and police had orders to shoot him on sight.

Complete story on page 10A

USA expecting test-tube baby

From USA TODAY Reports
NORFOLK, Va. — The nation may have its first test-tube baby early next year, according to an announcement Thursday from Eastern Virginia Medical School.

Doctors at the medical school's test-tube baby clinic said they have successfully impregnated a woman through laboratory fertilization after 14 months of frustrating failure.

The first test-tube baby, Louise Brown, was born in England in 1978; three more have been born since in England and Australia.

Dr. Howard Jones, who established the clinic at Norfolk with his wife Dr. Georgeanne Jones, did not name the expectant mother when making the announcement, saying he feared the publicity would endanger the pregnancy. He cited the recent case of a French woman who pregnanted artificially who miscarried and endangered her identity was revealed and news media attention focused on her.

The pregnancy was accomplished through the "in vitro" method in which the woman's egg is fertilized in a petri dish before being implanted in the womb.

Super cities of the '80s

COVER STORY

Jobs, migrants, lifestyles change face of nation

By JOHN HANCHETTE

HOUSTON — No one dreamed 10 years ago that this city's local newspapers would be two orders or newsstands in Detroit, 1,270 miles away.

But it is happening today for a variety of reasons — the air inflow in jobs that Houston offers and Detroit doesn't, and others as complex as energy and identities.

The great influx of centers of the hard are fading, and the sun belt cities are becoming as dominant as the prosper twin center of the country will soon shift west of the Mississippi for the first time.

These super cities and their suburbs are cities of the future. Here and beyond.

IN HOUSTON-GALVESTON, where the population jumped 24.5 percent between 1970 and 1980 from 2 million to 3,101,686, the story is a booming energy business and the sun's of generation.

IN SAN JOSE, where the population jumped No.1 percent in the last decade from 459,916 to 625,771, the story is also electronics.

IN PHOENIX-TUCSON, which grew by 52.1 percent in the same period from 1,575,634 to 1,765,099, the story is retirees.

IN MIAMI-FORT LAUDERDALE, where the population soared 20.3 percent from 1,607,862 to 2,644,232, the story is retirees.

CITIES continued on page 2A

Sinkholes spread in Florida

From USA TODAY Reports
WINTER PARK, Fla. — A sinkhole bigger than a football field suddenly opened here this week and by Thursday had grown to engulf several Florida businesses and homes.

Many journalists criticized the first front page. They disagreed with the news "play"—which stories were given prominence—and they found the page layout jumbled. With its many stories and promotional items, USA TODAY looked different: It did not conform to the horizontal, modular layout popular in many newspapers.

Despite its many standard features, editors found ways to make the front page flexible. For example, the March 31, 1987, issue gave two breaking stories—the NCAA basketball finals and the Oscars—equal importance.

Page one's make-up

Left ear:
The "lear" promotes sports stories and gives scores of hot games.

Newsline:
A digest of the day's news and an index of inside stories.

Left leg, right leg:
Stories that run on either side of the cover story. Topic depends on the mix on the remainder of the page.

Snapshots:
Often pegged to studies released that day. Gives a statistical look at some slice of life in the USA.

Blue band:
Added to check color quality, it is used to promote upcoming stories.

Right ear:
The "rear" promotes stories in Money, Life and sometimes the A-section.

Nameplate

Cover story:
Pegged to breaking news or to events scheduled that day or week.

Strip:
Also called the "talker," it may not be breaking news, but is either a story that people will be "talking about today" or a story that is fun and interesting.

Main color art:
At least one half should appear above the fold (top half of the page).

Lead:
It has a bolder headline than the other stories, and is the top news of the day.

Photos, illustrations:
Page one art work should represent a mix of men, women and minorities.

Off-lead:
Often called the "shoulder," it usually is the story that was in competition for the lead.

Hot corner:
A place for light, humorous or offbeat stories.

Above the fold:
All that a potential reader sees in the window of the newsrack.

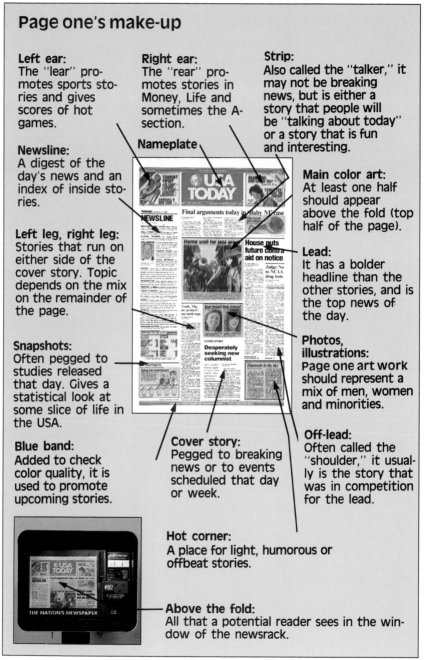

Occasionally, the strip story is replaced with a "Billboard Promo" to alert readers to a hot multipart story, a heavy sports weekend, or a special bonus section.

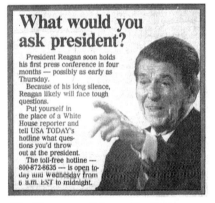

The "hot corner" is used to display bright or offbeat stories, or "hotline" features, such as the Reagan press conference above. Beginning in 1985, USA TODAY made an effort to get readers more involved in the newspaper by using "hotlines" to poll them or to put them in touch with experts, who gave them advice on topics ranging from drugs to exercise.

Small details are crucial on page one. Editors worked to make the "ears" stand out. First they added a gray background behind the headlines, but then they worried that it made the words harder to read. By mistake, a pink screen was used in an edition in early 1987, and editors noticed the type was much easier to read. So they dropped the gray background and went with a gray border.

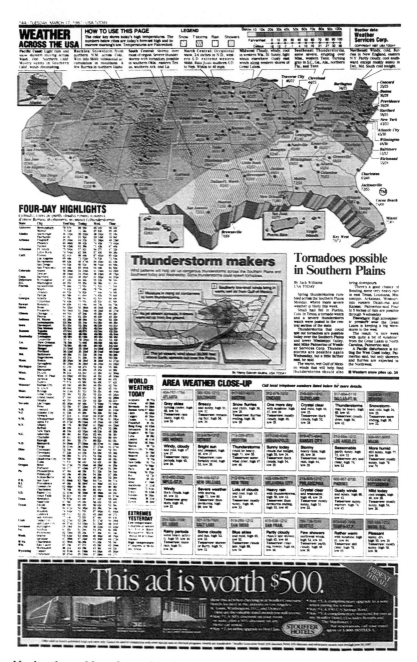

Neuharth would say later of the full page of weather news: "This is a direct, absolute steal from Willard Scott and other TV weathermen." An ad was added to the bottom of the page in February 1986.

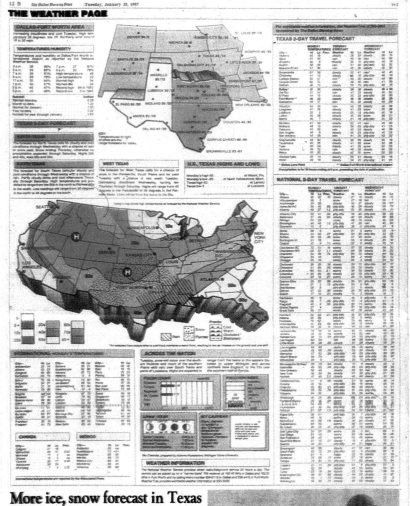

THE WEATHER PAGE

Probably the most imitated element in USA TODAY is its weather page. The Dallas Morning News was one of many newspapers that expanded weather coverage and added a color map.

More ice, snow forecast in Texas

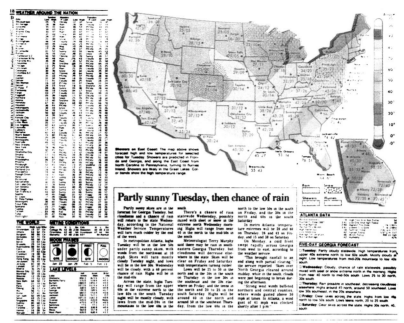

Edward Sears, former Atlanta Journal and Constitution managing editor, says, "We saw a lot of innovations in the USA TODAY prototypes. We stole the weather map before USA TODAY came to Atlanta."

In September 1986, The New York Times expanded its weather coverage, including a bigger black-and-white map.

instincts. That inevitably led to a lot of last-minute changes of direction and misunderstandings. USA TODAY had been launched, but its tone, its style, its very character were all still being invented and reinvented every day. "Sometimes it was hard for the editors and reporters to understand," John Curley says.

The editors "don't know what they want," one reporter complained to a writer for Columbia Journalism Review in the spring of 1983. The reporter, who asked to remain anonymous, added, "They might say something is important, then change their minds six times. The operative factor in whether a story runs is sometimes whether it has a color picture."

The mood in news meetings and the newsroom was often harsh. Part of it was a feeling that nothing was good enough. Neuharth wanted his editors to anguish over what went into the newspaper, to worry, to sweat over every headline and every lead. That produced a domino effect. John Curley says: "If Neuharth wasn't happy then Quinn couldn't be happy."

Curley had written an economics column at Gannett News Service, so he worked on business stories at USA TODAY. He remembers trying to rewrite the lead of one piece slated for page one. "No matter what I gave them, they didn't like it. Finally I walked away. Neuharth said, 'Don't get pissed off; there's no reason to.'

"I said, 'I am pissed off. I've rewritten it six or seven times. I don't know what else to do.' Then I went back and got the first copy of what I had written, waited until a quarter to eleven, and handed it in. Quinn said, 'Geez, this is pretty good.' I said, 'No shit' to myself; I didn't say it out loud. That was the first story; there was nothing wrong with it, that was just the process. They had to rework everything."

What Curley experienced was quickly becoming a way of life for USA TODAY reporters. Often they felt their copy had been butchered in the rewriting. Editors were trying so hard to make every story bright, to make every story scream "Read me!" that sometimes the facts the reporters felt were important got lost in the editing.

The reporters felt they had been dropped into some new, futuristic world where nothing was familiar. Part of it was their surroundings: Nice, expensive, but wildly different from the cozy newsroom atmosphere at many of Gannett's community newspapers. In her 1983 article for Columbia Journalism Review, Katharine Seelye wrote:

A visit to USA TODAY's offices is like going to the moon.
The thirty-story silver tower rises like a rocket among its
more sedate, rectangular corporate brethren. Although USA
TODAY rents only about one third of the building, it has its own
logo atop it—a royal-blue sign more than forty-four feet long
and five-and-a-half feet high. (Gannett wanted it bigger, but
other tenants in the building complained, and the Arlington
County Board restricted its size.)

Inside, escalators carry you on a mystifying journey above
a habitat of waterfalls and greenery. At the top, a curving
hallway seems to propel you toward what turns out to be
elevators. At the fourteenth floor, you step into the newsroom of the future: a total environment of black and white and
chrome all over. At the end of the long black corridors, raised
white letters tell you where you are: News, Sports, Money,
Life. Reporters, sitting at rows of white desks, type at black
Atex terminals. Their little file cabinets roll; reporters call
them R2-D2s. There are little glass offices with chrome-
trimmed chairs. Copy editors are grouped around a high-
shine, dog-bone shaped, black desk. What is not black and
white are the four television sets suspended above the copy
desk: the color is radiant, the reception immaculate. The
newsroom is airy with light from windows overlooking the
Potomac. It is orderly. It is quiet. It is sleek and efficient.

About 65 percent of USA TODAY's original reporters and editors
were loaners from other Gannett newspapers, from places like Rockford, Illinois; Tucson, Arizona; Marion, Indiana; and Boise, Idaho.
"Our people from across the USA came with a fresh approach to journalistic assumptions," Neuharth would say later, "different from those
that had developed through the years primarily in Washington and New
York. What they brought—and what produced the initial [critical] reaction from editors and publishers—was change."

That loaner policy made sense: If USA TODAY failed, or if reporters
or editors did not like working there, they could return to their old jobs.
They were given $125 a week in "walking around money," free lodging
at the River Place apartments next door, and one free plane trip home a
month. The company had rented 150 apartments in River Place, and
many were infested with bugs; the loaners called the complex "Roach
Palace" and had T-shirts made up with the legend, "I Survived River
Place," complete with color-coordinated pictures of cockroaches.

Many loaners remembered a paragraph from John Curley's letter to them. It was echoing in their heads: "We hope everything works to your satisfaction and ours. However, some people found during the prototype experience that it wasn't their thing. We also found that it doesn't always work for one reason or another from our point of view. But we hope it does."

Newsroom staff

USA TODAY had 218 professional journalists on staff when it began publication September 15, 1982. Here's a profile of those journalists:

• Loaners from Gannett papers	141	65%
Permanent hires from non-Gannett publications, including Forbes, Fortune, Business Week, The Washington Post, Detroit Free Press, New York Post	77	35%
• Men	133	61%
Women	85	39%
• Minorities	30	14%
Nonminorities	188	86%
• Average age	33	

• Members of the newsroom staff worked in twenty-nine states and three countries just before coming to USA TODAY. Here are the states and countries represented and the number of journalists from each:

Arizona	2	Nevada	1
California	16	New Jersey	7
Delaware	16	New York	37
District of Columbia	36	North Carolina	4
Florida	13	Ohio	11
Georgia	2	Oregon	1
Idaho	2	Pennsylvania	6
Illinois	2	South Dakota	1
Indiana	1	Tennessee	12
Kansas	1	Texas	7
Louisiana	2	Vermont	2
Maryland	9	Washington	1
Massachusetts	2	West Virginia	3
Michigan	12	Guam	1
Minnesota	2	Germany	1
Missouri	4	Japan	1

As operations chief for the A section, Anne Saul attended the morning news meeting with Nancy Woodhull. Curley, Quinn, and Martin wanted so many details in the budget meeting about stories, "we had to fake it," she says.

Most of the loaners were pedaling as fast as they could to keep up. Anne Saul, then thirty-eight, was a loaner from TODAY in Florida, where she had been managing editor. That job had been demanding, but as operations chief of the A section, she had even more to do. She was in charge of the copy desk, where stories were edited and headlines written; the layout desk, where pages were designed; the weather news desk; and the wire desk, where national and international stories were monitored. Each night, she helped Neuharth, Quinn, and Martin size headlines. None of them knew how to use the Atex computer terminals; they scribbled their headlines on little pieces of paper and asked Saul to figure out if the words fit in the assigned space. Often all three showed up with different heads for the same story. She wanted to say, "Why don't you guys get together and decide what you want to do?" but she never did. "I was exhausted," Saul says, "but it was fun."

In shaping USA TODAY, Neuharth's style was to tell people in general terms what he wanted, and let them figure out how to do it. "We gave people the broadest possible direction and told them to crawl into the trenches and do it," he says. Of course if they did it wrong, he and the rest of the "Gang of Four" were all over the mistakes. Quinn explains that's why all four of them were there every night in the beginning: To make sure the mistakes were corrected before they got into type, instead of inflicting the errors on the readers and second-guessing the staff later.

One of the first loaners to crawl into the trenches was George Rorick, who had been a jack-of-all-trades art director at the Lansing

(Mich.) State Journal. Rorick was assigned to design and produce USA TODAY's unique weather page. If there had been a daily deadline the first time he built the full-color map for a prototype, he would have missed it by about twelve hours. It had taken him a day and a half to make the page. With help from the production department, Rorick streamlined the process; by the end of October 1982, it took only half an hour to make the map.

The editor who had to figure out how "Voices Across the USA" would work on the Opinion Page was Kristin Clark Taylor, a young woman who had graduated from Michigan State and worked at the Detroit Free Press. The idea was to publish pictures of ordinary people every day with their opinions on the issue that USA TODAY was debating. But how would they get the photos? Trying to take pictures of seven people from all over the country the day they were interviewed would be a knotty logistical problem.

Editorial Director John Seigenthaler decided to gather pictures in advance. He sent Nashville Tennessean photographer J.T. Phillips to Opryland to snap mug shots of tourists. Phillips recorded their phone numbers on the back of the prints, and Taylor, then just twenty-three,

The weather page that George Rorick produced for Prototype III in the spring of 1982 established the design for the USA TODAY weather map. As circulation expanded westward, the map was tilted slightly so that the focus would not be on the East Coast.

Of the start-up frenzy, Jeffrey "Buzzy" Albert says, "It was the most exciting time. The camaraderie was great."

During the first months of publication, Kristin Clark Taylor had a hard time getting people to participate in "Voices Across the USA." Sometimes she would have to make thirty calls to get three people to talk. Some said they did not want to be quoted because they thought USA TODAY was "a Moonie paper."

selected seven photos each day and telephoned each person. The "Voices" were chosen to reflect the nation's diversity: young and old, male and female, black and white, from seven different states. Taylor became an expert at drawing opinions out of people, on subjects ranging from school prayer to the Sandinistas. For a few months, the "Voices" feature ran the photos of a lot of country music fans; later Gannett newspapers sent in photos and USA TODAY took pictures at conventions, and the result was a "Voices" photo bank with thousands of pictures.

Some loaners found working at USA TODAY nearly as strenuous as taking aerobics. Jeffrey "Buzzy" Albert lost thirty pounds in USA TODAY's first few months, "running up and down the stairs to the composing room." Albert, then thirty, came from the Wilmington newspapers. In the early days, he was the only Money staffer who knew the computer codes to set bar charts and tables. He came in about 10 A.M., met with content editors to find out what graphics were needed and ordered them. Afternoons, he laid out pages, edited stock market stories, and went to the composing room to make sure Money pages were pasted up properly. At 7:30 P.M. he stopped for a sandwich in the Great Eatery on the building's mall level. At 8:30 P.M. he retrieved specialized stock data from the Interactive Data Corporation's computer in Massachusetts. He usually finished by midnight and retired to Cisco's, a nearby restaurant, for a Monte Cristo sandwich and several gin and tonics. After a year, four people were assigned to do what Albert had done every day, and he helped supervise them. On Thursday nights, when the paper had been put to bed for the week, sports staffers would wind down by drinking and playing poker all night at Cisco's.

For the first six weeks, Neuharth was prowling around the newsroom nearly every night USA TODAY published. He was also a force in the afternoon news meetings. Louise Bernikow described one meeting in a 1983 article for Savvy.

> It is four-thirty in the afternoon. Thirteen people are seated around a chrome-based, tinted plastic table littered with Pepsi cans and Styrofoam cups. Only one person in the room smokes. There are four women, three sitting together. [John] Curley, in shirtsleeves and a red-striped tie, presides.

In seven days in August 1982, Karen Howze trained 235 newsroom staffers to use the Atex computer system.

Neuharth comes in a few minutes late.

There is no chair for him. Everyone jokes; laughter is a great bonding agent. Someone pulls a chair from the side of the room and Neuharth places himself next to Curley. It is the day after the last World Series game, and the group is discussing the front page of the next day's paper.

"Is there a parade in Milwaukee?" Neuharth asks.

The page will feature photos of parades in both St. Louis and Milwaukee, the winners and the losers. About a Wall Street report, he asks, "Why are we playing the losers over the winners? It seems a little early to pee on the rally."

He zeroes in on something missing in the coverage of auto tycoon John DeLorean, then in jail for allegedly dealing cocaine. "Why can't he come up with 250,000 bucks for bail? A man in that position ought to be out in a minute."

It is a good newsman's instinct. All of Neuharth's comments are good, nitty-gritty, tough editor comments. No one disagrees with him.

Nancy Woodhull told Neuharth he was spending too much time in the newsroom: "You intimidate everybody. You scare them to death, and as a result the wrong decisions are made. Everyone asks, 'What would Neuharth want?'" Neuharth knew there was some truth in her complaint, but felt he had to be where the action was. "There was no way I was going to let the thing be guided by somebody else; I'd have to take all the blame if it didn't work." And John Quinn adds that Neuharth's presence "gave people the feeling we were all in this together."

Midlevel editors found the process frustrating. Tom McNamara, a Life editor, says that waiting for Life Managing Editor Sheryl Bills to return from that afternoon news meeting was like waiting for the helicopters on M*A*S*H* to bring back the wounded. He never knew how mangled Life's story list would be when Bills returned. A Money editor recalls it was like being in a prisoner-of-war camp: One day you would obey the rules and then the next day "they" would announce new ones and punish you for having obeyed the old ones.

One reporter fell apart under the pressure: She broke down in tears and told her supervisor the cat had died, the laundry had not been done in weeks, that her personal life was nonexistent. He sent her home. The next day she came in at 11 A.M. and then disappeared; she rode the subway for four hours, physically unable to return to the USA TODAY building. She was given a different, less taxing assignment.

Reporters had to adapt. They had to learn how to quickly combine several elements from several sources to build one short, clear, concise story. That was difficult for people who were not used to the severe editing that went on, especially for page one. It was probably the only newspaper in the world where reporters sometimes fought to keep their stories *off* page one; they knew they would have more space, and less chainsaw-style editing elsewhere.

A staff guide titled "Writing for USA TODAY" concisely outlined the new newspaper's style:

> TELL THE STORY QUICKLY AND CLEARLY.
> DON'T WASTE WORDS.
> Because USA TODAY has a different mission than most newspapers, so do the reporters and editors. Our readers are upscale, well-informed and looking for a supplement to—not a replacement for—their regular newspaper. So our stories may contain less background on events, more emphasis on what's new. Our paper has less space. So every story, every word, counts.

Marie Saulsbury, Joe Urschel, and J. Ford Huffman listen to Sheryl Bills' (left) report from the afternoon news meeting. Bills said it troubled her that often the staff would blame changes in Life's stories on the higher editors, when in fact the changes had been her ideas.

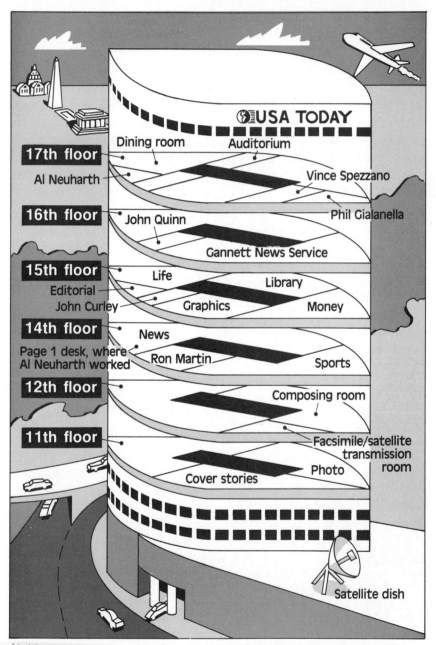

USA TODAY

17th floor — Dining room — Auditorium
Al Neuharth
Vince Spezzano

16th floor — John Quinn
Phil Gialanella
Gannett News Service

15th floor — Life — Library
Editorial
John Curley — Graphics — Money

14th floor — News
Page 1 desk, where Al Neuharth worked — Ron Martin
Sports

12th floor
Composing room

11th floor
Facsimile/satellite transmission room
Cover stories — Photo

Satellite dish

Unlike most newspaper operations, USA TODAY is scattered over a number of floors. It was important in the early days for the various sections to learn to communicate and not become isolated. This drawing shows where offices were in late 1982.

KEEP IT TIGHT.
Propel the story with punctuation. Colons, semicolons, bullets, and dashes can replace some words. . . . Condense background information. Don't prattle on for several grafs explaining what happened at Love Canal, or spend an entire graf telling who Phyllis Schlafly is. Our readers are well-informed.

While reporters were learning to write short, the managing editor of graphics, Richard Curtis, and his photo editors were scrambling to get enough color photos. The heavy use of color meant they suddenly needed color mug shots of almost everyone in the news, and in those days the wire services did not transmit much color. Photographers ran up big air express bills, and Gannett's corporate jets were sometimes dispatched to pick up film. Sometimes photographers even developed their film on the jets. The small darkroom on the fifteenth floor was grossly inadequate to handle all of the processing and storage; soon cardboard boxes filled with film overflowed into the hallway. Editors learned they had to plan very carefully for color, and eventually the newspaper built a library of tens of thousands of photos. By 1986, USA TODAY would publish more than fifty-two hundred color photos per year and its photographers would shoot and process nearly fourteen thousand rolls of color film.

Joe Urschel, an editor in Life, found himself panting to keep up with the pace. "I had come from the Detroit Free Press, which had a reputation for being a junior version of The Washington Post for encouraging 'creative tension.' But we went to lunch and we left at a reasonable hour. Here people were starting at 9 A.M. and they were still at their terminals at 10:30 P.M. I felt from the day I came in the door that I got caught in this updraft and I was just sucked away. I was pedaling as fast as I could."

Some people fell behind. In early October, Nancy Woodhull had to tell several loaners they had not made it, they had to go home. Some of them just didn't fit at this newspaper; its emphasis on tight, clear writing was not their style. "They weren't clear on how to write for USA TODAY," Woodhull says. "They were still fighting what we were. They really wanted to be at The New York Times."

In the supercharged newsroom atmosphere, the day the loaners went home came to be known as "Black Friday." Tom McNamara, who was working on the A section and living with other loaners in River

Place, remembers the tension of this extended tryout: "I've never seen so many people so frightened, so stressed. I saw people cry when they were sent back."

Going to the news meetings could be wrenching too. Tony Casale, the nightside national editor, wanted to crawl under the table the day he presented the A section budget and one dateline said Birmingham, Georgia, instead of Birmingham, Alabama. "What do we have to do," Neuharth asked, "give geography lessons to the goddamn national desk?"

Casale recalls the great pressure on his family life; for seven months, he was in Rosslyn and his family was in Rochester. "Once my wife and kids came down for a week and I saw them about two hours a day. And the last day they were going back to Rochester and I was going out the door to work and my son, who was then four, started screaming and grabbed my legs and wouldn't let go. I was trying to go out the door and here's this poor little kid screaming, 'Don't go.' It's probably the hardest thing I ever did in my life and I would never do it again."

In 1987, Casale left to join a polling firm. He was not the only editor who left. In the spring of 1986, after marrying John Heckler, a lawyer with an office in Boston and a seat on the New York Stock Exchange, Sheryl Bills made good on her 1982 pledge to quit newspapers. They live in the Virginia hunt country.

Because of his intense concentration on the project, Neuharth often wrote brutal memos on what he saw as shortcomings in news coverage or presentation. Quinn, Curley, and Martin usually did not share the critical notes with the staff—only the complimentary ones.

"Quinn was a big help in keeping Neuharth off people's backs," John Curley says. "I don't mean mine, because I don't have any problem with Neuharth and Martin didn't either. But just to keep Neuharth under control sometimes because you didn't want all those memos he wrote to get into the system. Some criticism is subjective anyway— whether headlines are good or bad."

While bearing the brunt of the criticism, Quinn sometimes put off reading Neuharth's "Orange Meanies." Once Neuharth spotted an unopened orange envelope in Quinn's back pocket and said, "See—he never even reads them!"

Despite what some felt was the craziness of the newsroom, people pushed on. Whether they believed the newspaper would succeed or

*Joe Urschel started as
entertainment editor in the
Life section in 1982
and became managing editor of the
section in the summer of 1985.*

not, they all felt they were experiencing the ultimate professional challenge.

"I'm a damn fool, I guess," Ron Martin says, "but I don't remember being scared. If I had realized the enormity of it, I would have run in the other direction. If you have a complicated job and you write down everything you do in a week, you'd say, 'I'll never get it done.' But you get some of it done, you do some later, some takes care of itself. It was exhilarating."

Jim Schulte, an editor in sports who came from San Bernardino, California, put it this way: "The whole idea of starting a newspaper was very seductive. Newspapers were dying left and right. This was a chance to create one."

Nancy Monaghan, then the national editor, remembers it as "the worst period in my entire life. But I would do it again."

It wasn't all stress. In the beginning, editors took people from every department out to dinner at some of Washington's best restaurants. There were occasional company parties, with sumptuous food and bars that never seemed to close, and frequent catered lunches for staff meetings. The change from life in the newsroom in Salinas, California, or St. Cloud, Minnesota, where a reporter might have to fight to get a chair fixed or find a free computer terminal, was so dramatic that some reporters felt they were working at a fantasy newspaper.

So it was not surprising that people believed there was going to be a swimming pool on the roof of the USA TODAY building. The rumor started in the Life department, and then department secretary Becky Holthaus thought it would be fun if there were a full-fledged memo on

Gene Policinski, left, helped set the short, punchy style for Page 1A stories when he worked as the page one rewrite editor. Tony Casale, night national editor, right, almost quit in October 1982 because of the second-guessing from higher editors.

the subject. She typed up a very official-looking document that said a limited number of applications were available for $150, and Holthaus signed it "Diane Large, vice president/personnel." Several people handed in checks before Diane Large found out; she did not think it was funny and wanted to fire Holthaus, but Sheryl Bills refused.

It was a few weeks before the A section enjoyed its first newsroom-wide laugh, and it came in the midst of the stress that had been there from day one. Anne Saul was editing briefs for the Washington page when she discovered she didn't have enough to fill the whole column. She called over to Gene Policinski, "Gene, your briefs are too short!"

"It was like a window cracked," Policinski says. "The entire room roared."

One day Neuharth and Quinn decided they needed to move Nancy Woodhull's office so they could use that space for their "war room," where they would huddle at night to write headlines. But no one told Woodhull until the movers arrived. Karen Howze filled her in as the movers were dragging Woodhull's desk out of the office. The newsroom began to buzz; everyone thought Woodhull had been fired. She climbed a stepladder that had been left in the middle of the room and said: "You're just seeing me move. This is all a surprise, but that's all there is to it, folks."

The early circulation returns were encouraging. A few days after launch, Neuharth wrote the directors that the Washington area circulation on the third day of publication was more than 130,000, above year-end projections for that market. "One market does not a season make," he said, "but we did avoid disaster coming out of the gate."

In its first few months USA TODAY managed to avoid making many serious mistakes, although other journalists made fun of its style—for example, its heavy use of personal pronouns in headlines. "We move less often," said one. "Census finds 228,800,000 of us," said another. The day after the census story ran, editors had to run a front-page correction. "Sorry, we missed 3 million of you," that headline read. The right number was 231,990,000 million. "We're sorry we miscounted," the correction said. "Welcome aboard to all of you!" Sometimes the attempt to be accessible and friendly was overdone.

"We said we had to be different," John Quinn says, "but we didn't have any guide going in. In the first six months we tried too hard to be different, and it kicked back at us. We were labeled as being too frothy."

Some of the froth that ended up on the front page was pretty fluffy: "USA is eating its vegetables," read one headline. "We're in mood to buy" was another. Summer brought a trip to the shore for USA TODAY's readers: "We're beachbound, bumper to bumper." The subhead said: "Ocean to ocean, time for lotion." And in May 1983, one of the newspaper's most naive headlines: "MEN, WOMEN: We're still different."

Naiveté played a role in the reporting of the Tylenol killer story.

Jim Schulte came to USA TODAY from The San Bernardino (Calif.) Sun. Of the mood in the Sports section at launch time, he says, "We wanted to hurt people. We wanted to take circulation away from the L.A. Times, because for years San Bernardino covered L.A. like a blanket but never got any respect."

Seven Chicago-area people had died after taking capsules spiked with cyanide. On March 9, 1983, the day the newspaper debuted in Chicago, USA TODAY's lead story said the police had the killer in sight. The story quoted "a source" who said, "We know who did it. We just have to prove it." The Associated Press moved a story on USA TODAY's report, quoting an FBI spokesman who said, "I don't know where the heck they're getting that from." Jim Head, TODAY's first editor in Florida, wrote a letter to Neuharth reminding him of a similar mistake they had made together at TODAY and added, "I understand a psychic in Chicago thinks the shade of Col. McCormick did it." Col. Robert McCormick owned the Chicago Tribune in the years following World War I.

"I was very, very skeptical of this story when it ran," Neuharth said in a memo to Quinn and Curley. "The best policy of course is not to go with these unattributed stories unless we have very, very solid reasons to believe that there is something to them and we are confident we can follow up. Any one-day story like this does great damage to our credibility if we cannot follow it up and substantiate it." Thus USA TODAY adopted a policy that severely restricted the use of anonymous sources; it was too easy for a newspaper to be misused by them. No one was ever charged in the Chicago Tylenol poisonings, and in the years to come, the words "sources said" would not appear in USA TODAY.

Despite the occasional mistakes, positive reaction from readers gave the staff energy. Henry Freeman's sports reporters lost time in interviews because athletes wanted to chat about how much they liked all the results, facts, statistics, and lists in the Sports section. Neuharth loved to read Sports; he was Freeman's biggest fan, and his biggest critic. As John Quinn had noted in offering his comments on Sports in the prototype days: "Only fools rush in where Jock Neuharth treads, but here goes."

On December 9, 1982, Neuharth wrote Freeman one of his typical memos: "Congratulations. Now that we have proved that we are human in the Sports department by blowing the NFL players' vote story this morning, we can relax and quit worrying about maintaining a perfect record. Our story was inferior in content and play to everything I saw anywhere else."

Neuharth read every edition very closely, and he was a bear on mistakes, especially in sports. Whenever the time of a TV program was wrong or a football team's record was misstated, Neuharth caught it

Clockwise, from lower left, John Bannon, Fred Meier, Henry Freeman, Rudy Martzke, and Curtis Riddle, with back to camera, discuss the day's stories. The 5 P.M. news meeting was preceded by section meetings, such as this one in Sports.

and Freeman heard about it. Every day USA TODAY's founder pored over the paper, often spending hours with it. He once asked the managing editors how long it would take a person to read everything in one edition of USA TODAY. "You don't know, because you don't have time to read it all," he said. The editors' guesses ranged from fifty minutes to two hours. Wrong, Neuharth said—it takes more than six hours to read every word in one edition.

Many journalists were used to hearing only complaints from readers: "You screwed up my dad's obit. You misspelled my neighbor's name. Can't you people get anything right?" At USA TODAY, reactions from readers were different. "It's the only newspaper I've ever worked for where people come up to you and say, 'I love your newspaper,'" said John Omicinski, a veteran Gannett News Service correspondent who sometimes wrote for USA TODAY. The flow of letters began as a trickle and grew to a steady stream. Although some found the paper superficial, the compliments far outweighed the criticism.

On October 15, David Roper of Duluth, Minnesota, wrote:

> After completely reading your October 15, 1982, edition, I must say it is the finest newspaper I have ever read. The color is great, the format is excellent, the stories and interviews are concise and enjoyable. Stock market coverage is

exceptional (equal or better than that of The Journal). I like
everything about it—I just wish there were more of it.

On October 19, Dennis Davenport of Washington, Pennsylvania,
wrote:

> We have had your paper in the Pittsburgh area for two
> weeks now. It has caused me to make several very important
> decisions—
> I am canceling my Time subscription.
> I am canceling my U.S. News subscription.
> I am canceling our local newspaper.
> I no longer need the Sunday New York Times.
> Most importantly, however, I am canceling my subscrip-
> tion to The Sporting News (which took me four years to
> convince my wife that I needed!)

While readers were praising USA TODAY, journalists christened it
"McPaper." One of the first articles to make the connection to fast
food appeared in Newsweek in January 1983. The headline labeled USA
TODAY "The Big Mac of Newspapers."

Not long after USA TODAY appeared, Jonathan Yardley, a columnist
for The Washington Post, wrote: "Like parents who take their children to a different fast-food joint every night and keep the refrigerator
stocked with ice cream, USA TODAY gives its readers only what they
want. No spinach, no bran, no liver."

"I think the 'McPaper' line was the best thing that happened in the
newsroom," John Quinn says. "It solidified the staff and gave them an
attitude that, by God, we're going to show them."

Even when the readers complained, they often sent bouquets along
with the brickbats. This positive reader reaction was more than
enough to make up for the negative reaction from fellow journalists
who thought "McPaper" was just television in print. What mattered
was what the readers thought—and they said they loved this new
newspaper.

Hitting
the streets

Getting a national newspaper on the streets required special tactics. Frank Vega and his people were USA TODAY's shock troops. They acted as if they were charging Normandy Beach; they burst out of the backs of rented trucks and suddenly, more than one hundred thousand news-racks were bolted to the sidewalks of America. Nothing could stop them: not lawsuits, not thugs with crowbars, not angry mayors or wor-ried competitors. And when it was over, the unique newsrack was ubiquitous. "McPaper's" blue-and-white boxes were as recognizable as McDonald's golden arches.

In the first two markets, Washington-Baltimore and Atlanta, news-racks were placed on the streets over a few weeks. In the third mar-ket—Pittsburgh—things got frantic.

Vega needed tens of thousands of racks to cover the country, so he went to three manufacturers to make them. One—K/Jack Engineering of Los Angeles—was behind schedule. On Wednesday, September 29—four days before the Pittsburgh launch—the racks still had not arrived. The pedestals were in, but not the boxes that held the news-papers. On Thursday at 7 A.M., the boxes came. Vega's people worked feverishly to put the boxes on the pedestals and load the assembled racks into tractor-trailer rigs and stepvans.

That Friday night, they started putting hundreds of racks on the streets—chaining them to posts and bolting them to sidewalks. They worked through Saturday and Sunday until finally, at 3 A.M. Monday, they placed the last rack on a Pittsburgh street corner, moments before the first papers arrived. Newsracks were usually tested before a launch; in Pittsburgh there was not time—and that led to trouble.

On Monday morning Neuharth looked out of the window of his downtown hotel, expecting to see the happy sight of a new reader discovering USA TODAY. As Neuharth watched, a customer put a quarter in and opened the door. But the quarter didn't stay in the machine; it dropped right through the coin return and bounced into the gutter. Neuharth saw other buyers insert quarters, open the door and retrieve their money from the coin return—"Hey, they're giving away newspapers here." The racks were defective.

K/Jack's owner flew to Pittsburgh and his people began repairing the racks. This was not Vega's only problem: Driving around the city, he discovered that vandals had ripped the doors off many newsracks with crowbars. They had poured pancake syrup down the coin slots. They had backed trucks up to racks and run over them; the pretty blue-and-white boxes looked like crumpled toadstools. Hundreds were damaged.

Many of the union drivers who delivered the Pittsburgh newspapers felt threatened by USA TODAY's non-union operation, and Vega suspected they were behind the vandalism. He arranged a meeting with the circulation director of those newspapers, and dropped a few hints that showed he knew how to damage racks, too. Vega mentioned that newsrack manufacturers were working overtime to fill USA TODAY's demand for racks. If any of the racks that belonged to the Pittsburgh newspapers were to get damaged, it would take a long, long time to get new ones. After that, Vega says, the trouble quieted down.

The cross-country invasion of the newspaper racks was enough to confuse some people. A Minneapolis woman wrote to the USA TODAY circulation department complaining that she had put a quarter into an empty rack and nothing had happened. She said she put in another quarter—and then another. Still, despite the "via satellite" boast on the rack, the satellite did not deliver. She said she wanted her money back. USA TODAY refunded her seventy-five cents—no questions asked. Another person complained that the post office had suddenly put out these weird-looking boxes that charged twenty-five cents to mail a letter.

Neuharth was USA TODAY's premier rack-checker—and certainly its highest paid circulation service clerk. Just after the Washington, D.C., launch, Neuharth and Editorial Director John Seigenthaler were riding through Georgetown. Neuharth saw a man buy a copy of USA TODAY

The Circulation department launched a sidewalk assault on the United States, often peppering a city overnight with hundreds or thousands of newsracks. Many cities and towns retaliated with proposals to ban the racks, but Gannett lawyers used a First Amendment defense and defeated the ordinances.

from a rack at the corner of Wisconsin Avenue and M Street. He stopped the limo and asked the man why he bought the paper.

"I put my quarter in the slot. I paid for the paper," the man said, unsettled by the question.

"I know, but *why* did you buy it?" Neuharth asked.

"I only took one."

"Okay, but I'd just like to know what caught your attention about USA TODAY. I'm curious."

"Sports," the man said, and walked away. Neuharth liked doing these man-on-the-street surveys; as a CEO, he was often skeptical of what subordinates told him, and it was fun to play reporter again.

When Neuharth found something wrong with a rack—and he checked thousands—he never let it pass unnoticed. On October 28, 1982, he wrote Vega:

> This morning, at 9 A.M., the vending machine kitty-corner across from the White House at Pennsylvania and Executive Avenue still had *yesterday's* USA TODAY in the window and in the box. Directly across the street, the vending machine had its door ripped off, stashed alongside, and the machine was

empty. This is the second consecutive day it has been in this condition. I did not report it yesterday because I wanted to see how quickly your efficient street crew would repair it.

This is one hell of an impression to make on those hundreds of Americans who mill around the White House every day, many of whom get their first impression of USA TODAY on those street corners. Some swift and solid ass-kicking is necessary around here—and probably elsewhere. I have started mine. Now it's your turn.

Neuharth's P.S. warned that "the lazy, the sloppy, the unenthusiastic, the uninspired will not be working around USA TODAY very long."

The scale of the project was so mind-boggling that it was impossible to avoid mistakes. Vega and his crew of people—Steve Johnson, Dick Hartnett, Carolyn Vesper, Tom Crowley, and many others—were racing from market to market bolting down racks. They left behind them brand-new circulation crews to supervise sales, distribution, and rack maintenance. Many of these new Gannett employees were new to newspapers; some were good, some were not. Vega's rack blitzkrieg left him little time to manage a market once it had been launched.

Neuharth sensed the problem and enlisted the help of a secret rack-checker—Bill Schmick, then a Gannett News Service editor. Schmick made two-day visits to Atlanta, Pittsburgh, and San Francisco. Traveling in a rented limousine, he inspected racks, newsstands, and convenience stores. The limo would pull into a 7-11 parking lot and take up half the spaces, and the dramatic arrival helped.

"I would say, 'Let me see your books on newspaper sales,' Schmick recalls, "and they'd open them up. They didn't know whether I was from the Mafia, the IRS, or what." He found lots of problems: large numbers of returns, racks selling yesterday's newspapers, airport vendors running out of papers or not getting them early enough. Sometimes a store owner would open a door and show Schmick a tall stack of unsold USA TODAYs. "Take these off my hands, will ya? I don't want 'em."

Union opposition was a problem in Pittsburgh, but in Philadelphia the confrontation turned into a war. Wherever it could, Gannett hired nonunion workers to distribute USA TODAY. Neuharth knew that the newspaper was not going to get launched if it was held hostage to

The fast pace of the launch schedule required intricate planning by the Circulation department. Frank Vega and his staff met frequently to review streetfighting strategy.

Vega wanted everything to go according to schedule on the first night. Impatient with the dock crew, he helped load newspapers onto trucks to ensure they'd reach the Washington–Baltimore area on time. He was so exhausted the next day, he slept through the celebration on the Mall.

restrictive union work rules. In Philadelphia, the union came out swinging and kept on fighting. Two months after launch, William Gullifer, secretary-treasurer of Local No. 628 of the Philadelphia Newspaper and Magazine Chauffeurs and Handlers, was still urging his members to continue the battle.

"Your local union has been engaged in an organizing campaign with the employees of USA TODAY," Gullifer wrote his members. "We must do everything legally possible to maintain the area wage standards and conditions that we all fought so hard to get. The sweat-shop conditions at USA TODAY must not be allowed to continue."

When Gialanella, Vega, and their people arrived in Philadelphia, the Teamsters had sent their people into the streets. "It looked like a scene from the 1940s," Vega recalls. "Pickets and people with clubs standing around fires burning in fifty-five-gallon drums. Everybody was singing 'Look for the union label.'"

Teamsters circled USA TODAY trucks and wouldn't let the drivers unload papers. There was some violence, too. Someone threw rocks through windshields. Firecrackers—big cherry bombs and M-80s— were used to blow up racks. One vandal mangled his hand when he couldn't get it out of the box before the explosion. Street vendors were afraid to carry USA TODAY.

Gannett had brought in fifty loaners from circulation departments in places like Marietta, Ohio, and Huntington, West Virginia. "After the first day, forty-six of the fifty wanted to go home," Vega says. Some papers for Philadelphia were printed at Gannett's newspaper in Lansdale, Pennsylvania. Bill McKinney, Jr., the Lansdale publisher, was so worried about violence he had the building's windows boarded up and hired one hundred extra security guards. A few were packing pistols. Other copies were printed in Bridgewater, New Jersey, and some of those trucks were run off the road on the way to Philadelphia.

The "drop sites," spots where bundles of newspapers were dropped for distribution to racks and newsstands, were the battleground. "We'd get to a drop site and there would be ten or twelve Teamsters there with clubs trying to intimidate our people," Vega says. A police captain called Carolyn Vesper and asked for the locations of drop sites so he could "protect" USA TODAY's people. Vega and Vince Spezzano didn't trust the police officer, so they gave him a bogus list. "At first the Philadelphia police were more help to the Teamsters than they were to us," Vega says.

Then Vega developed his "television incentive program." The security guards Vega had hired for USA TODAY's downtown headquarters were told that there was a reward for information leading to the arrest of anyone vandalizing a USA TODAY newsrack or harassing a driver—a free color TV. "We gave away twelve TVs," Vega says proudly. He considers the television incentive program a turning point in USA TODAY's relations with the powers-that-be in the City of Brotherly Love.

The Philadelphia launch was no fun for Randy Chorney, Neuharth's executive secretary. At 4 A.M. when Neuharth got to his hotel, he found an urgent note from Chorney. It said: "I've lost your briefcase. Please call me."

The briefcase contained a couple of thousand dollars in cash, all of Neuharth's credit cards, the only copy of his revised will, and the only copy of his latest contract—his first $1 million a year contract with Gannett, which the board had approved the day before.

Neuharth called Chorney at about 4:15 A.M. and asked, in very precise, measured words, "What does your note *mean*?"

What it meant was that in the middle of the night when Chorney had arrived on the corporate jet with all of Neuharth's luggage, luggage for other USA TODAY executives, and her own bags, there was only one cab. Its driver was asleep. She woke him up and talked him into taking her downtown. They loaded up and took off; the cab was filled with the aroma of marijuana.

The driver never stopped for a single red light. Once he reached across the seat, his hand dangling near Chorney's legs, and asked if she

Randy Chorney says of the hectic start-up: "To work from 7 A.M. to 7 P.M. was not a long day. It became 7 to 9 or 10 P.M."

wanted a cigarette. She was ready to jump out. They got to the hotel in
one piece, and in her rush to get out, Neuharth's briefcase was left
behind. Chorney called Vega for help, sobbing. He told her to calm
down, they would find it.

To get it back, Vega turned to Joe Mancuso, also known as Knuckles, who had worked in The Philadelphia Inquirer's circulation department for twenty-seven years before joining USA TODAY. Vega figured in
Philadelphia, he could use a little muscle. With his slicked-back hair and
veneer of sophistication, Knuckles looked a little like George Raft. But
there were a few unexpected turns to his nose that suggested he had
learned to take care of himself in a dark alley. Knuckles asked Chorney
a few questions and then told her: "Don't worry. We've put the reach
out."

Knuckles had a hunch it was an independent cab. He told an acquain-
tance at the cab company he would make it worth the effort to find the
briefcase. Within a few minutes, Knuckles' contact called back: He had
found the briefcase. Knuckles gave him forty dollars.

Fifteen minutes after Neuharth had called Chorney, Vega was at his
door with the briefcase. Everything—cash, cards, will, contract—was
still in it. Vega bragged, "When we wire a city, Al, it's wired."

The morning of the Philadelphia launch, Neuharth decided to do a
little rack-checking. He told his friend Barbara Whitney that the only
way to find out what was happening with the Teamsters was to go out
and check. To blend in, Neuharth donned a white sweatsuit, Nike
sneakers, and Porsche sunglasses. He was planning to hop in the limo,
hit the streets, and mingle with the Teamsters.

Whitney, who runs an art gallery and an interior design business
based in Cocoa Beach, said: "Allen, they're going to think you're a
screaming fag. They're going to beat you up." She talked him out of it.

Later that day, Neuharth learned that his son Dan, a USA TODAY
reporter, had appendicitis. After attending the launch party that night,
he left for Washington, leaving Vega and Phil Gialanella to get the next
day's papers out. They did it, and Vega was proud: "You know, fifty
years from now these racks are still going to be on the streets. The
rack may have lights on it; it may take an electric credit card, but my
descendants are going to say: 'My grandfather was the guy who put
these racks out in this city.'"

The little computer that couldn't

While the production, circulation, and news departments of the new paper forged new ground, USA TODAY's finance unit was nearly paralyzed, mired in chaos.

In November 1982—two months into publication—the business office was saddled with a computer system that was so inadequate it could not produce a bill. The office had about twenty-five people, half the staff it needed to keep up with its workload. And many of its employees had been hastily hired; some spoke English so poorly it was hard for them to communicate with the field.

During 1982 and for a good part of 1983, it was impossible for USA TODAY's managers to get timely, accurate information on anything—circulation, revenues, subscribers' names. Key financial systems had never been tested before launch, and now, when the newspaper was in dire need, they did not work.

One week, the newspaper could not even get out its own payroll. "We had people all over the United States clamoring for their money," recalls Dick Rumsey, who became vice president/finance in 1983. "There were four hundred district managers out there whose first thought was, 'Is this thing folding already?' We had vendors who threatened to cut us off. We had correspondents who threatened to quit writing articles for us because we didn't get checks out to them. It was real chaos."

The financial department's computer problems were making readers so mad they wanted to cancel their subscriptions—no matter how much they liked the newspaper. They either did not get billed or they got three bills. Or they paid, and then delivery was cut off. Or they didn't pay, and the newspaper kept coming. USA TODAY's ineptitude was driving customers crazy.

R.A. Fishbeck of Cherry Hill, New Jersey, wrote:

> Please cancel my subscription to USA TODAY. Why?
> 1. Three bills with three customer numbers and at least two names—all in one day. Really!!!
> 2. Arrival time on my driveway varies from 5 A.M. to noon.
> 3. On-again, off-again delivery. Some days yes, other days no.
> 4. The sweetest, most pleasant service representatives in the world, both here and in Washington, but totally incapable of getting the job done.
> 5. Cannot stop delivery of the paper for times I will be away from home. Result: Piles of newsprint on the drive to alert burglars.
> Not a bad paper folks, but I just can't cope with the bungling boobs who deliver it. So please cut it off upon expiration of my subscription—if you can. I am not at all sure you can stop it without locking up the delivery boy.

In a project that had been planned with the precision of a military invasion, with endless attention to detail, the finance department foundered. If finance did have a plan, it didn't work.

"I'm surprised Mr. Fishbeck got a bill at all," says Beth Silver, a USA TODAY accountant in those early days. Silver said a lot of subscribers figured out that they didn't have to pay for USA TODAY—it would just keep coming. When USA TODAY finally got a computer system that could track who was paying and who was not, more than half the names of its home delivery subscribers in many markets had to be dropped for nonpayment.

Why did a billion-dollar company with a reputation for excellent management buy the wrong computer? The answer is a tangle of good intentions entwined with bad decisions. The seed of the mistake was planted in 1980, when Neuharth held his very first meeting with the Project NN team. "Let's not waste any time in this phase of this thing trying to figure out whether you can home deliver such a newspaper or whether you can mail such a newspaper," Neuharth told them.

The message was clear: Think single-copy sales. That's all Frank

Dick Rumsey landed in the Finance department in the midst of computer turmoil that had vendors complaining about outstanding bills and employees panicking about past-due paychecks.

Vega was thinking about when Chuck Schmitt came to him in the spring of 1981 and asked what circulation needed from a computer system. Schmitt was an expert computer user, but had little experience buying a computer system; nevertheless, Moe Hickey had delegated that responsibility to him. And Neuharth and Spezzano had ignored Vega's request back in 1980 to add a data processing expert to Project NN.

In August 1981, Schmitt wrote a memo to some members of Gannett's capital appropriations committee—Jimmy Thomas, Larry Miller, Chuck Blevins, and Bill Malone—outlining what USA TODAY's computer system needed to do. Schmitt noted that the circulation base of the typical newspaper is composed mostly of home delivery subscribers, but USA TODAY would be "totally composed of single-copy sales. The problem of managing a data base of subscribers and deliverable addresses does not exist for USA TODAY."

Carl Fortson, who was Gannett's data processing director and helped Schmitt buy the system, agreed there was no need to store subscriber information: "You couldn't get anyone to talk about anything but street sales." John Palm, who succeeded Fortson when he left the company, says a cardinal rule in buying a system was violated: "Always plan for more than your present needs." And Gannett's needs were always changing, always expanding.

There was another element to this bad decision: the desire to save money. Two key members of the capital appropriations committee—Jimmy Thomas and Larry Miller—thought it was a mistake to start USA TODAY. They didn't want to "waste" any more money on it than they had to. Schmitt had come from corporate finance and was well aware of their concerns.

Tom Farrell, who worked in the Gannett's treasury department in 1981 under Jimmy Thomas, said that Thomas and other financial planners wanted to "minimize the investment in the computer." Doug McCorkindale had complained about the high costs of computer systems in his memo to Neuharth opposing the launch of USA TODAY. Their attitude was "Let's put a Band-Aid on it," Farrell says.

"Cost was always a factor," says Fortson, now a systems manager for Knight-Ridder. "IBM proposed dual computers for USA TODAY and the reaction from Chuck and the folks in Washington was, 'It's ludicrous, too expensive.' And corporate did not disagree."

Neuharth adds: "The financial folks went through the motions of setting up data processing operations, but they downscaled the hell out of it. The people who made the capital decisions didn't like the idea of USA TODAY in the first place." But Neuharth admits that his general ignorance about computers did not help either. He was deeply involved in the details in news, advertising, and circulation, but when it came to computers and satellite transmission, he trusted others to make the right decisions.

Thinking they needed only to track single-copy sales, Schmitt and

Lack of planning for home delivery caused what Chuck Schmitt calls "the biggest fiasco USA TODAY had." The computer system, purchased for its capability to keep track of single-copy sales, just could not handle home delivery subscriptions.

Fortson decided to buy Datapoint equipment. Datapoint, then an up-and-coming computer company, had a system that seemed ideally suited for their decentralized plan. Batches of numbers would be gathered in all markets and summaries sent to a computer in Washington.

But once USA TODAY began publishing, the mission changed. Circulation decision-making was centralized; managers at headquarters in Rosslyn needed detailed reports from the field, but the Datapoint system could not generate them. Then USA TODAY suddenly began offering home and mail delivery everywhere, but its computer system could not store subscriber information. "That change made what we thought was the best possible choice—Datapoint—the worst possible choice," Fortson says.

Instead of buying the equipment from Datapoint, it was purchased from a wholesaler. That was slightly cheaper, but it was another mistake. When things started going wrong, the wholesaler did not have the software experts to help Schmitt out. Then in the middle of the mess, the Securities and Exchange Commission accused Datapoint of inflating its sales and earnings. Without admitting or denying the charges, the company later signed a consent decree promising not to violate federal securities laws in the future. But Datapoint's sales suffered, its stock price fell, and the corporate turmoil didn't help USA TODAY solve its problems.

The result was a computer crisis. Top USA TODAY managers did not even realize the finance department was in trouble until two months after launch. Jerry Bean, then general manager of USA TODAY, suspected something was wrong. Chuck Schmitt had assured him everything was fine, but Bean called corporate for help: "I just get the feeling things aren't going right."

John Palm, Gannett's new director of corporate systems, flew down to Rosslyn from Rochester to investigate. When he opened the door to USA TODAY's data processing area, he found a roomful of zombies. They had been working around the clock trying to get their computer system to issue an accurate bill. "No bills had ever gone out," Palm said. He told them all to go home and get some sleep while he tried to pick up the pieces. It was the little computer that couldn't.

Despite what Neuharth predicted in 1980, USA TODAY plunged into widespread home delivery in 1983; that would add an element of predictable, consistent readership to the circulation base. But home deliv-

John Palm uncovered the computer crisis. "We fixed it," he says, "but it took some heavy dollars."

ery was started quickly, with little planning. And by then the Datapoint system was so overburdened that no one even considered putting new subscriptions on it. Instead, the national newspaper tried to piggyback on various kinds of computers at local Gannett newspapers. Many of them were swamped by the influx of orders; others had no room in their memory banks for USA TODAY's data.

Soon after USA TODAY began selling subscriptions in metro markets, Chuck Schmitt and Beth Silver flew out to Minneapolis to see how things were going. What they saw shocked them. Because data could not be put on the nearest Gannett newspaper's computer, the USA TODAY manager had hired four women and set them up at a card table in a rack storage area. The temperature was about forty degrees, so the women bundled up in heavy overcoats while they laboriously wrote out bills to thousands of new customers. Order forms had not been designed yet, so when calls came in, they recorded customers' names and addresses on scraps of paper.

Silver says their first reaction was to laugh—to keep from crying. "It was sad, very sad," she says. "It wasn't pretty," Schmitt says. The Detroit office was more advanced: Its temporary workers wrote names on index cards instead of scraps of paper. In Cleveland, twenty thousand subscriptions were done by hand for six months. USA TODAY had a twenty-first-century satellite delivery system, but a nineteenth-century billing system.

"The combination of the 'Band-Aid' approach to the computer and underestimating home delivery and mail really compounded our problems," Tom Farrell says. "It hurt circulation dramatically." Trying to fix things consumed vast amounts of management time.

Solutions were very expensive. Gannett had spent nearly $4 million on the Datapoint system. Eventually it had to abandon Datapoint and buy IBM equipment; that cost another $7 million. Having an inadequate computer system for a few years also made it much harder to figure out exactly how many copies USA TODAY was selling every day, and how much it cost to sell each copy. That didn't make running the newspaper easy.

"When I came to USA TODAY in 1983 the financial operation was terrible," says Jack Heselden, the newspaper division president who became the newspaper's publisher that year. "When I needed information to make decisions, I couldn't get it."

CHAPTER THIRTEEN

Waiting for the lead sheep

Paul Kessinger and Mike DeCarlo were on a sales call; it was the fall of 1982, and they were trying to sell a Dean Witter Reynolds ad director on USA TODAY. They talked about its upscale audience, its color, its uncluttered look, its impact. "He wanted to go," Kessinger recalls. "You could see it in his eyes. But he just didn't quite have the guts."

That was typical. Day after day, week after week, USA TODAY's salespeople walked the streets of New York and Detroit and Chicago and Los Angeles, pounding on doors, calling on prospects, telling anyone who would listen that this was a great new newspaper and they ought to be advertising in it.

But almost no one would. Kessinger knew the executives at the big Madison Avenue agencies acted like sheep: If no one else was advertising in USA TODAY, they were not going to be the first. It was safer to stay in the flock than step out on your own. And of course if everyone else was advertising in an established publication—say The Wall Street Journal—then they all had to be in The Journal, too. Just like sheep.

It was ironic. Madison Avenue agencies were constantly touting their creativity and innovation, their ability to come up with a "new" approach to sell a product. But when it came to spending a client's advertising dollars on a new, innovative newspaper, the agencies were very, very conservative. They were frightened to death. What if the agency advised a client to advertise in a new publication, and then it failed? That would be embarrassing, a black mark against the ad agency and its executives. It was far easier—and safer—to advertise in all of the same places that they advertised in last year.

*Mike DeCarlo made a
desperate sales trip to
Washington, D.C., the week
before launch, trying to drum
up ads for the second and
third editions.*

The timing for a new venture was tough, too. At about the same time USA TODAY was trying to attract advertising, several other new publications were trying to make it in the marketplace. The Washington Post had been pushing Inside Sports. Reader's Digest had introduced Families. And Time, Inc., introduced TV-Cable Week. Families and the TV magazine failed, and The Washington Post sold Inside Sports. "And here came Gannett with a really crazy idea," says John Quigley. He was trying to sell ads in those early days and later left to join Catholic Digest. Quigley remembers that in those first few months USA TODAY had no nationwide circulation numbers to sell: "It was like trying to sell a pig in a poke."

The sheep were nice to Joe Welty, the advertising director. They told him they would buy space in USA TODAY—someday. Welty was upbeat about the reaction he was getting: "An encouraging week and considerable activity," he wrote Phil Gialanella in September 1982. "We may have R.J. Reynolds coming our way. . . . I just left a meeting with American Express that was extremely encouraging." But he had to be downbeat about the actual results of all of those sales calls. Most days the paper was running only five or six pages of advertising, and most of that was free.

USA TODAY was not going to launch in New York until April 1983, and that was a problem, too. The executives who made the advertising decisions didn't see the newspaper on newsstands or on commuter trains from Westchester or Long Island, so they found it hard to believe anyone else was reading it.

"Nobody immediately said, 'Fantastic—I can hardly wait to get in

Mark Arnold, left, was a key player on Joe Welty's sales team. A seasoned Gannett advertising executive, Arnold helped outsider Welty learn the ropes of the company.

there,' " Welty says. "Everybody said, 'You guys either got a pair of balls or a hell of a lot of money. Who needs another source of news?' "

If he got beyond that then there was the problem of where USA TODAY fit in the established structure that Madison Avenue understood. Some agency people bought newspapers, some bought television, some bought magazines. "And here we were, saying we were somewhere in between," Welty says.

The sheep were all stuck on the same point: "What really concerns me is the niche that you fill," said Allen Banks during a USA TODAY sales call reported in Madison Avenue magazine. Banks, a senior vice president at Dancer Fitzgerald Sample, added, "I don't think there is a niche for this paper. I don't see anything unique in it like a Wall Street Journal."

Welty had a good answer. "As to our niche, take this important businessman. We think he has interests other than just corporate finance. Our twelve pages of sports every day will make this a very different product, not to mention the use of color. There are a lot of people who will get all the business news they need and want in USA TODAY plus a heck of a lot they won't find in The Journal."

If anything worked to sell Madison Avenue, it usually was the Partnership Plan—an offer of free advertising for the first 6½ months. "It was a revolutionary idea," Welty says. "Almost all new magazines have some going-in offer to make them attractive; this one made it almost risk-proof for the advertiser." One ad executive told Business Week it was "one of the best business plans for advertisers I've seen."

"Try it," Welty would say. "What do you have to lose?" They still wouldn't budge.

Welty did everything he could think of to keep Madison Avenue thinking about USA TODAY. Every time the newspaper started in a new market he had box breakfasts delivered to two hundred top agency people in New York. Each box contained orange juice, a croissant, and instant coffee, plus that day's paper and a USA TODAY coffee mug with the name of the latest market on it. Before long, desks on Madison Avenue had five USA TODAY mugs on them—but Welty had zip. During the early weeks, his people had to beg advertisers to let USA TODAY run their ads for free.

"Part of our pitch was 'Gannett has the resources to see this through,'" said Pat Haegele, who sold ads for USA TODAY. "They were not familiar with Gannett. Madison Avenue people buy media based on what they believe first, and then they get into researching what the rest of the country thinks. As New Yorkers, they figured The New York Times and The Wall Street Journal were all they needed."

Welty got his first circulation numbers on October 14, 1982. Neuharth announced that USA TODAY's circulation was 221,978 in its first four markets. In one month, it had surpassed its year-end goal of 200,000. That sounded good, but what many people on Madison Avenue were waiting for was audited circulation—numbers verified by the Audit Bureau of Circulations.

ABC is the industrywide authority on newspaper circulation; it was formed in 1914, when advertisers, ad agencies, and newspapers needed to verify circulation claims. ABC's auditors use strict rules, and their numbers are gospel. Those audited circulation numbers are crucial to newspapers and magazines, because advertising rates are based on them.

Unfortunately for USA TODAY, the audit bureau would not audit a new publication until it had been in business for one year. To verify its own numbers, USA TODAY hired the respected accounting firm of Price Waterhouse. That was not enough to make the numbers credible, for

Pat Haegele was one of the top sales representatives for USA TODAY. She later became publisher of USA WEEKEND, Gannett's Sunday magazine.

Madison Avenue or Wall Street. Or for publishers of other newspapers, who just couldn't believe USA TODAY could sell so many copies.

Joe Fuchs, an analyst of media stocks for Kidder, Peabody, remembers it was a circular argument. "If there wasn't any circulation, there sure as hell wasn't going to be any advertising. You had a continuing litany of Madison Avenue people saying 'No way' and a continuing litany of your fellow newspaper publishers saying 'The thing is a flaming disaster.' All the people at Gannett could say was, 'Believe us, believe us.' That really put a big focus on the ABC audit."

Simmons Market Research studied USA TODAY's readers, and reported in December they were the well-paid, well-educated people the newspaper needed if it was going to survive. Sixty-eight percent of its readers had attended college, a higher percentage than the readers of Time, Newsweek, People, or Sports Illustrated. Forty-three percent of USA TODAY's readers made more than thirty-five thousand dollars a year, again outpacing those magazines.

That reader profile—"upscale" in advertising lingo—helped. There was an increase in travel, computer, and corporate image advertising. "For people who wanted to throw stones, that took a lot of stones away from them," Paul Kessinger says. "But a lot of the agencies were still waiting for the lead sheep."

Even when Welty found a client who was willing to spend money in USA TODAY, he could not always get Neuharth to approve the ads. In December 1982 Welty worked out a deal with Radio Shack for a twenty-eight-page campaign that would run on seven Tuesdays from January until May. The first Tuesday Radio Shack would run one full-page ad, the second Tuesday two full-page ads in a row, and so on until on the seventh Tuesday, when it would run seven consecutive full-page ads. That meant some sections would have to be skimpy, others fat. Neuharth said no, turning down $250,000 in revenue.

In a private memo to Phil Gialanella, Neuharth wrote: "A very wise journalist-publisher once said, 'No single advertiser or group of advertisers is as important to the success of a new publication as the total reader audience.' I believe that; I said it. All of us at USA TODAY must believe and/or practice it." He pointed out that during the months when those ads would run, USA TODAY would be seeking hundreds of thousands of new readers in eight major new markets. "Discombobulation of the reader product during that period would be especially damaging long term. This is an easy-to-read, easy-to-find newspaper, with a place for everything and everything in its place—both news and advertising. USA TODAY is different. That's why it sells. We'll pass up the $250,000 revenue and protect the hold we have on present readers and must get on new ones."

Later, Welty thought he could sell the bottom of the weather page for a cigarette ad. Gialanella told him Neuharth would never approve it. Welty pressed. Finally Gialanella said, "I've got the feeling you don't believe what I have to go through on these ads. We'll go in together to see Neuharth, and I'll show you."

Welty flew down to Washington and pitched the weather page ad. Neuharth threw a fit: "You're ruining the newspaper. I won't have it."

All of this kept the pressure on Welty; it had been there from the beginning. At the very first dinner for the advertising sales staff in May 1982, Neuharth stood on the podium and said that he and his secretaries had been tearing advertisements out of the newsweeklies and business magazines for weeks. These were likely prospects. He reached under the lectern and pulled out a stack of color ads. "Here they are, Joe," Neuharth said, and dumped the tearsheets on Welty, who was sitting at the table beneath him.

As his friends at USA TODAY used to say, Joe Welty was in the trenches before they were dug.

The pressure was on Neuharth too, because the meter was running—USA TODAY's losses were mounting fast.

The October circulation number—222,000—satisfied the single "escape hatch" requirement in the business plan. If the year-end goal of 200,000 had not been met, they would have had to think about folding. Instead, circulation was well ahead of expectations, so Neuharth moved up the launch schedule. In November 1982 they moved into the Seattle and San Francisco markets, several weeks earlier than planned. Neuharth began saying: "Everything is ahead of our expectations—circulation, advertising, and of course, our losses." It was very similar to what he had said when TODAY in Florida started.

In the fourth quarter of 1982, Gannett reported its sixty-first consecutive quarter of comparative earnings gains. But the gain in net earnings was only 2 percent. USA TODAY's losses for 1982—$41 million—had significantly cut into Gannett's profits, nearly breaking its record run.

In the first quarter of 1983, the company managed to eke out another 2 percent net earnings gain, but that was remarkable since by then, USA TODAY was losing a little more than $10 million a month before taxes.

Nevertheless, during 1982 Gannett's stock recovered. Joe Fuchs, the Kidder Peabody analyst, was one of the first to recognize that Wall Street had overreacted to the impact of USA TODAY; he told his clients to buy the stock. Fuchs reported that Gannett was not betting the company, and the stock was very attractive when priced in the 30s, no matter what happened to USA TODAY. Other analysts issued similar opinions. On December 15, 1982, exactly one year after Gannett had decided to publish the newspaper, the stock closed at 60¼, double its low point in March.

Late in 1982, in an article for the bulletin of the American Society of Newspaper Editors, Neuharth asked the multimillion-dollar question: "Can all of this be brought together to make USA TODAY work as the nation's first nationwide, general-interest daily newspaper? Can we add a meaningful new dimension to journalism, give the industry a winner, pay the rent and return a profit? Only time and the readers can answer."

CHAPTER FOURTEEN

7-day/24-hour service

USA TODAY's debut in New York City on April 11, 1983, was the Big Apple of newspaper promotions, the launch party to end all launch parties. This upstart new newspaper had played well in the provinces, and now its managers desperately wanted to make it in the big time. They rented Radio City Music Hall, hired Dick Cavett as master of ceremonies, brought in the Rockettes to kick up their heels, and invited the obligatory mix of political leaders, celebrities, and advertising executives.

Vince Spezzano, who had polished his promotional skills at TODAY in Florida, planned this party, and he didn't miss a trick. There was patriotic music from the Wurlitzer organ; the Rockettes wore red, white, and blue costumes and danced to the "Stars and Stripes Forever" and then changed to white tuxedos and sang "I Love New York." Uncle Sams and "Samettes" mingled with the crowd, handing every guest a red "Big Apple" pin with USA TODAY written on it, while USA TODAY's radio-controlled robot cruised about the room.

The buffet was lavish and the liquor flowed. The revelers nibbled on roast wild boar from the "Hawaiian Luau," rare roast beef from the "South Dakota Picnic," and seafood from the "Grand Central Station Oyster Bar." As usual, money was no object: The new newspaper paid twenty thousand dollars for the hall, seventy thousand dollars for food and liquor, and ten thousand dollars for Dick Cavett.

To get opinion leaders talking about the newspaper, USA TODAY sponsored launch parties in many markets that were equal to the first gala held by the Capitol reflecting pool. It also touted its arrival with an

Radio City Music Hall's Rockettes kick up their heels at the New York City launch party.

Hundreds of New York City's business and political leaders packed Radio City Music Hall for USA TODAY's debut. Adweek magazine reported that Neuharth worked the crowd like a campaigning politician.

Phil Gialanella was worried the New York launch would be even tougher than Philadelphia.

ad campaign that saturated local television, radio, billboards, and newspapers. The high costs of this promotional blitz upset some insiders, like Gannett director J. Warren McClure. "I went to the Miami launch party," he recalls. "I had never seen such extravagances in my life. And I said to myself, 'My God, how can we afford this? Are we doing this in all of the cities?'"

Some journalists left behind at Gannett's local newspapers were offended, too. Mike Meyers, then a reporter at the Rochester Democrat & Chronicle, complained that his newspaper had given nine loaners to USA TODAY—and seven of them stayed. "They are spending money like water down there," he said of USA TODAY, "and profits from the [local] papers are directly subsidizing it."

Mayor Ed Koch stopped by the New York City party long enough to demonstrate his renowned political adaptability. Earlier that day he had complained bitterly to reporters about the sudden appearance of the USA TODAY newsracks on New York's streets. "It is outrageous that anyone would come in and dig up our sidewalks and bolt in our sidewalks," Koch told The Associated Press. Pat Cohen of the city's consumer affairs department added: "Nobody gave them permission. They just did it." Working around the clock, Frank Vega and his launch team had installed thousands of the boxes over the weekend.

Once inside Radio City Music Hall, where he was surrounded by USA TODAY and Gannett executives, Koch changed his tune: "The song says if you can make it here, you can make it anywhere. Any newspaper that can bolt down seventeen hundred newspaper boxes overnight without us knowing about it is here to stay."

A few days later, Koch jokingly told John Quinn at a civic breakfast that USA TODAY owed him a million dollars for the attention he had called to the newspaper's New York City debut.

Neuharth was upbeat about USA TODAY's first day in the Big Apple. The prolific writer of "Orange Meanies" was not above passing out compliments when he saw things done right. He wrote the editors: "Today's edition of USA TODAY was the best-planned, best-written, best-edited and best-presented in our seven month history. I predict the Big Apple will love it."

Neuharth was wrong. New York City was turning out to be the toughest market for the new newspaper to crack. New Yorkers were not used to seeing newsracks on their sidewalks and Koch's criticism had struck a sympathetic chord; they did not like stepping around all

*Master of Ceremonies Dick Cavett
called the new newspaper a "daring
and innovative venture."*

*Although he criticized the proliferation
of USA TODAY's newsracks, New York
Mayor Edward Koch was later a
guest columnist for the newspaper. He
wrote about the 1984 Democratic
Convention and New York "subway
vigilante" Bernhard Goetz.*

these strange boxes on street corners. "People looked like pinballs bouncing off of our racks," Vega recalls. Spezzano told the press the boxes had been bolted to the sidewalks because otherwise they might "topple over and injure someone." That creative explanation was a new one on Vega, who was just trying to keep college kids from stealing them for their dorm rooms.

Some New York City newspaper unions joined the chorus of complaints. "We woke up one morning and it was like mushrooms growing all over the city," said George MacDonald of the mailers' union. "If something isn't done, you will have automatic vending machines of every sort all over the place." Koch wanted to require a newsrack fee, but later agreed to guidelines that regulated placement. The mailers sued to ban additional racks, but their lawsuit was quickly thrown out. USA TODAY's victory encouraged other newspapers—from The New York Times to Jewish Week—to put even more newsracks on New York's streets.

The same destructive games that were played in Philadelphia got an even longer run in New York. Drivers ran over newsracks with big trucks; people set off M-80s inside racks and the boxes opened up like flowers. "In Queens or Brooklyn we could find whole lines of them— fifteen in a row—blown up," said David Mazzarella, who became general manager in New York in August 1983. The company estimated that more than one thousand newsracks had been destroyed or damaged in Philadelphia and New York over the summer. The racks cost $225 each; that was another $225,000 down the tubes.

Vandals used black markers to write "This is not news" on boxes on Fifth Avenue. Red and white stickers that said, "This is a nonunion paper," were pasted on many boxes.

Right after the New York launch, Don Derle, a USA TODAY circulation manager, got an anonymous phone call. The male caller warned that Derle was working for "a scab newspaper" and that USA TODAY newsracks were going to be destroyed. "He told me to take care of my health and be careful when the paper is delivered," Derle said. But there were no assaults on the newspaper's employees, and no delivery trucks were run off the road.

There was, however, a whole lot of stealing going on. It was common for half of the quarters from a box to be "missing" when the receipts were added up. Thieves would insert one quarter in an honor box, take a bunch of papers, and sell them for a profit. USA TODAY's managers caught one man on Park Avenue who was selling stolen newspapers that were supposed to have been delivered to homes; they still had the address labels on them.

A lot of people mistakenly thought USA TODAY was a "Moonie" newspaper. Just before USA TODAY launched in New York, the News World, controlled by followers of the Rev. Sun Myung Moon's Unification Church, changed its name to The New York City Tribune. Its managers may have been trying to benefit from all the attention the national newspaper was getting. Neuharth saw a reader ask for USA TODAY and the newsstand operator replied: "That damn Moonie newspaper? I keep it behind the counter."

Eventually, "Published by Gannett" decals were placed on all USA TODAY newsracks to promote the corporation and to help clear up confusion. Also, the Gannett G, a corporate symbol, was dropped from the upper left-hand corner of the front page. Neuharth was afraid it looked too much like the Moon and might cause some readers to think the newspaper was linked to the Moonies.

USA TODAY had to succeed in New York. If advertising decision-makers did not see people reading the newspaper, they would never buy ads in it. It was crucial for the new newspaper to be seen in New Yorkers' hands—on commuter trains, on the subway, and on Madison Avenue. Back in 1980 at the Cocoa Beach cottage, Paul Kessinger and Frank Vega had predicted that USA TODAY's appearance in New York City would be a big step toward success. They thought New Yorkers would stop reading the New York Post's sports pages and switch to USA TODAY's. That didn't happen; the newspaper's progress in New York was painfully slow.

The 1981 business plan predicted that USA TODAY would sell 227,000 copies in New York by the end of 1983. In September 1983, excluding the Gannett markets in Westchester County, New York, and Bridgewater, New Jersey, it was selling only 45,000 copies a day. "Everybody thought it was a disaster," says David Mazzarella, who had been an Associated Press correspondent in New York and editor of the Rome Daily American in Italy before joining Gannett. Mazzarella attended several New York City "focus groups," where the USA TODAY people sat behind a one-way mirror and listened to readers talk about the newspaper. "It was disheartening," he says. "People would say, 'Well, I read it sometimes. But on the subway I always make sure I carry it inside something else so no one can see I'm reading it.'"

New Yorkers were parochial; they were quite happy with the newspapers they had. The New York Times and the Daily News were well-edited papers and, despite sensationalism on the news pages, the Post had good New York sports coverage. This audience was not the mobile population USA TODAY was aimed at; many New Yorkers had never lived anywhere else and were not even that interested in the rest of the country. During the fall of 1983, Mazzarella says he saw only two people carrying USA TODAY on the streets of New York. He was distributing two thousand complimentary copies a day to advertising executives and potential advertisers, trying to get people hooked on it.

Things were so discouraging that the competition was not even worried. Like other New Yorkers, they treated USA TODAY's debut with lofty disdain. "We plan no special response," said Leonard Harris, a spokesman for The New York Times. "USA TODAY does not provide the in-depth, international coverage that our readers require."

In other cities, USA TODAY was doing well with readers. In February 1983, Neuharth reported that circulation reached 531,000—"nicely ahead of projections." By then USA TODAY was available in Washington–

Baltimore, Atlanta, Minneapolis–St. Paul, Pittsburgh, Seattle–
Portland, San Francisco–Sacramento, Houston–San Antonio, Denver,
and Los Angeles–San Diego. And besides New York and Philadelphia,
it was going full speed ahead with launches into Detroit and Chicago in
the spring of 1983.

Behind the rosy public statements, there were big problems. In late
March, Phil Gialanella wrote Joe Welty, the ad director, a memo about
their worries. The big accounts were not buying, and Gialanella
thought Welty was accepting too many cheap-looking ads from fly-by-
night advertisers. "We've got some crap in those pages," Gialanella
said, "some of which we are not going to get paid for and some of which
we have a responsibility to our readers not to carry." Gialanella was
also afraid that when the free advertising offer expired in April and USA
TODAY began charging full rates, the number of ad pages would
plummet.

"Joe, we ain't there!" Gialanella wrote Welty. "We have a hell of a
shortfall and there's no way we're going to pick it up within the next
three or four weeks."

Gialanella was right. There was no way ad executives were going to
flock to this newspaper after only seven months. "USA TODAY will be a
reckonable force when it hits a million circulation and has an ABC
audit," said Joe Magier, a print media supervisor for the ad agency
SSC&B, reflecting Madison Avenue's wait-and-see stance.

Neuharth had expected the advertisers' reluctance, but circulation
was proving to be a huge management headache. He told the Los
Angeles Times: "It's too damn early, and this is too big a country to
claim success after just four or five months." He was well aware of
what his secret rack checker had found: late arrival of the paper at
airports, damaged racks, high numbers of returns. And Neuharth had
checked enough racks personally to know that they could do a much
better job of managing circulation. They would have to if the newspaper was going to survive.

In April, Neuharth asked key executives to recommend possible
management changes. One had been made already. At Doug
McCorkindale's suggestion, Dick Rumsey was brought in from the
Westchester newspapers to try to straighten out the computer and
organizational mess in the business office. Rumsey was an experienced financial manager, and Chuck Schmitt, who had been responsible for the office since 1981, became his deputy.

Circulation's leadership was a knottier problem. Frank Vega had

done a superb job of getting USA TODAY on the streets; there was probably no one in the country who could have done it better. But Vega
needed help in managing and building circulation. And now circulation's
mission—which Neuharth originally had defined as only single-copy
sales—was rapidly changing. Readers were begging to get home and
office delivery of USA TODAY, but they could not because of computer
glitches and mismanagement.

"I have thoroughly enjoyed reading your paper," U.S. Rep. Daniel
Mica of Florida wrote Neuharth, "and can't wait for home delivery!"
About the same time, Siegfried Wolff of Milwaukee wrote: "I am sorry
to say this, but unless there is a considerable improvement in the delivery system, I am afraid USA TODAY will become the USA of YESTERDAY.
Maybe Washingtonians are arriving at their offices between 9 and 12
every day, but Milwaukeeans are early risers and like to have their
paper with their morning coffee between 6 and 7."

In a memo to Neuharth, Gialanella put it this way: "With the shift in
your marketing plans, I honestly don't know if Vega can do the job you
require to be done in *home delivery, office delivery, hotels, airlines,* and
Newspaper in the Classroom." They needed different players to get
that done. Vince Spezzano sent a memo to Neuharth describing Vega's
role this way: "Frank is one of our strongest and weakest links. He has
great ability and tremendous drive but an ego that makes his job most
vulnerable."

While Vega had moved mountains to launch USA TODAY, there had
been complaints that Gannett people in the field could not get him on
the phone to answer questions. And since he had no strong deputy, it
was hard to get help from anyone else. "I was a benevolent dictator in
my department," Vega says.

When Vega was on the road for weeks bolting newsracks, problems
festered. Some Gannett newspaper publishers felt Vega was not eager
to cooperate. If USA TODAY was going to succeed, it needed all the help
it could get from other Gannett newspapers. Vega did not have a good
sense of that: "I thought that my job and sole responsibility was to
launch USA TODAY and you know, fuck Gannett," he says. He concedes
he sometimes overplayed the benevolent dictator role. "I was getting
a little too big for my britches."

Ever since the research in the Cocoa Beach cottage, Neuharth
would periodically catch Vega in some bar where they would talk business. In one of these middle-of-the-night bull sessions after one glass

of wine too many, Vega informed Neuharth that he was too close to USA TODAY. You're interfering too much, Vega said, and you're not the greatest manager in the world, either. "You need to step back and let us operating executives run things." Corporate politics was not one of Vega's strong suits.

As their circulation and advertising troubles mounted, Neuharth appointed an ad hoc committee mainly composed of Gannett editors and publishers to study USA TODAY's business operations. "This will give us a 'new set of eyes' to make suggestions for possible improvements," he said.

By the spring of 1983, Neuharth had decided to give circulation to someone else. This was the first of many changes in circulation's leadership, and some Neuharth advisers felt the high turnover bordered on panic management. He brought in Paul Flynn, the publisher of the Fort Myers (Fla.) News-Press, who also had supervised fourteen newspapers in the Southeast as a regional president. Flynn had started out as a sportswriter and in the 1960s had been Vince Spezzano's assistant in the promotion department at the Rochester newspapers, but had never worked in circulation. Neuharth told Flynn he would be an executive vice president of USA TODAY and direct circulation. Vega would stay on as a consultant for the fall launches and then move to another assignment. Neuharth let Flynn break this unexpected news to USA TODAY's number one street fighter.

"I brought Vega up to my office on the seventeenth floor," Flynn recalls. "I closed the door because I thought he was going to scream, and he did. He called me every four-letter word you can think of; he questioned my heritage in about four different languages. He said, 'My God, I put my whole life into this. Instead of turning me into a second-class citizen, you ought to make me the boss.' "

The next day, an embittered Vega made a few phone calls and found out, Flynn says, that "just about every newspaper company in the country wanted him." Neuharth called Vega and got him calmed down: "You've got a great future with Gannett," Neuharth said, "but it's time for USA TODAY to move from a launch mentality to a management mentality."

At the same time—April 1983—Neuharth announced two other important promotions. John Curley, USA TODAY's first editor, was named president of the Gannett Newspaper Division; that moved him further along a fast track to eventually succeed Neuharth as Gannett's chief executive officer. John Quinn was named editor of USA TODAY, while retaining his role as Gannett's chief news executive.

Back in 1981 when he had worked on the Sports section of the prototype, Dick Thien used to ask, "Where's the white knight? We need the white knight." He was talking about John Quinn. Thien and others feared that if Quinn was not there every day, USA TODAY would place too much emphasis on feature news, soft news, and not enough emphasis on hard news, the news of the day. "Some of us had a strong feeling that the paper would be too soft if the white knight didn't ride in and get rid of some of the mush," Thien says. "And sure enough, it got a harder edge once he was there full time."

A frequent criticism Quinn and Neuharth had to battle in 1983 was the claim Gannett was "milking its papers dry" to start USA TODAY. Some of the grousing came from Gannett news staffers who felt their newspapers had been stripped of their best people by USA TODAY's loaner program. At The San Bernardino Sun, for example, Editor Wayne Sargent wore a button which said, "Free the San Bernardino Seven"—his loaners at USA TODAY. Some staffers complained that Gannett was squeezing local news budgets to pay for Neuharth's pet project.

Neuharth rebutted that charge often, once telling the Columbia Journalism Review: "USA TODAY hasn't hurt the papers at all. It has hurt the feelings in some newsrooms. There are two categories of unhappy people—those who hoped to be tapped and weren't, and those who aren't outstanding performers, those who have devoted more time to Newspaper Guild [union] activities. I don't believe the reader [of Gannett newspapers] has suffered just because the talent is down here."

Most Gannett editors agreed that while their newspapers were sometimes short-staffed, many loaners who decided that USA TODAY was not for them returned home refreshed and recharged. "It taught me how good a story could be in five inches or less," said Ken Paulson, a loaner who went back to the Bridgewater Courier-News to be managing editor. "It taught me the value of precision editing."

Jerry Laws, who was a loaner at USA TODAY before he left to join The Houston Post, told a reporter that his Rosslyn reporting experience "got me in the habit of asking for a multitude of details. I was the kind who tended to get certain elements, and once I got them I said, 'Okay.

Thanks.' But the USA TODAY editors wanted so many 'color' details. Now I get all the little things."

"I learned more about editing in a short time at USA TODAY than I did in fifteen years in the newspaper business," says Anne Saul, who worked on the A section and later became a managing editor at Gannett News Service.

To maintain its string of record profits while developing USA TODAY, Gannett had to keep budgets tight at its local newspapers. It also raised local advertising rates faster than it would have if there had been no USA TODAY. But the sacrifices the local papers made were relatively mild, considering the scale of the national newspaper. Don Hatfield, then publisher of Gannett's Huntington, West Virginia, newspapers, told a reporter in 1983, "Not one penny in our newsroom has suffered over USA TODAY."

John Quinn points out that although the Rochester newspapers sent twenty-six people to USA TODAY, in 1982 its editor still had twenty more people than Quinn had when he edited the same newspapers in the late 1960s. "He still had his own theater critic, who occasionally reviewed movies that were also being reviewed by Gannett News Service," Quinn says. "So my heart did not bleed too badly for folks who didn't have everything they wanted. The world is full of journalistic martyrs who are throwing themselves on the sword of management."

While editors outside Gannett were deriding USA TODAY as junk-food journalism, some of these same editors were quietly copying USA TODAY's most popular features. Edward Sears, managing editor of the Atlanta Journal & Constitution, had said reading USA TODAY "is nice, if you like reading the phone book." But, The Wall Street Journal pointed out on January 28, 1983, "This didn't stop him from swiping USA TODAY's splashy, colorful weather map format. The Atlanta papers also hit the streets with almost as much color as USA TODAY."

To illustrate its story on USA TODAY, The Journal ran a small map that showed the markets where the new newspaper was available—an unusual departure for the business newspaper. The story said:

> USA TODAY, Gannett Co.'s flashy new national daily, is becoming the Rodney Dangerfield of the newspaper business. It gets no respect from its rivals, at least for its news content. But as a commercial entry it is being taken more seriously.

As the color-splashed, graphics-laden new paper unrolls its distribution across the country, editors and business managers at some local dailies—though by no means all—are responding with more aggressive sales tactics and changes in news treatment, handling and display. These changes are making them look a little more like USA TODAY and a lot less like their old selves.

In terms of sales tactics, the Chicago Tribune asked its employees to call a special telephone number—"Hotline Today"—if they saw USA TODAY employees giving away free samples, making special home delivery offers, or opening new sales locations. The first employee to report a USA TODAY sales effort would get a cash award and a chance to win a Caribbean cruise.

And, as The Journal had said, after USA TODAY began publishing, newspapers across the country dramatically changed the way they handled and displayed news. The Washington Post added sports coverage and later redesigned the paper, making it easier to find various features. The Pittsburgh Post-Gazette got later sports scores to subscribers. The Miami Herald expanded weather coverage, beefed up its state-by-state news roundup, and improved color reproduction. The Chicago Sun-Times started a "Sports Facts" feature. Newsday on Long Island added a blue color logo, began printing full color, and expanded space for sports. The Richmond Times-Dispatch increased its use of graphics. The Dallas Morning News began running a full page of weather news and began running large, complex graphics. The San Francisco Examiner expanded the amount of space it gave sports. The Baltimore Sun started using more charts and graphs to illustrate stories. The New York Times began running a much larger weather map and added weather news, and eventually redesigned the front of its metropolitan news section.

Neuharth privately told associates that USA TODAY had become "the most imitated newspaper in the country." He saw that as a challenge. In a memo to editors, he said, "Imitation may be the best form of flattery, but . . . we must monitor closely all changes that other newspapers are making and see to it that we continue doing a better job than they can do."

J. Taylor Buckley, the editor of USA TODAY's Money section, told a California editors' conference in the spring of 1983: "The same newspaper editors who call us McPaper have been stealing our McNuggets."

Tom Holbein, who had studied USA TODAY's readers for Belden Associates, a Dallas consulting firm, told the same editors that the new national newspaper had become an important influence in American journalism. "The publication is called shallow, flimsy, and a rehash of TV news," Holbein said, "But we see newspapers scrambling to adopt USA TODAY-type capsulizing, indexing, and, of course, the weather map." He added that readers' reactions to USA TODAY were "much more positive than negative and higher than we usually find for local dailies."

Warren H. Phillips, the publisher of The Wall Street Journal and chief executive of its parent, Dow Jones, wrote a letter in the spring of 1983 to the trade magazine Editor & Publisher:

> Here's one newspaperman who believes the editors dumping so freely on USA TODAY should think again. It is a skillful execution of a well-thought-out concept. It offers readers a smorgasbord of lively reading of the People magazine, Money magazine, and Sports Illustrated genre, combined with a sum-up of the hard news tailored to a great many readers' interests and the tastes of a television generation. Is this necessarily bad? Does this not fill some readers' needs?
>
> The jury is still out on USA TODAY, the jury being American readers. In the meantime, editors so quick to heap scorn should think again whether they live in glass houses; circulation figures in recent years of most American newspapers, including those of some of the editors sounding off the loudest, are nothing to write home about. Are all our readers so satisfied that we can give USA TODAY sermons?
>
> Perhaps all of us in newspaper work ought to take some degree of comfort, even pride, in the fact that new newspapers can be started, that new kinds of newspapers can evolve, and that the American public still seems receptive to more use of the printed word on good old newsprint.

Those positive comments came from the publisher of the newspaper that USA TODAY was challenging for a national audience. Although Phillips urged the critics to "think again," most of them didn't. The negative drumbeat continued. Neuharth would say later, on the newspaper's first anniversary, that the critics "wrote our obit before we were born."

On April 24, 1983, Neuharth announced that in just seven months, USA TODAY had achieved a daily circulation of 1.1 million, making it the third largest daily in the nation. It was also the fastest growing newspaper in history. He timed his promotional announcement to coincide with the American Newspaper Publishers Association convention in New York City, a typical Neuharth touch. Eighty-four percent of its circulation was single-copy sales, 14 percent was home delivery, and 2 percent was mail. Home and office delivery would be stepped up in months to come, he said. The flurry of press releases also said that Phil Gialanella—although he was still eager to return to Hawaii—had been promoted to publisher. Vince Spezzano became USA TODAY's second president. But of course Neuharth was still in charge.

The skeptics questioned the 1 million circulation number. Communications Daily, a Washington trade publication, quoted an anonymous Gannett source as saying the circulation figure was "hyped" and that the real number was 850,000 to 900,000. As USA TODAY approached its first anniversary—September 15, 1983—the Los Angeles Times ran a story suggesting that the 1 million number was too high. The article said that USA TODAY typically suffered "a significant drop-off" of readers a few weeks after it was introduced in a market. John Curley and Neuharth told the skeptical reporter that circulation had "stayed above a million all summer."

But it was a struggle keeping it up there. Sometimes, because the circulation operation was so new and had been so loosely managed, they probably did not know how many copies they were selling. For Flynn, who had been worrying about a home delivery shortfall of a few hundred at his local newspaper in Florida, coming to a venture as complex as USA TODAY was a shock. "All of a sudden you're looking at something that was allegedly selling a million copies a day. I have no idea if we were or we weren't. But shortly after I got here the numbers had slipped to a point where we were very nervous."

In early June, Neuharth held a private meeting with Gialanella, Spezzano, and Flynn. Gialanella took notes on the decisions:

> 1. Neuharth insists that 1 million circulation must be maintained during June, July, and August even if we have to buy the papers. [They could do that by hiring hawkers and push-

ing offers of low-rate subscriptions, but the costs of these
promotions were likely to exceed the revenues.]

2. He further said he was not concerned with the long-
term goals but rather 1983 and 1984.

3. He also said that home delivery and metro markets not
covered by Gannett should be started as quickly and inexpen-
sively as possible.

In short, they were desperate. In the summer of 1983, they had to
go out and get the numbers "almost any way we could," Flynn says.
"Vega and I sat in a room for four hours one day and tried to come up
with everything we could think of."

Vega came up with the "cute kids" program. They would sell copies
of USA TODAY to wholesalers. The wholesalers would recruit a bunch of
kids, sell them the papers, and let the kids sell USA TODAY wherever
they could for whatever they could get. Flynn reminded Vega that this
kind of promotion would not count as audited circulation under Audit
Bureau of Circulations rules. Vega replied: "That's not important
because we're not ABC. We just gotta get the numbers." USA TODAY
had applied for membership in ABC, but it would not audit the new
newspaper until the last quarter of 1983. The "cute kids" promotion
got them a hundred thousand papers a day during that bleak summer.

"Cute kids" was Vega's last circulation brainstorm at USA TODAY.
As Neuharth had told him, he had a bright future with Gannett, and
later in 1983 he became general manager of El Diario-La Prensa, Gannett's Spanish language newspaper in New York City. After helping El
Diario turn a profit, he was promoted to publisher of TODAY in Florida
and president of Gannett South.

In mid-June 1983, the ad hoc committee of Gannett executives
studying circulation gave Neuharth its report. Its conclusion was simple: Circulation was a management disaster, of nationwide propor-
tions.

Across the country, the computer system to keep track of sales was
not working. In some cities, there were no reliable sales records. In
others, the records that did exist were being kept by hand. In many
markets, there were turf battles between the USA TODAY circulators
and those at local Gannett newspapers; sometimes it was hard to tell
they all worked for the same company.

Communications from circulation's head office in Rosslyn were confusing and contradictory. During a two-day period, five different Rosslyn staffers called the branch office in Atlanta to ask for the same piece of information, which already had been sent in a report to head-quarters.

There were no sales goals. Some offices did not know how many returns—unsold copies—there were at the end of each day. In some markets, theft was rampant—27 percent of the receipts in New York. Many people had been hired on the "warm body theory," with no training or skills for the job. Morale was low, too. Of course it was hard to place all of the blame on the employees for their lack of enthusiasm, since their paychecks sometimes arrived late or for the wrong amount because of the continuing chaos in USA TODAY's business office in Rosslyn.

In some markets, there was no cooperation at all between USA TODAY and local Gannett newspapers. For example, the publisher of the Gainesville Times, the Gannett daily outside Atlanta, had banned the USA TODAY Atlanta manager from entering the Times' printing plant. "Executives at the Gainesville Times, especially the publisher and the production director, appeared to be angry with everyone involved with USA TODAY," the report said. "The strongest antag-onisms were aimed at USA TODAY production." Chuck Blevins and his production people had bruised a few egos when they made over the Gainesville press.

Things were so disorganized in Detroit that USA TODAY was available at only three outlets inside that city's huge metropolitan airport. In Wilmington, Delaware, circulation employees of The News Journal had convinced a downtown hotel to buy copies of USA TODAY to give to guests. USA TODAY's people promised to manage the program but never contacted the hotel. The result: three hundred sales a day became zero.

To keep circulation up, Neuharth put new pressures on Gannett publishers. Back in 1981 at a Pumpkin Center brainstorming session, he had asked: "What if you could force circulation? What if you forced twenty thousand into Westchester, fifty thousand into New Jersey, with home delivery to Gannett subscribers?" Back when that was being discussed, the thought was that home delivery in Gannett mar-kets would be a bonus—extra circulation that would attract national advertisers. Now USA TODAY needed it to survive.

In a private memo to Neuharth, Gialanella wrote that USA TODAY had "a deteriorating single-copy circulation sales picture which carries with it a serious revenue shortfall and serious cost overruns." Home delivery was one answer, he suggested, "but it is not going to come easily—and certainly not as rapidly as we might think." Gialanella concluded that their original goal of 1.4 million daily circulation by October was "virtually impossible."

The disarray in the field was to be expected, Gialanella said. It came from the launch mentality. "Fourteen launches in twenty-nine weeks compelled us to Band-Aid a market and move on to the next," he said. The pace had taken its toll on people, too. Spezzano complained the lack of time had made things "crushingly tough." Jack Heselden, the veteran publisher who then was Gannett's deputy chairman, says the disorganization of that first year proves it would have been impossible to introduce USA TODAY everywhere at once. "Who would we have used to do it?" he asked. "We practically killed the people we had."

Gialanella wrote Neuharth that late "press times and irregular delivery have had a devastating effect on sales and costs. We lose sales when we are not available at the earliest hour possible—complete paper or not. As I've said in the past, Al, your paper deserves a fair test in the marketplace, and I honestly don't think you're getting it now."

They were trying to hold the presses until the last possible moment—1:30 A.M. in the East—to get all of the late sports scores and latest possible news into the paper. But many of the truck runs were long distances. For example, to get to the Miami market they were hauling USA TODAY about 150 miles—a three-and-a-half-hour drive—from Gannett's plant in Fort Myers. Both Knight-Ridder and Cox Enterprises, which published competing newspapers, had refused to print USA TODAY at their plants in the Miami area. If the pressrun was delayed for any reason, it was impossible to get USA TODAY to Miami by 6 A.M. And many newspapers that were mailed to remote areas arrived a day late because USA TODAY could not get its copies to the Post Office early enough. Day-late mail delivery was one reason Frank Vega was always pressing for earlier deadlines.

To fix that problem, USA TODAY went to three editions in August 1983. The presses would roll for the first edition at midnight Eastern time; a second edition would run at 1:30 A.M., and the third at 3 A.M. "The purpose of these changes is to make it possible to print, distribute, and sell more newspapers over a longer time frame in more

---

Deadline changes

USA TODAY has changed its deadlines twice to print more newspapers earlier so that additional readers could get same-day mail delivery or home delivery. The final edition is delivered to the central metropolitan areas:

Date	Editions	Press starts
September 15, 1982	one	1:30 A.M.
August 15, 1983	three	midnight, 1:30 A.M., 3 A.M.
November 17, 1986	two	11:45 P.M., with chase*; 2:15 A.M.

*Chase means that the press is briefly stopped so that some pages can be updated.

---

areas," Neuharth said. "We must make certain we do not permit any-one—in editorial, production, circulation—to use the first edition as an excuse for short-cutting readers of other editions. For example, those metro-area readers in the East who have been getting the replated sports final *must* continue to get it."

To attack the circulation glitches, USA TODAY named regional circulation managers for the markets and had them report to nearby Gannett publishers, dismantling Frank Vega's centralized system. As the summer wore on, the pressures mounted on Phil Gialanella. He says he was never sure what to think about USA TODAY's chances: "I didn't know whether it would fail or succeed. I just knew I was going to work my ass off for a year and make it work and then get the hell out of there."

Randy Chorney, then Neuharth's executive secretary, says that sometimes Gialanella thought Neuharth was asking for the impossible: "Phil would constantly say, 'Neuharth's crazy. He's not looking at the facts. He's not looking at reality. He's devising his own little world and he expects it to work. The company doesn't have the resources to do this.'"

All Gialanella wanted was to go back to Hawaii. He resigned four or five times, Chorney says, but Neuharth would not accept his resignation. Once when he tried to quit they got into a shouting match and Gialanella stormed out of Neuharth's office. The chairman chased him down the hall, shouting "Gialanella! Gialanella!" He rushed into

Gialanella's office and tried to slam the door but it was rigged to a hydraulic, remote-control mechanism. No matter how hard Neuharth pushed, he couldn't shut the door. Gialanella started laughing and finally pushed the button to close the door, and they went back to shouting at each other. "Neuharth was on an emotional roller coaster that whole year," says Gialanella, who has since retired from Gannett and joined a competitor, the Honolulu Advertiser Company. "But I gave as good as I got."

As the challenges multiplied, Gialanella realized there was going to be no end to the pressure: "Between the three of us," he wrote in a private memo to Vince Spezzano and Paul Flynn, "it looks as though there will be no interruption to seven-day/twenty-four-hour service."

Those were trying times. When they were having trouble reaching agreement with the unions in the Chicago Tribune plant where USA TODAY was going to print, Neuharth did not have time to be sympathetic. "We're going to launch in Chicago," he told Gialanella. "How are you going to do it? I don't know. But you will launch in Chicago or don't come back here. That's all there is to it." USA TODAY's March 1983 debut in Chicago was a success.

Gialanella was not in perfect health, either. He wrote Neuharth: "As you may know I've been nursing a duodenal ulcer with prescription drugs (Tagamet) for a long time. The most recent examination revealed that if the ulcer did not heal properly with care and medication the upper stomach would have to be removed. Now, I'm afraid, my stomach has paid the toll for the fast pace of the past weeks and months. Bleeding persists despite medication."

It was so serious that sometimes Gialanella had to get up from meetings and go deal with it. He wasn't the only one who was suffering. Nancy Woodhull, the thirty-seven-year-old managing editor for News, got cancer and had to have her uterus removed. Bob Dubill, the top editor at Gannett News Service, replaced her in the newsroom. Woodhull returned to work in May 1983 and went on to head Gannett News Service.

When it comes to stress, Paul Flynn, who headed circulation in 1983, remembers the tense, demanding atmosphere of the weekly operating committee meetings that Neuharth ran. Flynn left USA TODAY in 1984, but says: "I still look at my watch at 9:30 on a Monday morning and shiver."

To get ready, Flynn would come in on Saturday and Sunday and try to think of one hundred things that Neuharth might ask him about at the Monday meeting and develop an answer for each question. Inevitably, Neuharth would bring up the 101st thing. Flynn remembers one meeting when he thought he had done beautifully, had answered all of Neuharth's questions. "Then he stood up and started pacing back and forth, cracking his knuckles. I thought, 'Oh, shit—what has he found now?' He asked me, with no comment about all the good things, 'How come we don't sell papers at the airport in Missoula, Montana?'

"So I said, 'I don't know, Al. I didn't even know they had an airport there.' I was trying to be a little frivolous. That was the wrong thing to say. He climbed down my throat: 'Well, I want you to find out everything there is to know about that kind of airport and I want to know by the end of the day what airports we're in and what airports we're not in.' "

By day's end, Flynn had taken a graduate course in airports. He had discovered that there were 573 airports served by commercial airlines and USA TODAY was available in 80 percent of them—but it could be in 10 percent more and sell some more newspapers, which was Neuharth's point. It turned out Neuharth had given Tom Brokaw a lift back from

The relentless grind took its toll on Paul Flynn and Phil Gialanella. Both suffered from burnout—physical and mental—and eventually asked to leave.

*Although Malcolm Forbes
had big doubts when the
newspaper was launched, less
than a year later, he changed
his mind.*

South Dakota on the Gannett jet, and Brokaw had mentioned he couldn't find the paper in Missoula.

"Those meetings were the most stressful thing I've ever gone through," Flynn says. Yet in the midst of turning the screws, Neuharth could be sensitive. Once Flynn was planning to fly to St. Louis, where his daughter was going to have major surgery. In the middle of a meeting, Neuharth's secretary passed Flynn a note, telling him that Neuharth had arranged for a corporate jet to take him. When he got to St. Louis, Gannett executives from regional offices were there to help. "I had never even mentioned the operation to him," Flynn later told a reporter. "Neuharth handled all that himself. He is someone who never forgets what you do for him."

In August 1983, twenty months after he had signed Phil Gialanella up for USA TODAY, Neuharth finally let him return to Honolulu as publisher. In the press release Neuharth said that Gialanella "effectively quarterbacked the first year's successful launchings. We're grateful to him and pleased to honor his request to return to the Paradise of the Pacific." Neuharth named Jack Heselden, Gannett's deputy chairman, as USA TODAY's new publisher.

Even in USA TODAY's darkest days, there were always breaks in the clouds. In the summer of 1983, Malcolm S. Forbes, the editor-in-chief of Forbes magazine, made USA TODAY a prominent item in his Fact and Comment column. "HERE TODAY, AND IT WILL BE TOMORROW," the headline said.

Can you think of any newspaper anywhere, anytime, that from birth has enjoyed such phenomenal, near-instant success as USA TODAY?

When Gannett CEO Al Neuharth first got started on this project, I was among the multitudes who thought there was no way it could succeed. How wrong (again) can one be?!? The extraordinary and profuse use of color by the staff of this new daily is jolting a new awareness of graphics' importance in hundreds of editorial offices and news-printing plants. Its colorful, detailed presentation of weather in map and word has magnetic, countrywide appeal. Its sports section is winning coast-to-coast kudos. USA TODAY has captured a major segment of the higher-income itinerants who are constantly winging it. Except for Al Neuharth, who'd have thought it?

When the space shuttle Challenger *exploded, editors decided to tell the story on page one with one very large graphic.* USA TODAY *showed again it was "different," responding to a big story by using words and pictures instead of huge headlines.*

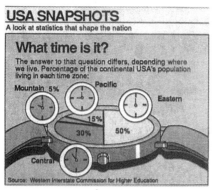

Snapshots were one of the innovations that evolved from Ron Martin's brainstorming sessions to find stories "about us." The snapshot was introduced in April 1982, on page one of Prototype III. Just before launch, Neuharth decided there should be four snapshots in the newspaper—one for every section front.

Originally, many snapshots were not timely, but later more and more emphasis was put on pegging snapshots to late-breaking news. The Hagler-Leonard snapshot ran on the day of the fight.

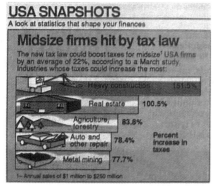

In five years, USA TODAY's graphics staff has produced approximately 5,500 snapshots, including some that were changed late at night, between editions.

All four sections have researchers who gather information for snapshots. The data are then edited by copy editors, and each snapshot is assigned to a graphic artist.

This "obit portrait," of Paul "Bear" Bryant, the legendary University of Alabama football coach, ran on the cover of the Sports section when Bryant died January 26, 1983. The illustration was done on deadline and took six hours to complete.

Every day the weather page includes an explanatory graphic that tells the reader more about some meteorological development. Here are two examples: One that explains smog and a second one on unusual temperature trends.

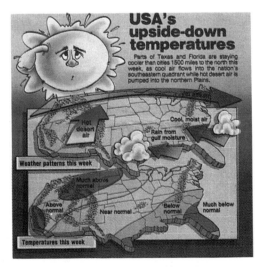

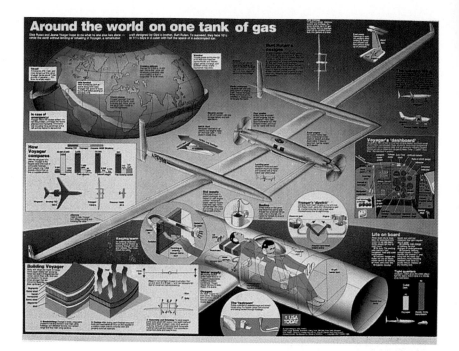

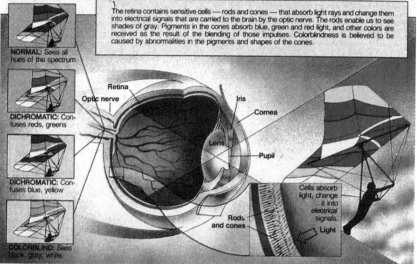

The Voyager *and color blindness graphics are examples of taking a complex topic and presenting it in easy-to-understand form.* The Voyager *drawing was two pages wide—a "double-truck"—and was prepared weeks in advance.*

BELFAST, MAINE: Harold Prentice, 32, wh speezes, lives with his wife Alice and their 9-year-old daughter Cora in a two-room shack. Heat comes from a stove fashioned from a barrel. His doctor tells him to work only 2-3 hours a day, but Prentice says "no blame around will hire me for that. If food stamps run out at month's end, the family gets help from a community program. Says his wife, 35: "We're just barely making it by the skin of our teeth.

THE FOE IS HUNGER

SEARCH FOR DAILY BREAD IS A CONSTANT STRUGGLE

By Denise Kalette
USA TODAY

Hunger exists in every state — from Maine to Mississippi, in cities and in hamlets.

Far from the political posturing over the budget issue are the quiet struggles of those who have not enough to eat or feed their children — or who can do so only with sacrifice and government aid.

While hunger proves difficult to measure, the poverty in which many families live is not. More than 34 million Americans live in poverty — 13 percent of the population. Hurt most often are the old, the young, blacks, single mothers.

Nearly half of all black children and a third of all households headed by women live in poverty.

The chronically poor are trapped in the cycle of illiteracy and lack of opportunity. "It's just simply hard to overcome that system," says Marianna Smith, 67, who cares for three of her grandchildren.

Five million people leave toilets into poverty before 1990 — nasty victims of the mess told. They are the new poor, learning to obtain food stamps and unemployment benefits.

Where there's hunger, you find people who can't pay for heating oil, people who face hard choices between food and shelter, food and fuel.

HINDS COUNTY, MISS.: Zachery, 2, above, eats a stew of beans and raccoon meat. He and siblings Sandra, 3, and Christopher, 4, below, are grandchildren of Marianna Smith, who lives in a wooden, three-room house with cracks wide enough to let the daylight in — a house where she has lived for 40 years. To get by, the Smiths plant beans and peas in their garden and raise chickens. "I try to raise me a hog each year for meat," it's gone "before you can look around," says Smith, 67. She disobeys her doctor's order to avoid strenuous labor. "How am I going to live if I don't? It's rough all right, but that's the only way we are making it," she says. "I strive to help myself." Smith's husband, Wilian, is retired and

draws Social Security. They also receive food stamps. Like many others in the sprawling country near Jackson, the Smiths have no indoor plumbing or running water or furnace, a fireplace provides heat. Surveying her surroundings, Smith says: "I've got figure needs fixing up — I guess some day. The children live with Smith's son, Herbert, who has just found a job in a nearby shack without heat or electricity. Many Washington outreach worker at a community health center, recently discovered that Smith has never seen the glistening shopping center only a few miles away. "I have lived in Mississippi all my life, and the poverty I see today, I've never known," says Washington. "And this is coming from a black Mississippian!"

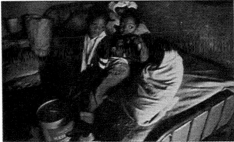

HIBBING, MINN.: Steelworker Tom Daniels, 23, who thought "I'm set for life, was laid off two years ago. Unemployment benefits have stopped. If it weren't for my wife, (Vicki) working, we'd be in pretty tough shape," says Daniels, who has a 2-year-old son, Joel. They get a box of free groceries from a community food shelf once a month "canned food, fruits, sometimes dates and peanut butter.

Hot Harold Prentice, Belfast, Maine "We make sacrifices," he says. "Sometimes maybe, but we make do," he says.

There is a stern pride among the hungry. Often they resist aid others who are some off. It takes up from the Bolton, Mass., Meyer Lawrence Buller, he to emphasize what poverty can mean; no indoor plumbing, a spare drum that volunteers fill through an empty refrigerator. Or a supper of "four bread" — a tried water-four mixture.

"I know they're hungry. Suffering," he says. "They're not going to tell you this."

Tom Smith: "We don't do a lot of kicking and worrying. We take it the best it comes."

WASHINGTON, D.C.: The six children of Catherine Sevier don't go hungry. Food stamps, free school meals and Aid to Families with Dependent Children (totaling $870 a month) keep them all by. In a pinch last month, she delayed paying bills to buy groceries. "A lot of people around me are hungry. In some ways, I'm better off," says the unemployed Sevier, 32. The spread winter front, Alfred, from left, Daniel, Sunny, Katayshia, Tamoya, Wilson, Carol.

COLUMBIA FALLS, MAINE: Tonya, 3, and Derek, Grant, 2, may eat nothing but eggs when the month's $151 in food stamps run out. A government program provides 4½ gallons of milk and 2 dozen eggs monthly for each of Danny and Angie Grant's two children. The food stamps aren't much, says Angie, 18. "You get four people eating. You can't really make it but only lasts about two weeks." Aid to Families with Dependent Children brings another $341 a month. Danny, 21, then is send odd jobs. "the digs worms and sells them. He only gets 6 cents a worm," says Angie, whose parents also were financially strapped. "My mother would go without (food). She always made sure we had something on the table. My mother had to sell things her mother gave her — jewelry." Angie says keeping her children comes before paying other bills.

How you can help . . .

NATIONALLY, some of the agencies that provide information or lobby on the issue include:
- Bread for the World (202-269-0200) is a 45,000-member national Christian citizens lobby.
- Department of Agriculture (703-756-FOOD) is a hotline for people or groups interested in distributing government surplus commodities, such as cheese and butter.
- Food Research and Action Center (202-393-5060) lobbies Congress on hunger issues.

IN YOUR LOCAL AREA, churches and synagogues often donate food. Or you can telephone a local food bank — it will accept donations of food or money, or tell you how to volunteer time. Among organizations in selected cities that are involved in hunger issues, want donations, and need your help or want referrals to others are:
- Albuquerque: 505-247-2052 Atlanta: 404-688-4540 Baltimore: 301-837-9667 Boston: 617-523-7010 Chicago: 312-733-0666 Cleveland: 216-441-1252 Dallas: 214-330-1396 Denver: 303-371-9250 Detroit: 313-923-2552 Houston: 713-926-2700 Kansas City: 816-471-2211 Los Angeles: 213-442-0554 Memphis: 901-345-7663 Miami: 305-945-9402 New York: 212-561-4300 Philadelphia: 215-223-2777 Portland: 503-294-5437 Raleigh, N.C.: 919-834-4227 St. Paul: 612-224-9431 San Francisco: 415-668-5444 Seattle: 206-344-0300 Ext. 225 Washington, D.C.: 202-526-5344
- Second Harvest Network (312-341-1303) has compiled a directory of local food banks across the USA.

Editors used full-color photos to show the plight of the hungry.

THE SUPERFIGHT: SUGAR RAY'S SWEETEST VICTORY

FIGHTLINE

The officials

The scoring, round-by-round

Leonard had right tools to 'boggle history'

By Angelo Dundee
Special for USA TODAY

Earth-shaking upsets

| Feb. 25, 1964 | Oct. 30, 1974 | April 6, 1987 |

Arum shows King no mercy in Promoter-mania

By Jim Brown
USA TODAY

FIGHT SCENE

Show went on and on

Fight replays a hit, too

Arum keeping count

Guerra defends his card, favoring Leonard by 10-2

By Larry Weisman
USA TODAY

> I really believe Sugar Ray Leonard made a beautiful fight.
> — Juis Guerra

Commission: Scoring system fine

The Sports section's extensive, full-color coverage of the Leonard–Hagler fight included a story by trainer Angelo Dundee. Sports pioneered the use of celebrity writers. The first was Bill Veeck who wrote a guest column during the 1982 World Series. Other sections also have used celebrities: Nancy Reagan kept a diary for the A-section during her China visit in April 1984.

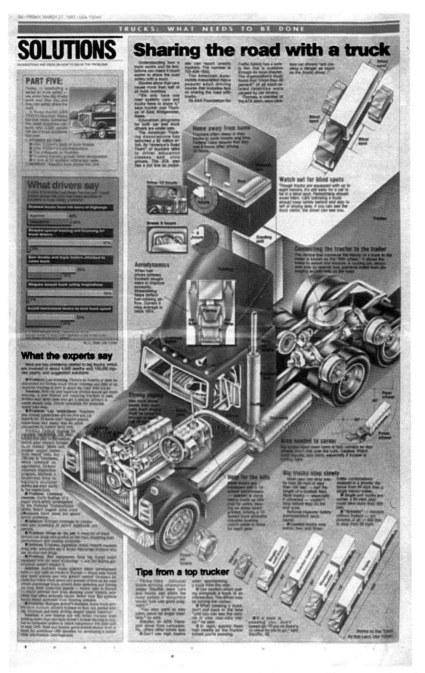

A series on truck safety, "Semi-safe," included a full-page graphic presentation of how a truck works and what life is like for the driver.

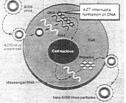

Other newspapers have improved their use of full-color graphics and photos since USA TODAY began publishing, as this Sunday edition of the Seattle newspaper shows. The New York Times drawing on AIDS is an example of the kind of informational graphic now seen frequently on the front pages of newspapers across the country.

CHAPTER FIFTEEN

Paying
the price

Cathleen Black, the peppy, enthusiastic publisher of New York magazine who was a rising star in the business, was working in the garden of her weekend cottage when the phone rang.

It was a summer Saturday in 1983, and her husband answered: "Just something about a delivery," he said. "It's probably the dishwasher repairman," Black said. "I've been waiting thirteen weeks." Minutes later, a long black limousine turned up the driveway of her Lakeville, Connecticut, cottage. The driver said he had come all the way from New York and gotten lost—it had taken him three hours. He handed her a huge basket of herbs from a chic gourmet food store in SoHo; in the middle was a bottle of champagne and a peach-colored envelope.

"It must be from Neuharth," Black said. She had heard about his peach stationery. The letter said: "I still think you ought to think about the Gannett Company. Enjoy your time with your guy and give us a call."

Cathie Black's first brush with the Gannett Company had been early in 1982, when Phil Gialanella and Vince Spezzano were knocking on doors on Madison Avenue looking for an ad director. Black later told an associate that it felt strange to be interviewed by such an odd couple— "the midget and the greaseball," she called them.

"I couldn't believe that these were the two people they had trotted out in New York City," she says. "Phil with his dark glasses, a scarf around his neck, looking like the Mafia, and Vince being Vince. I didn't take them real seriously."

More than a year later, in the summer of 1983, she got a letter from a

243

headhunter. Gannett was looking for someone to head Gannett Media Sales, to sell advertising packages combining USA TODAY, local newspapers, television, radio, and billboards. Black said she wasn't interested. The headhunter did manage to persuade her to have lunch with Madelyn Jennings, Gannett's head of personnel. "I was impressed by Madelyn," Black recalls. "I liked the way she talked about what women could do in Gannett." Now Black was interested in the company, but she wasn't excited about the Gannett Media Sales job.

So she made a suggestion: "The most logical place where I could make a difference would be at USA TODAY, but all of the titles are filled and I understand that."

A couple of weeks later, she met Neuharth at his Waldorf-Astoria suite. He asked: "Is it true that you are now seriously interested in the Gannett Company, that you have finally seen the light?" "Yes," Black said. "Is it true that we have not yet been smart enough to think of the right job?" "Yes," Black said. "Well," Neuharth said, "I think we now have the right job. How would you like to be president of USA TODAY?"

"You could have saved yourself a lot of fancy dinners if you'd talked about that in the beginning," Black said. She mentioned she was considering another possibility: heading a New York ad agency.

Jack Heselden, USA TODAY's new publisher, was at the meeting. He told Black, "That would be interesting, but let me tell you something about this company. You will learn how to run an ad agency in a year or so, but then all that will be ahead of you will be more of the same. The one thing I can guarantee you about the Gannett Company is that you will never be bored, because we are always pushing out in new directions. There will always be something new to learn. You will always be challenged."

That September, Cathie Black was named president of USA TODAY. That title meant she was in charge of advertising; Heselden was in charge of all other business operations, and they both reported to Neuharth. In the press release, Neuharth said she brought a "special dimension" to the newspaper because of her extensive magazine experience, some with start-ups. After graduating from Trinity College in Washington, D.C., Black started by selling classified ads over the phone at Holiday magazine. After working at other magazines, she moved to Ms., where she rose to associate publisher. Then she was named publisher of New York magazine and helped restore it to profitability.

Black had established herself as a rising star, and her USA TODAY appointment was well received by ad executives and the trade press. As Richard Scheinin put it in a profile of her in Washington Journalism Review:

> She has moved steadily to the top of the world of publishing and advertising not by goofing off at lunchtime but by working relentlessly—building an awesome network of friends in advertising, setting world records in the number of sales calls made per day, writing small mountains of follow-up notes and establishing a reputation as an advertising executive who is easy to get along with. In an industry famous for chutzpah and ego, she is a rarity, an ad person other ad people actually seem to like and want to help. She will need to call on all of that goodwill in her new job as president of USA TODAY.

Black, however, was not lacking in chutzpah herself. For example, in the mid-1970s, a reporter once asked her if being a blonde had made a difference for her. "Absolutely," she said. "All my life I've felt better, special because I'm blonde. . . . I used to have a brunette roommate, and even though she was prettier than I, when we walked down the street people looked at me first."

"Is it important to be blonde?" the story asked, and then reported Black's reply: " 'Of course,' she says emphatically. 'Did you ever hear of a brunette described by her hair color? Nobody says 'the brunette publisher.' But they all say 'the blonde publisher.' ' "

To give Black the title that she wanted, Neuharth shifted Spezzano to the Gannett corporate role of senior vice president for communications. The chairman was still struggling to put together the right combination of people to move USA TODAY from a launch mentality to a management mentality. The New York Times reported Black's appointment with the headline: "USA TODAY names third president," and its article noted that she was the third president "in little more than a year."

In October 1983, on her first full day on the job, Black must have wondered how long she was going to last. To fill the Gannett Media Sales opening, Neuharth and John Curley had hired Ray Gaulke, an experienced sales executive who had been president of a New York ad agency, InterMarco. Black and Gaulke were about to get their feet wet together. Neuharth was presiding at a USA TODAY meeting in the thirty-second floor conference room of Gannett's New York offices on Madison Avenue, and it was cold. The chairman liked to keep the thermostat at about sixty degrees.

"The first thing I learned was that a 9 A.M. meeting is really an 8:55 A.M. meeting," Black recalls, "and you damn well better be there on time or they'll be calling to find out where you are. In an ordinary meeting, you'd have small talk for five minutes and somebody would wander in at 9:05 and it wouldn't be a big deal. Not here. Bang, into it, no small talk. Meeting begins."

Gaulke remembers what happened next: "Al burst into the room waving a piece of paper that was apparently an invoice for billing subscribers to USA TODAY. He ran up to the front of the room and said, 'I can't believe that you dumb SOBs could have let this goddamn invoice be created. This is the stupidest thing I've ever seen in my life. I can't believe that you people I pay all this money to and trust have let this go through. This is just the worst thing I've ever seen.'"

Then Neuharth ripped the invoice into pieces, wadded it up, and threw it in the general direction of Paul Flynn, who was then in charge of circulation. "Cathie looked across at me and we didn't say anything," Gaulke recalls, "but our body language was, 'Jesus Christ, we have joined a bunch of maniacs.'"

"It scared us shitless," Black says. "We were like little kids. Ray and I were facing each other, looking straight ahead, not looking to the right or the left, thinking, 'Oh my God, are we going to get yelled at like that?'"

Certainly there was a theatrical element to Neuharth's tirades in those days. Doug McCorkindale, Gannett's chief financial officer, recalls that sometimes after one of those tough meetings Neuharth would step into the limo and say, "Pretty good act, huh?" But Neuharth usually planned his temper tantrums to accomplish a serious purpose.

During the first two or three years of publication, every USA TODAY management meeting was crucial. "You had to be right on the edge of your chair because every single little item was critical," Editor John Quinn says. "Everything—from what we were putting on the top of page one to whether we were sending complimentary copies to key advertisers in New York. We would be in a meeting and find out that the person in charge of advertising had put together a list of key adver-

Ray Gaulke says of his first Gannett meeting: "I'd never seen anything like it. It was frightening."

In addition to her USA TODAY responsibilities, Cathie Black was later named executive vice president/ marketing of Gannett and was appointed to its board of directors in 1985.

tisers who were supposed to get the newspaper at home, but had not followed up to find out whether they had received it or not. The circulation director said he had assigned it to somebody, but he didn't know who was delivering them. It was a small—but critical—move. You couldn't blame Neuharth for saying, 'Get the goddamn thing rolling.'"

Neuharth was pacing back and forth across meeting rooms from coast to coast, cracking his knuckles and crumpling up invoices. Sometimes he managed by persuasion, sometimes by fear. During creation of the USA TODAY prototypes, one editor called Neuharth "Ming the Merciless," after the old Flash Gordon character, because of the way he remade pages. McCorkindale remembers many tense meetings, but says he and others in the finance department were working long hours "trying to figure out where we could get the money from the rest of the company to pay for the thing."

Quinn thinks the first years of USA TODAY were a period when some of Neuharth's management skills failed him. "Al's great talent for getting the best out of people faltered a little bit," Quinn says. "When it came to his leadership team, he didn't have time to conduct the orchestra. He was spread so damn thin and had so many tough challenges that he was looking for people who could take the job, go away, and move things to the next plateau. But that didn't work, particularly in circulation, because we tried to do more than we were ready to do and we didn't do any of it very well. And then we got into that terrible rollover of people."

While McPaper's managers struggled, the flow of negative publicity quickened. A lot of it focused on the lack of advertising. The Los Angeles Times article on USA TODAY's first anniversary noted that during July 1983 the newspaper was running only six ad pages per day. That estimate was probably high, media analyst John Morton said, because of all the discounts and special rates. Even the business neophytes on the News staff were counting ad pages every day and worrying about their big mortgages.

The Audit Bureau of Circulations had not yet verified USA TODAY's circulation numbers, and that made it hard to sell ad executives. Gannett had hired respected accountants to verify the numbers, but the ad buyers did not believe them. "Price Waterhouse means nothing in the advertising business," Welty admitted to the Los Angeles Times reporter. "ABC is the accepted standard. It is a very conservative industry."

The story noted that John Morton had estimated that USA TODAY would lose $70 million in 1983, "making it one of the most costly publishing ventures of all time." Morton was a little off—the real number for 1983 turned out to be $121 million.

In his story, Times reporter Thomas B. Rosenstiel touched on the circulation troubles.

> The reasons for the vast expenses are legion. Neuharth spends lavishly on parties and promotion whenever he introduces the paper in a new market. The paper also uses a blanket approach to sales, installing its boxes on hundreds of street corners and giving thousands of newspapers away free at airports. As a result of that technique, USA TODAY prints, distributes, and then must pick up, hundreds of thousands of papers every day that are never sold.
>
> The return rate for the paper is unusually high. Los Angeles Times circulation officials estimate that in Southern California about 40 percent of the USA TODAY copies are returned unsold, and officials at papers in other markets report it as being even higher. The Los Angeles Times has a return rate on street-sale copies of less than 15 percent, and the industry average is about 8 percent.

The Times story was accurate: USA TODAY's return rate often was around 40 percent.

Rosenstiel also quoted Paul Warren of the trade newsletter Communications Daily. Warren, who had worked for Gannett's Times-Union in Rochester, had written the early stories in Satellite Week that predicted Gannett would launch USA TODAY. Warren told the Times reporter that "Gannett insiders" had informed him "that it may take five years and a circulation of 3 million before Gannett breaks even."

The Wall Street Journal's first anniversary story echoed Rosenstiel's theme. Its headline said: "Despite progress, USA TODAY finding advertisers skeptical." The story said: "As cable TV networks, dozens of fledgling magazines, and other new ventures seeking advertisers' money have learned, Madison Avenue isn't a friendly place for start-ups. The latest to find that out is USA TODAY."

The Journal quoted an anonymous print buyer for a large New York agency who said he was waiting for the ABC audit results. "Once we get them," he said, "we'll probably still be looking for reasons not to buy USA TODAY."

There were a few bright spots. Charles Schwab was using the Money section regularly for ads for his discount brokerage business and to promote financial products, and the response from investors was excellent. Seagram's used USA TODAY to introduce a new rum, and its wholesalers complained when the ads did not run for a month. "Why aren't you using our newspaper?" they asked Seagram's executives.

But in the summer of 1983, there were not enough Charles Schwabs to help Joe Welty. Madison Avenue's attitude was terribly frustrating to him. In August 1983 Welty wrote Doug McCorkindale a memo that said that it was unlikely the ad department would make its $22 million target—a $2 million shortfall was possible. He was right. His department didn't make its goal. The shortfall turned out to be $5.7 million.

That summer, USA TODAY's advertising salespeople were "hitting the wall." "That was my lowest point," said Pat Haegele, Welty's top ad producer. "There wasn't any advertising. Very, very little. Welty would be at my door almost every day saying, 'What are we going to do to fill the book?' We were literally giving pages away so it looked like we had some advertising. If you give it away too often, nobody's going to buy any."

The pressure of being the advertising director for a start-up newspaper had worn down Joe Welty. "He was getting it from both ends," Haegele said, "You could just see it in him."

"I did get a little sick at one point," Welty says. "Somehow Al had given everybody the feeling that we were coming out of the trenches with bayonets. How he did that I'm not sure, but that was part of his magic. He got a bunch of people together who he either drove or conned into being committed to this, as being terribly important to it. They were willing to work very long hours, driven to make it successful. But there was a physical price paid."

Outwardly, Neuharth appeared unruffled. When people asked him about the lack of advertising—and sometimes he was asked that question several times a day—he would often reply, "I'm not worried, because I remember what happened in Florida when the Sears manager said he wouldn't advertise in TODAY. And eventually, he did." But insiders could see the frustration growing in Neuharth's eyes. He had to be worried: His newspaper was a hit with readers and still a flop with advertisers.

When Cathie Black took over the helm of the advertising department from Joe Welty, the transition did not go well. "I made it very clear to Joe that he was number two and she was number one," Neuharth says. "That went down pretty hard with Joe."

Welty recalls the transition this way: "It was not clear to me and I suspect to Cathie exactly what we were supposed to be doing to and with each other. That was a difficult period."

Black mentioned her transition problems to Neuharth; he told her Welty must have misunderstood the situation. To solve that problem, Black and Ray Gaulke concocted a plan to shift Joe Welty to Gannett Media Sales, where he would work for Gaulke selling USA TODAY in conjunction with other media. They had dinner with Neuharth and Heselden to spring the idea on them. Neuharth raised several objections. "For about an hour, Cathie and I answered all of them," Gaulke recalls. Then Neuharth reached into his pocket and pulled out a draft press release that said Welty was going to work for Gannett Media Sales. Neuharth asked them, "Is this what you had in mind?"

That experience convinced Gaulke that "if you have any ideas about what's right to do, you better move fast because chances are if you've thought of it, he's already thought of it a couple of months ago."

Her position secure, Black attacked the advertising problem. Outside observers began suggesting she was the person who could turn

*Valerie Salembier was a
leading force behind USA
TODAY's advertising drive.
She had worked at Inside
Sports and Ms. magazine,
and after joining USA TODAY
in 1983, rose quickly to
become senior vice president.*

things around. Susan Duffy wrote in Barron's: "Talk to Cathie Black for five minutes and you *want* to believe. She's earnest, undauntingly enthusiastic, a classic salesperson."

Black said she realized advertisers were leery of new publications, but said, "We're going to wear down some of that resistance with enthusiasm, optimism, and water torture."

While the advertising was a trickle, the steady stream of enthusiastic letters from readers continued. C. Rich Diffenderffer, an executive with DuPont, wrote: "After reading in Business Week about USA TODAY's financial difficulties, I wanted to write and say I have been addicted to your paper since I first received a complimentary copy on the front seat of a rental car in Detroit—please don't give up!"

"Your paper is great," wrote Judi Moussa of Los Angeles. "Having moved from Detroit, Michigan, to Los Angeles several years ago I often wondered what was happening news-wise in the Motor City. Your paper keeps me informed. Keep up the good work—I LOVE IT!!!"

That reader reaction persuaded Neuharth to press on with expansion plans. On USA TODAY's first anniversary—September 15, 1983—he announced that by July 1984, the newspaper would be able to print a forty-eight-page daily edition, up from forty pages. That would double the number of color pages available to news and advertising, from eight pages to sixteen, allowing full-color news and advertising for the first time in the Money and Life sections.

His decision was a bit of a shock to Chuck Blevins and his production people. They had barely finished getting the presses up to the point where they could produce forty pages, now they were going to add eight pages and eight color positions. "I knew we could do it, mechanically," Blevins says. "But we were running out of steam. The rest of the newspaper industry really thought we were crazy, going to forty-eight pages." Blevins and his crew went back on the road, bought more press units, trained more operators, and got it done.

At the 1983 year-end meeting of Gannett executives, Neuharth announced that USA TODAY had grown "to be a healthy fifteen-month-old baby." He said it was now the "third largest daily newspaper in the USA and by far the fastest-growing newspaper in the history of the USA." Neuharth added that while "1982 and 1983 were planned as the years of the reader, 1984 and 1985 are planned as the years of the advertiser."

He also reported that Lou Harris had done a survey of four hundred opinion leaders. It showed that "Gannett has a substantially more favorable image in the eyes of the USA's opinion leaders than it did three years ago. Sixty-four percent of those who have heard of Gannett view the company favorably. Seventy-two percent say the launching of USA TODAY has strengthened the company's growth potential."

In 1982 and 1983, USA TODAY had lost a total of $162 million. But the effort was beginning to pay off. The Harris survey was one of the first concrete signs that starting the new newspaper would bring significant noneconomic benefits to the company. Gannett was fast acquiring the national reputation its executives had yearned for for so long.

CHAPTER SIXTEEN

The numbers game

Behind the flow of positive news that Neuharth was feeding the world in 1983, USA TODAY was fighting for its life. The last three months of 1983 was the period when the Audit Bureau of Circulations would certify the new newspaper's circulation. It was hard to overstate how important that audit was to "McPaper's" future: If its circulation numbers did not check out, it had no future.

Madison Avenue was still waiting. Frank McDonald, a senior vice president at Cunningham & Walsh, told Advertising Age: "We need to get an answer on the circulation numbers. I'm not really sure where their numbers are coming from and if we are accepting them."

In mid-November 1983, Neuharth called Jack Heselden, his current publisher, from Florida. They both had been studying USA TODAY's circulation reports, and the numbers were running under 1 million. They had to keep circulation above 1 million. That was the minimum number Madison Avenue had told them they had to have, and they had been saying since April of that year that they had it. If the ABC audit found that the circulation was only 950,000, they were in big trouble.

On the phone Neuharth and Heselden talked about the numbers. "We realized we were going to be short," Heselden says. "He got very, very firm, as firm as he's ever been with me." The rest of the conversation went like this:

"So, what are you doing about it—other than wringing your hands?" Neuharth asked.

"Al, we've opened New Orleans, Mobile, and Jackson. Paul Flynn is getting the paper into Kentucky—Louisville and Lexington. John

Curley has a contest going to get the home delivery numbers up for the Gannett papers."

"That isn't enough," Neuharth said.

"I'm afraid you're right," Heselden said.

"Did you ever think about offering five weeks for five dollars?" Neuharth asked. "Five for five. Just make sure they pay for it up front. What do you think of that?"

"Well, that certainly would add some numbers all right," Heselden said.

"You better get going on it then," Neuharth said.

Heselden spent the afternoon on the phone: "Nobody knew how they were going to bill for it or how they were going to collect," Heselden recalls. "We told everybody, 'Get the money in advance,' but you know how that goes. Some of them did, some of them didn't. We scrambled and worked like hell and the numbers came in. Then after five weeks, an awful lot of the new subscribers quit. That gave us another problem: How do you replace those people?"

The business office was completely unequipped to handle the torrent of orders. "It raised havoc," says Dick Rumsey, that department's chief. "We had problems getting the orders into the system. We had many, many problems trying to get the papers delivered, trying to get the bills out." In some cases, USA TODAY was sending its drivers ten miles to deliver one newspaper.

"It was a bleak situation," Rumsey says. "There were a lot of customers who were really unhappy." Rumsey was working from before 7 A.M. until 10 at night, trying to bring a semblance of order to the business office.

Part of the difficulty, of course, was the very short time frame Neuharth had set for USA TODAY to be successful. In five years or less, they were trying to create a new national newspaper and persuade millions of readers to buy it; no company had ever tried anything like that before, much less actually done it.

But, as Jack Heselden points out, getting big circulation numbers fast was crucial to success. If USA TODAY did not make a big impact on Madison Avenue quickly, within a couple of years, it would die. "We would have been just another new publication that nobody gave a damn about. We never would have gotten any advertising. I don't think it could have been done any faster, and it should not have been done any slower, yet we got into an awful lot of problems because of that speed."

In November 1983, George Dastyck, the publisher of the Gannett Rochester Newspapers, who also had responsibility for some USA TODAY operations in the Northeast, wrote Heselden a letter unloading a catalog of woes:

> Several Gannett locations were simply not prepared to handle the incredible volume of transactions that resulted from immense sampling programs, far in excess of any prior experience any of us had. In Rochester, we were sampling forty thousand a day at some points. We had a week's notice to prepare for it. Obviously, this means forty thousand follow-up phone calls, forty thousand entries on records, perhaps the addition of as many as four thousand subscribers to process from the circulation, billing, and data processing standpoint. In Rochester, as in some other locations, our data processing structure was not programmed to handle this. Temporary manual operations had to be put in place.
>
> If we had stayed with our original selling plan, I'm quite certain we would have come out as well in terms of the net number of subscribers with more stability in those subscribers at less cost, less confusion, and less customer alienation. We are getting to the point where nonsubscribers are getting their second, third, and fourth phone calls to subscribe to USA TODAY. Some become angry about the repetition.

In just over a year, forty-four thousand subscriptions to USA TODAY had been processed in Rochester alone, and twenty-eight thousand of those customers had dropped the new newspaper. USA TODAY had churned and burned a good portion of all of the newspaper readers in Rochester. George Dastyck had a final suggestion: "Care in establishing realistic and achievable goals without the need to use extreme measures would also help."

The indiscriminate sampling Dastyck complained about took its toll. Over three months in the winter of 1984, USA TODAY had to reduce its circulation by 318,000 copies per day—credit kills for readers who subscribed to the paper but never paid their bills. It certainly would have been easier to go slow and set "realistic goals."

But, of course, there wasn't time. No one at Gannett had realized what an enormous logistical job it would be to sell and service more than 1 million customers per day across the country. Every time they changed an offer or a billing procedure, the number of changes managers had to make—in instructions to employees, in forms for customers, in programming for computers—was awesome. "It's like trying to turn the *QE II* around in a small river," Rumsey complained.

Rumsey did not have much experience working with ABC's rules, and his accountants had never been told they were supposed to make sure those rules were followed in the field. Rumsey had assumed the people in the circulation department would take care of that. They didn't. Most of the circulation people in the field had been hired to install and service racks; many had no experience or training in how to keep track of circulation data.

In January 1984, the ABC auditors arrived in Rosslyn. The circulation records were a mess. "They couldn't figure them out," Rumsey recalls. "ABC had never dealt with an organization that had so many delivery locations."

The head auditor for ABC was Dick Deneen. He had audited many of Gannett's local newspapers and found few problems. Every Gannett circulation director knew how to keep the ABC records straight. "But when we got out to the USA TODAY clusters," Deneen says, "no one had a hint of what they were supposed to do. Records were not re-capped as they should have been. There was big disarray, pieces of paper here and there."

Beth Silver, a USA TODAY accountant, remembers John Kracsun, a meticulous auditor from ABC, running out of patience; he almost got up and walked out a couple of times. The information he needed was not available and no one could seem to get it.

To sort it out, ABC hired a statistics expert from the University of Chicago to calculate how many copies they should check in each market to make sure the audit would be a large enough sample to reflect an accurate count. Back in Rosslyn, Rumsey made his deputy, Chuck Schmitt, the troubleshooter. Whenever ABC ran into a problem at one of the cluster offices, Schmitt flew out and fixed it.

Just about every competing circulation manager in the country suspected that USA TODAY was cheating on its numbers. Howard Kutz, ABC's executive vice president, often attended meetings of circulation directors. "No matter where I went, a competitor of Gannett would come up and ask, 'How in the world are you going to audit this?' There would always be innuendoes that USA TODAY was doing something wrong someplace. It was a semivicious campaign that was going on at the time."

As the months dragged on, it became obvious that the ABC audit was going to take a lot longer than anyone had expected. Neuharth and Heselden had hoped ABC would report USA TODAY's circulation in its regular semiannual report at the end of April. But the new newspaper's numbers were not included, because ABC had not finished.

Without the ABC numbers, advertising buyers continued to sit on the sidelines. In the first three months of 1984, which Neuharth had proclaimed as "the year of the advertiser," USA TODAY was averaging only about six ad pages per day, well off the goal of ten pages per day he had set.

Several disputes over ABC's rules flared during the audit. Sales to hotels, airlines, and rental car companies, which the newspaper had started out calling its "amenities" program before Madelyn Jennings thought of calling it "blue chip" circulation, had grown to about forty-one thousand per day. For example, Hertz would buy several hundred copies at a slightly lower price—say fifteen cents per copy instead of twenty-five cents—and give a newspaper to each customer who rented a car. Hotels, airlines, and some restaurants also participated. The "blue chip" program eventually would sell nearly 240,000 copies a day and newspaper marketing would never be the same.

USA TODAY's executives wanted this circulation counted in the daily ABC total. ABC refused, noting that these "bulk sales"—as it called them—could not be counted as regular paid circulation under its rules. The figure was included, but as a separate category on an inside page of ABC's circulation report. Gannett fought to get the rules changed, noting that under ABC rules, bulk sales to prisons counted as paid circulation, but bulk sales to hotels, where the newspapers were read by well-paid executives, did not count. Even though some Gannett newspapers pulled out of ABC for a few months, it refused to change the rules. But every time Neuharth reported USA TODAY's circulation, he added in the blue chip sales, a habit that irritated ABC officials.

Inadequate records were the real stumbling block to finishing the audit. There was one point, Dick Rumsey remembers, "where we and ABC didn't really know how we were finally going to come up with a number. But we did and it was audited and we found out that our record-keeping had been pretty accurate."

The competitors' claims about hyped circulation at USA TODAY were false. "We never found any evidence at all of fraud," said Dick Deneen of ABC. "It was strictly overenthusiastic people who didn't know what the rules were."

Finally, in late June 1984, ABC reported the results. The number, Paul Flynn told Editor & Publisher, had Gannett executives "doing handstands." Neuharth drafted the press release that would show USA TODAY with a daily circulation of 1.33 million if blue chip sales were included, and 1.28 million if they were not counted. His draft read:

> The first Audit Bureau of Circulations report for USA TODAY was released today and confirms that newspaper's dramatic growth since its establishment in September 1982.
> The ABC figures match those released earlier by USA TODAY. They confirm that USA TODAY ranks a strong third in the country, behind The Wall Street Journal and very close to the New York Daily News.

In the last paragraph of the draft press release he wrote about the ABC report, Neuharth decided to have a little fun. He wrote:

> Allen H. Neuharth, chairman and founder of USA TODAY, said he is pleased at the belated ABC report and said "I hope this puts to rest all that bullshit that cynics and competitors have been spreading about our circulation claims. Anyone who knows Gannett and me knows we cannot tell a lie because we are not smart enough to cover our tracks."

Then he added a "chairman's note" to the public relations department which said, "The last paragraph is optional. If you opt to use it directly, you will probably be reprimanded and/or fired. If you opt to spread that *theme* discreetly and intelligently, you will certainly be applauded and/or rewarded."

The early response from the advertising community to the ABC audit was encouraging. "It was a very important step for USA TODAY," said Michael Drexler of the Doyle Dane Bernbach agency. "I was a skeptic, but right now I feel much more confident about USA TODAY both as an advertising medium and as a viable product in the marketplace, and I think that's reflective of a lot of people in the advertising community."

Madison Avenue heard about
the long-awaited results of the
ABC audit.

But that reaction was not universal. "The jury is still out on whether USA TODAY will succeed," said John Reidy, a media stock analyst for Drexel Burnham. John Morton added: "ABC doesn't say who USA TODAY's readers are, and their demographic studies are only partially satisfying. Also, the figures don't say how stable their circulation is. There is concern that it's a revolving door and that a substantial portion of circulation is always a new bunch."

Over Memorial Day weekend in 1984, Jack Heselden's family was struck by tragedy. His daughter, Nancy, who had been under psychi atric care, was arrested and charged with killing her two daughters, ages six and five, in her home. Neuharth cut short a trip to Europe and flew back to try to help. This awful event removed Heselden from USA TODAY's day-to-day management. He stood by his daughter, saw that she got the best care, and tried to help his son-in-law, too. Heselden's daughter later pleaded guilty to manslaughter. She received a sus- pended sentence and was confined to a private mental hospital for twenty months before being released on probation.

Heselden had been the steady hand at the publisher's helm that the newspaper needed. But just when the right people were beginning to get into the right jobs, Heselden had to leave. They were forced once again, as John Quinn put it, "to jump from one instant solution to another." That was a flawed strategy, and there were more rocky days ahead.

CHAPTER SEVENTEEN

The enemy within

David Shaw, the media writer for the Los Angeles Times, uncovered this description of Al Neuharth by a friend: "He's the sort of man who would go after Moby Dick with a rowboat, a harpoon, and a jar of tartar sauce."

There are Gannett managers who think that's no exaggeration. Many people who have worked closely with Neuharth have been struck by the strength of his will, by its nearly palpable force. "When he wants something to happen," says Randy Chorney, who worked closely with Neuharth for several years, "it has to happen. He's not a person you bring problems to, only solutions."

Through most of 1984, Neuharth was willing USA TODAY to succeed—with all his might. He was struggling to overcome formidable difficulties in advertising and circulation, but he was also fighting on another front.

"There was a category of people who were enemies from within," he says. "They took a hell of a lot of my time keeping my backside covered, time that I could have used more productively. There were people in finance who would ask, 'Why do you need 135,000 vending machines? Couldn't it be 99,000? And why can't we spend $165 apiece for them like The Washington Post does instead of $225?' That was disruptive. The enemy from within didn't keep the job from getting done, but it made it a hell of a lot more difficult."

Much of Neuharth's ire was focused on Doug McCorkindale and his lieutenants in the corporate financial department. They had been against the project from the beginning, but what angered him now was that nearly two years had passed since USA TODAY began publishing, and some of the newspaper's internal opponents were still holding things up.

Carl Fortson, who had been Gannett's data processing director when USA TODAY was launched and who later moved to Knight-Ridder newspapers, remembers "the enemy within." Fortson reported to Gannett Treasurer Jimmy Thomas, and through him to chief financial officer McCorkindale. Fortson says:

"Within the entire finance group—I never figured out if this advice came from McCorkindale or from where—we were advised to stay as far away from USA TODAY as we could. If that wasn't a quote, it was that explicit: We don't want to be involved in it."

While McCorkindale and his people may not have done anything to deliberately sabotage USA TODAY, they took a hands-off stance that hindered its progress. This standoffish attitude was quite different from the approach other Gannett executives took toward the project. For example, when USA TODAY was announced, chief news executive John Quinn did not stay in Rochester and leave the news job to a Washington-based editor; he plunged into the fray and made sure things were done right. Quinn left his Rochester corporate office and flew to Rosslyn in the spring of 1982, expecting to come back in a few days. Two years later he returned to clean out his office and found there was still a note to himself on his desk, written the day he had left. "Talk to John Curley about loaners," it said. Chuck Blevins and his production people took the same hands-on approach, and Jack Heselden mobilized corporate circulation and advertising experts to pitch in and help.

During three important years when the real action in the Gannett Company was going on in the USA TODAY building in Rosslyn, the corporate financial executives were back at headquarters in Rochester. They viewed USA TODAY from a distance of several hundred miles, and they saw it as one more Gannett newspaper among all of its other newspapers. They treated it as Gannett Unit 121—not that different from Unit 120 or Unit 122. When Chuck Schmitt and USA TODAY's business office got into trouble, the corporate accountants did not drop what they were doing and rush to Rosslyn to help. Instead they kept their distance and dispatched Dick Rumsey from Westchester to deal with it. And when corporate finance did get involved in the newspaper's problems, the approach some executives took complicated things as often as it solved them. As Quinn puts it, where USA TODAY was involved, they would "tie sandbags to their accounting procedures."

Tom Reynolds, a Chicago lawyer and Gannett director, says he noticed a "marked lack of enthusiasm" by the financial people at board meetings during those years. "There was an appearance—albeit very light—of disassociating themselves from it. 'That's Project X.'" Randy Chorney recalls that in those days corporate finance vigorously examined every USA TODAY expense: "Everything was questioned. Their attitude was, this whole project was a Neuharth lark and it was costing the company a lot of money. You do your own thing down there in Rosslyn and we'll do our own thing up here in Rochester, and never the twain shall meet."

The flip side was the wholehearted support USA TODAY got from other departments. The spirit in the newsroom in the early days was described by the wife of a loaner as akin to "a campus crusade for Christ." That enthusiastic support, Neuharth says, helped attract outsiders to the project. The chairman kept saying that one group within Gannett was planning for success, the other was planning for failure.

In August 1982, Neuharth had formed the "Project S" task force, led by Louis A. "Chip" Weil III, a McCorkindale lieutenant who was an early opponent of USA TODAY. Neuharth announced the group would study possible "spinoff" products from USA TODAY, but did not mention publicly its other purpose—to figure out what could be "salvaged" if the newspaper failed. For example, the group figured out how many newsracks could be repainted and used by Gannett's local newspapers if USA TODAY flopped. There was a lot of internal speculation about what the S in Project S really stood for: Success, Synergy, and Spinoff—or Salvage and Shutdown.

The split between believers and nonbelievers had a dramatic effect on the careers of two top Gannett executives, Doug McCorkindale and John Curley. Carl Fortson says, "I thought Doug's opposition to USA TODAY was the best thing that ever happened to John Curley." McCorkindale had been a wunderkind at Gannett. He had become, at thirty-seven, one of the youngest chief financial officers of a Fortune 500 company. In the late 1970s, many thought McCorkindale was a strong contender to succeed Neuharth as chief executive.

McCorkindale had no peer in legal and financial matters, but he lacked one important ingredient to lead a media company—newsroom experience. In Neuharth's view, Gannett's next chief executive really

With Neuharth just a few years from retirement, all eyes were on John Curley, right, and Doug McCorkindale to see which one would be named his successor.

needed that. Even if the candidate to be CEO had not worked in news, that person ought to understand it and have a sure sense of what might work in the media business and what might not. USA TODAY was a chance for McCorkindale to show he understood and could help lead a news-oriented operation.

But McCorkindale did not seem to grasp the significance of the new venture's news potential; he did not attach much weight to the phenomenal reaction USA TODAY had received from its readers, but focused instead on its heavy financial losses. That positive reader reaction, which never waned, was enough to keep Neuharth, Curley, and John Quinn thinking that they eventually would be able to make the newspaper a financial success. Then it would be worth the considerable investment.

But what if the newspaper failed and Neuharth had to quit in disgrace? If that happened, McCorkindale was in a good position, as the venture's most prominent opponent, to succeed Neuharth as Gannett's chief executive. If USA TODAY bombed, the board of directors would have to think about turning the company over to the executive who had argued all along that starting it was an unreasonable risk.

This combination—Doug McCorkindale's opposition and John Curley's enthusiastic support—gave Neuharth the confidence to push Curley ahead, and he passed McCorkindale on the corporate ladder. In January 1982, Curley became editor of USA TODAY. In April 1983, he was named president of the newspaper division. In March 1984, he was named president and chief operating officer of Gannett.

McCorkindale read that last promotion as a sure sign Curley would be Gannett's next chief executive officer. Neuharth broke the news of Curley's promotion to his chief financial officer over lunch, and McCorkindale said, "You've picked your successor." Neuharth was cagey. "I've picked a president and chief operating officer," he said. He didn't want McCorkindale to quit; the company needed his talents.

In the spring of 1984, the continuing reluctance of some of Gannett's corporate executives to get on the USA TODAY team was really begin ning to gnaw at Neuharth. He knew the newspaper faced huge problems, and he was ready to start knocking heads.

Neuharth called a meeting of what was then called the USA TODAY Umbrella Committee—the forerunner of its management committee—at his vacation home at Lake Tahoe. The top leadership of the newspaper was there: Jack Heselden, the publisher; John Quinn, the editor; Cathie Black and Ray Gaulke from advertising; Paul Flynn from circulation; Vince Spezzano, who was planning the new international edition; and Doug McCorkindale from finance.

Neuharth told them that USA TODAY would increase its single-copy sales price from twenty-five cents to thirty-five cents on Monday, August 27. This was a crucial test, because asking people to fumble with two different coins at the vending machine would cost them many sales—probably more sales than a 40 percent price hike normally would cost them. In his own notes for the Lake Tahoe meeting, Neuharth underlined some of their continuing difficulties. He wrote: "Costs! Returns! Finances/Hold Down! Promotion—Think!" Then his notes defined what he thought the Gannett/USA TODAY relationship should be. When he spoke to the group, he followed this outline he had written:

> Gannett IS USA TODAY; USA TODAY IS Gannett.
> USA TODAY is *not* Neuharth.
> USA TODAY has put the Gannett Company in the *major*
> leagues.
> USA TODAY can keep Gannett there, OR can dump Gannett
> back into the *minor* leagues—to *stay!*
> YOU in your 40s and 50s better think about that—HARD!
> YOU will reap the benefits—in prestige, stature, financially,
> or YOU will suffer the consequences.

Neuharth and Heselden will be gone and pretty much forgotten, win or lose . . . us guys in our 60s will retire, enjoy
life.
YOU in your 40s and 50s will live with *it*—whatever *it* is! IT
is USA TODAY.
IF IT succeeds—YOU are stars and run a prestigious, major
league media company with a flagship, USA TODAY, that is the
envy of all.
IF IT fails—YOU (Gannett) are resigned to being a minor-
league outfit—in prestige/stature for the rest of your careers!
You have a great opportunity to cash in—or to Blow It!!!

Neuharth hoped that message—delivered, as usual, with a
sledgehammer—would sink in, and that McCorkindale would carry it
back to his associates in corporate finance, but the sniping from
Rochester continued. Neuharth called another meeting to try to get
the corporate finance people to help bail out USA TODAY's rowboat.
"It was McCorkindale's whole crew and I landed pretty hard on
them," Neuharth recalls. "That was when this planning for failure had
gotten to the point where it was just too much for the camp that was
planning for success to overcome."
So Neuharth flew up to Rochester to give a group of key corporate
staffers a little lecture on corporate organization. The corporate staff,
he explained, was "support staff." The support staff existed to help
the "line" people—the operating executives who brought in the
money. USA TODAY was a "line" operation. As corporate staffers, their
primary duty was to support it. Neuharth's message was simple:
Either help row the boat or jump overboard.
The chief executive's explanation of a corporate staff's responsibilities offended Larry Miller, the capable accountant who worked
closely with McCorkindale. At the meeting, Miller pointed out to Neuharth that many corporate "support" staffers helped Gannett make
money every day: Treasurer Jimmy Thomas got a better return on
Gannett's investments; Bill Metzfield of Gannett Supply cut the cost of
newsprint purchases; John Jaske, the labor relations lawyer, negoti-
ated favorable union contracts.
But that day, Miller recalls, Neuharth wasn't interested in discussing those details. "He wanted to talk philosophy. He just pissed us
off." In Miller's view, Neuharth was too close to USA TODAY: "He

would have been better off if he had backed away a little and let people help him. Every time we try to critique USA TODAY and give him suggestions he thinks we're peeing on his project, and we're not. I think I'm as devoted to Gannett as anyone else around here—we're in the ball game together. And it hurts when you want to be helpful and the end product is that you feel you have to keep your mouth shut. That's not good."

Given the heavy pressure from Neuharth, one would have expected the financial people to shut up and pull the oars. Not all of them did. In July 1984, Doug McCorkindale wrote John Curley, now Gannett's president and chief operating officer, a memo about the money Curley and Neuharth wanted to spend for two new USA TODAY print sites:

> I was surprised to receive your memo of July 12 approving in principle two new Gannett facilities for Cocoa and Rochester.
> Neither location has submitted any requests for such facilities. To my knowledge, no analysis has been done on the business and economic impact of the expenditures, which I estimate would be between $30 million and $40 million.
> Our established procedures provide for review of all capital expenditures, followed by submission to Al for consideration, in light of the company's overall cash flow, debt, and earnings picture. After he's considered these factors, we submit a memorandum to the board of directors for their approval. Only after we've gone through those procedures do we grant approval in principle for capital expenditures.

"That's the way they would try to stymie the project," John Curley says. "They would try to delay it, delay it. The phrase that Doug sometimes uses is to 'beat it to death.'"

McCorkindale sees it differently: The financial rules that Gannett makes its newspapers follow serve a useful purpose, and USA TODAY needed the same controls. As chief financial officer, he had a responsibility to enforce the rules, to look out for the shareholders. And he thinks the big spending at USA TODAY dampened the desire of Gannett's managers in the provinces to perform.

"There's a lackadaisical attitude toward a lot of things now because of what many in the company saw as the inordinate waste involved in that project," McCorkindale says. "They say, 'Why should we kill ourselves in Gitchagumee, Idaho [to make money] when they'll just waste it over there anyway.'"

The entrepreneurial spirit that this huge project needed was bound to clash with the finance department's "by the book" mentality. Spending money that way "just inherently went against the grain, the law-and-order framework of most financial folks," says Tom Farrell, who worked under McCorkindale and later became USA TODAY's general manager. "Those financial executives, myself included, are not entrepreneurial by nature. We're used to managing existing operations."

Neuharth agrees that the two sides—news versus finance—took fundamentally different approaches. "Why did the guys in news—Curley and Quinn—immediately jump aboard with both feet? Why did these other guys in finance drag both feet? It's their basic nature, the tunnel vision most financial people have. That's their natural instinct, as opposed to the natural arrogance or supreme confidence that editors have."

McCorkindale's memo on the print sites was "the last straw," Neuharth says. He decided to lay down the law one more time, so he summoned McCorkindale, Larry Miller, and Jimmy Thomas to his office in Rosslyn. His notes from that meeting say:

> We talked about the *past* in Rochester. There was some sensitivity or testiness about Rochester—"back here"—and Rosslyn—"down there." TODAY we are here to talk about the future—and where it's at. The future is down *here*; there ain't no more back there.
>
> Anyone who wants to play on Gannett's team plays *here*. And, plays by the rules—some new, some just clarified. All policies are set by the *Boss*. I am the boss; I lean on lots of help—Jack Heselden, John Curley, Doug McCorkindale, others—But, I decide . . . then y'all carry out the policies. Some in operations, some in services.
>
> *Operations* are the people who run newspapers, broadcast, outdoor—the LINE people. *Services* are the financial, legal, personnel, administration—the STAFF people.
>
> There will be no more services/staff getting in the way of operations, policies. There will be *no more* service policing of operations. HELP—don't police. *Counsel*—don't impede. Don't cover your ass, save the ass of operations.

> USA TODAY is a healthy kid who needs help—not a whipping
> or a scolding or policing.

Once again, Larry Miller stood up for his point of view. "I've offered
to help, but no one's asked me to do anything," he said. Neuharth
quizzed John Curley and Bill Keating, the new president of the newspaper division, to make sure that was true. It was.

"Fine," Neuharth said. "Then we're all on the same team. Let's
get to work."

The good public reaction to the ABC audit in June 1984 may have
lulled some people into thinking USA TODAY had it made, but not Neuharth. At a meeting of the Gannett board that summer, he gave the
directors a sober update. His notes show he made a point to be candid:

> It sounds like we're really on a roll, but the facts are quite
> different. The public perception is that circulation is booming,
> with the ABC audit. Advertising really moving—some are
> saying "they have it made."
>
> The reality is that circulation *was* booming. Now, it's lag-
> ging. In June, it slipped below 1.3 million. Circulation in the
> Gannett newspaper markets is *dismal*. Advertising is
> upbeat—9 plus pages a day versus 7½ for last year but—rates
> are being cut to get volume. *Much* better picture than circula-
> tion, but long ways to go.
>
> Most important—the overall management picture is *shaky*.
> Jack Heselden was stable, sound, experienced—the right
> boss in transition from launch to management. It was neces-
> sary for him to leave; it was nearly a year premature.

A committee had replaced Heselden; John Curley, John Quinn, and
Bill Keating were its key members. Keating, a former judge and member of Congress from Ohio, had been publisher of The Cincinnati
Enquirer. When John Curley was named president of Gannett, Keating
followed him as president of the newspaper division.

Neuharth handicapped USA TODAY's future for the directors. "We
have created a product that has very high acceptability and popularity,
with readers and leaders. Believability has improved with advertisers.
But—manageability is the big question."

He told the board a revised business plan for USA TODAY would be
presented at the August meeting. "The long-term outlook is still very

Before becoming president of the newspaper division, Bill Keating was president of Gannett/Central, helping direct USA TODAY's circulation and marketing efforts for that region.

good," Neuharth said. "But, it ain't gonna be easy. Things will get worse before they get better. I'm telling you this not to discourage you, because there is absolutely no reason to be discouraged. Quite the contrary. But it is important to know that the *ruthless reality of this roller coaster* is that we are again on a slight downhill trend rather than uphill. And that roller coaster ride will continue for quite a while before we go over the top and into a nice steady climb."

On July 27, 1984, USA TODAY published its first forty-eight-page edition. That Monday, Neuharth flew into Dulles International Airport from Florida and rode into Rosslyn with Tom Farrell, who had just been named USA TODAY's business manager. Farrell had been a banker in upstate New York before joining Gannett's treasury department in 1979. Neuharth sat down in the limo and snapped open his copy of USA TODAY. He looked at every page, checking the color; he had already read the paper early that morning at Pumpkin Center. Then he finished it, folded it, and threw it into Farrell's lap with a flourish and said: "If I had listened to some of your dumb fucking friends in the financial department, Farrell, there wouldn't be a forty-eight-page newspaper to read today."

That August, the directors reviewed the revised business plan. Bill Keating presented the numbers for USA TODAY. He predicted that the newspaper would lose $108 million in 1984; $70 million in 1985; $22 million in 1986 and then turn the corner and make $5 million in 1987. "We really think we can make this budget," Keating said, with enthusiasm. "I give you my word that we can make this budget next year."

Then the board went into executive session, for board members only. "What you've seen and heard so far represents what our operating people believe they can achieve," Neuharth said, speaking from notes. "Because we want maximum motivation for them, we decided to let those projections stand as their goals." Then he briefed them on "reality."

"Most of us have been around this track quite a few times," Neuharth said. "from that small, slow track with Gannett's first new newspaper venture in Brevard County, Florida, to all those relatively easy and rewarding tracks around the Gannett empire, to this fast, tough new track that runs clear across the USA. We must tell you we simply do not believe we can run quite as far, quite as fast, as our operating people have projected."

Neuharth estimated that USA TODAY's losses would be $124 million in 1984; $81 million in 1985; and $25 million in 1986, but then the newspaper would break even for all of 1987. He estimated USA TODAY's cumulative losses at the end of 1987 would be close to $400 million, before taxes. That August 1984 re-evaluation of USA TODAY's finances, Neuharth says, was "as close as we ever came to folding the tent."

There had never been any public announcement of USA TODAY's losses. Reporters asked for those numbers often, and Neuharth would say only that the losses were "exceeding our expectations, like everything else." He explains that the losses were kept secret because "I didn't want Wall Street or the media critics making the judgment to shut it down for us. You had to have an overview." And John Curley adds that if the huge losses had been made public, "Everybody would have been thinking about that instead of doing their jobs."

Despite the magnitude of the losses, the directors say a decision to close USA TODAY was never imminent. "I never had any expectation that at one of these meetings we would turn it off. Not at all," says Andrew Brimmer, a Gannett director who is on the boards of several other large companies, including DuPont and United Airlines. "The circulation was always pretty good. The advertising, while it started slowly, we could see that getting better after Cathie Black got there."

"The truth is that I always thought we would make it," Neuharth says. "I thought so from the very first day, because we produced that first edition and it sold." Even when the losses were at their highest, Neuharth was always buoyed by how much readers liked the newspaper. He was especially encouraged on those rare occasions when a fellow journalist praised it.

One of the first reporters to do that was Charles Kuralt of CBS News. In April 1984, when Neuharth received an award from the Center for Communication in New York City, Kuralt helped present it. While "On the Road" for CBS, Kuralt read USA TODAY regularly. Two of his favorite features were the news from every state and the editorial page debate, but what he really liked was the heartland flavor that the newspaper gave him. "I guess what really knocks me out is the girls' [high school] basketball scores," Kuralt said at the awards ceremony. "That is sort of showing off. People complain that USA TODAY is not The New York Times. I cannot find the girls' basketball scores anywhere in The New York Times."

Neuharth knew the job now was to translate that reader loyalty into business success. His concerns about lack of management strength propelled him to look for more help, especially in circulation. Paul Flynn had struggled hard, but the self-imposed strain of trying to think of an answer for every question Neuharth might ask had worn him out. While swimming after work one night, Flynn aggravated a hernia, and now he needed surgery. He told Neuharth he would like to go back to what he did best, being a community newspaper publisher. One of Flynn's last assignments was to handle part of the August presentation to the board. In it, he pointed out that it had taken The Wall Street Journal seventy-seven years to become a 1 million circulation newspaper, and "we did it in one year."

"I don't know if I suffered a classic case of burnout," Flynn says, "but I did have a lot of the symptoms you read about. You're just totally tired. You do strange things. You drink coffee in the morning to wake up and then you drink liquor at night to go to sleep. I think that burnout was all over the place. Our circulation executives around the country, it's astounding that so many of them are still with us."

After the Heselden tragedy, Neuharth promoted Cathie Black from president to publisher, but she was still only in charge of advertising. Flynn was then president, in charge of circulation. Now, to replace Flynn, Neuharth looked outside Gannett. He found Lee Guittar, a newspaper executive with seventeen years of circulation and general management experience. Guittar had been president and publisher of The Denver Post and now was chairman of the Dallas Times Herald and a vice president of its parent, the Times-Mirror Company.

Over Labor Day weekend, Cathie Black the new publisher—

*In November 1984, newly
appointed president Lee
Guittar set out on a cross-
country tour of USA TODAY
operations, trying to get
control of distribution costs.*

learned that Lee Guittar was going to be the new president. That was
evidently a shock to her; somehow, she expected to get the job of
running the circulation department even though she then had only one
year of newspaper experience. Circulation was a bear of a job. It
already had ground up and spit out four people who had worked on it—
Frank Vega, Phil Gialanella, Vince Spezzano, and Paul Flynn. Black
wrote a "highly personal and confidential" memo about her disappointment to John Curley; he shared it with Neuharth.

Her memo to Curley read:

> With an-about-to-be-named president, I feel compelled to
> tell you how I really feel. I'm frustrated. And discouraged.
> And in doubt as to my near-term growth at Gannett/USA
> TODAY.
> On the one hand, I appreciate and accept the involvement
> of every executive in Gannett for the running of USA TODAY.
> First, I have no choice! And second, there is the scope of the
> project. In many ways, I don't see my authority increasing.
> How can it grow or be expanded when USA TODAY is really run
> by both you and Al (plus Bill Keating) and now circulation,
> production, and manufacturing will be controlled by Lee
> Guizzar [sic].

For Neuharth, this was just too presumptuous. He began furiously
marking up Black's memo, as only an old city editor could. He never
sent her the copy he "edited," but the comments he scribbled show

just how angry Neuharth could get. USA TODAY was fighting for its life, and he had no time to hold anyone's hand. On the cover sheet, Neuharth circled the "CB:mm" notation that showed the memo had been typed by a secretary and wrote: "Nothing any secretary handles is 'highly personal and confidential.' Type it yourself *or* talk privately about it."

"Wasted Time!" Neuharth proclaimed at the top of the cover sheet. "Too long Labor Day Weekend." In the margin, he wrote: "Too much time with personal concerns rather than professional solutions!" Black had noted on the cover sheet that she had written her memo "after a great deal of thought" and it had not been done "in haste." Neuharth circled the words "in haste." "Maybe," he said, "but it's full of errors and bullshit."

Turning his attention to the second paragraph, Neuharth inserted a huge exclamation mark next to "Lee Guizzar," the new president's misspelled name. He circled Black's observation that USA TODAY was really run by Curley and Neuharth. "You're damned right!" Neuharth wrote. "*We* started it. *You* were invited aboard later."

Black's third paragraph said:

> In our brief conversation, I've been told Lee comes as number two, underneath me. At least that's how Al presented it to me in Dallas. But does he really? Last year, I joined USA TODAY with the title of President—only later to discover it was a title with no authority or responsibility. It never occurred to me (dumb on my part) that with that title, no authority was conveyed over advertising or circulation, the two major areas over which a Publisher or President would exercise control. The advertising side was corrected soon in 1984, but not circulation.

In the margin, Neuharth wrote: "Titles are what we want them to be!" Black's memo continued:

> I now sense that the same situation is being repeated. The fact is that I'm a Publisher in title only. I'm really the Advertising Director with a little circulation promotion thrown in.
> You may think I'm bold to lay all this out. But, if I don't tell you what I think and how I feel, then I have no one to blame but myself.

The first page of Cathie Black's September 6, 1984, memo to John Curley, with Neuharth's markings on it.

Neuharth, who had brought dozens of talented women into the Gannett Company, showed the height of his frustration when he leveled his parting shot at Black: He circled the word "bold" and wrote in the margin: "Bold? NO. Fucked up? Yes."

Beyond a doubt, Neuharth had demonstrated that he could be just as tough with female executives as he was with males. Instead of sending the copy back to Black, he returned it to Curley. He was sensitive enough to have a "fatherly chat" with Black, but he made many of the same points in that conversation.

"Early on, she had begun to believe her own press releases," Neuharth explained later. "She needed to realize that her expertise was in advertising, but if she played her cards right, we'd teach her something about the rest of the newspaper business. When Cathie went back to concentrating on advertising and quit pretending she could run the whole show, she became a super performer."

Black was hardly the first Gannett executive to run into Neuharth's buzzsaw. Similar up-or-out conversations, of varying intensity, had been a factor in the departures of some top managers—J. Warren McClure, who was once Gannett's vice president/marketing, and John "Jack" Purcell, who had been Gannett's chief financial officer before he joined CBS. The issue of being a team player, with Neuharth as quarterback, coach, and *boss,* had also been a factor in Karl Eller's departure. The difference between those who stayed and those who left Neuharth's inner circle was the difference between those who could play on a team with only one star, and those who could not. Black managed to resolve her frustration over titles and stay on the team, while building a high-profile image in advertising and social circles in New York and Washington. By 1986, U.S. News & World Report would call her "one of the best-known women in publishing."

As USA TODAY began to attract advertising, Black was the star of many feature stories in the trade press which noted the first signs of success. In one 1984 article, she was asked what it was like, working at Gannett. "It's not a company for the weak of heart," she said, a veiled reference to how hard Neuharth could come down on people. A year after she joined the company, Black had learned something new about what Neuharth liked to call Gannett's "philosophy, policy, and style."

CHAPTER EIGHTEEN

Wall Street 101

In July of 1984, another year in which USA TODAY's losses were averaging more than $10 million a month, Neuharth returned to Rosslyn from the Democratic Convention in San Francisco and began catching up on the local news. One of the first things he picked up was a Washington Post article on the prospects for Gannett stock.

The Business section story carried the headline: "Gannett Cut From List of Stock Buys." The lead said:

> Asserting that losses from USA TODAY would prove far higher than expected, a leading investment firm has cut Gannett Co., Inc. from its list of recommended stocks.
> Salomon Bros., a top Wall Street investment banking firm, said that advertiser acceptance for the 18-month-old national daily had proved "disappointing" and it contended that Gannett will be unable to reduce the paper's losses significantly.
> . . . As a result of this [advertising] shortfall, Gannett's overall future profitability will be affected, the investment firm asserted.

The Post's story did not mention any reports from analysts at other investment firms, but did quote Gannett Treasurer Jimmy Thomas as saying, "I don't agree with" the Salomon Brothers report. The reporter also quoted other media analysts who "agree that USA TODAY will continue to be a drain on Gannett's resources but say the company's growth will be relatively unaffected."

Neuharth was furious. "He went batshit," John Curley remembers. Neuharth ordered research done on all recent reports by analysts on media stocks—there had been many—and sat down at his black Royal, still steaming. He wrote The Post's editor, Ben Bradlee, this letter:

Dear Ben:

I've spent the last couple days, after returning from the San Francisco Demo bash, catching up on reading of old news and old *non*-news, published hereabouts while you and I were away.

In the latter category, I thought you might be interested in a factual review of circumstances re the attached Washington Post story about Gannett which appeared in your Business section on July 20, under the headline "Gannett Cut From List of Stock Buys."

The story and headline were contrived from a Salomon Brothers report on Gannett, issued by Ed Dunleavy, a leading Wall Street analyst. What Dunleavy's report said, in fact, is that he was changing his designation for Gannett from O (expected to *Outperform* the S&P 500 market average for the next 6 to 12 months) to M (expected to *Match* the S&P during the same period).

As you may know (or perhaps you may not) reports and recommendations from stock analysts occur daily from many, many different sources. Most of them, like Dunleavy, are quite knowledgeable and respected.

Among them are John Morton of Lynch, Jones and Ryan and Ken Noble of Paine, Webber, both of whom are quoted in your non-news story with generally favorable comments about Gannett.

To help you understand how Wall Street works, in the last few weeks, analyst reports on public media companies have included, but probably not been limited to, the following:

On June 26, Salomon Brothers reported on The Chicago Tribune Company, changing its designation from O to M. (No story in The Washington Post.)

On June 28, Salomon Brothers changed its designation for Knight-Ridder from O to M. (No story in The Washington Post.)

On June 29, Salomon Brothers changed its designation for

Times-Mirror from O to M. (No story in The Washington Post.)

On June 29, Donaldson, Lufkin & Jenrette issued a report that recommended deferring further purchases of several media companies, *including The Washington Post Company*, but continued to recommend buying Gannett. (No story in The Washington Post.)

On July 9, Salomon Brothers changed its designation for Gannett from O to M. (The basis for the story in The Washington Post eleven days later.)

On July 10, Donaldson, Lufkin & Jenrette recommended the purchase of Gannett stock. (No story in The Washington Post.)

On July 11, Drexel Burnham Lambert issued a report on Gannett titled, "Strong Second Quarter/Purchase Recommendation Reiterated." (No story in The Washington Post.)

On July 12, Donaldson, Lufkin & Jenrette issued another report recommending the purchase of Gannett stock. (No story in The Washington Post.)

On July 18, Drexel Burnham Lambert issued another report that said: "We continue to recommend strongly purchase of the Gannett common stock." (No story in The Washington Post.)

Yet on July 20, The Washington Post weighed in with a 15-inch story that was a misrepresentation of one analyst's eleven-day-old recommendation and failed even to explain what the recommendation was.

That story about Gannett didn't even get the day's stock closing price right. By-liner Michael Schrage reported that Gannett stock closed at $40^3/_8$, down one-quarter. Your own stock tables on following pages showed Gannett closed at 40, up one-eighth.

Please do not misunderstand the purpose of this note. It is by no means a request for any retraction, correction or clarification. (Your clarification column already threatens to become the most rapidly growing section of your newspaper and I do not wish to add to that burden.)

Since we are now a "local" company, with your boss Don Graham having solicited my United Way pledge card, we welcome closer coverage of Gannett in The Post. And, you well know, that as a newsman I understand and am more willing than most CEOs to accept the spotlight of publicity, good or bad.

But, my friend, it grieves me to see a good newspaper like The Washington Post, with its potential for greatness, so embarrass itself on its pages.

I don't expect all your financial reporters to have the same sophistication as the business reporters for The Wall Street Journal, or The New York Times, or USA TODAY.

But I suspect that is your goal. Therefore, in the spirit of brotherhood, if you are interested in having some of your business staff people sit in on an elementary lesson on Wall Street Analysis 101, I'll be happy to arrange it. I've a hunch we could even prevail on such a distinguished guest as Ed Dunleavy of Salomon Brothers to explain to y'll the difference between O and M and buy and hold and sell.

In the meantime, a friendly suggestion for when all you pros at The Post leave town next month to party with the Republicans in Dallas, as you did last week with the Democrats in San Francisco:

Instead of letting the amateurs play with your newspaper again in your absence, we'd be happy to provide a professional temporary "loaner" or two to help guide your ship on a more steady course.

This offer is not based on any worry that your folks might again pee on us poor people across the Potomac. It is prompted instead by my genuine concern about that unsuspecting public out there that doesn't understand how a good newspaper can sometimes be so bad.

Affectionately, if not admiringly,
Al Neuharth

Neuharth sent copies to Katharine Graham, the chairman of The Washington Post, Don Graham, its publisher, and three analysts, Ed Dunleavy, John Morton, and J. Kendrick Noble. He sent blind copies to all Gannett directors, several USA TODAY and Gannett executives, several other media stock analysts, and to his children, Dan and Jan.

Bradlee wrote back:

Dear Al:
Thank you for your condescending and fundamentally unpleasant letter of July 24.

Ben Bradlee says USA TODAY "redefined the news"—but it isn't his idea of news.

Now that you have moved your headquarters out of Rochester, you must expect that we will cover you as a major business in our area (the fifth largest compared to ourselves, a tenuous tenth). You certainly cannot expect to be covered as you were by the Rochester papers. Nor can you expect our Business & Finance section to run the stock-touting service that we read in USA TODAY's financial advice to the lovelorn.

I have looked at all the points in your letter, and I feel you are simply wrong about the Salomon recommendation. Dunleavy is the representative of one of the largest, most prestigious investment houses in the country. It is my understanding that he specifically told Salomon Brothers' clients not to buy Gannett stock. Not because it was a bad, money-losing company, but because the expected losses from USA TODAY were such a drain on the Gannett operation that the company no longer warranted an "O" rating. This in turn is newsworthy because they blamed the drain on the losses created by the unusual experiment that is USA TODAY.

As I understand the "O" and "M" designations—and I make no claim to match you on expertise and experience and involvement with the Wall Street crowd—an "O" means that a company is expected to outperform the market. An "M" means, therefore, that there is no real point in buying the stock because you can probably do better elsewhere.

The Salomon Brothers report became newsworthy for precisely the reason you outline in your letter: The other brokerages had been advising clients to buy, and suddenly

here comes a major investment house that warns against
such a purchase.

There is no way I can misunderstand the purpose of your
letter, what with its copies to Katharine Graham, Don
Graham, and Messrs. Dunleavy, Morton, and Noble. I don't
know how it will go over with them. It grates in my craw.
When I need help in Wall Street Analysis 101, I can promise
you I will turn to someone other than yourself to arrange it.

Now about these "loaners" which you offer us. Would
they be journalists who are already on loan to USA TODAY?
Which editor of which paper would I reimburse?

Yours in truth,
Ben Bradlee

P.S.: We did have one error. The stock did close at 40, up
an eighth. And I can't tell you how much I appreciated your
cheap shot about our clarification column. That is class.

Bradlee copied the same people Neuharth had, but of course he
didn't know about the blind copies. Neuharth replied:

Dear Ben:

Aw shucks, I didn't mean to ignite your short fuse!

Your misguided missile of July 27, obviously hip-fired in
quick retaliation for my note of July 24, missed all the marks.

Neither you nor I have the time to get involved in a pen-pal
relationship. Therefore, I won't prolong this exchange by
commenting specifically on your comments.

Suffice to say, I understand that you don't understand.

But Ben, the air of arrogance you exhale really is polluting
The Post's reputation. Think about it.

A lot of the rest of us in this profession think about it a lot,
because as a high visibility player, what you and The Post do
or say rubs off, or rubs in, on all of us.

Please remember, I ain't mad at anybody. Not at you.
Certainly not at The Post. The particular story I wrote you
about simply was a matter of human judgment error. I understand those things happen.

I also believe that journalists should be as willing to admit
their own errors as they are to point out mistakes of others.
You've done your share (or more) of the latter; you ought to
think about the former.

In the twilight of your career, my friend, you still have the
opportunity to balance your well-deserved reputation for
toughness with some late-blooming fairness. Think about it.

In any event, I still believe that a good, albeit frequently
erratic, Washington Post will some day be great. Smart
young turks like Don Graham, Len Downie and others will
build on one legacy and overcome the other.

Love, but no kisses,

Al Neuharth

Neuharth copied Kay Graham, Don Graham, and Len Downie, The
Post's new managing editor. He sent blind copies to everyone who had
gotten the other letters. Then Neuharth had the correspondence
leaked to several magazines. Washingtonian magazine devoted a page
to the "Neuharth-Bradlee Letters: A Sneak Peek at the Battle
Between These Titanic Egos." Advertising Age said, "Neuharth &
Bradlee make poison pen pals."

In Advertising Age's August 6 edition, James Brady included the
following item in his "Brady's Bunch" column:

> Salomon Brothers wants it known it hasn't issued a "sell
> recommendation" on Gannett stock because of USA TODAY's
> costs. Salomon tells me it doesn't issue such advisories.
> What it does is rate stocks "O" for those outperforming the
> market, "M" for those matching it, and "U" for stocks that
> underperform. What Salomon did was drop Gannett from
> "O" to "M."

Bradlee had discovered, as Fred Christopherson in Sioux Falls and
Martin Andersen in Orlando had learned decades earlier, that Neuharth was a formidable adversary in a pissing contest. In 1987, three
years after the exchange of letters, Bradlee was still wary. When
asked to give a reporter his opinion of USA TODAY, Bradlee started to
talk and then hesitated: "I'd better shut up before I get in trouble." He
said he didn't want to fight with Al Neuharth anymore.

CHAPTER NINETEEN

The Last
Supper

USA TODAY's darkest days came just before Thanksgiving, 1984. Neuharth was not sure whether they would be able to turn things around or not.

At the August board meeting, he had told the directors that the "ruthless reality" was that USA TODAY would probably lose as much as $124 million in 1984, $16 million more than the "maximum motivation goal" he had let the operating executives pursue. Neuharth's pessimistic estimate turned out to be true. In 1984, it was losing more than $10 million a month.

Put another way, the newspaper was losing $339,726 every day, $14,155 every hour, $236 every minute, $3.93 every second. Although advertising had improved, heavy discounts were being used to keep volume up, and that held revenues down. In October 1984, the paper was getting nine or ten ad pages per day, but it was giving away an average of three pages a day.

Wall Street analysts realized the losses were much larger than anyone had expected. Drexel Burnham issued a report that predicted Gannett would shut down USA TODAY if it did not turn the corner soon. In Drexel's view, that possibility made Gannett's stock a good bet—the company was finally going to wise up and cut its losses. Earlier in 1984, in his newsletter on advertising trends, Bernard Gallagher said: "We predict demise of paper within six months. Reason: Advertisers not convinced USA TODAY viable alternative to newsweeklies."

On November 10, 1984, a day or two after he had received October's financial results which showed USA TODAY had lost another $10 million that month, Neuharth called John Curley at home. It was late Saturday morning, and Curley was about to walk out the door to drive to the Delaware-Lehigh football game. "These numbers are a fucking disaster," Neuharth said. "We've got to do something dramatic to get people's attention. We've got to turn the thing around." He told Curley to arrange for every member of USA TODAY's management committee to be at Pumpkin Center by midday Sunday. Late Saturday night, Cathie Black returned home from a day with her husband in Virginia's Blue Ridge mountains to find a message on her recording machine, telling her to be on a corporate jet that was leaving from Dulles Airport Sunday morning.

When the managers walked into the conference room at Pumpkin Center, none of the usual amenities were on the table—no water, no coffee, no hard candy. Skipping the small talk and the usual jokes, Neuharth began the meeting. Choosing his words carefully, he spoke slowly and deliberately. He mentioned the "promises" they had made to the board in August, and reminded them that USA TODAY was hemorrhaging red ink; the losses were way beyond their projections. These excerpts from his notes for that meeting show he was blunt about the bleak outlook:

> Thanks for giving up a Sunday. Why are we here? Because we have a little problem. We can no longer afford to run USA TODAY the way we've been running it.
>
> We can't afford it financially, we can't afford it in terms of our credibility, we can't afford it emotionally. Is this fun? To be losing money this way?
>
> We have two alternatives. We can (a) quit it, or (b) change it. Alternative (a) would mean that we declare defeat and move on to other dull things. Alternative (b) means we make a major effort at changing many things in many areas—to try to win. So we need major—some drastic—policy changes. I make the policy changes, you implement them. It won't be easy. It won't be pleasant. *Some* of you may not want to keep playing. If so, I understand.
>
> Everything boils down to a few simple, ruthless realities. Overall, we must now substitute management for money.
>
> We must produce and present even more news, with fewer people, in less space, at lower cost.

> We must sell and present even more advertising, at higher
> rates, with fewer people, at lower costs.
> We must produce and print more newspapers, with even
> better quality, with fewer people, at lower cost.
> We must circulate and sell even more newspapers, at
> higher prices, with fewer people, at lower cost.
> We could decide we have been passed over by the ruthless
> realities, declare defeat, and go on to other things; or renew
> and revise our approach to this adventure and pass on to win.
> We arc opting for the latter.

Neuharth ordered a 5 percent cut in payroll costs that had to be
carried out by the end of 1985. "Naturally this means the departure of
some nonproductive and marginal personnel so we can continue to
properly reward productive people," he said.

He told them that USA TODAY's loss for 1985 had to be under $75
million. To make sure it was, they would police all costs line-by-line.
Before any new hires could be made, approval was required in writing
from Neuharth or John Curley. Neuharth added a warning: Any deviation of more than 5 percent from the plan "will be considered
unsatisfactory and the executives responsible for such deviation subject to dismissal."

After this grim meeting, they adjourned for dinner to Bernard's
Surf, a Cocoa Beach restaurant that was locally famous as a hangout of
the astronauts, a place where Gannett had hosted hundreds of company dinners—but never before or since a company dinner like this
one. Neuharth had summoned them to town to shock them, and shock
them he did.

The restaurant was run by a Jewish friend of Neuharth's, Rusty
Fischer. When the USA TODAY executives arrived at the Surf, the door
to their private dining room was closed, and Neuharth was not around.
Thirty minutes later, the door opened and there was Neuharth: He
was wearing a crown of thorns. There was a huge wooden cross leaning against the wall behind him.

Neuharth and restaurateur Fischer had arranged the room so it
resembled the scene of the Last Supper. Gannett executives were
used to drinking Pouilly-Fuisse, but this long, sparse table had jugs of
Manichevitz wine and pieces of unleavened bread on it. "I am the cru-

cified one," Neuharth told them. Then he presided at what he called "The Service for the Passed-Over," which he had based on the Jewish observance of Passover.

Neuharth had decided upon a loose, theatrical adaptation of two religious events, and the result was a mixed religious metaphor. He superimposed the service for the Jewish feast of Seder, a Passover ritual which commemorates the Jews' escape from Egypt, on top of a setting in which he played the role of Jesus at the Last Supper. "Passover" appealed to him because if USA TODAY did not cut its losses soon, they were all going to be "passed-over." Then this meal at Bernard's Surf might indeed prove to be their "last supper." In addition to the cross and other props, Neuharth also passed out scripts to the somewhat stunned executives.

He read some lines from the Seder service, which Fischer had given to him. He asked the ritual question, "Why, on this night, do we eat especially bitter herbs?" Each member of the group was supposed to respond, reading from the script, "This bitter herb is eaten because we are threatening to embitter our lives and the lives of our children," but there wasn't much enthusiasm from the "followers."

Some of them watched, John Quinn remembers, with "benign amusement." Quinn, a lifelong Roman Catholic and former altar boy,

Among those attending the "Last Supper" were, from left, Cathie Black, Tom Farrell, Lee Guittar, Barbara Whitney, Al Neuharth, John Curley, and Tom Dolan.

spent most of the evening outside in the main dining room with his wife Loie; he saw the "Last Supper" as another Neuharth attempt to dramatize the need for better management with a dash of humor.

Others were shocked. "I was appalled," said Charles Overby, the former editor of the Jackson, Mississippi, newspapers who was then Neuharth's special assistant. Overby, a Southern Baptist who sometimes taught Sunday School, says "It was the most offensive thing I have seen in my adult life. I was waiting for lightning to strike that place down, I was so mortified." After the "service," they ate an ordinary seafood dinner.

Neuharth explained later: "Some USA TODAY executives were getting lethargic. They were beginning to think our money supply was unlimited. They needed to be jarred into reality. A simple statement would not have done it. The 'Last Supper' drama got their attention. Those who got the humor of it laughed; those who were offended didn't get it."

■

Earlier that day, Neuharth had ordered several specific steps to cut costs. One memo went to Lee Guittar, USA TODAY's fifth president, who was in charge of circulation. Neuharth said: "While every dollar spent in every phase of the USA TODAY operation is important, the big, back-breaking bucks are those spent in field circulation operations." He asked for a report outlining how Guittar was going to reduce costs. Field circulation costs—to place and repair racks, service newsstands, and truck newspapers around the country—were running more than $80 million a year.

The good news in circulation was that USA TODAY had come through its first price increase, from twenty-five cents to thirty-five cents, with minimal losses. In the fall of 1984, the newspaper reported that its circulation was 1.25 million, off 5 percent from the March number of 1.33 million. Guittar told reporters the drop was modest, considering that the price had been raised 40 percent and customers had to "fiddle with two coins instead of one." By now, the newspaper's circulation was about 70 percent single-copy sales; the remaining 30 percent was home, office, and mail delivery.

The News department did its part by producing a barrage of special stories accompanied by a logo that said "More." The campaign included special features on "summer boom towns," a weekly USA Calendar, a personal finance feature called "Your Money Plan," and a special on couples and their relationships. The added features and heavy promotion continued for several weeks; it was another example of how the different departments, even those that were sometimes at odds, pulled together to try to help the whole survive.

During that fall Tom Curley, who had been promoted from editor in Norwich, Connecticut, to publisher in Bridgewater, New Jersey, did a survey of the newsracks. His conclusion was that "one of USA TODAY's most wonderful and heralded innovations—its vending machine— needs to be rescued. The company has failed to make maintaining this hallmark a priority. About a fifth of the racks are filthy and another fifth are dirty."

The company had bought 135,000 newsracks. Each one was about four feet high. If all of the racks were stacked on top of one another, they would reach 102 miles into the sky, or an altitude equal to 366 Empire State Buildings. Maintaining all of those racks was a huge job; it was no wonder some of them got dirty. By the end of 1986, the company estimated that 19,666 racks—worth $4.4 million—had been lost, stolen, or destroyed.

Neuharth was not the only one who had a "morning job" checking newsracks. Many Gannett and USA TODAY employees routinely reported sell-outs or delivery problems. For example, Doug McCorkindale told Paul Flynn that some of his friends who had vacation homes on Long Island were unable to buy USA TODAY in East Hampton. "It might be worth supplying some copies there next summer," McCorkindale said. Another early opponent of USA TODAY, Treasurer Jimmy Thomas, wrote his old friend Bob Crandall, the president of American Airlines, asking him to buy copies for his customers.

John Curley reported counting twenty-one empty newsracks on a Friday afternoon in San Francisco. Cathie Black spotted a box on 72nd and Lexington in Manhattan that had been surrounded by scaffolding. Gannett lawyer Alice Neff Lucan once used spit and a handkerchief to clean off the dirty window of a USA TODAY rack in Georgetown. Gannett's busiest executives found time to fix minute details.

Even while he was deeply worried about USA TODAY's finances, Neuharth was still going over its news content every day with a fine-tooth comb. On October 5, 1984, he fired off another zinger to John Quinn:

Damnit! After two years, can't we find someone on the Page 1 desk who can add, subtract and read and think, and can't we find someone in the Sports department who can think and double-check things?

Screwing up the World Series schedule as we did in Rudy Martzke's Page 1 story today is absolutely inexcusable. Anyone who follows baseball knows that for years and years games 1 and 2 are played on Tuesday & Wednesday; Thursday is an open date; games 3, 4 and 5 are played on Friday, Saturday and Sunday; games 6 & 7 are played on Tuesday and Wednesday. *Nobody* with any knowledge whatsoever should have let this screwup re games 5 & 6 on Tuesday and Wednesday get in the paper. Actually, that screwup fits the rest of the Page 1 strip story—which was a contrived nothing.

We simply have too many examples of sloppy writing and editing of stories which should have accurate facts in them— especially when it comes to television viewing of sports or anything else. Damnit! Everyone in a position of responsibility in editing this newspaper must put himself or herself in the place of the reader or viewer and tell those readers what they want to know.

Unless we can figure out a fool-proof system to have this done right by our Sports people and our Page 1 people, you will find me back haunting all of you in the Sports department and on the Page 1 desk every night, pretty damn soon.

Sports editor Henry Freeman got a copy of Neuharth's note. "We didn't used to make these kinds of mistakes," he complained in a note to his top associates. "I don't care whose ass you have to kick to get this fixed, but *fix* it. I'm getting tired of getting notes like this from the chairman."

CHAPTER TWENTY

The journalism of hope

By creating a brand-new publication that fit in no conventional category, Neuharth had thrown down a gauntlet for advertisers, challenging them to think again about how they bought advertising. But he did not stop there. He threw down his gauntlet for journalists too, daring them to think again about the way they presented news to readers.

In October 1983, when USA TODAY was a little more than one year old, Neuharth made a controversial speech at the Overseas Press Club in New York City. In it, he asked whether what he called the "old journalism of despair"—"the derisive technique of leaving readers discouraged, or mad, or indignant—should survive or thrive in the eighties and nineties."

To replace the "old journalism of despair" Neuharth proposed a "new journalism of hope." He defined it as an approach that "chronicles the good, the bad, and the otherwise, and leaves readers fully informed and equipped to judge what deserves their attention and support."

That was the philosophy Neuharth used to guide USA TODAY. The new national newspaper, he said, seeks "to cover all of the news, with accuracy, but without anguish, with detail but without despair." He added that he hoped the newspaper's voice would "advocate understanding and unity, rather than disdain and divisiveness." The "unity" idea was there again, a strong strain in his life.

A story on death rates on January 7, 1983, helps illustrate what Neuharth meant by the "journalism of hope." USA TODAY's lead read:

WASHINGTON—Advances in science and better health habits have produced dramatic drops in the death rates for almost all age groups in the USA, the government said Thursday.

In the headline over the story, the Page One editors tried to emphasize the positive side of the news. The head said: "Death rate drops but not for 15–24 group."

The Detroit News ran a similar wire-service version of the story, but its headline said: "Death rate up for the young." In Neuharth's view, that was an example of the "journalism of despair."

In fact, Neuharth did not think USA TODAY's headline had gone far enough to highlight the bright side of that health story. The day that it ran, editors were attending the annual "brainstorming" session at Pumpkin Center. Neuharth focused on Page One Editor Ray Gniewek.

"Gniewek," Neuharth said, "today's front page has a horrible headline on it."

"Which one?" asked Gniewek tentatively.

"'Death rate drops,'" Neuharth said. "It should have read, 'We're living longer.'"

Gniewek said nothing. Quinn had written the headline, but he didn't say anything either. Two years later, on the day editors arrived for another Pumpkin Center brainstorming session, another story about a drop in the death rate happened to make the front page. Gniewek made the most of this coincidence. This time the headline read, "We're living longer." Neuharth never said a word.

Gniewek later joked, "The journalism of despair is death and taxes. The journalism of hope is living longer and tax avoidance."

Ray Gniewek designed a program on his home personal computer that could generate a Page 1A layout and position stories and headlines in minutes.

Neuharth's approach rankled some critics. Ben Bagdikian, dean of the Journalism School at the University of California at Berkeley, derides the "journalism of hope" as the "journalism of joy." Bagdikian says: "At best, I think that's a meaningless phrase for journalism. It's just an inappropriate way to look at the news, as it would be to say that we should have the journalism of doom and gloom. News tends to accentuate conflict. Some of that is inevitably negative."

Del Brinkman, a University of Kansas vice chancellor who was dean of its journalism school, says he thinks Neuharth's philosophy is simply a plea for balance—balancing the bad news with some good news, answering the negative with the positive. "USA TODAY represents that kind of balance," he says.

In its early days, USA TODAY may have carried the "good news" philosophy too far. In a Washington Journalism Review article assessing the newspaper after four years, Barbara Matusow wrote: "Many journalists were particularly disturbed by the paper's relentlessly upbeat tone—a reflection of Neuharth's philosophy that news is something more than a recital of hurricanes and other calamities. He has a point, but the early USA TODAY sounded mindlessly breezy at times; one headline, following a plane crash proclaimed: 'Miracle: 327 survive, 55 die.'"

The former editor of The Boston Globe, Thomas Winship, thinks that "from a commercial point of view, bad news has hurt newspapers. But I was never much on labeling news and putting it into categories. You shouldn't be self-conscious about how you pick and choose news."

James D. Wilson/Woodfin Camp

Journalism professor Ben Bagdikian says of USA TODAY: "It is not a very good paper with which to keep abreast of serious news."

USA TODAY's drive for balance did help attract readers; many mentioned they liked the way the newspaper "gave both sides" and "kept opinion out of the news columns." Frank Middleton of Denver wrote: "USA TODAY's headlines are looking for the bright side of the news, and that can do more to help the positive attitude of Americans than most anything. Keep up the positive news!"

Neuharth often told his staff that newspapers should work harder to provide fair, balanced coverage. At news meetings he sometimes asked if editors were overplaying the negative news. In a 1983 note to Quinn, he complained about the lead on a cover story about a price increase for first-class stamps. It began with a quote from a retired Chicago man who said: "The mail comes late—and then they deliver it to the wrong apartment." Neuharth wrote in his memo that the man's comment "belonged deep down in the story. . . . When we pee on news developments with this kind of negativism we are guilty of everything that we accuse some others of doing. Please rub all the proper noses in this so we can learn from it. Thanks."

USA TODAY did not ignore negative news. But a review of early editions shows that it did put most of it on the "Second Front Page," page 3A. Most of the mass murders, hostage situations, and child molestation stories appeared on 3A, while 1A tried to emphasize a brighter, more optimistic tone, balancing the hard news of the day with lighter fare of wide interest.

Neuharth said often that USA TODAY's devotion to balance was partly responsible for its popularity. "The most frequent comment we get in reader surveys is that USA TODAY is 'an enjoyable reading experience,'" he said in a 1984 interview. "Apparently, we are able to inform them without offending them. There's a very fine line to balance the good and the bad, the glad and the sad, if we are to truly mirror the USA every day. Most readers think USA TODAY does that."

While USA TODAY's founder was aware of that "fine line," he was also quick to seize every opportunity for a commercial advantage. For example, the newspaper's heavy use of "USA" in its news columns to identify what other newspapers called "America" or "American" grew out of his desire to promote the newspaper. Even though he had personally written the front-page headline on the first day—"America's Princess Grace Dies in Monaco"—Neuharth later felt that was a mistake. He wrote in a 1985 memo to editors:

I'll explain it *one* more time. America is made up of Canada, the United States of America, Central America, South America, and more.

The USA is made up of the United States of America. All 50 of them. And its territories. No more. No less.

Any poll, any news story which refers broadly to Americans, when it really means only the people in the United States of America, is subterfuge. It represents inexcusably sloppy reporting and editing.

Perhaps equally important, it flies in the face of the philosophy, policy and style clearly spelled out by the Founder of USA TODAY. In our news columns, it is never appropriate to refer to America or Americans unless we mean *all* of the Americas or *all* Americans; it is *always* appropriate to refer to the USA when we mean the United States of America.

I do not expect all reporters always to know about philosophy, policy and style. I *do* expect *all* editors always to know. Please make sure all editors understand. If anyone does not, I'll be happy to arrange a transfer for him/her to Calgary, or Cuzco or Curitiba so that he/she can practice journalism for a different audience in The Americas than that which we serve in the USA.

Earlier Neuharth had not been so sensitive to the concerns of other "Americans." When hundreds of newsracks were placed on street corners in Canada, there was a barrage of complaints from Canadians. "USA TODAY isn't this nation's newspaper," snapped Jack Layton, a Toronto alderman. Black tape was used to cover over the motto, "The Nation's Newspaper," on two thousand boxes in Canada.

Editorial Director John Seigenthaler told Neuharth that he thought the "USA" edict went too far, although he would enforce it on the Opinion Page. Seigenthaler said that when Moses came down from the mountain and announced "Thou shalt not commit adultery," some married couples stopped copulating just to be on the safe side. That kind of overreaction sometimes occurred in the newsroom, as when reporters referred to the "USA Department of Agriculture." At Neuharth's direction, the Sports department renamed its "All-American" teams "All-USA" teams. The word "American" was banned when referring to people living in the United States. Instead of using "Americans," editorials had to say "we" or "the people of the USA."

Caesar Andrews joined USA TODAY as a loaner from TODAY in Florida, and was promoted to senior states editor, then deputy managing editor of bonus sections. In early 1987, he returned to Brevard County as managing editor of FLORIDA TODAY. About 550 journalists have participated in the loaner program.

The Associated Press Stylebook handles the "American" issue this way: "Do not limit the description to citizens or residents of the United States. It also may be applied to any resident or citizen of nations in North or South America."

Some wordsmiths disagree with Neuharth's premise. William Safire wrote in his New York Times column on language that it is permissible to call U.S. citizens "Americans" because other residents of the Americas—Mexicans and Canadians—do not refer to themselves as "Americans" or even as "North Americans." Safire added, with a quick twist of his knife, that the letters USA "are the initials of the name of the country and are not the trademark of a subsidiary of the Gannett Newspapers."

But Neuharth stuck by his "USA" philosophy, partly because he believed in it and partly because he thought it helped sell newspapers. "I started it because it's a good way to promote USA TODAY," he says. Late-night headline writers like Quinn also felt "USA" was much easier to work with while trying to wedge words into a small space.

When it came to photos, Neuharth thought page one should occasionally have some sex appeal; he had not forgotten how much the male readers of SoDak Sports had liked those shots of Mamie Van Doren. In January 1983, Neuharth attended his first news meeting in several weeks. In the window of the newsrack in the conference room, the smiling face of a leaping cheerleader was above the fold—the top half of page one. After all of the editors were seated, Neuharth strode over to the newsrack. He opened the door and then slammed it violently. He did that again and again, banging the door against the rack.

Each afternoon, Sunday through Thursday, fifteen states' editors talk to sixty correspondents across the country and read the wire-service reports from each state to compile the Across the USA package.

The assembled editors stared, wide-eyed. He had their attention now. "When you run a picture of a nice clean-cut all-American girl like this," Neuharth announced, *"get her tits above the fold."*

Neuharth's penchant for promoting USA TODAY led to the newspaper's decision to be an official sponsor of the 1985 inauguration of President Reagan, a move that drew criticism. Inaugural planners were given $336,000 worth of advertising space. In return, USA TODAY received tickets to the inaugural balls and was mentioned as a sponsor of a positive, patriotic event. Gloria Cooper, managing editor of the Columbia Journalism Review, told The Washington Post, "My first reaction is to laugh. It seems to me the paper sort of put itself in the same league as M&Ms or Snickers, like the official sponsors of the U.S. Olympic team."

While the newspaper's basic format remained constant, its editors began a drive to improve its content, and "McPaper" began to win respect. Barbara Matusow wrote in Washington Journalism Review: "Now almost four years old, USA TODAY sounds less boosterish, although it consciously pursues a different editorial agenda from other papers, using more features and 'news you can use' on the front page."

In the first few months of publication, some readers had complained that the front page was too "soft," that it lacked urgency. Ed Cony, a top Wall Street Journal editor, said: "Our light feature probably has more depth than anything on the front page of USA TODAY."

"I enjoy USA TODAY," wrote Ron Coolbaugh of Long Beach, California, "but the paper could have more emphasis on hard news on the front page. As the main story recently, you have 'Big Easter hints at travel season boom.' Without more hard news, the paper begins to take on a less credible appearance."

Realizing that, Quinn made himself a permanent fixture on the Page One desk after he became editor in April 1983. Most nights he was there until midnight or later, tinkering with headlines, packing in hard news, envisioning how the front page would look in the newsrack. Quinn loved his work. He said later, "In this working world, there is no better title than editor and no better life than working at being one as the newspaper goes to bed."

As the front page groped for that harder edge, what evolved was USA TODAY's special spin on the news—the "look ahead." Quinn says: "About the time I became editor, we realized we were going to have

John Quinn is the quintessential hands-on editor, making last-minute revisions late at night even as Page 1A is being pasted up in the composing room. Editors scanned early editions of other major newspapers every night, frequently picking up stories. For example, on April 8, 1987, USA TODAY ran this line: "The Reagan administration and supporters raised up to $97 million for the contras between 1984 and 1986, The New York Times reports today."

to deal with the hard news of the day on page one. Then we had experiences when you'd pick the paper up in the morning and we'd gone from being too different to being not different enough. So from that emerged what was our own 'spin' on the story, to look ahead to what happens next."

Quinn, Ron Martin, and other editors gradually defined USA TODAY's special approach to the news. It would try to tell the reader what happened in the past twenty-four hours, what was likely to happen in the next twenty-four hours, and what it all meant to the reader. "McPaper" was finding the identity it had lacked in the beginning.

Martin was in charge of enforcing USA TODAY's emphasis on clear, concise writing. He did it with his own special communications— "Rongrams." These were notes or page proofs marked up with brown ink; no one else used that color. An ongoing nervous joke was: "I saw a Rongram in the mail with your name on it. It had a bus ticket attached

to it." Rongrams always carried a little sting. For example, Martin
wrote Taylor Buckley in late 1982:

> Taylor: This INSIDERS package is about as big a mess as
> I've seen yet. The copy is overwritten, it is poorly edited,
> and the content mix is just a package of rehash. I propose
> that:
> —Starting today, we get a look at this page in advance.
> Why not just produce two pages today—one for Tuesday and
> one for Wednesday—and stay one ahead. We can always sub
> items out if we have breaking news; god knows we rarely do,
> at this point.
> —You need to consider getting a writer and an editor for
> this page. The material needs to be better and more brightly
> written, and some editorial judgment needs to be exercised.
> Consistently, I'm sorry to say, this is about the most trou-
> blesome page in the newspaper. It has the potential to be one
> of the best.

Another detail Martin monitored daily was diversity. Neuharth had
long preached that Gannett's leadership had to reflect its readership;
he also believed news content had to mirror the nation's diversity. He
did not want USA TODAY full of photos of middle-aged white men, the
way many newspapers were. Early in 1983, Neuharth sent top editors
a memo about the page 2s, which ran short features on people. "Page
2 in each section is coming around with the female flavor," Neuharth
said. "2A today, excellent; 2B, excellent; 2C, excellent; 2D, bad. The
female flavor that we must have on these pages *every* day will be there
consistently *only* if you tell all four section editors that they *must* have
at least one female illustration every day. Please fix."

One night after 9 P.M., long after page 2B had left the composing
room floor bound for the satellite, Martin called the Money desk and
said he wanted a woman's face on 2B "tomorrow morning." Deputy
Managing Editor Monte Trammer scrounged a story out of a trade
magazine and remade the page. It was a long time before 2B neglected
the "female flavor" again.

Editors also worked hard to get the faces of minorities into the
newspaper and to hire talented minority journalists. At the beginning
of 1987, 15 percent of USA TODAY's newsroom managers were from
minority groups, and 18 percent of its newsroom professionals were

minorities. Nationally in 1986, only 3.9 percent of newsroom managers and only 6.6 percent of newsroom professionals were minorities. Forty-one percent of USA TODAY's managers and 40 percent of its newsroom professionals were women. The newspaper's hiring record for women and minorities was much better than that of most other newspapers, but as Neuharth and Quinn said often, "We can do better still."

At the 1986 Operation Push convention, Chuck Stone, a senior editor at Knight-Ridder's Philadelphia newspapers, praised USA TODAY for having "the largest percentage of blacks, Hispanics, and women in positions of responsibility. That's only half of it, hiring black people. The other is how you depict the news, how do you portray blacks and Hispanics. You look at USA TODAY and every day in its pages . . . you always find blacks, Hispanics, and women and minorities portrayed as just normal people. They're not singing and dancing or stuffing a basketball or being sexist. . . . [It is] the fairest newspaper in the country."

An example of USA TODAY's sensitivity to racial concerns, and willingness to correct errors, appeared on the Inquiry page on January 29, 1986. Called "Anatomy of an error," the article was one of the most thorough explanations of an error ever run in a newspaper. It explained how a false statement got into an Opinion page column by Morris B. Abram, then vice chairman of the U.S. Commission on Civil Rights. Abram had written that, in 1979, the Reverend Joseph Lowery of the Southern Christian Leadership Conference, Benjamin Hooks of the NAACP, and Georgia State Sen. Julian Bond had given the "decoration of Martin Luther King" to Libya's Col. Muammar Khadafy.

That never happened. A Harvard professor, Glenn C. Loury, had made a speech in which he made the error. He based his comments on a book, *Jesse Jackson and the Politics of Race,* by Thomas Landess and Richard Quinn. An abridged version of Loury's speech was published in Commentary magazine and Abram picked it up from there. The error was adopted as fact in his USA TODAY column, and in columns by Albert Vorspan in The New York Times and the Palm Beach Jewish World. In 1986 Khadafy had been blamed for terrorist attacks against Americans, so tagging civil rights leaders with giving Khadafy an award was a very serious charge. The error had taken on a life of its own, but John Quinn's idea to run a half-page explanation, which let everyone involved comment, helped put the mistake to rest.

A misjudgment in July 1983 was harder to correct. USA TODAY's editorial board was preparing a daily debate on tuition tax credits—whether the Supreme Court was right when it approved a Minnesota law allowing taxpayers to take tax credits for tuition paid to private and parochial schools. The board reached a consensus that it would be a mistake for the government to subsidize private and parochial schools with public money. David Seavey, USA TODAY's cartoonist, drew a cartoon that showed a Supreme Court justice presenting a communion wafer—the body of Christ in Roman Catholic theology—to a clergyman wearing a clerical collar. The wafer came from a chalice labeled "tax break" and the clergyman wore a mortar board labeled "church schools."

Peter Prichard, then USA TODAY's deputy editorial director and this book's author, reviewed the cartoon. It was awfully strong, but then, it certainly made the point. He showed it to Dan Martin, then editor of The Port Huron (Mich.) Times Herald, who was on loan to USA TODAY as an editorial writer. Martin, a practicing Roman Catholic, was not offended. "I thought it was a great cartoon," he says. So Prichard let it go, never realizing how many Catholics it would deeply offend.

Hundreds of letters of outrage poured in. The Reverend Virgil Blum, of the Catholic League for Religious and Civil Rights, spoke for many when he wrote: "The July 5 editorial cartoon was defamatory and viciously anti-Catholic. . . . Such blasphemy and bigotry is hardly consistent with USA TODAY's purpose to foster 'better understanding and unity to help make the USA truly one nation.'"

Editorial Director John Seigenthaler wrote Blum a long letter explaining that no one on the editorial board had intended to insult Catholics or demean a sacred religious ritual. A few weeks later, when a study found parochial schools were doing a better job than public schools, the editorial board did a page on the value of religious education. Blum wrote Seigenthaler back, praising the commitment to balance.

In 1984, the editorial board had to decide whether to endorse a candidate for president. After two days of discussion, the board decided not to endorse. It was not a close call: Only two or three people on the ten-member board felt USA TODAY should back a candidate. The majority felt it would be a mistake for a newspaper that had built a reputation for fairness and balance, in part because it published an "opposing point of view" to its own every day, to back one candidate or one

*Hundreds of outraged
readers wrote to USA TODAY
in response to this cartoon by
David Seavey, above.*

political party. "That would be like putting a political bumper sticker on
our masthead," Seigenthaler said later.

While he did not participate in the editorial board's decision, Neuharth was pleased with it. He announced the news the day before it was
published when he spoke at the National Press Club. Neuharth said
that "as the only national general-interest daily newspaper, USA TODAY
has a unique role. Our mission is to inform, to enlighten, to provoke
debate, but not to dictate. We seek neither to be king-makers nor king-
breakers."

Like every newspaper, USA TODAY made its share of run-of-the-mill
mistakes in the early years. Many errors involved photos. It mixed up
senators, identifying Sen. John Heinz as Sen. Joseph Biden. It mixed
up spies, identifying convicted spy Johnny Walker as his brother who
was also convicted, Arthur Walker. It mixed up stock prices. On
August 17, 1983, due to a computer operator's error, it printed the New
York Stock Exchange results from the wrong day—every price was
wrong. And the Sports staff allowed a joke to get into the newspaper.
One night Edmonton Oilers' star Wayne Gretzky had another great
game, scoring the game-winning goal. A news assistant working on the
game's statistics asked who had scored the winning goal. "God,"

someone said. So the news assistant typed "God" into the box score instead of "Gretsky." No one caught it and Managing Editor Henry Freeman put two people on probation.

Even on everyday flubs, the correction policy was firm. Quinn made sure errors were corrected quickly. Corrections ran on page two of the section where the mistake occurred, and on page one of the section if that was where the error was made. When a picture was wrong in the Newsline column on page one, Quinn corrected it with the proper photo in the same spot the next day.

The Sports section had won compliments from the critics from the beginning. In the fall of 1983, the Washington Journalism Review called it "The sports section that rolls over its rivals." Fred Barnes wrote:

> Almost from the paper's first day of publication it has,
> arguably at least, been the best sports section in the country.

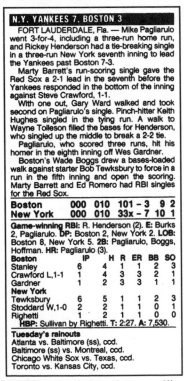

N.Y. YANKEES 7, BOSTON 3

FORT LAUDERDALE, Fla. — Mike Pagliarulo went 3-for-4, including a three-run home run, and Rickey Henderson had a tie-breaking single in a three-run New York seventh inning to lead the Yankees past Boston 7-3.

Marty Barrett's run-scoring single gave the Red Sox a 2-1 lead in the seventh before the Yankees responded in the bottom of the inning against Steve Crawford, 1-1.

With one out, Gary Ward walked and took second on Pagliarulo's single. Pinch-hitter Keith Hughes singled in the tying run. A walk to Wayne Tolleson filled the bases for Henderson, who singled up the middle to break a 2-2 tie.

Pagliarulo, who scored three runs, hit his homer in the eighth inning off Wes Gardner.

Boston's Wade Boggs drew a bases-loaded walk against starter Bob Tewksbury to force in a run in the fifth inning and open the scoring. Marty Barrett and Ed Romero had RBI singles for the Red Sox.

Boston	000	010	101 – 3	9 2
New York	000	010	33x – 7	10 1

Game-winning RBI: R. Henderson (2). E: Burks 2, Pagliarulo. DP: Boston 2, New York 2. LOB: Boston 8, New York 5. 2B: Pagliarulo, Boggs, Hoffman. HR: Pagliarulo (3).

Boston	IP	H	R	ER	BB	SO
Stanley	6	4	1	1	2	3
Crawford L,1-1	1	4	3	3	2	1
Gardner	1	2	3	3	1	1
New York						
Tewksbury	6	5	1	1	2	3
Stoddard W,1-0	2	2	1	1	0	1
Righetti	1	2	1	1	0	0

HBP: Sullivan by Righetti. T: 2:27. A: 7,530.

Tuesday's rainouts
Atlanta vs. Baltimore (ss), ccd.
Baltimore (ss) vs. Montreal, ccd.
Chicago White Sox vs. Texas, ccd.
Toronto vs. Kansas City, ccd.

An example of "how they scored" coverage.

Bob Barbrow says, "On any given day, agate we produce could fill up to 60 percent of the section." The Sports section is now linked by computer to the NCAA, NHL, and the Elias Sports Bureau, which handles the NFL, NBA, and National and American baseball leagues.

Arguably because it follows a different formula. If flashy writing and the sociological approach to covering athletes, prevalent on many sports pages, are required, USA TODAY falters badly. . . . But if what matters are results, old-fashioned scores and averages and standings, and far more of them than you can get anywhere else, USA TODAY routs all its rivals. Its sports section is a cornucopia of results. And it is just what hard-core sports fans have been craving for years—but not getting.

Barnes and other critics were beginning to realize that USA TODAY offered depth and detail, but in a different way from traditional newspapers. The depth came in thousands of facts, rather than single stories that were thousands of words long.

The Sports section, Neuharth said proudly, published more facts than any other newspaper. Many of those facts were in USA TODAY's thorough report on sports statistics. That report's editor was Bob Barbrow, who came to USA TODAY in July 1982 from the Westchester newspapers. Henry Freeman told Barbrow to develop, by September 15, a "how they scored" feature for baseball games, special standings, and team-by-team statistics for every baseball and football team. "It was a hellacious job because there was no role model," Barbrow recalls. As a first step, he and Freeman set up a network of Associated Press writers and stringers to phone in information every three innings for baseball games. USA TODAY made a specialty of gathering inning-by-inning, quarter-by-quarter statistics from ball parks and stadiums.

Barbrow and his staff of six changed the way sports results are reported. After many newspapers expanded their sports sections in response to USA TODAY, The Associated Press began a sports agate wire, using USA TODAY's report as a model. One of Barbrow's 1983 boxscores reported that an umpire left a game to join his wife at a hospital, and now he was the father of a new daughter. That detail made a 1986 Sports Illustrated story which described how far USA TODAY would go to report results.

"McPaper's" brand of journalism required an entirely different way of thinking about reporting, writing, and packaging news. For example, Money Managing Editor Taylor Buckley talked about "information delivery systems," when he counseled reporters. "I hate those words," Buckley says, "but they are the best way to describe what we do." He thought a reporter should always ask: What is the best way to present this information? Should some of it be presented as a graphic? Should some be put in a list? Should some be packaged in a sidebar—a separate, short story with bullets [heavy periods] to set off the high points? How much should be presented in traditional text form? Editors and reporters spent a good deal of time and energy thinking about how best to present the information to the reader. At USA TODAY, the text plus the photos plus the graphics equaled the story.

Reporters were used to the traditional way of presenting news: Weave the facts through a lot of flowing prose and then wrap the whole thing around a couple of photos. Neuharth called that method "dumping type"; little or no thought was given to readers' needs. Reporters were asked to produce copy that got to the facts immediately and kept the prose to a minimum. Sometimes they gathered news for two days for a story that filled six inches. One story on air fares resulted in a note from Neuharth—a Pumpkingram—that said: "Too much prose, not enough facts."

And while "McPaper's" critics sneered at the "McNuggets," these short news stories were crammed with facts and details. For example, a March 1987 story of less than two hundred words on a couple driving a pickup truck from Denver to Managua, hauling food to Nicaragua's poor, packed this detail in: "On the road, the couple fight boredom by reading to each other. Their favorite authors: Charles Dickens and Carlos Fuentes." A profile of billionaire Jack Walton, founder of the Wal-Mart drugstore chain, noted, "Still, he drives a 1979 Ford pickup, its upholstery well-chomped by his bird dogs." "McPaper" had little room for flowing prose, but its attention to details made for interesting reading. Taylor Buckley, who was promoted to senior editor and became the newspaper's writing critic, began an internal contest, the "McNugget Awards," to encourage tight, clear, fact-filled stories. Monthly winners collected $100 each in various categories, including best brief, best story, and best headline.

Readers liked digging for nuggets from their home states. A woman who grew up in North Dakota told an editor that while vacationing in Florida, she bought USA TODAY and was amazed to read that her favorite high school teacher in a small North Dakota town had won a teaching award. That find kept her reading the North Dakota part of the "news from every state" for several weeks.

□ **THE CARRIL FILE**

□ **FAVORITE SMOKE:** $1 Baccarat cigars, a Honduran blend. "My only contribution to the trade deficit."

□ **FAVORITE FOOD:** Pizza, ordered extra dry, with onions, sausage, mushrooms, garlic.

□ **FAVORITE TV:** Basketball; loves to watch Congress on C-SPAN.

□ **FAVORITE MUSIC:** Tastes range from flamenco to Herb Alpert, from Linda Ronstadt to the Drifters, from Bob Seger ("I love *Night Moves*") to Simon and Garfunkel. Says Butch van Breda Kolff: "At my daughter's wedding he sang *Old Black Magic* and *People Will Say We're in Love.*"

□ **ON RECRUITING:** "Some coaches love to go into homes. They make about 63 visits. I say that's the same thing a burglar does, make a lot of home visits. I have the same attitude that Bob Cousy had. You get so involved stroking some of these kids that . . . you have to do the same thing to get them to play."

□ **EDUCATION:** Bachelor's degree from Lafayette College; master's in educational administration from Lehigh University.

□ **SIMPLEST BASKETBALL PHILOSOPHY:** Always coach and play like you're two points ahead or two points behind.

□ **HOME:** One-story house in West Windsor, N.J., with a room for watching game films. Family crest from Spain over the fireplace.

□ **THEORY OF REBOUNDING:** "Rebounding is proportionately related to the distance of your house from the railroad tracks."

□ **PERSONAL DATA:** Born July 10, 1931, in Bethlehem, Pa.; divorced; has two adult children.

USA TODAY has been both praised and criticized for its unorthodox way of presenting news. A list, like this one about Princeton basketball coach Pete Carril, is often used in place of a conventional story.

"McPaper's" headline style evolved too, catching a tone reminiscent of the New York Daily News. When the St. Louis Cardinals won the World Series, USA TODAY's front-page headline was "It's in the Cards." Another example, over a story about IBM: "Fourth quarter puts Big Blue in the pink." Or the head for a pro football game on a freezing Sunday: "Chicago puts Green Bay on ice."

By 1986, the newspaper developed its own brand of investigative journalism, state by state. Using laws that require records to be open to the public, editors wrote thousands of letters to public officials in every state, asking for information on compensation paid to college presidents and coaches. The probe found that many football coaches had salaries and perks comparable to or better than those of university presidents or governors. And in March 1987, USA TODAY found another way to use its state-by-state approach to the news, publishing a series of reports on unsafe trucks and the thousands of people they kill. That series, with the catchy title "Semi-safe," contained reports on accidents in every state and led to calls for new federal laws to regulate trucking.

On January 29, 1986, USA TODAY pulled out the stops and devoted almost the entire A section to the explosion of the space shuttle *Challenger.* That blanket coverage, which included a graphic that covered much of page one, recalled the way TODAY in Florida had covered an earlier Cape Canaveral disaster in 1967. Neuharth saluted his staff in a memo:

> The USA TODAY news staff really came of age today. No
> other newspaper came close to the superb overall job you did
> on the Shuttle story. Other newspapers did OK. A couple
> even used a little more space in which to dump type. None
> had a final product as comprehensive, colorful and readable as
> USA TODAY. Even those doubters who hadn't previously rec-
> ognized your ability to cover a major news story in a
> dramatically different way will grudgingly give you credit for
> this one.

Unlike the critics, readers often wrote to say they thought USA
TODAY was a substantial newspaper, crammed with information. Much
of it was dense, not easy to skim; it was better to read some portions
slowly, carefully, the way many readers—but not all journalists—read
newspapers.

Michael Hetherington of Bozeman, Montana, wrote in September
1984: "In lieu of a birthday card, permit my editorial comments on your
fine newspaper. Initially attracted by your graphics, I have become
totally immersed in your paper. I devote about an hour a day to it,
considering that a fine investment for both enlightenment and recrea-
tion. Your concise, neutral news approach is like fresh air after the
miasma of political vitriol spewing from most major papers."

McPaper's success with readers like Hetherington began to affect
editors' thinking. Larry Tarleton, an editor at the Dallas Times Herald,
told Time magazine in 1985: "Editors are now aware that you can get a
lot of information into a chart or a graph rather than a 10- or 15-inch
story." Even so, Time observed that some editors "still treat the

Patty Rhule, who came to the newspaper as a
loaner from Huntington, West Virginia, says
headlines should be snappy and conversational.
"It's like you're telling a friend what's
happening in the news that day." Here are some
examples:
  It was in the Cards
  Players walk, talks balk
  There he goes again
  Career women on sex: Twice is nice

From left, Bob Laird, Karren Loeb, and Julie Stacey use an Apple Macintosh to create a graphic. USA TODAY has twelve artists on staff, and they produce an average of one hundred graphics a week.

paper as a leprous intruder. 'It's not our kind of journalism,' says James Greenfield, an assistant managing editor at The New York Times."

By 1986 USA TODAY's influence on the nation's newspapers was widely acknowledged. "The single most important development in newspaper design in the first half of the 1980s is undoubtedly the debut of USA TODAY," said newspaper design expert Mario Garcia in the Journal of Graphic Design, which named the newspaper one of the ten best designed papers in the country. Overall, the national newspaper and its staff have won more than fifty professional awards.

A Washington Journalism Review article concluded that USA TODAY has had a "profound impact on newspapers across the country. Many editors decided it was time to put colored weather maps on their pages, while others began using shorter stories, more photographs, expanded sports coverage, and op-ed debates. USA TODAY is 'held up as an example in newsrooms,' says Harold Livendahl, publisher of the Orlando Sentinel. 'Editors say, here's how they took the NFL drafts and condensed them into a quick, easy read.'"

A 1987 survey of 109 newspaper editors by Douglas Anderson, an Arizona State University professor, showed that more than half of those newspapers had increased weather coverage since 1984. More than one-fourth of the editors said USA TODAY's example had spurred them to improve their weather packages.

Neuharth didn't mind the imitations. He told one audience: "After all, that's exactly what USA TODAY did. We simply stole the best ideas and concepts from television, from news magazines, and newspapers across the USA, gave them a national perspective, and added a few different twists for a unique USA TODAY sparkle.

"If there has been an overriding misinterpretation of USA TODAY by some journalists," he said, "it has been to confuse brevity with fluff and to focus on story length rather than on story count and information. The readers know the difference. Some editors and reporters do not."

For example, Leonard R. Church of Pittsburgh wrote Neuharth: "It has become my habit to snip articles [from USA TODAY] and mail them to our adult children around the country, urging them too, to become readers. When do I read USA TODAY? In the early evening of course, instead of watching the purveyors of doom and gloom on TV news. Keep it just the way it is." For Neuharth, that was the real journalism of hope.

Early in 1986, there were more signs of the growing—if grudging— acceptance of "McPaper" by the nation's journalism establishment.

In accepting the William Allen White Award, John Quinn told the luncheon audience the public wants all the news it can get: "It wants the bad and the sad news along with the good and the glad. It wants to enjoy the best of the news and it wants to learn how to cope with the rest of it."

The National Press Foundation named John Quinn its "editor of the year," one of the most prestigious awards in journalism. Quinn added that honor to other highlights of his career; earlier, he had been president of The Associated Press Managing Editors' Association and president of the American Society of Newspaper Editors. And in 1987, Quinn received another accolade: The University of Kansas gave him the William Allen White National Citation Award, named for the crusading editor of the Emporia (Kan.) Gazette.

Accepting that award, Quinn poked fun at himself and his newspaper. He confessed that William Allen White might not approve of him, since he was "a groupie, a bona fide member of the chain gang, a media-merging monster." He added that he worked for USA TODAY, the newspaper that had won renown for "bringing new depth to the definition of shallow." After all, Quinn said, USA TODAY has been called:

—The titan of tidbits.

—The explosion in a paint factory.

—The near-beer of newspapers.

—The flashdance of editing.

—The junkfood of journalism.

Quinn sometimes joked that if "McPaper" ever won the Pulitzer Prize, it would be for "best investigative paragraph." The year before, when he had been named "editor of the year" by the National Press Foundation, Quinn suggested how various newspapers would write headlines for the story of the end of the world.

In The Wall Street Journal, the headline would read:

STOCK EXCHANGE HALTS TRADING AS WORLD ENDS.

In The New York Times:

END OF WORLD HITS THIRD WORLD HARDEST.

In The Washington Post:

WORLD ENDS; MAY AFFECT ELECTIONS, SOURCES SAY.

In USA TODAY, Quinn said, the end-of-world headline would be:

WE'RE GONE . . . STATE-BY-STATE DEMISE ON 6A . . .

FINAL FINAL SCORES ON 8C.

The audience laughed and applauded, and settled back to listen to Quinn's serious message: that the "public wants all the news it can get—when it wants it, where it wants it, how it wants it." USA TODAY— that "crazy idea" which the critics said would never work—had found its niche.

CHAPTER TWENTY-ONE

Turning
the corner

If it was a struggle for USA TODAY to win a measure of acceptance from journalists, it was even harder to get financial analysts to change their minds about the new newspaper. But by mid-1984, John Morton's doubts about USA TODAY's future had begun to fade.

The respected media analyst wrote:

> Gannett's USA TODAY is the slickest, most talked about, most colorful, and most unprofitable daily newspaper in the history of the world. In its short life since September 15, 1982, USA TODAY has:
>
> —Shocked other newspapers into trying to match its high-quality printing and use of color.
>
> —Pushed many newspapers into rethinking their traditional stodgy, haphazard makeup.
>
> —Become the third largest daily in the nation, and is likely to pass up the New York Daily News later this year to become second only to The Wall Street Journal.

Then Morton asked: If it has been so widely imitated and such a success with readers, why was USA TODAY losing so much money? Time magazine noted in September 1984 that the losses "McPaper" had piled up in just two years "are believed to be the biggest ever sustained by a newspaper." The losses were staggering, Morton said, because advertisers were still not convinced USA TODAY was here to stay. But he added, "There are signs that this could be changing."

It was. The ABC audit, which was completed in June 1984 and showed USA TODAY had a circulation of 1.33 million, including Blue Chip circulation, had removed many of the doubts. The first sign of real advertising progress came during the 1984 Olympics, when the paper ran a record sixty-three pages during the last week in July, an average of more than twelve pages per day. Twenty-two new advertisers— including Federal Express, Nissan Trucks, United Artists/MGM, and Mutual of Omaha—used USA TODAY during the Olympics.

That August a survey done by Simmons Market Research, a firm whose work was considered authoritative by Madison Avenue ad agencies, gave the newspaper another boost. Simmons said that although USA TODAY's circulation then was 1.3 million, each copy was read by four readers; that made the newspaper's total audience 5 million people per day. Simmons found that 43 percent of USA TODAY's readers had household incomes of more than $35,000 a year, compared to 42 percent for the average newsweekly.

Those results are likely "to aid the paper's drive to attract advertisers," said The Wall Street Journal. The same Simmons study showed that The Journal had suffered a 7 percent decline in readership in 1984, to 6.3 million from 6.8 million the year before. The total audience of The New York Times was down 5.5 percent, to 2.7 million from 2.9 million.

All of this progress was not lost on executives of the nation's largest media companies. At the annual American Magazine Conference, S.I. Newhouse Jr., whose family-run media empire includes newspapers,

Ten largest newspapers as of June 1984

Newspaper	Circulation*
1. The Wall Street Journal	2,081,995
2. New York Daily News	1,374,858
3. USA TODAY	1,138,030
4. Los Angeles Times	1,057,536
5. The New York Times	970,051
6. New York Post	963,069
7. The Washington Post	768,288
8. Chicago Tribune	762,882
9. The Detroit News	657,015
10. Detroit Free Press	631,087

*Daily net paid circulation.
Source: Audit Bureau of Circulations

magazines, and broadcast stations, said of USA TODAY: "I think it is the greatest entrepreneurial tour de force in our times. It came out of an organization, Gannett, which is a fine organization but up until USA TODAY they have done nothing but buy these wonderful high-profit, small-town newspapers. I think the real triumph of USA TODAY is in its distribution system, which is absolutely extraordinary."

At the same meeting, Malcolm Forbes of Forbes magazine said that when USA TODAY started, "I wouldn't have put a nickel in it. In fact, I would have sold Gannett stock when they announced it. I thought it was sort of an ego trip. But I think now it has been an extraordinary success. USA TODAY has broken through in journalism in an extraordinary way, I think, in graphics. . . . It isn't a substitute for a magazine; it's just a better daily newspaper, outside of a half-dozen, than you'll find if you travel around the country. USA TODAY looks awfully good next to [newspapers in] most smaller and middle-sized cities in this country."

One early fan helped change the way the newspaper promoted itself. He was George Lois, a Madison Avenue character actor who thought he knew how to get the attention of his ad agency colleagues. When Cathie Black took over advertising, she met with the heads of major Madison Avenue ad agencies. One call was on Lois, who had started as an art director at Doyle Dane Bernbach. Later he created a TV spot that sold a lot of Xerox copiers. His commercial showed a Xerox machine that was so simple to run that a chimpanzee could make copies. After leaving Doyle Dane, Lois formed his own agency—Lois Pitts Gershon Pon/GGK.

Black's aim at that luncheon was to persuade Lois to start using USA TODAY for his clients' ad campaigns. Instead, Lois was so enthusiastic about the newspaper that he persuaded Black that he should do USA TODAY's advertising. An energetic, free-spirited type, Lois began raving about the newspaper, waving his hands and pulling at his tie. He told Black: "I've only worked on two things where the product was better than the competition's—Xerox and Volkswagen. Your product is better than the competition's—but you're not communicating that to the advertiser!

"The truth is," Lois said, rising out of his chair at the Four Seasons restaurant, "your advertising sucks."

USA TODAY's advertising was then done by Young & Rubicam, the world's biggest ad agency. Y&R had done a good job for "McPaper" in

*One of George Lois' biggest
successes was the "I want my
MTV" campaign that put the
new music video channel in
the public eye.*

its early days; its design subsidiary came up with the distinctive blue
block that became the newspaper's nameplate. Its executives had
helped develop a strategy to sell ads and had coined the motto, "The
Nation's Newspaper." But by 1984, the quality of Y&R's advertising
for USA TODAY had dropped a notch, and the managers of its campaign
lacked a keen understanding of the newspaper or its audience. USA
TODAY had to find a way to persuade Madison Avenue to start using the
newspaper; George Lois thought he was the man who could do it.

"I understood the paper from the beginning as a big marketing idea,
as a big new idea," Lois says. "I remember buying the paper on its first
day in New York and saying, 'This is a whole new ball game. These
guys know what they're doing. It's a graphic presentation of news, TV
turned into print.' We would get a bunch of copies and circulate them at
work. Guys were cutting things out and Xeroxing them.

"Most ad agencies, especially the big ones, don't want to touch a
new publication. They don't know how to talk to their clients about it.
They want a winner before they go into it."

Black asked Lois if he could prepare a few sample ads for her to look
at. USA TODAY was about to launch a new campaign in the trade press,
ads designed to induce media buyers to buy space in the newspaper.
Y&R had presented a few ideas, but its first pass at a campaign had not
bowled anyone over.

A week later, Black and Ray Gaulke went over to Lois' shop. "He
showed us thirty-five ads, and each one was better than the last,"
Black recalls. "Plus he was fun and he was engaging."

But once they had seen Lois' ads, Black and Gaulke got a little nervous. They had not mentioned their bright idea about switching ad agencies to Neuharth, and in the corporate world, that is not a decision to be made lightly. "We felt a little like kids who were stealing the old man's car for a drive," Gaulke says. A few days later Black told Neuharth what she had done. "He looked a little startled," Black recalls, "but then he said, 'Well, that's why you're here. We brought you in to have new ideas.'"

They arranged a sudden-death playoff. The Y&R people made their presentation for a trade campaign, and then George Lois, who had been hidden away in a different room so the Y&R people would not see him, came on for his act. He was performing for a group of Gannett's key executives: Neuharth, John Curley, John Quinn, Cathie Black, Madelyn Jennings, Ray Gaulke, Jack Heselden, and others. Right from the start Lois was excited, he was fired-up, he was rolling. He read each pitch and then tossed the samples around the room, ad after ad which proclaimed his theme: "The Advertising Might of USA TODAY."

Flailing his arms, Lois read the short, snappy copy:

> USA TODAY is a powerful advertising medium unlike any
> other in the history of advertising. We offer wonderful size,
> dazzling color, superb reproduction and a unique, graphic
> look. We also offer advertisers a remarkably responsive,
> involved, *action* audience—3.7 million sophisticated, intel-
> ligent, upscale readers who prefer a newspaper that's quick
> instead of slow, interesting instead of dull, visual instead of
> verbal.
> USA TODAY. As a newspaper and as an advertising medium

Not all of Lois' ideas landed
in print; Neuharth quickly
rejected this ad.

we proudly admit to being different. But we also, humbly,
suggest that we are better.

Lois proposed a series of four full-page ads that would run in one
edition of The New York Times, and in all of the advertising trade publications. Another ad said:

An insertion in USA TODAY is . . .
—an ad
—a poster
—a commercial
—all of the above.

Some of Lois' suggestions were too radical, too smart-alecky for
even this upstart newspaper to accept. One proposed ad advised people to "Fly Eastern" because the airline bought copies of USA TODAY
for its customers; it looked like an ad for an airline, not a newspaper.
Another was an idea for a TV spot which showed a baby crawling
toward a TV set, reaching with one finger for the "power" switch,
which was meant to be an allusion to Michelangelo's Sistine Chapel
scene of man reaching toward God to receive the gift of life. The message, Lois said, was that USA TODAY was "the first modern newspaper
for readers who grew up as viewers."

Lois relished this competition for Gannett's business. "You walk in
and you see a lot of hard asses. Enemy territory. People sitting there
saying, 'Show me.' And your ass is grass if your work's not terrific.
This was right up my alley. I love accounts that are in trouble—they're
forced to let me do exciting work.

"If I've got work I know I want to show and I've got a point of view
and I know I can do something for somebody," Lois says, "I'm hyper
and I'm strong and I get up there and there's no fear at all."

Lois finished his spiel. He was standing there, surrounded by a pro-
fusion of ads, and no one said a word. The Gannett executives just sat
there, stone-faced. "George put on an Academy Award presentation," Cathie Black says. "And of course what you would expect from
any normal company with normal people is that everybody would have
clapped. Not here. And I am sitting there thinking, 'I can't believe this.
What is wrong with all these fuckers?'"

For twenty seconds, no one said anything. Lois knew what was
going on. "People are afraid to react," he says, "They're trying to

figure out what the top guy is thinking." Neuharth was silent, wearing shades—no one could read his eyes. "You've got to understand the thinking of any corporate guy in America," Lois says. "His business depends on advertising. And the idea that you might fire a big agency like Y&R—that's a horrendous move."

Lois finally said to an aide, "Okay, let's go," and started to pack up. "Hold it a minute," Neuharth said, breaking the ice. "I think we've seen some pretty good stuff here."

John Quinn asked a question: "Mr. Lois, we are now with Young & Rubicam, the world's largest advertising agency. You are with Lois Pitts Gershon. Where does your agency stand?"

"We are probably one of the fucking smallest," said Lois, never one to mince words.

"What would people say if we moved from the world's largest advertising agency to one of the smallest?" Quinn asked.

"They'd probably say you're finally getting your heads screwed on straight," Lois said. "You're doing pussy advertising now. You ought to be doing *triumphant* fucking advertising."

"I thought, 'Oh, my God, he's lost it with this language,'" Ray Gaulke recalls. But he hadn't. Neuharth concluded that Lois should refine the advertising, and they would take another look at it. A few weeks later, Neuharth gave Lois part of USA TODAY's advertising, the part aimed at the trade press. "That got him off the hook because he didn't want to fire Y&R," Lois says. "This way, he let Y&R fire themselves."

Lois had some lessons to learn about how Neuharth operated,

George Lois tackled the identity problem head on.

*NBC's "Today" show
weatherman Willard Scott
was one of several celebrities
who sang about USA TODAY in
TV commercials.*

though. One was that USA TODAY's founder could match Lois "f" word for "f" word, especially when Lois' ads were more clever than correct.

Eventually Lois won all of USA TODAY's advertising, as well as Gannett's corporate advertising business. He soon created a series of testimonial TV commercials for USA TODAY which featured Joan Collins, Joe and Deborah Namath, Wilt Chamberlain, hotel executive J.W. Marriott, Jr., and former Senate Majority Leader Howard Baker. Later, Lois produced singing testimonials which starred Willard Scott, Jane Byrne, Charles Schwab, Diahann Carroll, Willie Mays, and Mickey Mantle. They all crooned, with varying degrees of talent, "I read it every day."

Lois' trade press campaign, which cost $934,000, ran just before the ABC audit results were released in June 1984. "It was almost as if everything we said in our previous nine ads was proven correct by the ABC numbers," Lois said in a memo to USA TODAY executives during that summer. "Ad pages are up and positive momentum is building."

Another reason the momentum was building was that Neuharth had changed roles, from editor to huckster, and gone on the road with Black, shilling for his newspaper at dinners USA TODAY hosted for big advertisers in nearly every major city. "While you're having fun editing USA TODAY," he told Quinn, "I have become a goddamn pitchman."

Finally, USA TODAY had gotten the attention of Madison Avenue's media buyers. Advertising linage began to grow, slowly at first, but with steady gains from month to month. The stream of negative stories about USA TODAY's advertising woes, once a deluge that dampened even the enthusiasm of Cathie Black, began to dry up. "Ads picking up at USA TODAY," said the headline in The New York Times. "Hopes on Rise at USA TODAY," said Advertising Age.

John Morton wrote in his newsletter at the end of 1984 that the newspaper's fourth quarter advertising performance of fourteen pages per day was "quite impressive." For all of 1984, USA TODAY carried 2,100 ad pages, a 37 percent increase over 1983. "Most Monday and Friday papers are now completely sold out for four-color advertising and often are sold out for all advertising space," Morton wrote. And he noted that just seven weeks after the August 1984 price hike to thirty-five cents, circulation had recovered completely, matching July's numbers when the newspaper cost a quarter.

On July 10, 1984, USA TODAY began air-freighting 30,000 copies of a scaled-down, two-section edition to Europe and parts of the Middle East. The international edition was a tightly edited, sixteen-page newspaper designed to serve the needs of U.S. travelers, expatriates, and military personnel. The colorful weather page showed the world's weather, but otherwise the content was the same as the domestic edition, although condensed; there was no special world coverage. "It is not designed to be a money-maker but to enhance the prestige of the paper," Morton told readers of his investment newsletter. If this test was successful, USA TODAY would explore satellite distribution to Europe and Asia later. Being everywhere was another way to win new readers who otherwise might not try the newspaper.

As late as 1985 there were still people living in the USA who did not know about USA TODAY. Shirley Louw of Wadena, Iowa, wrote to say, "I first read your newspaper USA TODAY while I was living in Sicily. Now that I am back in the States, I was wondering if I could subscribe to the newspaper—is it available here in the States?" If Frank Vega had been around to read Louw's letter, he would have planted a newsrack in the cornfield closest to her home.

By the spring of 1985, signs of progress were strong. The week of March 12, the newspaper ran a record eighty-one pages of advertising, with every color position sold out. For the first quarter of the year, advertising pages increased 97 percent over 1984. In April, the newspaper ran its first "special bonus section," a special fifth section containing news and advertising. It was on "Baseball '85," and was seen as yet another way to attract more advertisers to the newspaper. Neuharth told Black she ought to be able to sell fifty-two special sections a year—another "maximum motivation goal."

In May 1985, at the annual meeting of Gannett shareholders, Gannett President John Curley announced that USA TODAY would expand its capacity from forty-eight to fifty-six pages by November. A week after that announcement, the newspaper had the biggest advertising week in its 2½-year history, selling an average of nineteen pages per day.

"We like USA TODAY," Carole Book, Motorola's director of corporate advertising told Advertising Age. "It's timely, with an upscale audience, and the fact that we can get color reproduction is just right for us."

William F. Gloede, a reporter for Advertising Age, assessed the newspaper's chances for a Columbia Journalism Review article: "The advertising agencies which can make you or break you are just beginning to come around, creating a whole new category in the budget for this newcomer. It just might be able to get back the thunder television stole from newspapers in the fifties."

USA TODAY had given newspaper readership a needed lift. In a 1984 column about advertising problems at some newspapers, John Morton noted that daily circulation for the entire newspaper industry rose 1.6 percent in 1983. "All of the growth was accounted for by USA TODAY," Morton said. "Take that out, and daily circulation for the rest of the industry actually declined slightly." By itself, USA TODAY had contributed to a significant gain in newspaper readership.

Morton added that because of an oversupply of newsprint, the cost of the raw material for newspapers declined in 1983, for the first time in many years. That price break helped; "McPaper's" losses would have been even higher if newsprint prices had increased as usual.

Wall Street analysts sensed that the tide was turning. C. Patrick O'Donnell, Jr., an analyst with Furman, Selz, Mager, Dietz & Birney, wrote in the spring of 1985 that USA TODAY, which he called "the most ambitious project in the modern history of the American press," had in the last few months "turned an important corner. We think the paper is poised for a major decline in losses."

Things were going well enough in the summer of 1985 that Neuharth began a "little experiment" with the newspaper he had founded in Florida in 1966—TODAY. Back in 1981 he had asked if it were possible to "force" USA TODAY's circulation in markets where there were Gannett newspapers. That effort had never been as successful as Neuharth thought it should have been. When the total circulation of Gannett's newspapers was 3 million, Neuharth thought USA TODAY's circulation

Cathie Black presents some ad campaign ideas to Lee Guittar, left, and Tom Farrell at a meeting of USA TODAY executives.

should be 10 percent of that in those markets, or three hundred thousand.

It never got that high. In 1987, even when USA TODAY's circulation was averaging more than 1.6 million per day, USA TODAY was only selling 230,000 copies a day in the Gannett markets. By then, circulation of Gannett's local newspapers totaled more than 5 million, so 10 percent would have been five hundred thousand.

When USA TODAY first appeared, some editors suspected Neuharth had a hidden agenda. "I have my doubts that it's going to succeed in its present form," said Eugene Patterson, then editor of the St. Petersburg (Fla.) Times. "But if it fails . . . it can't miss in another form."

What Patterson thought it would evolve into was a one-section newspaper, filled with national and international news, beamed to all Gannett newspapers. Patterson speculated this section of national news would be wrapped around the local reports produced by Gannett newspapers.

That was not quite what Neuharth had in mind for TODAY in Florida. He hoped instead to put two newspapers in every home, USA TODAY and a completely revamped local newspaper. Using a task force of Gannett editors, he ordered his creation, TODAY, transformed to emphasize local and state news on nearly every page. Almost all national and international news was taken out. The idea was to force readers to take USA TODAY if they wanted to read anything that happened outside Brevard County or Florida. To underline the change in emphasis, TODAY was renamed FLORIDA TODAY and given a new look; its nameplate was an orange companion to USA TODAY's blue one.

To encourage readers to buy two newspapers, USA TODAY was distributed free to FLORIDA TODAY subscribers for six weeks. After that sample period, they could subscribe to both newspapers for a low price—$3.25 a week, just 75 cents more than the weekly price of either newspaper.

FLORIDA TODAY added some features readers liked: short pieces on local folks on every section front, with color photos; reports of every crime in every community, and detailed information about mortgage and interest rates at every financial institution. It was an exhaustive local news report, and for a time it exhausted even the expanded local staff's ability to fill it with solid local news.

But many readers were outraged that Gannett had changed what they viewed as a perfectly good newspaper that had been consistent every day for twenty years. They did not like the all-local-news A section, and these angry readers wrote more than three thousand letters of complaint. FLORIDA TODAY lost eight thousand home delivery customers, from seventy-eight thousand to about seventy thousand. Marie Dudley of Cocoa Beach and seven other readers wrote a joint letter "to protest what you have done to our newspaper. It bears no resemblance to TODAY, which was perfect. Had we wanted to subscribe to USA TODAY, we would have done so. We resent having an orange-colored replica forced upon us. Bring back TODAY!"

The change did produce one big plus for USA TODAY. Its circulation increased thirteen-fold, from twelve hundred copies per day to about sixteen thousand.

"Neuharth was just too rigid on FLORIDA TODAY," Quinn says. The abrupt switch to all-local news was too drastic for readers to accept. But, Quinn adds, "Nobody bothered to tell Neuharth this because it was clear he didn't want to hear anything that would discourage the test."

The first edition of the
revamped FLORIDA TODAY
appeared on August 26, 1985.

To try to stay on top of the FLORIDA TODAY experiment, Neuharth traveled to Cocoa Beach frequently for meetings. And no matter where he was in his travels, the chairman insisted that the morning newspapers be delivered to him no later than 5 A.M. He regularly set aside an hour between 5 and 6 A.M. to read, and there was always a price to be paid if his papers were late. One morning in November 1985 his copy of FLORIDA TODAY arrived, but no USA TODAY. At 5:15 A.M. he telephoned Frank Vega, the new local publisher. "Mr. Publisher," Neuharth asked the sleepy Vega, "where is my copy of USA TODAY?"

Vega began laughing. "We didn't print it today, Al," he said.

"Why not?" Neuharth demanded.

"Because, Al," Vega said, relishing his rare moment of advantage, "it's Saturday."

But by the fall of 1986, Neuharth was ready to admit, despite all of his efforts, that the "little experiment" with FLORIDA TODAY had failed. That November, editors restored national news to the A section, put the stock prices back in, and moderated the emphasis on local news. Early in 1987, Neuharth told a Florida audience: "What we learned in

Brevard is that you cannot force an unwanted object down an unwilling
throat." After national news was restored, FLORIDA TODAY's circulation recovered. And the fears of many Gannett editors that Neuharth
might try similar tests in their towns eased.

But in the summer of 1985, Neuharth's big experiment—USA
TODAY—was starting to turn the corner. In the second quarter ending
June 30, Gannett reported a 20 percent earnings gain—a testament to
the company's underlying financial strength. The turnaround was well
under way at USA TODAY; its advertising revenue for the first half of
1985 increased 106 percent compared to 1984.

"The trends at USA TODAY are very encouraging," Neuharth wrote
in his quarterly letter to shareholders. On August 26, 1985, the newspaper raised its cover price from thirty-five cents to fifty cents. That
same Monday, it published its biggest edition in its three-year history,
sixty pages, in six sections, with twenty-six pages of advertising. In
September, on the eve of its third anniversary, USA TODAY reported
that its circulation was averaging more than 1,350,000 daily, more than
100,000 ahead of the year-earlier figure.

The price increase to fifty cents had been planned very carefully. It
was phased in for some wholesalers and convenience store operators.
These merchants were offered an incentive, an extra nickel for every
copy sold, if they displayed USA TODAY prominently and carefully
explained the price increase to customers. The News department
launched another campaign to boost readership, this time called "Must
Read."

All of that effort paid off. When the newspaper had gone from
twenty-five cents to thirty-five cents the year before, early circulation
losses were more than 10 percent. Now the price had gone from thirty-
five cents to fifty cents, and the losses were only 5 percent. In less
than three years, its cover price had doubled. A few weeks after the
increase, the newspaper had recovered and was growing again. The
move to fifty cents would bring in an extra $22 million in circulation
revenues in the next year.

Some readers hated to pay the extra fifteen cents, but once they
were hooked, it was hard to kick the habit. Alex Canja of Lansing,
Michigan, wrote Lee Guittar:

> None of your glib arguments, explanations, or rationale for
> your announced price increase will dissuade me. Your com-

pany's actions are not only sneaky but also insidious. First it
was just twenty-five cents. Then it moved up to thirty-five
cents. Now you urge your readers to "hurry" to take advantage of today's "low" subscription rate in order to save
money and beat the price increase of fifteen cents! Your M.O.
is obvious. Lull your audience into a sense of false security
and then hit 'em!

  Well, I don't give a damn what you do. I'll continue to buy
and read your product!

  Neuharth predicted in a September news release that USA TODAY's
losses for 1985 would be "substantially below 1984 and are expected to
drop dramatically in 1986. The original five-year business plan which
called for the newspaper to be profitable by the end of 1987 now seems
quite achievable."

  But late in 1985, behind the newspaper's progress, a potential disaster lurked. Its executives did not realize they were about to embark on
a free sampling program that would turn out to be the largest, most
expensive promotion in newspaper history—and USA TODAY's biggest
mistake.

CHAPTER TWENTY-TWO

$12 million mistake

After three years of launches, Carolyn Vesper—the woman who had thrown out her white linen suit after USA TODAY's first day—considered herself thoroughly "Gannettized." There had been moments when she wanted to quit: like the night of the Atlanta launch, when her only sleep was a two-hour nap on a couch in the ladies' restroom at the Gainesville Times plant, or the time two huge Teamsters confronted her in a Philadelphia hotel elevator and demanded to know where USA TODAY's command post was. She didn't tell them, and she didn't quit.

One reason she kept going, she says, was that Frank Vega had made a bet "that Carolyn Vesper wouldn't last eighteen months."

"He thought I was too soft," Vesper says. "You know, this is street work. I was determined that Frank was going to lose the bet, that I would make it through New York. The bet kept me going. I became obsessed. This job—making USA TODAY succeed—literally became my life."

The eighteen-hour days and her brother's illness eventually forced Vesper to reassess things, and near the end of 1984, she took a six-week leave. When she came back, one of her first tasks was to work out a circulation promotion with General Mills. The basic idea was simple: A consumer would buy several General Mills products—cake mixes, cereals—and send in the proof of purchase seals. For doing that, the shopper would get a free six-month subscription to USA TODAY.

At first, General Mills wanted USA TODAY to spend several million dollars to help pay for advertising inserts to announce the promotion in

The General Mills promotion put Carolyn Vesper in the hot seat. "It started taking on a Watergate kind of feeling," she says.

Sunday newspapers. Vesper said no: "We had never done a circulation promotion where we had spent a dime upfront." She told the General Mills people USA TODAY could provide creative support and help produce the advertising insert, but would not help pay for the cost of the ads. General Mills' executives at first called the deal off, but then called back with a question: "Can we put a limit on the number of free subscriptions we have to pay for?"

Vesper figured if USA TODAY was going to do the promotion, it had to pick up part of the costs. It seemed smarter to let General Mills pay for the first portion of the costs—for the advertising and for a fixed number of subscriptions. If more people than expected sent in their box tops, USA TODAY would foot the bill for the excess, above a certain limit. "Then if the offer bombed," Vesper says, "the only company to lose money would be General Mills. If it worked well, we would get more subscriptions. That would cost us more, but we were getting something."

During the summer of 1985, they worked out a deal. Consumers would have to send in proof-of-purchase seals for eight of twelve General Mills products to get USA TODAY free for six months. The products were Cheerios, Honey-Nut Cheerios, Total, Fruit Bars, Chewy Granola Bars, Fruit Roll-Ups, Au Gratin Potatoes, Creamy Deluxe frosting, Bisquick baking mix, Brownie Supreme mix, SuperMoist cake mix, and Hamburger Helper. Some of these items were already in people's cupboards.

General Mills would pay for the first fifty two thousand free subscriptions. USA TODAY would pay for everything beyond that. "We would pay for the next three hundred thousand subscriptions or whatever it turned out to be," Vesper says. "Getting three hundred thousand was a possibility the lawyers and I laughed about, literally laughed." Getting that many seemed out of the question, impossible.

USA TODAY had just done a promotion with Procter & Gamble that required the consumer to buy three products and send in two dollars. About forty-nine thousand people signed up and got free thirteen-week subscriptions to USA TODAY. At a meeting to discuss the new promotion idea, Vesper says the General Mills people "contended that they had absolutely no idea how many subscriptions would result." Considering the results of the Procter & Gamble offer, Vesper says, "the General Mills contract seemed very reasonable to us." So after discussing some minor changes with Lee Guittar, who headed circulation, Vesper signed the contract—Guittar was traveling that day. He expected the deal would generate, at the very most, seventy-five thousand orders. If that happened, the additional costs USA TODAY would have to pay would be minimal.

To advertise the offer, General Mills placed inserts in just about every Sunday newspaper in the country. At the same time, USA TODAY was getting a lot of publicity; there were articles all over the place, from Time to Advertising Age, assessing the newspaper's fast progress as it approached its third birthday. And because USA TODAY was planning to increase its price to fifty cents, the newspaper was promoting itself aggressively. "All these forces came together with a boom," Guittar says.

Carolyn Vesper was the first to feel the shock waves. She was tracking how many people took advantage of the General Mills offer. In the first week, forty thousand people signed up for free subscriptions; there were twenty-one thousand orders in *one day*. Chuck Schmitt recalls when Vesper came to tell him what was happening.

"She was scared," Schmitt says. "She was literally white." The possibility of getting three hundred thousand orders was not so funny anymore. John Curley told Neuharth what had happened, and then Lee Guittar sat down with USA TODAY's founder to assess the damage.

"I can't say he was happy about it," Guittar says. "He was reasonably calm; he asked all of the right questions. How many could we count? Under ABC's rules, you could count only the first fifty-two thousand as paid circulation. Al allowed as how it was a mistake that shouldn't have happened. Somebody should have recognized the potential liability we had and brought that to him. He's right."

On September 13, 1985, 48 million free-standing inserts promoting the USA TODAY subscription offer appeared in newspapers. Neuharth says, "If General Mills had happened in year one or two, we probably would have folded our tent."

It became an insiders' game to guess and make small wagers on how many people would get free subscriptions to USA TODAY as a result of the General Mills offer. The number turned out to be awesome: 512,000 people sent in eight proof-of-purchase coupons and asked for the newspaper.

"We built the fifteenth largest newspaper in the country in three months, just ahead of The Boston Globe," Vesper says with a pained smile. She meant that a newspaper with a circulation of 512,000 would be slightly larger than The Globe, which in 1985 had a circulation of 509,000. That 512,000 people would buy eight products to get USA TODAY indicated how popular the newspaper was. "It took the Globe 113 years to get that big," Vesper says. "It took us three months and General Mills."

The deluge of orders nearly crushed the whole operation. Every department had to help figure out how to print 512,000 extra copies of the paper every day and how to get those extra 512,000 copies to the readers. USA TODAY's Datapoint computer system, which had just begun to function reasonably well in 1985, was competely overwhelmed now. "General Mills just killed our Datapoint computer," Chuck Schmitt says. "There wasn't enough time on the clock to process the mail. No matter how fast that computer moved, it wasn't fast enough. We had to turn around and upgrade the central IBM system because that wasn't big enough to hold half a million orders."

Tom Curley, who had been promoted from publisher in Bridgewater, New Jersey, to assistant to USA TODAY President Lee Guittar, was a member of the General Mills crisis committee. Curley remembers traveling early one evening to Minnesota to discuss how Gannett's St. Cloud Times could print enough copies to service all of the new General Mills subscribers in the Minneapolis area. Still wearing suits and ties, the group sat down for a meeting in St. Cloud at midnight, did the best they could to iron out the problems in two or three hours, and then flew back to Washington and worked a normal ten-hour day at the office.

They tried to fulfill as many orders as they could by using same-day mail or home delivery. If that service was a day or two late in the subscriber's area, then they issued coupons good for a free copy of the paper at a newsstand or convenience store.

One good effect of the deluge of orders was that USA TODAY had to upgrade its computer, distribution, and production facilities yet another notch. "General Mills forced real efficiencies in our system," Vesper says.

The best thing about the General Mills promotion was that it exposed millions of new readers to USA TODAY; the worst thing about it was that it cost Gannett another $12 million. It was the largest unscheduled circulation promotion, the largest free sampling program, in newspaper history.

"I'm probably the only guy in the world today who still thinks that the General Mills promotion was one of the great things that happened to USA TODAY," says Lee Guittar. "People outside say, 'If only we could have come up with something like that.' What's wrong with it, obviously, is that there can be too much of a good thing."

Neuharth and Curley told the board of directors what had happened. The reaction of the board to this $12 million slip-up was typical of their confidence in Neuharth; the directors were planning for success, not failure. Howard Baker, who had joined the Gannett board after he gave up his post as Senate majority leader, said, "I'm waiting to see how USA TODAY can turn General Mills to its advantage." Julian Goodman, the former NBC chairman, said, "It is a wonderful problem to have— all these new readers."

For a few months, the General Mills mistake stopped USA TODAY's momentum. "We had to stop and do a lot of back filling," John Curley says. Instead of pushing the newspaper over the top, their attention was focused for months on filling half a million unexpected orders.

USA TODAY picked up some lasting circulation gains from the promotion. Of the 512,000 people involved, more than 93,000—or 18 percent—paid to renew their subscriptions when the free offer expired.

In November 1985, Neuharth hosted USA TODAY's annual "brainstorming" session at Cocoa Beach and took his share of the blame. By that time, Carolyn Vesper thought some people were looking at her as if she were the woman who had made "the $12 million mistake." In her speech on national circulation sales at Pumpkin Center, Vesper didn't mention General Mills: "I skirted the issue."

After she finished, Neuharth raised it. "I want to talk about General Mills," he said. "I don't want to pretend that it didn't happen. It did, and I want to talk about it."

"I remember my heart stopped then," Vesper says. "I was afraid to move. I was hoping the floor would open up and my chair would disappear because now it was all going to be on the table. Neuharth was fairly eloquent. He said, 'General Mills shows the entire Gannett organization at its best and its worst. At its best, let's not forget that a very well respected Fortune 500 company agreed to do a program with us, and that's not insignificant. At its worst, we did a lousy job of evaluating the potential cost.'"

Neuharth mentioned that there were rumors that someone was going to get fired over this. "If anybody gets fired, it will be me," he

---

Changes at the top

By its fourth anniversary, USA TODAY had already had six presidents:

Phil Gialanella
January 11, 1982–April 24, 1983
Vince Spezzano
April 24, 1983–September 27, 1983
Cathie Black
September 27, 1983–June 15, 1984
Paul Flynn
June 15, 1984–October 1, 1984
Lee Guittar
October 1, 1984–March 17, 1986
Tom Curley
March 17, 1986–

said. "I'm responsible because nobody brought the contract to me. Since this happened I've reviewed the contract a number of times, and if it had crossed my desk, I probably would have signed it. I have no intention of firing myself. Does anybody think I should be fired?" No one said a word. The meeting ended; they went downstairs to have lunch.

Vesper felt she was still suffering from "corporate contagion." She thought her peers did not want to be seen near her, although several top executives had gone out of their way to talk to her. She was eating alone, and felt a tap on her shoulder. It was Neuharth. He asked: "Do you think I should be fired, Carolyn?"

"Look, I made a mistake," Vesper said. "I think I learned from it and I don't think it will happen again."

"We appreciate what you've done for us so far," Neuharth said.

A few months later, in March 1986, Lee Guittar left Gannett to join the Hearst Corporation. Tom Curley, one of Project NN's original "four geniuses," was named to head USA TODAY's circulation operations; he was USA TODAY's sixth president in less than four years. Carolyn Vesper was later promoted to vice president for national circulation sales.

Neuharth says now: "A lot of people point fingers at Carolyn Vesper or people at that level, but they went out and sold a deal that they brought to Guittar, and he didn't look at it in the way the head of circulation should have examined it. We were ready to forgive that and figure out how to get out of it. But I think Lee began to realize, with that kind of thing behind him, it wasn't too good an idea to stay much longer."

General Mills executives are generally close-mouthed about the whole affair. "We consider the promotion to be successful," said Randy Mayer, director of promotion services. "It had a good impact on the volume of our brands."

CHAPTER TWENTY-THREE

Here
to stay

In January 1986, Neuharth stood at the podium at the University of Pennsylvania's Wharton School of Business, smiling out at a sea of eager young MBA candidates, while Wharton honored him for his entrepreneurial leadership in launching USA TODAY. His newspaper was growing, so Neuharth was crowing.

He told the business school students that "McPaper" was now "the second largest newspaper in the country, with a circulation of 1.4 million and growing." And he added:

"We believe that USA TODAY now is here to stay, that it has found a niche, and the foundation for its financial success has been laid."

By 1986, the relentless pressure of USA TODAY's massive losses and management nightmares—which at times would have overwhelmed anyone, even Neuharth—had begun to ease. Neuharth was getting back to his old self. He was more relaxed, more cocksure than ever, and although still involved in every phase of operations, he was not so insistent on orchestrating every detail. The losses had been cut. The "management mentality" Neuharth had worked so hard to build had finally taken hold.

Now in his sixties, Neuharth was not as cocky as he had been in his twenties at SoDak Sports, but he could not resist bragging a bit. He knew USA TODAY was going to succeed.

The newspaper's operating loss for all of 1985 was $102 million. By the end of 1986, that had been cut to $70 million. Advertising continued its dramatic growth and circulation recorded steady gains, while costs remained stable.

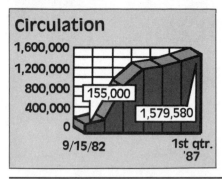

Circulation

1,600,000
1,200,000
800,000   155,000
400,000
         0   1,579,580
      9/15/82   1st qtr.
                          '87

"Blue chip" sales are an important part of USA TODAY's circulation. For the first quarter of 1987, they averaged about 238,000 copies per day.

Back in 1981, Neuharth had said Gannett would launch the newspaper only if management was convinced it could achieve a daily circulation of 1 million to 2 million, annual revenues of $250 million, and operate at a profit in three to five years. It was going to take nearly five years instead of three, and the losses had been much higher than predicted, but in 1986 it looked certain that USA TODAY would achieve those basic goals. It would not meet the 1981 business plan's original goal of 2.3 million daily circulation, but as long as the newspaper's circulation was well over 1 million and it attracted well-educated, well-paid readers, advertisers would flock to it.

"It's the most widely imitated newspaper in the USA," Neuharth told his Wharton audience, "but I'll let you in on a secret: USA TODAY's appeal is not its color or its graphics or its quality of offset printing. USA TODAY's secret is very simple. It communicates with the reader on a personal level, very quickly, clearly, and directly in an upbeat, exciting, positive environment. It's giving the readers information that they want and need in order to form their own opinions. USA TODAY has made reading a newspaper an enjoyable experience again.

"And much of USA TODAY's success has been from listening to the reader—not editors and publishers and other so-called experts—and giving those readers what they say they want."

An important step forward was a July 1986 survey of newspaper readership done by Simmons Market Research. It showed that "McPaper" had 4,792,000 readers per day, more than any other daily newspaper in the country.

That was a 14 percent increase in readership over 1985. Readership of USA TODAY's main competitor, The Wall Street Journal, had dropped 17 percent since 1985—to 4,030,000 readers. According to Simmons, since 1984, The Journal had lost 2.2 million readers. The study showed that an average of three people read each copy of USA TODAY; The Wall Street Journal was read by an average of only two readers per day.

In response to that study, USA TODAY rushed out an advertisement with the headline: "Simmons says we're No. 1. The MOST daily newspaper readers in the USA." The Wall Street Journal refused to run that ad, although The New York Times and advertising trade magazines accepted it. After The Journal refused to run the "No. 1" ad, George Lois made its refusal the subject of a new ad. "Our numbers are driving The Journal up the wall!" it proclaimed. Ever the promoter, Neuharth quickly added this line under USA TODAY's nameplate: "No. 1 in the USA . . . 4,792,000 readers every day."

In the months following the Simmons survey, circulation continued its steady climb—the nice smooth climb Neuharth had been dreaming about back when he talked about the "ruthless reality of this roller coaster." In February 1987, USA TODAY announced that it was selling an average of more than 1.5 million copies per day and was raising its ad rates to adjust for the increased circulation. A full-color page in USA TODAY would now cost nearly $45,000, but that was still less than half

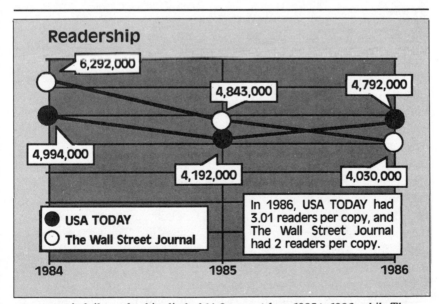

Readership

6,292,000

4,843,000

4,792,000

4,994,000

4,192,000

4,030,000

● USA TODAY
○ The Wall Street Journal

In 1986, USA TODAY had 3.01 readers per copy, and The Wall Street Journal had 2 readers per copy.

1984   1985   1986

USA TODAY's daily readership climbed 14.3 percent from 1985 to 1986, while The Wall Street Journal's readership dropped 16.7 percent. This is a comparison of the two newspapers' readers per day.

Another George Lois ad that ran in 1987.

USA TODAY *took on* The Wall Street Journal *in an ad when that newspaper refused to run an ad proclaiming* USA TODAY *number one in readership.*

the cost of a color page in Time or a black-and-white page in The Wall Street Journal. The edition published for the 1987 Super Bowl weekend, which included a bonus section pegged to the big game, sold 2,030,313 copies—the first time the newspaper had broken the 2 million mark.

USA TODAY's weekend newspaper was its best-seller. Because it was available Friday, Saturday, and Sunday, by early 1987 the weekend edition was selling an average of 1.7 million copies per day, compared with the 1.5 million sold on a typical weekday. Editors planned that edition carefully to try to give it a longer "shelf life," emphasizing news and features that would stand up for three days. In the week ending April 1, 1987, circulation set another record—a daily average of 1,725,000. "McPaper" was gaining on the 2 million mark.

As Neuharth had predicted, the herd of advertisers had begun to move, following the readers. The December 22, 1986, issue carried more than twenty-nine pages of advertising and generated more than

$1 million in revenue, a record. For all of 1986, USA TODAY's ad revenues rose 38 percent; ad linage was up 3 percent, in a year when ad volume at the newsweeklies was flat or down. USA TODAY ran a total of 3,484 ad pages in 1986, more than Time, Newsweek, U.S. News & World Report, or Sports Illustrated. In the newsweekly and business magazine field, USA TODAY's total number of ad pages was second only to Business Week.

In the first quarter of 1987, the newspaper chalked up strong advertising gains. Ad pages for the quarter were up 24 percent, and revenues were nearly 50 percent ahead of the same period in 1986. The newspaper was averaging 14.98 pages a day of advertising, up from 12 pages per day in the first quarter of 1986.

USA TODAY was close to making a profit, and Cathie Black was widely credited with helping turn USA TODAY's fortunes around. Adweek magazine picked her as one of five "business leaders to watch" in 1987, noting that USA TODAY "is changing the face of newspapering and threatening to upset the delicate economics of several national magazines."

As the advertising flowed in, Neuharth relaxed some of his strict ground rules. For example, he allowed Black to sell a strip on the bottom of the weather page to Nestle, a piece of space he had not let Joe Welty sell earlier. But Neuharth held firm whenever he thought a proposed ad would, as he wrote in one memo, "screw up the product by jerking the readers around at the mercy of advertisers." He rejected a

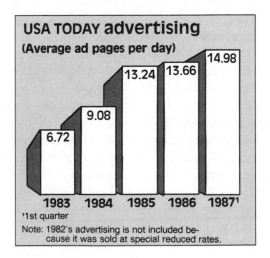

USA TODAY advertising
(Average ad pages per day)

14.98
13.24   13.66
9.08
6.72

1983   1984   1985   1986   1987¹

¹1st quarter

Note: 1982's advertising is not included because it was sold at special reduced rates.

Reader profile

Here's a profile of USA TODAY's readers in 1986, according to Simmons Market Research Bureau:

- 33 percent held professional/managerial positions, compared to 28 percent for the average newsweekly.
- 31 percent earned $30,000 or more a year, compared to 22 percent for the average newsweekly.
- 32 percent had annual household incomes of $50,000 or more, compared to 25 percent for the average newsweekly.
- 61 percent were between 25 and 49 years of age; 64 percent male, 36 percent female.

proposal from RJR/Nabisco to buy a strip on the "For the Record" page in Sports every day for three months, forgoing $550,000 in revenue. Neuharth's policy for regular pages was a one-year commitment.

After he quit personally laying out USA TODAY every day—deciding how much news and advertising the paper would have—Neuharth gave that job to USA TODAY's editor, not its publisher. It was yet another indication that at USA TODAY, the reader was king. The amount of news that it ran each day—the "newshole"—was not a percentage based on the number of pages in the newspaper. Instead, it was a fixed number: twenty-seven to twenty-eight pages of news in the early years, and when the ads came in, that was tightened slightly, to twenty-five or twenty-six pages of news per day.

The test of the International edition was a success. In October 1985, satellite transmission of USA TODAY to Singapore began, with distribution throughout Asia. In May 1986, the first satellite-delivered copies of the European version of the International edition came off a press near Lucerne, Switzerland. Neuharth was there, snapping open the pages, checking out the color. He said that the Swiss printing site "means that readers in most European capitals will receive their papers in time for breakfast, with fresher news than ever before."

By mid-1986, USA TODAY was available in more than fifty countries. "McPaper" had become a global newspaper. Melvin M. Belli, Sr., the San Francisco lawyer known as the "King of Torts," wrote: "A few weeks ago, I was in Australia on business. There was a USA TODAY at my door. I've had it at my door in Singapore, Paris, New York, Mexico City, indeed all around the world, and I'm grateful for this 'letter from home' whenever I'm abroad."

Another good sign that delighted Neuharth was the decision by Harvard Lampoon editors to publish a parody of USA TODAY in September 1986. Joe Armstrong, the Lampoon's publisher, said they picked USA TODAY because "it's the hottest newspaper in the country. Because it is important, because it is hot and fresh, because it has appeal and recognition, because it has a vision and a personality and it is friendly and fun." It also was the youngest publication the Lampoon editors had ever picked to parody. Life was forty years old when it was Lampooned, Cosmopolitan eighty-six, Time almost forty-one, and People, ten.

USA TODAY was easy to parody: "Reagan, Gorbachev Swap Wives" read one teaser headline. "Four Out of Three College Jocks Can't Count" said another. The "USA Snapshot" at the bottom of the front page told "Why we love our country: 1. Freedom 41% 2. Good food, reasonable prices 23% 3. Big tits 18%." The Lampoon sold more than 750,000 copies of the young Harvard humorists' work.

Neuharth plunged into the fun, inviting the Lampoon's editors to a sumptuous reception and dinner in the thirtieth floor dining room of Gannett's lavish new corporate headquarters, in a tower that was a

This photo, taken for Gannett's 1986 annual report, shows American vacationers reading USA TODAY. Daily sales of the international edition in Europe and the Middle East rose after USA TODAY began printing in Switzerland.

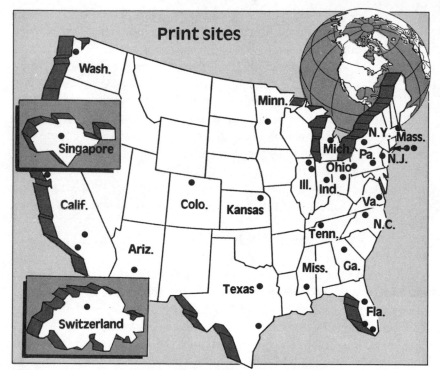

When USA TODAY celebrated its first anniversary, it had twenty print sites. By 1987, it had thirty-two, including one in Lucerne, Switzerland, and one in Singapore.

twin of the USA TODAY skyscraper overlooking the Potomac. The Washington Post story on the dinner said:

> Some people may have seen the Harvard lampooning of USA TODAY that went on sale yesterday as a stinging parody, and it was, but Gannett Co. Chairman Allen H. Neuharth loved it. He celebrated the parody as a recognition and acceptance of his 4-year-old creation, the subject of so many "McPaper" jokes.
>
> Among the guests at the Washington celebration were Secretary of Defense Caspar Weinberger, FBI Director William Webster, and Sens. Alan Simpson, Larry Pressler and John Warner. They were among the several hundred, mostly media, who wandered through the corporate dining room nibbling on fillets of rare beef and exotic cheeses.
>
> But with their marble fountain and unsurpassed panorama

At the Washington, D.C., reception celebrating the Harvard Lampoon's parody issue, Neuharth joked: "I was afraid the parody would be just a cheap imitation of USA TODAY. It is not. It's a very expensive cheap imitation."

of Washington, the corporate offices were the event of the evening. What was unique was an opportunity to visit Neuharth's vast personal office-corporate boardroom, up a spiral staircase to the 31st floor. At the far end of the room with bands of windows overlooking Washington and Northern Virginia was a massive (big enough to roast a steer) white onyx fireplace with dozens of logs blazing. William Randolph Hearst's ghost must be green with envy. Or as WUSA TV (a Gannett station) anchor Gordon Peterson said as he took his first look at the room: "This is a 'holy cow' by a factor of ten." To clean up the quote slightly.

Joking with the Harvard kids, Neuharth was the picture of the relaxed corporate titan. He was at the pinnacle of his career, a long, long way from Alpena and Eureka and the South Dakota prairie.

He was relaxed enough to commission a piece of sculpture for the newspaper's lobby: a larger-than-life-size bust of USA TODAY's founder. Neuharth, the living legend, could stroll by a statue of himself while he was still in charge. A wag soon posted a New Yorker cartoon on the newsroom bulletin board that showed a man talking to his boss. "The job is fine," he said. "It's the lobby sculpture I can't stand." David Seavey, the USA TODAY cartoonist with a sense of artistic proportion, sputtered: "That bust is so big it belongs on a, on a . . . mountain!" It turned out there were three busts: one at USA TODAY, one outside Neuharth's corporate headquarters office, alongside similar busts of Gannett's other chiefs, Frank Gannett and Paul Miller, and a third at FLORIDA TODAY's new plant in Brevard County.

As USA TODAY cut its losses, the parent Gannett Company kept charging along. In the first quarter of 1987, it reported its seventy-eighth consecutive increase in quarterly earnings gains, more than nineteen years of uninterrupted growth in profits. This record, combined with the vigorous financial strength of the company and declining losses at USA TODAY, produced rosy forecasts from Wall Street analysts.

"If USA TODAY breaks even by 1988 (which it probably will), this [Gannett stock] could become the glamour stock of the decade," said Louis Ehrenkrantz, of the money management firm of Ehrenkrantz and King.

During 1985 and 1986, Gannett completed what Neuharth called

The Neuharth bust quickly became a landmark. Just as New Yorkers used to say, "Meet me under the clock at the Biltmore," USA TODAY staffers now say, "Meet me at the Al-head."

the "triple crown" of acquisitions. It bought The Des Moines Register for $200 million, The Louisville Courier-Journal and Times for $320 million, and the Evening News Association of Detroit, which included The Detroit News and other newspapers and a TV station in Washington, D.C., for $717 million. Gannett did all of this despite USA TODAY's huge losses; the financial department's prediction that launching USA TODAY would slow acquisitions was wrong.

The company's newspapers now had a combined circulation of more than 6 million copies per day. Early in 1987, Gannett completed a two-for-one stock split. If an investor had bought one hundred shares of Gannett stock for $2,900 in 1967 and held it until 1987, that investment would be worth $65,306.

In a January 1987 report, John Kornreich, an analyst with Neuberger and Berman, "strongly recommended" the purchase of Gannett stock. "The fundamentals are getting better and better," he said. "With 77 consecutive quarters of up earnings (and the next four probably up strongly) Gannett is a model of consistency—through recessions, newsprint shortages, high initial costs of start-up ventures and dilutive acquisitions. . . . By the end of 1990, USA TODAY should be a national publication with a daily circulation of 1.8 to 2 million, total revenue of about $400 million, cash flow of perhaps $60 million and an asset value of perhaps $600-$700 million." The rosy financial forecasts made back in 1981, the numbers Chuck Schmitt had to craft out of "air," looked real now.

Praise from outsiders was flowing in, too. "USA TODAY has had an extraordinary effect on the business," said J.D. Alexander, executive editor of the Seattle Post-Intelligencer. "Any paper that can generate that kind of reader loyalty in such a short time must be doing something right."

USA TODAY, said CBS News media critic Peter Boyer, has "been taking the rest of America's newspapers to school. It's taught them that there's nothing wrong with being colorful. There's nothing wrong with using graphics to enhance the news. The USA TODAY weather page is the most imitated feature in American journalism, with the possible exception of the USA TODAY Sports section. Even if you've never read USA TODAY, you've probably seen its influence in your own paper, and your own paper is probably a better read because of it. Maybe USA TODAY should get a prize for that."

In May 1986, Gannett's annual meeting of shareholders was drawing to a close in the grand ballroom of the Capital Hilton Hotel in Washington. Frank Fantanza, a shareholder from Rochester, had saluted Neuharth: "Whatever you're doing," he said, "just keep on doing it. You're making a rich man out of me."

Then Neuharth made an announcement that startled many in the room. His voice began to break as he said: "My instincts as an investigative reporter and editorial analyst tell me that the time has come to take another step in the planned and orderly transition of Gannett's leadership to the next generation. Accordingly, I will recommend that President John J. Curley be elected chief executive officer, succeeding me in that role.

"I am not going away," Neuharth said, his voice full of emotion. He seemed to be holding back tears. "I love this company and the business and profession we are in. I plan to continue as your very active chairman until my contract expires in March of 1989, when I will be sixty-five. During the next three years, I will be devoting more of my time to long-term policy and planning, especially in the areas of acquisitions, mergers, new ventures, and other such major Gannett matters."

Neuharth had been through a long, drawn-out transition with Paul Miller in 1973, when he was grasping for the reins of power and Miller did not want to let them go. He was determined that this transition of chief executives would be orderly and effective. And Neuharth had made it absolutely clear that a news executive—John Curley—not a financial executive—Doug McCorkindale—would be running the Gannett Company.

In the spring of 1987 Neuharth set off on a six-month, fifty-state bus tour. The purpose, he said, was to "report on the mood of the USA . . . to find and present an accurate reflection of places and people all across this nation—what they are thinking, doing, and wishing for themselves, their communities, and their country." He called the tour "BusCapade USA." He returned to his first love—reporting and writing—with two columns a week created on his 1926 Royal typewriter in an office in the back of the bus. His reports were published in USA TODAY and also made available to Gannett's ninety-one other daily newspapers and its twenty-six radio and television stations. Another purpose of the trip, Neuharth told associates, was "to get me out of John Curley's hair."

Out on the road, he discovered McPaper's growing popularity firsthand. In the nation's heartland, Neuharth told a rally of USA TODAY advertising executives, people "are hooked on USA TODAY. This newspaper is very, very hot, especially when you get away from New York City and Washington, D.C."

After he gave up the title of CEO, Neuharth seemed more reflective—still driven, but some of the hard edges had been softened. One day, while he and his associates were talking about USA TODAY, he leaned back in his chair in his office overlooking Washington and said, "I don't think even *we* can screw this up now." USA TODAY was here to stay.

In March 1987, in a speech to financial analysts in New York City, Neuharth predicted that USA TODAY would make a profit sometime in 1987. "Yes, we are on a roll," he said. "Yes, we will move from red ink to black this year, at least for a period—or two, or three." And he could not resist twitting them: "No, we could not have done it without your constant encouragement from the beginning."

If Neuharth's prediction turns out to be true and the newspaper becomes profitable by the end of 1987, that will be fast progress compared to many other new ventures in the media. For example, it took Sports Illustrated ten years to become profitable; Money magazine took eight years; and Newsweek, nine years. One Time, Inc., publication—People magazine—turned a profit in just eighteen months, but that was unusual.

Through 1986, USA TODAY's pretax operating losses, not counting some costs incurred by Gannett's local newspapers, were about $458 million. That was by far the greatest deficit any newspaper had ever run up; it was more than the annual gross national product of several Third World nations.

In addition, Gannett's capital spending—long-term expenditures to buy printing plants and equipment that had some application to USA TODAY—totaled more than $208 million over five years. All of these dollars cannot be assigned to USA TODAY, however, because most of the money was spent on plants and equipment that had multiple uses. Some new presses were used to print Gannett's local newspapers as well as USA TODAY; others also did commercial printing for the Gannett Offset network.

During USA TODAY's history, some costs were borne by local Gannett newspapers. For example, Gannett newspapers paid the salaries of loaners who worked in Rosslyn for months at a time, while during the first few years, USA TODAY paid their travel and living expenses. Neuharth thought it was perfectly fair for the local newspapers to bear some of these costs. He insisted that those newspapers reaped benefits when reporters, editors, and other executives returned home, enriched by their USA TODAY experience.

The financial department and Gannett's independent accountants wanted to add other costs borne by local newspapers for USA TODAY's production and distribution to the new newspaper's losses, but Neuharth was vehemently against that. He pointed out that it was hard to precisely determine these costs. For example, a local newspaper might add an extra person in circulation whose job was divided between USA TODAY and the local newspaper. Local publishers estimated how much time that person spent working for each newspaper. Some publishers were tempted to overestimate the costs assigned to USA TODAY to make their own budgets look better, while others underestimated those costs. Finally Neuharth and the accountants compromised and added an extra line near the bottom of USA TODAY's financial reports that separately listed an estimate of costs assigned to Gannett's local newspapers.

At first glance, the national newspaper's operating losses look awesome. When looked at from another perspective, however, the losses do not seem nearly so large. During the years when USA TODAY was developed, Gannett's effective income tax rate was about 48 percent.

That means, as Neuharth said often, that most of the dollars spent on USA TODAY were "50 cent dollars." After taxes through 1986, Gannett's operating losses as a result of launching USA TODAY were only about $230 million, not counting costs incurred by some Gannett newspapers.

That was quite a bit less than the $305 million Gannett paid in 1986 for one newspaper franchise—the Louisville Courier-Journal—with a daily circulation of 309,000. Even if the estimated expenses incurred by Gannett newspapers are added to USA TODAY's losses, the company spent less, after taxes, on USA TODAY than it did on Louisville. The after-tax costs were much less than the going rate for a single television station in the nation's seventeenth largest market, Tampa–St. Petersburg. In the spring of 1987, Nashville investor George Gillett agreed to pay $365 million for WTVT-TV in Tampa, and analysts said that was a bargain.

How valuable is Gannett's investment in USA TODAY? Neuharth often predicted that if it becomes profitable, "I could sell it with one phone call for more than a billion dollars." Of course, he doesn't want to.

Looked at over the short term—five years—Gannett's return on its investment in USA TODAY is a huge negative. But if USA TODAY turns its red ink to black soon, its future is bright. It is quite reasonable to expect that within the next five years it could return a very substantial profit. Eventually, if the newspaper grows and prospers as The Wall Street Journal did in the fifties and sixties, it could become a big money-maker.

As Jeff Greenfield of ABC News said in 1985: "USA TODAY could be the richest, most profitable newspaper in the country within the next several years." Music to the founder's ears.

During the 1970s and 1980s, managers of U.S. companies were often accused of "short-term thinking"—maximizing quarterly profits, milking the business while neglecting long-term investments. That short-sighted approach left many businesses in a weakened or damaged condition later. USA TODAY is an example of the opposite philosophy: innovative, long-term thinking by management.

In spite of the obvious risks to the company and to his own career, Neuharth was impelled to make a new newspaper. His vision changed journalism, added value to the Gannett Company, and brought pleasure and satisfaction to millions of readers. As R. Joseph Fuchs, a media analyst with Kidder, Peabody, put it: "Al Neuharth exhibits the best balance between creative and editorial ego and sound business judgment—those two very different masters."

In the fall of 1986, Neuharth returned to the University of South Dakota as Honorary Grand Marshal of the homecoming parade. He spoke at a big dinner on campus at Vermillion and another the night before in Sioux Falls, and many of his old friends showed up. Gordon Aadland, the SoDak Sports humor columnist, came all the way from Washington state, where he was a retired professor. Always the prankster, Neuharth arranged for Aadland to be met at the airport by a pickup truck loaded with hay. Aadland had to sit on hay bales when he rode into town, where Neuharth met him.

For writing that SoDak Sports column, Neuharth had paid Aadland twelve dollars a week and three dollars in SoDak Sports stock. "The stock part I'm still reminding Al of," Aadland says.

In the late 1940s, they were in journalism classes together at USD. "It has occurred to me in recent years," Aadland says, "that when the professor lectured about prestige newspapers, I and the kid next to me probably wrote down the names—Des Moines Register, Louisville Courier-Journal, etc. But I was preparing for a test; the kid next to me was making out his shopping list."

At that same dinner was Fred C. Christopherson, now in his eighties, the former editor and part-owner of the Sioux Falls Argus Leader whom Neuharth had feuded with. Aadland remembers the situation in the 1950s this way: "In those days the unchallenged god of the media in South Dakota was the publisher of the Argus Leader, Fred C. Christopherson, pipe smoking, pontifical, pudgy. He developed a dislike for Al and considered the little sports newspaper a threat. It was a sort of David and Goliath situation, this time with Goliath winning."

That October evening, Christopherson was holding court after the dinner. Neuharth went over to his table to say hello, and the conversation turned to newspapers. Christopherson looked at Neuharth and said: "I have to tell you something. I get three newspapers. I get the Argus Leader every day, and I read that. Then The Wall Street Journal comes in the mail. And then USA TODAY is delivered, a little later. The Wall Street Journal is all right, but, to tell you the truth, if I had to choose between the two, I'd read your paper."

Neuharth's eyes glistened as he told the story. He had worked and struggled a lifetime to win the respect of readers and journalists, and when that kind of a compliment came from an old adversary, a former competitor like Fred Christopherson, it was a sweet thing to hear.

Back in 1982, Neuharth wrote an article on USA TODAY for the American Society of Newspaper Editors. In it, he asked the multi-million dollar questions: "Can all of this be brought together to make USA TODAY work as the country's first nationwide, general-interest daily newspaper? Can we add a meaningful new dimension to journalism, give the industry a winner, pay the rent, and return a profit? Only time and the readers can answer."

By April 1987, some answers were in—and they were all yes. Through the efforts of thousands of people, efforts which can only be described as heroic, Neuharth and his troops had created something of value. Led by a visionary, driven man who had an insatiable desire to succeed, they had scrapped and suffered to bring a new publication to life. They had invented a new newspaper, improved journalism, and informed millions of readers.

Neuharth's obsession with winning, with achieving, with "doing a little bit better tomorrow than you did today" touched the lives of thousands of Gannett's employees. For a few months or a few years, many of them put the fate of this new newspaper first in their lives. They put it ahead of family and friends, ahead of leisure and the good life.

Taylor Buckley, the senior editor whom Neuharth once kicked out of a page one news conference because he didn't bring a written news budget, remembers the struggle to create USA TODAY: "Sometimes, while spanking his baby to life, it looked as if Neuharth and his team of journalistic obstetricians might beat the poor thing to death. But Neuharth kept telling us we could do it if only we would 'newspaper as well as we know how.' And I think there were very few of us who ever doubted we could whip together Al's Spruce Goose someday, and make that sucker fly like the Concorde."

In November 1986, many of the newspaper's top editors and executives met for their annual "brainstorming" session at Cocoa Beach. They were all there: John Quinn, John Curley, Cathie Black, Doug McCorkindale, Nancy Woodhull, Taylor Buckley, John Seigenthaler, Tom Curley, Karen Howze, Henry Freeman, Richard Curtis, Nancy Monaghan, and many others.

As usual, Neuharth had the last word. The benediction, he called it. USA TODAY's founder was nearly sixty-three, two-and-a-half years from retirement. Near the end of his career, his eyes misted over sometimes and emotion crept into his voice. The iron control, the icy self-discipline, was not as powerful as it once was. "As I look around this room," he said, his voice breaking, "one thing that I feel good about is that damn near all of you were here at the beginning. I hope it makes you feel good, too."

McPaper was going to make it. That was an accomplishment they would remember, with pride, for the rest of their lives.

Epilogue

On June 15, 1987, John Curley sent this telegram to Al Neuharth, who was on the road with BusCapade USA in the Black Hills of his native South Dakota.

```
     LU LU LU                                    Telegram
     western union

    IPMWGW2 WSH1-010683A166 06/15/87
    ICS IPMWGWD WSH
    01331 WASHINGTON DC 58 06-15 1234P EDT
    ICS IPMWGW2
    PMS AL NEUHARTH
    BUSCAPADE USA, SYLVAN LAKE LODGE
    HILL CITY SD 57745
    CARE WU YELLOW CAB CO (WPU)
    408 5TH ST
    RAPID CITY SD

    DEAR AL:
    NCPAPER HAS MADE IT. USA TODAY BROKE INTO BLACK WITH PROFIT OF
    $1,093,756 FOR MONTH OF MAY, SIX MONTHS AHEAD OF SCHEDULE.
    STAFF BETTING YOU'LL FORGIVE US FOR RUINING YOUR PREDICTION THAT
    WE'D HAVE TO WAIT UNTIL END OF YEAR.
    HOPE YOU'LL FLY BACK TO WASHINGTON FOR CHAMPAGNE CELEBRATION TOMORROW

    JOHN CURLEY
    PRESIDENT AND CHIEF EXECUTIVE OFFICER
    GANNETT CO., INC.

    W.U. 1201-SF (R5-98)
```

USA TODAY
timeline

1952	November 21	*SoDak Sports* begins regular weekly publication.
1954	September 24	*SoDak Sports* announces a "Time Out" period to last one month; it never resumes publication.
1966	March 21	TODAY begins publication in Brevard County, Florida.
1978	August 21	Westchester TODAY begins publication.
1979	November 5	Eastbay TODAY begins publication.
1980	February 29	Project NN task force members meet for the first time with Al Neuharth at Pumpkin Center.
	October 28	Project NN members make presentation to Gannett's board of directors in Reno, Nevada.
	December 16	Gannett announces the formation of GANSAT.
1981	June 11	USA TODAY prototypes printed.
	August 19	GANSAT installs satellite earth station at Army Times plant in Springfield, Virginia.
	August 25	Board of directors meets in Oakland; Neuharth announces "encouraging public response" to USA TODAY prototypes.
	December 15	Board of directors unanimously approves launch of USA TODAY. Gannett stock closes at 37.75.

1982	January 11	USA TODAY executives named: President: Phil Gialanella Executive Vice President: Vince Spezzano Editor: John Curley Executive Editor: Ron Martin Senior Consultant: Moe Hickey General Manager: Jerry Bean
	January 28	USA TODAY operations executives named: Vice President/Telecommunications: Larry Sackett Vice President/Circulation: Frank Vega Planning and Research Director: Paul Kessinger Personnel Director: Diane Large Public Affairs Director: Linda Peek Finance Director: Chuck Schmitt
	February 26	Joe Welty named USA TODAY's vice president/advertising.
	March 1	Moe Hickey leaves USA TODAY to become Gannett regional president and publisher in Reno, Nevada.
	March 15	Gannett stock closes at 29.88 after hitting low of 29.5.
	April 20	Gannett announces it will launch USA TODAY on September 15, 1982, in the Baltimore-Washington area.
	May 13	John Seigenthaler is named editorial director.
	June 14	USA TODAY's key editors named: News: Nancy Woodhull Money: Taylor Buckley, Jr. Sports: Henry Freeman Life: Sheryl Bills Graphics and Photo: Richard Curtis Systems: Karen Howze Special Projects: John Walter Washington Page: Gene Policinski Director/Newsroom Administration: Donna Rome
	September 15	First edition of USA TODAY hits the streets in the Washington-Baltimore area; the issue is a sellout.
	September 20	Atlanta launch.
	September 27	Minneapolis launch.
	October 4	Pittsburgh launch.

	November 8	Seattle launch.
	November 15	San Francisco launch.
	November 29	Circulation hits 362,879, double year-end projections.
	December 15	Gannett stock closes at 60.25.
1983	January 10	Houston launch.
	January 17	Denver launch.
	January 24	Los Angeles launch.
	February 7	Circulation hits 531,438; Neuharth says that's "nicely ahead of projections."
	February 9	Miami launch.
	February 23	Dick Rumsey is named vice president/finance. Detroit launch.
	March 9	Chicago launch.
	March 23	Philadelphia launch.
	April 11	New York City launch.
	April 24	Reorganization of USA TODAY management announced. Publisher: Phil Gialanella President: Vince Spezzano Executive Vice President: Paul Flynn Editor: John Quinn
		John Curley named president of Gannett Newspaper Division.
		Neuharth announces USA TODAY's circulation tops 1 million at 1,109,587.
	August 22	Jack Heselden named publisher of USA TODAY. Phil Gialanella returns to Hawaii.
	September 12	Boston launch. Cleveland launch.
	September 15	Neuharth says 1984 launches will make USA TODAY available to 80 percent of U.S. population.
	September 21	Joe Welty promoted to executive vice president/ advertising.

	September 28	Cathie Black named president of USA TODAY.
		Vince Spezzano named Gannett's vice president/corporate communications.
	October 3	Dallas/Ft. Worth launch.
	October 10	New Orleans launch.
	October 18	Frank Vega leaves USA TODAY to become assistant to Gannett regional president Robert Collins.
	October 24	Neuharth gives "journalism of hope" speech to Overseas Press Club.
1984	February 2	Joe Welty joins Gannett Media Sales.
	February 27	Carolinas launch.
	March 27	John Curley named president and chief operating officer of Gannett.
	April 2	Kansas City launch.
	June 15	Cathie Black named publisher of USA TODAY, replacing Jack Heselden.
		Paul Flynn named president.
	June 25	The Audit Bureau of Circulations reports that USA TODAY circulation was an average of 1,179,834 for the period October 1–December 31, 1983.
	July 10	Distribution of USA TODAY's international edition begins in Europe.
	July 27	First 48-page edition published.
	August 3	USA TODAY runs 63 pages of advertising for the week, a record.
	August 27	Cover price increased from 25 cents to 35 cents.
	September 10	Cincinnati launch.
	October 1	Lee Guittar named president of USA TODAY.
		Paul Flynn becomes publisher of Gannett newspapers in Pensacola, Florida.
	October 15	Phoenix launch.
	September 9	Nashville launch.
	November 11	USA TODAY executives attend "Last Supper" at Bernard's Surf restaurant in Cocoa Beach.

1985	April 3	USA TODAY announces that ad pages are up 97 percent for first quarter.
	April 16	Circulation reaches 1,276,334, counting Blue Chip.
	May 23	Ad pages for week averaged nineteen per day, a record.
	July 17	Ad revenues up 106 percent for the first half of 1985 compared to 1984.
	October 8	International Edition begins printing via satellite in Singapore.
	October 21	Circulation passes 1.4 million.
	November 7	USA TODAY moves to fifty-six-page capacity.
	December 9	Gannett and General Mills report that response to joint nationwide sales promotion "exceeded expectations."
1986	February 6	Gannett reports that during the fourth quarter of 1985, USA TODAY became the second-largest newspaper in the nation, with more than 1.4 million daily circulation during the quarter.
	March 17	Tom Curley named president of USA TODAY. Lee Guittar leaves to join Hearst Newspapers.
	April 15	ADC reports USA TODAY's circulation is 1,417,077, including Blue Chip.
	May 6	International Edition begins printing via satellite in Switzerland.
	May 20	John Curley named chief executive officer of Gannett, succeeding Neuharth, who remains as chairman.
	July 20	Simmons Research reports that USA TODAY has 4.8 million readers per day, the most of any U.S. daily newspaper.
	September 16	Harvard Lampoon parody of USA TODAY published.
	December 22	USA TODAY runs twenty-nine pages of ads in one issue, bringing in more than $1 million in revenue, a record.
1987	January 20	USA TODAY published 3,484 ad pages in 1986, finishing second among newsweeklies and business magazines.

February 4   USA TODAY's circulation passes 1.5 million.

March 20   First report from Neuharth's fifty-state
                    "BusCapade USA" tour is published.

March 30   Ad pages in USA TODAY increased 24 percent in the
                    first quarter.

April 16   Readership survey by Mediamark Research shows
                    USA TODAY has nearly 4.8 million readers each day,
                    more than any other U.S. daily.

Index